Pragmatic Sustain

In the short time since the turn of the millennium, the notion of "sustainable development" has been distilled to the specific battle against climate change. The tools for waging this battle are largely technoscientific and linked to market-based strategies. Such grand plans suggest a simple technological fix is not only possible, but profitable.

The authors gathered here, leading thinkers from architecture, business, economics, engineering, history, philosophy, planning, science and technology studies, welcome action toward solving this clear and present threat. However, they are skeptical of the assumption that a single approach, model, or list of best practices can be universally applied in a diverse world. Instead, they advocate a pragmatic and pluralist approach to environmental and social change, demanding constant adaptation to changing conditions.

The pragmatic attitude and tools investigated in this collection contribute to the development of a much needed transdisciplinary conversation to emphasize the long-term consequences of our actions, not their ideological or disciplinary purity. Despite the often failed attempts to incorporate the insights of others, here we step beyond narrow disciplinary incentives to offer a new understanding of how we all might live sustainably.

Steven A. Moore is Bartlett Cocke Professor of Architecture and Planning, Director of the Graduate Program for Sustainable Design and Co-Founder of the University of Texas Center for Sustainable Development, Austin, TX.

Pragmatic Sustainability

Theoretical and practical tools

Edited by Steven A. Moore

LONDON AND NEW YORK

First published 2010
by Routledge
2 Park Square, Milton Park, Abingdon, Oxon OX14 4RN

Simultaneously published in the USA and Canada
by Routledge
270 Madison Ave, New York, NY 10016

Routledge is an imprint of the Taylor & Francis Group, an informa business

Typeset in Univers by Wearset Ltd, Boldon, Tyne and Wear
Printed and bound in Great Britain by MPG Books Group, UK

British Library Cataloguing in Publication Data
A catalogue record for this book is available from the British Library

Library of Congress Cataloging-in-Publication Data
Pragmatic sustainability: theoretical and practical tools/edited by Steven A. Moore. – 1st ed.
p. cm.
Includes index.
1. Sustainable development. 2. Sustainable urban development. I. Moore, Steven A., 1945–
HC79.E5P677 2010
338.9'27–dc22 2009025088

ISBN10: 0-415-77937-5 (hbk)
ISBN10: 0-415-77938-3 (pbk)

ISBN13: 978-0-415-77937-1 (hbk)
ISBN13: 978-0-415-77938-8 (pbk)

To those interdisciplinary graduate students at the University of Texas who shaped this book by refusing to recognize the traditional categories of knowledge.

Contents

Contents

Figures

Tables

Acknowledgments

This book began in 1999 when two students from the McCombs Graduate School of Business at the University of Texas, Bruce Wilcoxen and Derek Bensen, knocked on my door with a question. In the most polite of terms they wanted to know if I would contribute a lecture to a new inter-disciplinary graduate seminar they had proposed, *Topics in Sustainable Development*. I said, "yes, but..." It is, as they say, a long story, but the earnest request by these students eventually resulted in a course and lecture series that I have taught for ten consecutive years. It was also through Wilcoxen and Bensen that initial funding was secured from the Shell Oil Corporation in Houston to support a series of visiting lectures by significant voices in the field of "sustainable development." To these former students, and to Ralf Brand, who was a key organizer, I owe my thanks for conceiving an opportunity that I might not have invented myself.

In 2004 funding from the Henry Luce Foundation enabled the creation of a graduate minor degree, or "portfolio in sustainability," at UT and this support continued the series for another three years. As of the spring of 2009 there have been better than forty scholars, activists, and business people who have contributed to our education and well over two hundred graduate students who have challenged what we think we know. I am grateful to them all.

In the early years of the course I concluded that it would be foolish indeed not to publish the fine lectures delivered by our distinguished guests. But because the lectures were, by design, conflicting and diverse, it took several years to find the glue that might make for a coherent book on such a broad topic. That glue is, as the title suggests, the pragmatic attitude demonstrated by the twenty authors represented herein. With this theme in mind the contributors have revised their initial lectures into a more conversational format. The remaining lectures, which rest upon different assumptions, await another opportunity to be published in an appropriate context. I am grateful to those authors for their patience.

I must also acknowledge the support of my colleagues at the University of Texas, both in the School of Architecture and elsewhere. Successive Deans, Larry Speck and Fritz Steiner, provided the space in my teaching schedule to teach non-design students from seven other disciplines. From across campus, biologist Dick Richardson, geologist Jay Banner, public policy analyst David Eaton, economist Don Fullerton, geographer Kevin Anderson, and poet Betty Sue Flowers have contributed significantly. Within the School of Architecture planners Kent Butler, Elizabeth

Acknowledgments

Mueller, and Bob Paterson; architects Dason Whitsett, Sergio Palleroni, and Michael Garrison; as well as landscape architect Hope Hasbrouck have lectured and contributed scarce time to projects. And from the City of Austin, numerous activists including Fred Blood, Jim Walker, Susana Almanza, Sylvia Herrera, and Robyn Rather have contributed generously with their time and ideas.

Finally, interdisciplinary learning requires an environment both rich in knowledge and heterogeneous in its allegiances. For this I am grateful to the University of Texas which is one of the few institutions I know that pays more than lip service to interdisciplinary scholarship.

About the Authors

David Allen is the Gertz Regents Professor of Chemical Engineering and the Director of the Center for Energy and Environmental Resources at the University of Texas at Austin. His work focuses on gas phase atmospheric chemistry, the chemistry of fine particles in the atmosphere, and the development of educational materials that bring environmental issues into the chemical engineering curriculum.

Braden R. Allenby holds several positions at Arizona State University: Lincoln Professor of Engineering and Ethics; Professor of Civil and Environmental Engineering, and of Law; and founding director of the Center of Earth Systems Engineering and Management. His areas of expertise include sustainable engineering, earth systems engineering and management, industrial ecology, and design for the environment.

Samuel D. Brody is Associate Professor in the Department of Landscape Architecture and Urban Planning and Director of the Environmental Planning and Sustainability Research Unit at Texas A&M University. He received his Ph.D. at the University of North Carolina at Chapel Hill. Dr. Brody's areas of research interests are environmental planning, coastal sustainability, ecosystem management, and geographic information systems. He has a particular interest in the role of industry in ecosystem management.

Vincent B. Canizaro is Associate Professor of Architecture at the University of Texas, San Antonio. His publications include *Architectural Regionalism* (2007), the *Journal of Architectural Education* (issues on architecture, landscape and sustainability), various articles in *Texas Architect* and the *AIA San Antonio Guidebook*. He is recipient of the UTSA President's Distinguished Achievement Award for Creative Production in 2008.

Sean B. Cash is Assistant Professor in the Department of Rural Economy at the University of Alberta. He received his Ph.D. in Agricultural and Resource Economics at the University of California, Berkeley. Dr. Cash's research interests include: socially responsible consumption and production; environmental regulation; health, natural resources and development; and public choice on environmental and agricultural issues.

Jeffrey M. Chusid is a preservation architect and an associate professor in the Department of City and Regional Planning at Cornell University. His recent research has focused on early modernist architecture in California and India; while he has consulted for towns, cities and historic sites in China, Bosnia, Ukraine, Fiji, and the United States.

Cliff I. Davidson is Professor in the Department of Civil and Environmental Engineering and the Department of Engineering and Public Policy at Carnegie Mellon University. His interests are the measurement and modeling of airborne particles and education and research on sustainable development.

Andrew Feenberg is Canada Research Chair in Philosophy of Technology in the School of Communication, Simon Fraser University, where he directs the Applied Communication and Technology Lab. He is recognized as the author of five influential books, numerous book chapters and articles in the philosophy of technology, and as an early innovator in the field of online education.

Simon Guy is Professor of Architecture and Head of the Manchester Architecture Research Centre (MARC) in the School of Environment and Development at the University of Manchester in the UK. His research is aimed at critically understanding the co-evolution of design and development strategies and socio-technical-ecological processes shaping cities.

David J. Hess is Professor and former Chair in Rensselaer's Department of Science and Technology Studies. He is the recipient of two Fulbrights, a Social Science Research Council fellowship, and the Diana Forsythe Prize. His research focuses on the anthropology, history, and sociology of science, technology, health, the environment, and social movements.

Andrew Jamison is Professor and Director of the Graduate Program in Science and Technology Policy at Aalborg University, Denmark. His recent research has been especially concerned with the political implications of what he calls "green knowledge" – that is, the ideas and practical experiments that are to be found in the world of environmental politics.

Holly Jordan Lanham is a Ph.D. candidate at the University of Texas at Austin, McCombs School of Business. Holly studies organizations as complex adaptive systems with a focus on understanding information technology use in professional organizations.

Andrew Light is Associate Professor of Philosophy and Director of the Center for Global Ethics at George Mason University and a Senior Fellow at the Center for American Progress in Washington DC. Light's research focuses on environmental ethics and climate, energy, and science policy.

Reuben R. McDaniel Jr. is the Charles and Elizabeth Prothro Regents Chair in Health Care Management and Professor of Information Management at the University of Texas at Austin, McCombs School of Business. Reuben studies organizations as complex adaptive systems with a special focus on knowledge-intensive organizations.

Martin V. Melosi is Distinguished University Professor of History and Director of the Center for Public History at the University of Houston. He has written or edited fifteen books and written more than eighty proceedings, articles, and book chapters. His areas of research interest include urban environmental history, city services and urban technology, environmental racism, environmental politics, and energy history.

Steven A. Moore is Bartlett Cocke Professor of Architecture and Planning at the University of Texas at Austin where he serves as Director of the Graduate Program in Sustainable Design. Moore is Co-Founder of the University of Texas Center for Sustainable Development and is the author of many articles and five books on the topic of sustainable architecture and urbanism.

Cynthia Folsom Murphy is a research associate at the Center for Energy and Environmental Resources at the University of Texas at Austin. Her research interests lie in the area of environmental and economic assessments of emerging technologies, particularly for electronics and energy systems.

Michael D. Oden is Associate Professor of Community and Regional Planning at the University of Texas at Austin. His teaching and research areas include local and regional sustainable economic development, regional growth dynamics, and affordable housing policy.

Frederick Steiner is Dean of the School of Architecture at the University of Texas at Austin. He was a Fulbright scholar at Wageningen University, The Netherlands, and a Rome Prize Fellow at the American Academy in Rome. Dean Steiner received his Ph.D., M.A., and Master of Regional Planning degrees from the University of Pennsylvania. He earned a Master of Community Planning and a B.S. in Design from the University of Cincinnati.

Paul B. Thompson is W.K. Kellogg Chair of Philosophy in Agricultural, Food and Community Ethics at Michigan State University. He is the author of three books related to sustainable agriculture, he has served on many national and international committees related to agricultural biotechnology, and he contributed to the National Research Council report The Environmental Effects of Transgenic Plants. Thompson has a continuing interest in environmental and agricultural ethics.

Langdon Winner is Professor of Political Science in the Department of Science and Technology Studies at Rensselaer Polytechnic Institute in Troy, New York where he serves as co-director of the Center for Cultural Design. He is a political theorist who focuses upon social and political issues that surround modern technological change.

Introduction

Pragmatic Sustainability

Steven A. Moore

Not long ago, I had breakfast in an old diner that my family has frequented for years, but had recently changed hands. The old place, which we loved, served grease liberally and was just as filthy. The new place seemed completely transformed, yet still held the welcoming intimacy that is an essential part of the diner format. As I ate my first breakfast in this new context I overheard a lively conversation taking place at the counter between two large and loud young men, the distracted cook, and the new owner – an attractive if tired woman in her 50s – who answered questions about the menu. The two young men must not have noticed the new sign outside, or the new décor inside, because they expected their habitually stout breakfast. And to be accurate, it wasn't the new menu per se that animated their talk but the attitudes and choices that led to serving, to the degree possible, only locally grown organic food as was announced by the banner outside – "Local Food and Global Love."

Theirs was a good and thoughtful conversation. When one young man asked why she couldn't just serve sliced potatoes fried in Crisco, the owner instead served up a brief explanation of the health problems associated with trans-fats along with an exacting distinction between isomer fatty and vaccenic acids. When her abstract explanation drew only blank stares from the young men, she laughed at herself and said, "Here, try these." As she handed her hesitant prospects something that looked like slices of dark orange potatoes baked in a seasoned batter, the owner told them about the farm where the vegetable came from. With a now full and smiling mouth the other young man said, "oh yeah, I know the place, nobody's worked those fields for years and I use to…"

In the fast-paced conversation that followed the young men offered their own very different perspectives about farming, water scarcity, the price of gasoline, real estate development, and taxes – all of which the four conversants could see as related to food. As they talked, the cook offered a taste of hand-ground local pork sausage which, in turn, inspired the young men to order more, along with poached organic eggs, whole wheat biscuits, and, of course, more tubers. By the time other new customers joined the counter conversation the young men were recommending menu items on the basis of their own experimentation.

From my vantage point at one of the seven small tables I marveled at this small drama, not because the young men were converted to "sustainability" by rational argumentation – they weren't. They did, however, like the food and its association to conditions they knew. I marveled because these four people had found common ground in their talk, despite the dramatically differ-ent cultural associations announced ahead of time by their clothing, coiffure, and manner of speak-ing. The success of their tentative agreement about such important topics was forged, not by the abstract or formal argumentation initially offered by the owner, but by a willingness to engage in ad hoc experimentation with life's ever-changing menu. It is on the basis of such experimentation that old habits are changed. The empirical evidence of this claim is that I have seen the young men at the diner several more times.

And so it is with this book – we are a diverse group of conversants. But as geographers are fond of saying, "events take place." This is to say that diner, office, or classroom conversa-tions are always specific to the places where they occur – the difference between conversants is mediated by the social and environmental context of our talk, by our expectations of decorum. Outside the ivied halls of my university the contributors to this conversation may look very much alike to those who frequent diners, but viewed from the inside the ivy camouflage we represent groups that rarely talk to each other, let alone agree. And as in the diner drama, I am somewhat surprised that there are substantial areas of tentative agreement among us. The two conversa-tions are, of course, different. Not only are there many more conversants in this book, but our talk has taken place over years, not minutes and the food we have shared in our various meetings hasn't been as good. As a result our agreements are partial, hinted at, and incomplete. They are, however, serious and point the way to new intellectual and institutional habits.

In all, our accord is constructed as a warp made up of five vaguely parallel perspec-tives. These perspectives are generally disciplinary in character – meaning that they originate in the training we have each received. Our perspectives are, however, made far richer by the discov-ery of seven reconstructed themes that weave across our conversation. The structure of the book is, then, a cloth made of both warp and weft which I'll describe in turn in what follows.

To begin the book, four of my colleagues have engaged in the "struggle to define terms." In this first section philosopher Paul B. Thompson, economist Michael D. Oden, business scholars Reuben R. McDaniel Jr. and Holly Jordan Lanham, and historian Andrew Jamison parse the term "sustainability," question "social equity" as one of the three "balanced" dimensions of sustainable development, and question how we could "know" sustainability even if we saw it. In the end these contributors are not convinced that trying to define terms and conditions such as these is a very good use of our time.

In the second section of the book philosopher Langdon Winner, engineer David Allen with his colleagues, and Science and Technology Studies (STS) scholar Simon Guy investigate three "technological cultures" in which sustainable development is contested at different scales. In Winner's chapter, the Hudson River Valley of New York is a scene of struggle. In Guy's, Japan is a scene of misunderstood possibilities. And in the chapter by Allen *et al.*, the entire world is a scene of technological uncertainty. This group of collaborators finds no single formula that will guide our cultural choices.

In the third section, philosopher Andrew Light, architect Vincent B. Canizaro, and pres-ervationist Jeffrey M. Chusid investigate the cultural content of technology from another perspec-tive – by trying to understand the relationship between "sustainability and place." In sum they argue that it is an historical error to think about sustainable development from a single Cartesian or abstract perspective. In lieu of a grand, single-point perspective, all three argue in favor of multiple, local perspectives.

The fourth section considers, not wilderness, preservation or the patterns of regions, but "sustainability and cities." Planner Frederick Steiner and historian Martin V. Melosi investigate the very social process of making long-term decisions about the urban infrastructures that render cities sustainable or not. Although there are patterns of decision-making and rapid feedback loops that over the short run seem to yield better results, both contributors recognize that decisions over the long run are never repeated in the same historical circumstances.

In the fifth and final section, STS scholar David J. Hess, planners Sean B. Cash and Samuel D. Brody, and philosopher Andrew Feenberg investigate "civil society, industry, and regulation." The shared perspective of these three contributors is that the rules by which we regulate industry are an index of social change and not inherently technological.

Collectively, these five perspectives add up to something I refer to as "pragmatic sustainability." But rather than limit our discussion to the warp constructed of these common perspectives at the outset, it will be even more helpful to examine the weft of experience that weaves them together. The weft is constituted of seven themes found repeated in our conversation over several years – respectively these are *history, consequentialism, pluralism, determinism, secularization, disciplinarity*, and *storylines*. By relating these themes to those that appear in the works of such pragmatists as William James, Charles Sanders Peirce, John Dewey, and Richard Rorty the pragmatic attitude shared by the contributors to this volume will become clearer. I can then conclude by making a case for *pragmatic sustainability*, not as a coherent environmental philosophy, but as a useful tool for people with very different attitudes toward life's ever-changing menu.

On history

Among the contributors to this volume there is no agreement, as there is in doctrines of orthodox Marxism or its antithesis, the Manifest Destiny of capitalism, that history will unfold in a particular way. But it would be equally incorrect to say that history is entirely contingent – that there is no order that we can perceive and influence. Rather, our view toward history is somewhere in between – we share a sense that the path of history is uncertain and we will influence it, but not in the manner we may intend. This is, of course, a grand epistemological topic that we need not resolve here. The agreement among the contributors to this volume is far more limited in scope, but also of more immediate concern – it is that mainstream environmental discourses in North America have failed to halt advancing environmental degradation. Even more, these same discourses have failed to halt advancing social degradation. In spite of our overall optimism, we hold that things are getting worse, not better, and the trajectory of history is directly tied to, if not entirely caused by, the development of liberal capitalism as a means of production.

In the shadow of this sobering reality is our shared understanding that "sustainability" is less a scientific concept than an historical discourse through which we might imagine more hopeful futures. Elsewhere I have argued this point at length, but in these pages there are other possibilities offered (Moore 2007). My colleagues also make clear that the sustainability discourse has been with us far longer than the nuanced way that we now use the word itself. Architect Vincent B. Canizaro, for example, demonstrates that architectural regionalism is a proto-sustainability conversation that has been with us for at least a century. Historian Jeffrey M. Chusid and planner Frederick Steiner look to the history of preservation and planning in North America and arrive at similar conclusions. And historian Martin V. Melosi reminds us that, although cultures may experience recurrent problems, those problems always return to altered conditions. Collectively their observations suggest two things: first, that contemporary talk about how we might develop sustainably must be understood, not as a new conversation, but an old one. And second, gnash and talk tough though we have, the logics we have articulated to date have failed to do the job. Philosopher Andrew Light, engineer David Allen, and anthropologist David J. Hess are particularly vehement on this point. We need, they argue, new ways of talking about sustainability that will galvanize diverse and experimental forms of action because it is through such experimentation that we will find the vocabulary we need. Beyond this initial agreement about history there are six other accords that grasp our attention.

Consequentialism

Philosophers generally acknowledge three traditions of determining moral rightness or wrongness – *deontology*, *virtue ethics*, and *consequentialism*. Those who favor the first tradition, deontology, argue that moral judgment favors the quality of the act being judged – how pure, brave, or selfless it was. Those who favor the second tradition, virtue ethics, argue that moral judgment favors the quality of the actor – were her intentions pure, brave, or selfless. And those who favor the third tradition, consequentialism, argue that moral judgment favors the consequences of the action taken – did it result in conditions that are life-enhancing. Although none of the contributors to this volume invoke the term "consequentialism" per se, their singular focus on the environmental and social outcomes precipitated by our habits make them consequentialists by default.

Another way to say that we are concerned more with consequences, rather than the qualities of acts or actors, is to define rightness as *successful*, or life-enhancing action. A corollary would be to define wrongness as unsuccessful action – action that leads to degraded social and environmental conditions. This bias derives not only from theoretical affiliation and personal experience of the contributors, but from empirical research that is *action-oriented*. By this term I mean research that blurs the traditional barriers between objective scientific knowledge production and social or environmental activism.

In the practice of traditional science, scientists are considered responsible only by distancing themselves from what they learn to hear and see. This is the core principle of the scientific method – objectivity. But in the kind of science favored by the contributors to this volume, Andrew Jamison most explicitly, one becomes responsible for the conditions heard and seen in the act of learning. In other words, sustainability science is not understood as an activity that takes place outside of society or one that is disengaged from the conditions being studied. Rather, it is understood as a social activity that has consequences for the phenomena being studied. It is in this sense that action is more important than the isolated creation of facts – in making truth claims that have no immediate consequence to our communities.

In all, the collective argument in this volume is that the contemporary idea of sustainable development is first an ethical one that derives from the history of how we determine rightness and wrongness. In the face of catastrophic collapse of the ecosystem, upon which all life depends, it is not the quality of actions or actors that matters most, but the consequences of those actions.

Pluralism

In the essays that follow nearly all of the authors hold that successful actions, as I have defined them on p. 4, tend to come from problem-solving groups that share three qualities: heterogeneity, informality, and trust. In general we can say that these qualities characterize an attitude best described as pluralism.

By heterogeneity I mean that in decision-making, or determining a course of action, many minds are better than one. A frequently used term to describe such conditions is *diversity*. The logic employed here is not an overly optimistic assessment of the intellectual capacity of regular citizens. Dewey, for one, recognized that successful states must be constituted of "a plurality of social groupings, good, bad and indifferent" (Dewey 1927). Rather, arguing in favor of heterogeneity is to recognize that we each approach situations from a particular vantage point and with a particular set of interests. Accepting the value, if not rightness, of diverse perspectives will provide insight about the nature of reality and increase the likelihood of taking successful actions. Heterogeneity is, of course, a foundation for democracy.

The second quality of successful action groups, informality, is specifically suggested by planners Cash and Brody in this volume. By "informality" they refer to a lack of formal, rule-bound behavior and the predictable expectations that accompany such rules. If we can set these norms aside we are far more likely to find the unexpected. Getting at this point another way, Dewey argued that,

> And so it is with mathematical knowledge, or with knowledge of politics or art. Their respective objects are not known till they are made in course of the process of experimental thinking. Their usefulness when made is whatever, from infinity to zero, experience may subsequently determine it to be.
>
> (Dewey 1916)

For Dewey, knowledge emerges in anticipating how it will be used, how it will solve a problem, and is only confirmed in the act of testing one's anticipation in the material world. This is not a "formal" process in either a social or philosophical sense – it is "experimental thinking" that happens most often when many minds are focused on solving a common problem rather than on the forms of accepted protocol. It is a social, not an individual or purely mental process.

The third quality of true pluralism is trust, which derives from informality, and is more difficult to find in heterogeneous than homogeneous settings. One might argue that the trust found in homogeneous settings is tribal or habitual, rather than earned. Learning to trust the insights of others, no matter how limited we may think their insights may be, requires setting aside familiar forms – it is adopting an experimental attitude.

The argument for pluralism in the essays by Guy, Thompson, Hess, and Jamison is brought into full focus by economist Michael D. Oden who explicitly argues that social equity is a necessary if insufficient condition for sustainable development to occur. The kind of "complex social equity" championed by Oden, and most of the authors collected herein, is the heart of social pluralism. But to be clear, our argument is not that one must accept the rightness of plural truth claims (which is philosophical relativism), but it is prudent to accept them as relevant to problem-solving (which is political pluralism).

It is a short step from arguing that many minds are better than one, to arguing in favor of citizen participation in the making of successful public choices. Successful actions are more likely to result from diverse insights and recommendations that are rationally deliberated in public space. Dewey (1927: 207) argued this point in saying,

> The man who wears the shoe knows best that it pinches and where it pinches, even if the expert shoemaker is the best judge of how the trouble is to be remedied.
>
> A class of experts is inevitably so removed from common interests as to become a class with private interests and private knowledge, which in social matters is not knowledge at all.

Nearly all of the contributors to this volume explicitly employ similar logic. They hold that heterogeneous, informal, and trusting relationships lead to more successful action – action that is life-enhancing and sustainable.

Determinism

Elsewhere, contributor Langdon Winner has pondered the sadly predictable enthusiasm with which North Americans await the next technological innovation – the railroad, the automobile, atomic power, solar power, the iPhone, and more (Winner 2004). In his view we remain convinced, in spite of a history filled with unexpected and negative consequences linked to technological change, that surely the next wave will not only solve the immediate problem at hand but make us somehow better, more democratic, or even thinner. Winner's description of this phenomenon makes a compelling definition of technological determinism. Also elsewhere, contributor Andrew Feenberg (1995: 7) has held that technological determinism amounts to the inability to imagine that our tools and our lives might be different than they now are. In both estimations we imagine that the technological choices that we will make in the future are somehow already determined – already decided by a logic that lurks within the things themselves – water power must replace human muscle power, steam engines must come after water power, internal combustion engines follow steam, hybrid electric follows gasoline, and so forth. In the "hard" version of this logic society has no power itself to alter the menu served up by physics. In the "soft" version society has agency, but it is limited by the momentum of our prior choices. In both versions we are less free than we would like to think.

The same deterministic view of history is also applied to economics, but in this version we imagine that it is money that holds within it a logic that is independent of human agency. In other words, we imagine that economics precedes politics because politics are preconditioned by a universal human nature hard-wired to greed – we are free to make only those choices that lead to greater material wealth. In this sense, orthodox capitalists and Marxists interpret history through the same deterministic lenses. Dewey (1927: 156) criticized both versions of economic determinism by arguing,

> The doctrine of economic interpretation [determinism] as usually stated ignores the transformation which meanings may effect; ... It thinks in terms of antecedents, not of the eventual; of origins, not fruits.

In this volume there is at least implicit agreement that technologies and economies are socially constructed phenomena – they are not predetermined by logic inherent in the scientific laws of physics or human DNA. Rather, they are historical, meaning that existing technological and economic situations limit our choices.

Andrew Feenberg, in this volume, builds on these agreements to argue for the regulation of our technological and economic future. If history, as I argued on p. 3, has demonstrated that the market has failed to maintain a life-enhancing balance between social and ecological interests, then it is time, Feenberg argues, we recognize that regulation is not a "trade-off" between environmental integrity and some other social good. Rather, regulation is a rational choice about how we want to live that can be made before economic interests are taken into account. Technological and economic regulation, in Feenberg's proposal, is not conducted in the service of some higher truth handed down by the nature of physics or human biology, it is a question of how we would like to live in the places we inhabit.

On the basis of this collective insight, there is little interest among the authors represented here in grand plans or sweeping theories intended to correct the injustices or wrong-turns of history. Rather, our proposals for action tend to be local or limited to particular situations. For example, in their assessment of the debate raging among engineers regarding "long-lived" vs. "rapidly-evolving" designs for large technological systems, David Allen, Cynthia Folsom Murphy, Braden R. Allenby, and Cliff I. Davidson find no certainty in selecting one design over the other. Were they technological determinists they would likely find certainty in systems designed to operate for very long periods of time. Were they economic determinists they would likely find certainty in the fast-changing conditions of the market. They find, however, that certainty is nowhere to be found. Rather, both long-lived and rapidly evolving systems will each find niches within a sustainable world. Rather than adopt a deterministic logic they opt for an experimental one.

Our collective skepticism toward the doctrines of technological and economic determinism can be translated into a proposition which holds that ecological and social degradation is neither caused nor cured by technology and/or the market. If we are to construct a sustainable world it will be by assessing, on a case by case basis, how particular technologies and particular markets might contribute to the outcomes we desire. This is to say that we must secularize them by recognizing that technologies and markets are tools made by us, not laws that we have discovered.

Secularization

Richard Rorty holds that the United States is the first nation state to attempt the complete secularization of politics as first imagined in the era of Enlightenment (Rorty 1998). In drafting the

Constitution the framers determined that rather than relying upon a higher order of gods, kings, or their worldly representatives to make decisions on our behalf, we would be the first society to take upon ourselves the responsibility for how we should live. In retrospect, reconstructing the rules of causality in this way must have been a frightening prospect for the framers because, from that moment forward we would have only ourselves to blame for the consequences of our choices.

The far more recent discourses of "critical theory" and "science studies" have not only accepted the American attempt to secularize politics but extend that logic as a parallel attempt to secularize science. In this view, science, far from being an objective practice outside of society, has only become politics by other means (Latour 1987, 2004). This is to say that modern society has only substituted the authority of science for that of gods and kings. If we really believe in the life-enhancing qualities of democracy, Bruno Latour argues, we must be willing to challenge the authority of science as well. Recognizing the humanness of the King requires that we see scientists through the same lenses. Both have been enthroned by laws of our own making, but in the end both are naked. By the mid-twentieth century, Herbert Marcuse argued that if we desire to live in harmony rather than in conflict with nature, we need "a new science" (Marcuse 1966, c1964). Latour has built upon Marcuse's critique by distinguishing between "Science" and "the sciences." In this project he defines "science as *the politicization of the sciences through epistemology in order to render ordinary political life impotent through the threat of an incontestable nature*" (Latour 2004, italics original). Latour argues that we surely need the skills and insights of "the sciences," but the very idea of democracy is inconsistent with "Science" as an authority elevated above human ethics. Such reasoning concludes that we need the sciences to understand the likely consequences of our actions, but science cannot tell us what to do. In the end there is only we citizens who can interpret the findings of the sciences and propose what action to take. But this insight does not suggest that all we need is the political will to turn things around. Elsewhere Latour (1993: 5) argues that,

> scientific facts are indeed constructed [not revealed to us], but they cannot be reduced to the social dimension because this dimension is populated by objects mobilized to construct it.

His is, then, not an argument for social determinacy, but an argument that we have our categories wrong. It is not enough to recognize that science has politics embedded in it from the outset. Latour's point is that, in lieu of claiming the autonomy of science and nature as moderns have done, we should confront "nature-culture" as a single entity – we have not gone far enough. In Latour's view, the secularization of politics has been productive – some of us have acquired more liberty. The secularization of science is now underway – this too will create more liberty for others. Now we should focus on completing the job – we must secularize not only Politics and Science, but Nature too if we hope to be successful in constructing a life-enhancing or sustainable world.

In this volume, related arguments are made by architect Vincent B. Canizaro, planner Frederick Steiner, preservationist Jeffrey M. Chusid, and philosopher Andrew Light. It is Light's essay, however, that most directly adopts the logic, if not the language of secularization. In it he distinguishes between the abstract devotion to "Nature" promoted by deep ecologists in the 1980s, and the particular allegiance to "place" promoted by regionalists like Lewis Mumford in the middle decades of the last century. The difference, he surmises, adds up to something akin to a historical error made by North American environmentalists. In pragmatist terms, Light assesses the error on the basis of the consequences resulting from the sanctification of Nature as a force distinct from culture. From his perspective, it is less important that we know the final cosmological status of other living things than it is how our attitudes and actions affect their well-being. In shifting our focus from the myth of wilderness to the actual condition of the places we inhabit, Light sees not salvation, but "the creation of an intentional community of people dedicated to the places around us as an extension of themselves." As for Canizaro and Chusid in this volume, such a proposal requires the radical secularization of nature.

One might argue, I suppose, that the positive benefits that derive from the secularization of politics – which we have enjoyed for better than two centuries – do not automatically require us to treat science and nature in the same way. In this view it will require far more lengthy and careful arguments to make our case for the secular character of sustainable development. Not only this, but I doubt that all of the contributors to this volume will agree to the project of radical secularization as I have begun to sketch it here. Even so, the tentative agreement between at least some of us is that partitioning the worlds of politics, science, and nature has had unintended negative consequences. Simply put, unsustainability is not a scientific or technological problem, it is a social one. And as Dewey put it on p. 6, knowledge that claims to be asocial is not knowledge at all because, in the end, it has to be applied in a social context. Such holistic thinking requires us to question the partitioning of knowledge into the traditional disciplines.

Transdisciplinarity

The structure of this book was conceived as cutting across disciplinary lines in anticipation of finding fresh insights into the old problems of environmental and social degradation. Albert Einstein is reported to have said that we cannot hope to find new solutions by employing the same old tools and habits of discovery used to concoct the mess we wish to escape. The explicit bias of this book is, following Einstein, that the disciplines and tools we have created to produce new and salient knowledge have not lived up to their potential – they have been both less objective and less useful than we imagined (Fischer 2000, 2009).

The term "discipline" has, of course, layered meanings. In the most ordinary sense it refers to "training that is expected to produce a specified character or pattern of behavior." In the academic or professional worlds it refers to "a branch of knowledge or teaching" ("discipline" 1969). In both usages, kinds of knowledge are linked to preferred behaviors. From the dictionary, experience, and popular cartoons, we can predict that engineers and philosophers, for example, neither know the same things nor behave in the same way. This is to say that our training in one discipline tends to blind us to the insights and behaviors developed in others. In one discipline we are rewarded for thinking and behaving in a manner that would be cause for "disciplinary" action in another. This is, of course, hardly a new observation. The assets and liabilities of disciplinarity have been the subject of much scholarship and policy initiatives in both business and academe.

In this volume Andrew Jamison makes a particularly helpful distinction between "interdisciplinary" and "transdisciplinary" knowledge. By the first term, interdisciplinarity, he refers to the kind of hybridized knowledge produced in "collaborative" or "cooperative" teams seeking ways to transgress established intellectual boundaries for political purposes – to open our eyes.

By the latter term, transdisciplinarity, he refers to the kind of hybridized knowledge produced by "nondisciplinary" or "subdisciplinary" teams seeking ways to solve real problems for real people – to be useful. In Jamison's view, both forms of hybrid knowledge are necessary and I believe that the other contributors to this volume would generally agree because sustainability is an inherently inter- and transdisciplinary concept. This observation suggests a trajectory, or storyline for sustainability studies in general, which is the final theme reconstructed in the conversation of the contributors.

Storylines

Elsewhere I have argued that sustainable conditions show up in places, not because the citizens of that place have meticulously followed an abstract map or idealized model of sustainable development, but because they have, over time, articulated stories about how they want to live in relation to each other and in relation to nature that influence their habits in a manner that turns out to be "sustainable" (Moore 2007). Simply put, Science has no maps or models to give us. The sciences can, however, imply alternative futures we can try out for ourselves. In this volume, compatible claims are made by several contributors.

In his essay, David J. Hess rigorously and empirically documents four experimental or "alternative pathways" taken by advocates of social change in North America that have demonstrated at least partial success in achieving a more just and sustainable society. Hess's argument is not that these success stories can be replicated per se, but that we can learn from our fellow citizens the processes through which they came to invent and test novel "organizational, technological, and market relationships."

In his investigation of Japanese urbanism, Simon Guy tells us that we have been looking in the wrong places for indicators of sustainable development in Japan. As a result, we have been telling the wrong stories about what it might look like. Rather than look to the well-known, if little understood, history of Japanese attitudes toward timeless nature, Guy argues, we should look at the messy, ad hocism of Japanese attitudes toward the city. If we look at what the Japanese actually do, rather than at romanticized projections from the West, we will tell very different stories.

From an entirely theoretical perspective Paul B. Thompson finds that, although "sustainability" has little philosophical coherence as an idea, it does something more important – it provides a framework for action as a shared conception of where we have come from and where we might go. In other words, the very concept of sustainable development implies a hopeful storyline – it is a common narrative of what we would like life to be.

In the view of these three contributors, the stories told by citizens trying to make sense of their world are privileged over knowledge claims thrown in from the sidelines, from academia. The use of "context-dependent knowledge" in social affairs is far more likely to be successful than the use of rule-bound or "context-independent knowledge" borrowed from elsewhere. As Bent Flyvbjerg has argued, "narrative is an ancient method and perhaps our most fundamental form for making sense of experience" (Flyvbjerg 2006). Making sense of the actions we are about to take is more important than being right about actions taken in the past by others. Sustainable development requires stories to make new habits attractive.

Conclusion

At the outset I said that this introductory essay would reconstruct the warp and weft of our conversation before having anything to say about the nature of pragmatism or sustainability. Having fulfilled the first task I will rely on Richard Rorty to summarize the common or meta-characteristics that tie together the themes found in this volume. Together, these characteristics add up to a down payment on pragmatic sustainability.

Rorty (1989: 105) holds that pragmatism is constituted of three attitudes: First, pragmatists share a "simple anti-essentialism" toward categories like truth and knowledge. As I argued on p. 3, pragmatists in general don't find it particularly helpful to make grand claims – humble, concrete actions are preferred. Second, they find "no epistemological difference between truth about what ought to be and truth about what is." This is why constructing collaborative stories about the future is preferred by the contributors to making technoscientific claims about what happened in the past. And third, "there are no constraints on inquiry save conversational ones." This is to say that there are no sacred texts, no authorities that cannot be transgressed because we have constructed them all ourselves – we have only ourselves to blame.

There is, of course, an inherent problem in characterizing such a diverse group of people – whether found in the diner or this book – in this way. As Rorty recognized, to claim that there is no competing authorities "out there" to guide us is in itself an authorial claim. And this is a trap that besets pragmatists of all stripes – how to secularize our stories, how to be useful, without writing history for others before it unfolds.

From my own perspective, Rorty's characterization of the attitudes shared by pragmatists is consistent with the seven perspectives found in the essays in this collection. Nonetheless, I will avoid claiming that these seven views toward reality constitute, in themselves, a pragmatic philosophy of sustainability. Susan Haack and her colleagues have clearly demonstrated the inconsistencies and tensions between the "old and new" pragmatisms, between Peirce and Rorty for example, and I agree that any attempt to define the fundamental assumptions of pragmatism, as if it were a single idea, is not a very good use of our time (Haack 2006). I can, however, recommend the seven themes that turned up in the essays time and again as helpful heuristics, or tools, that we can use to test the menu of choices presented to us.

If we return to the diner where this introduction began, I can now say that the diner and its owner have become successful, like the conversation they catalyzed, because they are examples of what the Greeks referred to as *mētis*. To be successful in life, the Greeks certainly recognized the value of *episteme*, the kind of formal, abstract, or symbolic knowledge that the diner's owner demonstrated in parsing the distinction between kinds of trans-fats. But unlike our own culture, the Greeks valued practical knowledge over the abstract. *Mētis* refers not just to the cunning use of practical knowledge required to create a healthy substitute for French fries, but to "a wide array of practical skills and acquired intelligence in responding to a constantly changing natural and human environment" (Scott 1998). This is the kind of skill required of a diner owner who must alter her menu based on what local farmers can grow seasonally in an undependable climate and yet attract a constant flow of customers in a shifting demographic area. This is not the kind of intelligence or constant experimentation one can find at restaurants like Denny's or McDonald's, or even at the old diner where the saturated trans-fat potatoes were always the same. But it is the kind of knowledge that is privileged by the contributors to this volume. It is not that the themes of conversation will be precisely the same in this book as in the diner, but that both conversations are hopeful, future-oriented, and just might catalyze other successful experiments and new habits that will turn out to be sustainable.

Bibliography

Dewey, John. (1916) *Essays in Experimental Logic,* Chicago, IL: University of Chicago.

——. (1927) *The Public and its Problems*, New York [reprinted in Athens, OH]: H. Holt [reprinted by Swallow Press, Ohio University Press].

"discipline". (1969) In *The American Heritage Dictionary of the English Language*, edited by W. Morris, Boston, MA: Houghton Mifflin.

Feenberg, Andrew. (1995) "Subversive Rationalization: Technology, Power, and Democracy," in A. Feenberg and A. Hannay (eds.) *Technology and the Politics of Knowledge*, Bloomington, IN: Indiana University Press.

Fischer, Frank. (2000) *Citizens, Experts, and the Environment: The Politics of Local Knowledge*, Durham, London: Duke University Press.

——. (2009) *Democracy and Expertise: Reorienting Policy Inquiry*, New York: Oxford University Press.

Flyvbjerg, Bent. (2006) "Five Misunderstandings About Case-Study Research," *Qualitative Inquiry* (12): 219–245.

Haack, Susan with Robert Lane, (ed.) (2006) *Pragmatism, Old and New*, Amhearst, NY: Prometheus Books.

Latour, Bruno. (1987) *Science in Action*, Cambridge, MA: Harvard University Press.

——. (1993) *We Have Never Been Modern*, translated by C. Porter, Cambridge, MA: Harvard University Press.

——. (2004) *Politics of Nature: How to bring science into democracy*, translated by C. Porter, Cambridge, MA: Harvard University Press. Original edition, *Politiques de la Nature*, Editions de le Couverte.

Marcuse, Herbert. (1966, c1964) *One-Dimensional Man: studies in the ideology of advanced industrial society*, Boston, MA: Beacon Press.

Moore, Steven A. (2007) *Alternative Routes to the Sustainable City: Austin, Curitiba and Frankfurt*, Lanham, MD: Lexington Books, Rowman & Littlefield.

Rorty, Richard. (1989) *Contingency, Irony, and Solidarity*, New York: Cambridge University Press.

——. (1998) *Achieving Our Country*, Cambridge, MA: Harvard University Press.

Scott, James C. (1998) *Seeing Like a State*, New Haven, CT: Yale University Press.

Winner, Langdon. (2004) "Sow's Ears from Silk Purses: How Enthusiasts Betray the Promise of New Technology," in M. Sturken (ed.) *Technological Visions: Utopian and Dystopian Perspectives*, Minneapolis, MN: University of Minnesota Press.

The Struggle to Define Terms

Editor's Introduction to Chapter 1

We depend on philosophers to help us assess the meaning of our words. And when it comes to a word so used and misused as "sustainability," we can generally count on a philosopher to provide a substantive account. In this essay Thompson classifies sustainability into three dominant meanings. The first, resource sufficiency, points toward an interpretation of sustainability as a measure of the duration of practices that produce well-being. In this model, resource sufficiency is little more than the nineteenth-century utilitarian maxim proposed by Bentham: choose practices that maximize total well-being. A problem associated with this option is that it leaves open questions about whose well-being and the relative measure of different forms of satisfaction.

The second model, functional integrity, describes the mechanisms that allow whole systems (such as human societies or human-dominated ecosystems) to regenerate themselves over time. It is generally expressed as prudential advice to be cautious about taking uncertain risks in altering social institutions or ecological interactions, but the contrast between these two approaches can reveal important value judgments.

Thompson holds that the third model followed in the sustainability literature is "non-substantive" – sustainability is either just a way to endorse and condemn certain practices, or a banner under which the various groups interested in environmental and social justice might assemble. In either case, this notion lacks empirical content: claims about sustainability are neither true nor false. He argues, however, that these non-substantive uses do in fact matter for mobilizing publics in pursuit of important social goals. It is in this way that Thompson, like the pragmatists, privileges action over contemplating the meaning of words, even words like sustainability, because it is through action that meaning is created. William James put it this way:

> ...if you follow the pragmatic method, you cannot look on any such word as closing your quest. You must bring out of each word its practical cash-value, set it at work within the stream of your experience. It appears less as a solution, then, than as a program for more work, and more particularly as an indication of the ways in which existing realities may be changed.
>
> (James 1904)

Chapter 1

What Sustainability Is (and What It Isn't)

Paul B. Thompson

The variety of views on what it means to be sustainable has multiplied since critics of conventional agriculture began to claim that it was "unsustainable," and ecologists and wildlife biologists were developing models of "sustainable yield." The debate is no longer confined to agriculture and natural resource management. Others now want to talk about "sustainable cities," "sustainable capitalism," "sustainable medicine," "sustainable manufacturing," and even "sustainable architecture." The most significant expansion in the dialog occurred following the Brundtland Report, which precipitated two decades of debate and discussion on the idea of "sustainable development" (WCED 1987). Yet few that participate in these conversations about a given "sustainable X" have the time, inclination or skills to step back and analyze whether what separates them is a difference in values and perspectives, or a simple verbal dispute. The (possibly) contentious title of this chapter is intended to direct readers to the discipline of philosophy's main contribution to any "sustainable X." Philosophy can at least help clarify what is being disputed, even if it cannot resolve disputes or specify definitions in full.

It is possible that the philosopher's task ends when the terms of debate have been clarified, but a second aim of this chapter is to argue that sustainability is becoming a contested concept of more enduring and fundamental interest. In some cases, our thinking and communication can be clarified simply by attending closely to a specific definition. Other times we find that a particular concept is so important to the way we understand ourselves and our world that we cannot gain mastery over it simply by specifying a definition for a given context. Concepts like "truth," "objectivity," "causality," and "justice" have been contested throughout human history. These ideas have resisted our attempts to specify them in any final sense, yet it seems we must use them to think and to act collectively. As we come to think more deeply and carefully about the impact of human activity on the broader environment and on the opportunities of future generations, competing conceptions of sustainability have a tremendous impact on the way that we frame the central problems. In short, philosophy encounters sustainability first by offering tools to better understand disputed visions of what sustainable practices might involve, and second because debates over what is sustainable and what is not may well be the opening to an important new set of philosophical inquiry.

Steven A. Moore has argued that we can understand sustainability as a storyline, a narrative thread that people use to understand how the past, present, and future can be connected in different ways (Moore 2007). Although I will take issue with that view on p. 26, I will begin the argument with a bit of biography, describing my own past encounters with the idea of sustainability en route to a more argumentative discussion of why sustainability is important, and why it is important to debate what it is as well as what it is not. I will argue that the most productive debates will revolve around conceptualizations of sustainability that I characterize as *resource sufficiency* and *functional integrity*, respectively. But a fair amount of the talk currently circulating with respect to sustainability adopts neither of these frameworks, and appears, in fact, to be calculated toward political, ethical, and cultural concerns that actually have nothing to do with sustainability as such. This *non-substantive sustainability* has to be taken into account, and even contributes to our pursuit of real sustainability in important ways. But in the end, I will argue, this *is* in fact what sustainability is not, and the possibility of really learning from a debate over sustainability depends upon particip-ants' willingness to move toward a more substantive way of understanding it.

Sustainability: a personal storyline

Philosophers generally began to take an interest in the concept of sustainability in the late 1980s, and I have been working on it myself for over twenty years. My early research was framed exclu-sively within the context of debates over the future of agricultural production in the United States. That context of thought gradually came to encompass debates over the methods and structure of crop and livestock production in other industrialized countries, especially Europe, and eventually on a global scale. The Brundtland Report was primarily responsible for helping me think through sustainability as an issue of importance to developing nations, but it is, in fact, only in the last five years that I have come to appreciate how much my focus on agriculture has shaped my thinking on sustainability. As readers will see, agriculturally oriented examples and citations still continue to dominate the following discussion.

Before turning explicitly to my journey with sustainability I should mention that my per-sonal storyline also includes a longstanding commitment to pragmatism. Other chapters in this volume take up the task of explaining pragmatism more explicitly than I do in what follows, but perhaps it will suffice to note how the classical pragmatism of William James and John Dewey has always maintained a relentless focus on specific problems, never allowing the detritus of lin-gering theoretical perspectives to block a critical re-conceptualization of ends in view. At the same time, pragmatists are capable of tolerating a fair amount of ambiguity and vagueness when doing so seems to serve the interests of communication. Thus, Dewey, an inveterate opponent of supernaturalism, once wrote,

> There is a time and place to see ghosts and a time and place to see scouts of the enemy, and the great thing is to observe the conveniences about the proper time and place. To think of things rightly or wrongly is to think of them according to or contrary to social demands.

> (Dewey 1911: 1)

The interest I have taken in "defining sustainability" throughout my encounter with it should be read in that spirit.

My thinking on sustainability has three main phases. From about 1986 until about 1994, I was fairly skeptical and even cynical about the idea of sustainability. This is not to say that I was ever opposed to sustainable agriculture, for I was always "with" the critics and activists who were promoting a change in farm production. However, for about six years I believed that the debates over sustainable agriculture and sustainable development were not really about sustainability at all. To be sure, there were genuine differences in the participants' conceptions of social justice, though there were also plenty of occasions when it seemed like it was just underlying economic interests in a contest for markets and political influence. (That is, big companies thought that sustainability meant profitability for big companies, small farmers in Nebraska thought that sustainability meant being able to continue farming at a small scale in Nebraska, advocates for Latin American peasants thought that sustainability meant social justice for Latin American peasants, etc.). My writing from this period argued there was little ethical significance to sustainability, as such. It was, I believed, much better to articulate the genuine differences in outlook on social justice in more direct and conventional language (Thompson et al.).

However, this work is most notable for recognizing both an empirical and a normative (or ethical) dimension to sustainability (Thompson 1992). By "empirical" I meant that it is meaningful to question how long one would be able to continue doing what one was doing before scarcity of resources or some internal contradiction in one's practice would lead to its undoing. By "normative," I meant that even if people's value judgments are grounded in beliefs about social justice, they were using claims about the sustainable or unsustainable nature of practices to say something more than just saying whether they could be continued. When the TV news anchor says that the current prices for gasoline are unsustainable, he or she is simply saying that they will go up or down. When agriculture, architecture, land use, cities or development trajectories are said to be unsustainable, the person who says this is saying that they are ethically, politically or in some other way inappropriate, improper or bad.

There are two other dimensions to this early work that should be summarized. First, I believed then and still believe that it would not be possible to answer empirical questions about sustainability without taking a systems view. That is, no particular production technology, form of land tenure or other human practice is either sustainable or unsustainable in isolation. One examines a practice within a system context and then asks whether the total system is sustainable, presuming that what happens outside system borders remains stable. It is, thus, possible for an agronomist to assess sustainability at the level of a farmer's field, looking only at soil chemistry and its impact on biota. But doing this presumes that the farmer is "outside" the system, and will always be there to manage inputs. One can reframe the question of sustainability by asking what system has to be in place to ensure that a farmer (either a particular farmer, or any given farmer) will always be there to farm. Here, farm policies and the availability of credit become the exogenous elements that one treats as "outside" the system, always there year after year. How one defines system borders involves a value judgment that frames the empirical assessment of sustainability (Thompson 1995).

Second, because of this systems approach, I have argued that it is possible for a person who is morally committed to sustainability to be overwhelmed by a more comprehensive and unsustainable system. It is also possible for someone who neither thinks nor cares about sustainability to farm (or engage in other practices) that nevertheless contribute to the sustainability of the overall system. As such, it matters less that we promote sustainability as a personal ideal than that we pursue sustainability at a system level. This may mean that we are careful to maintain norms and beliefs that contribute to sustainability, even if they are not articulated as injunctions to pursue sustainability as such (Thompson 1986).

In 1994, several colleagues and I undertook a fairly extensive review of the way that people were defining and using the concept of sustainability in a variety of problem-solving and policy contexts. Many of the authors we read were trying to find ways of answering the empirical questions that I had already identified as meaningful. This research did not lead me to reject my earlier views, but it did lead me to recognize that any attempt to answer these empirical questions would not be straightforward, and that it would involve a number of subtle value judgments. Furthermore, I came to the view that although there are dozens, perhaps hundreds, of distinct methodologies for measuring and pursuing sustainability through technical research, there are two broad paradigms for conceptualizing sustainability. These two paradigms did not contradict one another so much as they represented alternative approaches, each of which would tend to subsume the other. They differed in which questions they took to be most fundamental, and this difference had implications for how one would organize and conduct research on sustainability, how one would understand our ethical responsibility to make our practices more sustainable.

Many of the technical approaches my colleagues and I reviewed conceptualize sustainability as a problem of *resource sufficiency*. People working within this paradigm arrive at working definitions of sustainability through two measurement problems. First, they measure the rate at which a given production or consumption practice consumes resources. Second, they estimate the stock or store of resources available. The relative sustainability of a practice is then determined by predicting how long the practice may be continued, given the existing stock of resources. The other approach conceptualizes sustainability in terms of the *functional integrity* of a self-regenerating system. On this view, a practice that creates a threat to the system's capacity for reproducing itself over time is said to be unsustainable. This approach requires an account of the system in question that specifies its reproductive mechanisms, as well as an account of how specific practices, conceived as system activities, place those mechanisms at risk (Thompson 1997; Thompson and Nardone 1999).

The third phase of my thinking began to take shape as I began working on the first draft of the manuscript that became this chapter around the year 2000. I recognized that the literature on sustainability contained a third group of people writing and talking about sustainability who seemed to be making a *non-substantive* use of the word. Here, the normative dimension is retained, but the descriptive or empirical dimension has virtually disappeared. Calling a practice or a pattern of conduct unsustainable becomes a way of saying, "You may get away with that this time, but eventually you'll be sorry!" This *might* point toward a deeper sense in which the practice or conduct will lead to its own undoing, but more frequently it is just a very general form of moral or prudential rebuke. While I had been very critical of such talk in my earlier phases, I began to appreciate the fact that there was more to this usage than I had originally thought.

In 2005, Bryan Norton published an enormous tome intended to be the definitive statement of his general approach in environmental philosophy under the title *Sustainability: A Philosophy of Eco-System Management.* I had long been an admirer of Norton's work, and was shocked to discover the turn in his thought (see Norton 1992). His final chapter summarizes over four hundred pages of analysis with the statement that, "Sustainable activities are ones that can be carried on in the present without negatively impacting the range of important choices that should be left open to the next generation" (Norton 2005: 432). Norton goes on to say that in many respects, sustainability is very close to what we have always meant by autonomy or freedom. So to promote sustainability is basically to promote freedom. Was Norton caving in to a non-substantive notion of sustainability, devoid of empirical content? Or had I missed something in my earlier work?

This chapter, along with two other recent papers thus represents the third phase of my work on sustainability (Thompson 2007a, 2007b). I still believe that the contrast between resource sufficiency and functional integrity is important, and I still believe that conceptualizations which depart wholly from either of these approaches are lacking in important respects. However, I will also probe the value of non-substantive uses of the word "sustainability," a little more deeply. This way of talking about sustainability enables and promotes some very healthy activities within local *and* global debates.

Sustainability as resource sufficiency and functional integrity

Dale Jamieson traces the concept of sustainable development from a 1980 report from the International Union for the Conservation of Nature and Natural Resources, through the 1987 Brundtland Commission Report, to its current plethora of uses and applications. Jamieson concludes that the word is useful in structuring popular discussions and debate, but that it has little philosophical content or motivational power (Jamieson 1998: 188). Jamieson's indictment amounts to the claim that conceptualizing human activities in terms of sustainability does nothing to enhance our understanding of moral and prudential obligations associated with those activities. The second claim, that sustainability has no motivational power, amounts to the claim that characterizing one course of action as more sustainable than another will have little effect on human behavior. This second point will be reviewed in connection with the non-substantive meaning identified on p. 25, but first it is important to rebut Jamieson's claim that there is nothing of much importance added to a political or philosophical analysis of human practice by asking whether it is sustainable.

It is possible that Jamieson is simply rejecting the idea that sustainability represents some sort of intrinsic good, or some comprehensive synthesis of goods. If this *were* the case, information about sustainability would be important because we would have an ethical obligation to pursue sustainability as such (George 1992). In previous work, I concluded that this is not the best way to characterize the ethics of sustainability (Thompson 1992, 1995). The argument can be reformulated by considering an extreme question: is murder sustainable? We can answer in terms of resource sufficiency by measuring the rate at which murder consumes human lives, and the number of victims available. We can answer in terms of functional integrity by determining whether murder threatens the human population's ability to reproduce itself. It seems likely that murder would turn out to be relatively sustainable on either approach, so long as more people are born than killed off. This fact about murder does nothing to recommend our approval of the practice. We are not inclined to say, "Well, at least it's sustainable; that's something in favor of murder." This suggests that we must first deem a practice to be worthwhile on grounds other than sustainability before attempting to find more sustainable ways of securing the values or achieving the goals that make a practice worthwhile in the first place (Thompson 1992, 1995).

The argument so far implies that sustainability is not intrinsically valuable. However, information about the sustainability of a given activity might be important in assessing the costs and benefits of that activity. Measuring sustainability might, for example, help us understand how long a benefit stream can be maintained, or it might alert us to future risks or costs that will be incurred as a consequence of personal or policy decisions that we make today. This suggests that sustainability over time is just a dimension of the general utilitarian maxim proposed by Bentham over two hundred years ago. The maxim states that we should choose practices that maximize total well-being or utility, and Bentham describes several ways to measure utility. One of these is to increase the duration of pleasurable or satisfying experiences, but increase in duration can be swamped by increase in intensity or extent (i.e., in the number of parties experiencing satisfaction) (Bentham 1789: 30). The underlying principle is optimization, not sustainability. If sustainability simply points us toward the duration of well-being over time, it is worth including in a comparison of alternative social policies, but there is nothing really new that is added to planning by expressing the importance of how long a given level of well-being can endure in terms of sustainability.

So far, the argument does not provide any basis to contradict Jamieson's judgment that there is nothing novel or interesting about sustainability, but perhaps this is simply a result of the resource sufficiency approach implicit in utilitarian thinking. To examine this possibility, consider again the practice of murder. Taking first the sustainability-as-duration idea suggested by the resource sufficiency approach, we can argue that society's capacity to sustain a murder rate over time is of little value because the costs or harms associated with almost any given murder outweigh its benefits. Lengthening the duration of a murder rate for society might be a good thing in comparison to an alternative where the murder rate increases, but not because of sustainability. The moral judgment is simply a matter of the total welfare produced by each alternative. Duration, again, is only a dimension of the increase or decrease in total utility, total benefit and harm.

Switching to a functional integrity approach, we ask how murder threatens a society's ability to reproduce itself. We might first assess the question in terms of biological births and deaths, but we will quickly recognize that this is a more complicated question than whether there are enough victims to keep up the killing. We are led quickly to ask whether a given murder rate (or perhaps murders of a particular kind or within a particular sector of society) might threaten the stability of political, religious or family institutions. Answering these questions might, in turn, lead one to conclude that murder *does* threaten a society's ability to regenerate its fundamental institutions, and this conclusion adds something to the way in which murder is understood as a social problem. The harm done by murder is sufficient reason to expend resources on police and courts, but the stakes are even higher when we become convinced that it threatens fundamental institutions. Indeed, there would be outrage if people found out that police only expended resources to curtail murders when the harm threatened by a given murder exceeded the cost of conducting the investigation (though of course cities that neglect crimes against the homeless may in fact do exactly that). Here, even being seen to make decisions on a cost–benefit basis "poisons the wells" (Baier 1986).

A similar comparison can be made for ecological, environmental, and agricultural applications of the resource sufficiency and functional integrity approaches, though the issues are more complex. If we take a resource sufficiency approach to food production, the problem is still one of balancing costs and benefits. The accounting becomes very complicated and contentious, in part because we know too little about the environmental costs of food production. Yet if we did reach consensus on the costs and benefits of food production, the value associated with sustainability (e.g., how long we could produce food a given way) would be entirely subsumed in this larger optimization problem. We would compare the relative costs and benefits of different ways for producing food. The comparison would be difficult in virtue of the disparity between different kinds of cost or benefit (e.g., gustatory vs. nutritional value; producer vs. consumer benefit; human vs. ecosystem health), but sustainability-as-duration would certainly be one of the least difficult aspects of the comparison to make.

Consider then how food production affects our society's ability to reproduce itself. This, too, is a problem of almost overwhelming complexity because society must be understood as a system comprising many subsystems that are threatened in different ways by different approaches to producing food. The human population's biological need for food sets one system parameter, but in meeting this parameter it is possible to deplete soil, water, and genetic resources used in food production. Since each of these is a regenerative subsystem, threats to these subsystems represent threats to total system sustainability. Similarly, farms and rural communities represent subsystems. If farming is unprofitable, or if the local institutions that support farming are not regenerated, the sustainability of the larger system is threatened. Our desire to maintain the functional integrity of all these subsystems might make us cautious about tampering with any subsystem that seemed to be functioning for fear that what we would do might upset the complex interconnection of the whole.

Far from understanding sustainability as one dimension of optimization, we would understand it as a relative equilibrium among social and natural subsystems, an equilibrium that we challenge at our peril. We might say that we value these natural and social subsystems because they provide the context or the constitutional basis for personal and group identity, and for the formation of preferences that would give rise to a given conception of well-being. While this might make us reluctant to introduce changes in pursuit of greater system output, it does not make sustainability into an intrinsic value, for we would feel little compunction about interfering in a system that did not seem to be functioning well. It might be worth some risk to change a social system that produces wretchedness and social injustice in large measure. And if our knowledge about threats to system integrity indicated that our food production system was headed for collapse, sustainability-as-functional integrity would provide a basis for even extreme restorative measures.

We may summarize and tie this discussion to a broader literature in ethics and political philosophy. Resource sufficiency points toward an interpretation of sustainability as a measure of the duration associated with practices that produce well-being. It leaves questions about whose well-being and the relative measure of different forms of satisfaction open. It is consistent with the general form of the utilitarian maxim, and indeed seems to specify nothing more than the temporal dimension of it. It is therefore an important component of the information we need to carry out moral and political duties conceptualized in utilitarian terms, but it is not particularly interesting from a philosophical perspective. Functional integrity, however, describes the mechanisms that allow whole systems (such as human societies or human-dominated ecosystems) to regenerate themselves over time. System level stability manifests itself in social institutions, renewal of soil, water and genetic resources (including wildlife), and cultural identity. The basis of our obligation to maintain this stability is sometimes obscure but can be expressed as prudential advice to be cautious about very uncertain risks. It may also be expressed in more communitarian terms as a duty to maintain the integrity of institutions and natural processes that are the basis for our collective sense of identity and purpose.

Debating sustainability

There is more that can be said about the relationship between resource sufficiency and functional integrity. It seems likely that there will be situations in which the data and models – the science – used to determine whether a given system meets resource sufficiency and functional integrity criteria do not differ. Classical models of sustainable yield in fisheries, for example, could be articulated under either paradigm. The choice of one approach or the other would appear to make little difference in such cases. But one could argue that even here, the accounting orientation of resource sufficiency will direct one to normative questions such as "How much sufficiency, and for whom," while the attention to system vulnerabilities in functional integrity will direct one to normative questions relating to the way that system boundaries have been constructed. As such, the "debate" between these two approaches concepts may be better described as a dialectical approach to thinking about sustainability that is most effective in surfacing normative issues when each paradigm is put into dialog with the other (Thompson 2007a).

This is not, however, the way that debates over sustainability are routinely described. Allan Holland reviews the debate between advocates of *strong sustainability*, who insist that natural capital must not decline over time, and those who advocate *weak sustainability*, that is, that human well-being does not decline over time (see Holland 2001; Jamieson 1998). In Jamieson's treatment, both groups operationalize their respective conceptions of sustainability by sketching accounting arguments of a resource sufficiency kind. The primary difference is that weak sustainability presumes that one means for maintaining human well-being is as good as any other. Crucially, advocates of weak sustainability believe that it will be possible to maintain well-being by substituting human for natural capital (see Pearce 1993; Simon 1998). Advocates of strong sustainability believe that future generations have a right to the same amount of natural capital as present generations, and that protecting this right places a prior constraint on preference maximization by present generations (see Howarth 1995; Bromley 1998).

Strong and weak sustainability represent significantly different perspectives for evaluating any "X," be it agriculture, cities, or manufacturing. Specifically, advocates of weak sustainability may see science and technology as a way to compensate for consumption of non-renewable resources, or for perturbation of an ecosystem's ability to regenerate renewable resources. To say that human capital is substituted for natural capital is economists' talk for saying that science will continue to increase yields, even as the renewable resource base declines. Advocates of strong sustainability such as Norton reject this strategy, claiming that it violates the rights of future generations (Norton 2005). Holland emphasizes the way strong sustainability might be understood to include concern for sentient creatures beyond human beings, or perhaps even for the integrity of nature itself (Holland 2001). But this objection can still be interpreted in light of both paradigms. As an expression of resource sufficiency, the objection states that the interests or needs of some affected parties (e.g., future generations; sentient non-humans; ecosystems) have been left out of the accounting. One can certainly debate how far one should go in one's inclusiveness, and such debates are very familiar in environmental ethics. But extending concern to future humans or to non-human animals and ecosystems is fully compatible with resource sufficiency's key normative question, "Sustainability for who?"

A focus on functional integrity might point toward a totally different kind of normative problem. First, if science is generating the technology crucial to meeting needs in the future, we must be sure that the subsystem that supports science is itself secure. Yet funding for agricultural science, at least, has declined steadily over the last decade, and as the number of farmers who lobby for research declines, it is not at all clear that social apparatus needed to support the research system is clear (Buttel 1993). If we maintain the focus on agriculture, we can note a second issue. Increases in per acre yield of staple crops have been accompanied by patterns of industrialization in agriculture that deplete rural populations, and that shift farmers' economic livelihood away from dependence on soil, water and genetic resources, and toward dependence on finance. This shift is central to an alternative conception of sustainable agriculture. Bearing the 2008 credit crisis in mind we may question whether making our food supply depend upon Wall Street is a good idea. Those who believe that farming has shifted toward greater dependence on an inherently risky system for regenerating financial capital will not be impressed by accounting calculations which show that projections of food production by industrial agriculture include the food needs of future generations.

The case of agriculture thus illustrates how the value judgments rising to the surface for debate and conversation will be different when one takes one of the perspectives implicit in the resource sufficiency and functional integrity paradigms. This difference lurks beneath the surface of a characterization that sees the debate over sustainability in terms of weak and strong approaches, but a philosophical interpretation of sustainability that seizes upon the weak/strong dichotomy fails to articulate the point. It is worth stressing how empirical (or descriptive) and normative (or ethical) points are interlinked here. Resource sufficiency and functional integrity are alternative paradigms for answering the empirical question, "Is X sustainable?" In many cases, they will utilize the same data and models to answer that question. But what is most important about the difference between these perspectives is the way that each surfaces a different set of value judgments about what sustainability means. Thus, the weak/strong dichotomy is certainly not *equivalent* to the dichotomy between resource sufficiency and functional integrity, and one reason for stressing the latter way of understanding the debate over what sustainability is (and what it is not) lies in the way that more profound and fundamental value judgments are made obvious.

Non-substantive sustainability

Jamieson notes that "sustainability" is a good conversation starter, and a way to bring different interests to the table. What I call *non-substantive* uses of the word "sustainable" can be important in bringing people with different interests and values together. When this use generates definitions of sustainability, they tend to be highly general. Two economists offered this definition:

> We define sustainable agricultural development in this paper as an agricultural system which over the long run, enhances environmental quality and the resource base on which agriculture depends, provides for basic human food and fiber needs, is economically viable, and enhances the quality of life of farmers and society as a whole.
>
> (Davis and Langham 1995: 21–22)

This definition acknowledges that agriculture feeds the human population, provides income for farmers and rural communities, and affects the environment, and in doing so it at least acknowledges multiple interests and multiple objectives. But *every* agricultural technology is intended to be sustainable in this sense. Not every project meets these goals, of course, but here the difference between a sustainable and an unsustainable X seems to devolve down to the difference between a good X and a bad one.

There is also a widespread tendency to represent sustainability in terms of a triangle with ecological, economic, and social vertices. Here, X would be sustainable if it is ecologically, economically, and socially sustainable (Thrupp 1993; Dlott *et al.* 1994; Bell and Morse 1999; Armstrong and Pajor 2001). Authors who use this tripartite characterization often go on to develop extensive discussions of how each dimension should be understood, but a simplified summary suffices for present purposes. Ecological sustainability means something akin to functional integrity of ecosystem processes, as described on p. 19. Economic sustainability means that those participating in an activity can recover their costs. In business settings, their activities are profitable; in household and other non-profit settings, they remain within budget. A resource sufficiency approach would clearly speak to economic sustainability in most cases. Social sustainability is intended to call attention to issues of equity, fairness or social justice.

In some instances, authors simply assert that socially unjust practices are unsustainable (see George 1992; Barkin 1998). Patricia Allen and Carolyn Sachs defend this use of the term "sustainable," when they describe sustainability as a "banner" under which a number of groups interested in environment and social justice have assembled (Allen and Sachs 1992). Allen and Sachs argue that an adequate conception of sustainability must include the interests of labor, of the poor and of marginalized groups (Allen and Sachs 1993). Their usage is consistent with that of others who suggest that we understand sustainability as a social movement (Peet and Watts 1996; Bartley 2003). Thus, social sustainability can be a way of adding normative criteria that may have little to do with either resource sufficiency or functional integrity as such in order to stress that "mere" sustainability (as one would derive it from either paradigm) is not enough. This is (as noted on p. 21) exactly what I had previously endorsed in seeing sustainability as an "add-on" value. Or it can become a "banner," a label that unites people concerned with environmental and social justice concerns into a more effective social movement.

I don't think that one can deny that sustainability-as-social-movement has become somewhat effective as an organizing principle for many groups. This suggests that Jamieson was just mistaken when he wrote that it lacked motivational power. Steven A. Moore's suggestion that sustainability can be understood as a storyline also illustrates how the idea has organizational and motivating power. Comparing the way that goals of sustainability have been used to frame and orient urban development policies in three cities, Moore suggests that the idea of sustainability is effective in helping people collectively envision the route from a given community's past toward an envisioned future. Because people envision this route (and indeed the future itself) somewhat differently, sustainability gets contested in any given locale. What is being contested, however, may have very little to do with resource sufficiency or functional integrity, and everything to do with competing conceptions of democracy, justice or the good life (Moore 2007).

I am insisting on calling all of these "non-substantive" conceptions of sustainability precisely because of the way empirical issues seem to be wholly irrelevant to the debate over whether a given X is sustainable or not. The basic problem with social sustainability or sustainability as a storyline is that when calling something sustainable or unsustainable, we generally think that we are making a statement that could potentially be shown to be true or false. We thus need some conception of sustainability that does more than indicating approval or that reiterates claims and disputes familiar to contested concepts such as social justice. Furthermore, important issues are overlooked when the functional integrity paradigm is limited to the ecological domain. What are the institutions that are truly critical to the reproduction of our social world? How does placing too much reliance on a potentially fragile credit system, the continued existence of employment or tax revenues associated with a given industry, or upon a traditional family structure for inculcation of norms such as honesty or industriousness threaten the continued existence of social systems?

As a resident of Michigan, I am keenly aware that something is amiss in the "social sustainability" of the community in which I live. Is it a deficit in our local commitment to democracy or social justice? Arguably not. Arguably, accounting practices based on the assumed vibrancy of the US auto industry resulted in resource sufficiency calculations for many households as well as state and local governments that were badly mistaken. One might describe the problem this way: The resource sufficiency models in use a decade ago were wrong; they overestimated income flows for households and tax revenue into the future. Might an inquiry into the economic and social forces that kept the auto industry solvent for so many years have revealed vulnerability in the subsystems that were critical to the functional integrity of Michigan cities? Arguably so. Here, the functional integrity paradigm calls attention to the way that fixing the boundaries of Michigan's economy too narrowly allows one to overlook key vulnerabilities.

I would also argue that the Michigan problem is not just about economic sustainability. Tax revenues have declined and the ranks of the jobless have swelled, but this is clearly more than just an economic problem. Migration out of the state threatens a number of community institutions, and the general malaise extends to spiritual as well as monetary resources. Although the less well-educated and less well-off do indeed suffer more than the rich (as advocates of social justice might stress), the displaced autoworkers who are bearing the brunt of this transition are members of the middle class. This strike against the middle class threatens social stability and quality of life even more fundamentally and pervasively than do nagging deficits of social justice in regard to the poor. Functional integrity and resource sufficiency therefore are both relevant to the continuation of social and economic institutions, but a conceptual approach that sees "social sustainability" solely in terms of normative commitments, effective social movements and the "goodness" of a particular solution is liable to serious deficiencies and mistakes.

Conclusion

Yet in the end, it seems clear that the motivational effectiveness of sustainability as a social movement may compensate for the vagueness and lack of specificity one associates with non-substantive sustainability. Here, Moore's idea that sustainability is a storyline actually seems more hopeful than vague. Developing a shared conception of where we have come from and where we are going will clearly require conversations that bring in a number of historically contested concepts. "Democracy," and "social justice," will be prominent among them, and I, for one, would not want to participate in any storyline where they are absent.

My "early stage" thinking left me with a paradox. On the one hand, the human polity ought to act sustainably. On the other hand, the human polity cannot mobilize around the goal of sustainability. Looked at in one way, there is no contradiction here. It is just a way of saying that it is better to be lucky than smart. If we have simple norms that provide little insight into the regenerative systems of ecology and society, but that guide our behavior in ways that allow those systems to function, we should retain those simple norms. We ought *not* replace them with complicated conceptual or mathematical models that are "smart" in providing predictive knowledge of system failure, but that are too complex for people to follow on a day-to-day basis (see Grant and Thompson 1997). My middle stage thinking left me with irony. Though we ought to improve our understanding of sustainability in a deep sense, and though non-substantive discussions of sustainability make this more difficult, non-substantive talk about sustainability may be more sustainable than reforming the public discourse with an ecologically and philosophically richer idea.

My third stage thinking leaves me with solidarity, and I am very happy to be included among the authors in this volume. I am wholly "with" Moore when he wants to build a storyline around commitments to democracy and social justice. I am wholly "with" Oden when he writes that we should envision a future where our own and others' children's children have at least as much opportunity as we did. I am wholly "with" Light when he claims that we should rethink our understanding of environment in terms of place. I will continue to interject the need to think through the questions that arise in pursuit of non-substantive sustainability in terms of the functional integrity of the ecological, economic and social sub-systems on which we depend, and will submit, politely, that we have not fully understood what sustainability is until we have done so.

Questions for further consideration

1   If, as Thompson argues, the meaning of "sustainability" cannot be defined scientifically, why should we consider the concept to be of interest?

2   Without an agreed upon definition of "sustainability," isn't action toward such an elusive goal likely to be counterproductive?

3   Is "sustainability" anything other than "hyper-efficiency"?

4   Thompson and others argue that "sustainability" must be considered from "a systems view," but how do decision-makers even begin to assess what, or who is or is not inside the system?

5   "Good science" routinely distinguishes "facts" (those conditions that can be verified empirically) from "values" (those conditions that we either do or don't like). Does the consideration of "values" – social equity for example – to be a dimension of sustainability make the concept hopelessly vague and "nonsubstantive"?

Bibliography

Allen, P. and Sachs, C. (1992) "The Poverty of Sustainability: An Analysis of Current Discourse," *Agriculture and Human Values* 9(4): 30–37.

—— (1993) "Sustainable Agriculture in the United States: Engagements, Silences, and Possibilities for Transformation," in Patricia Allen (ed.) *Food for the Future: Conditions and Contradictions of Sustainability*, New York: John Wiley and Sons, 139–167.

Armstrong, J. and Pajor, E. A. (2001) "Changes in Animal Welfare Needed to Maintain Social Sustainability," in R. R. Stowell, R. Bucklin and R. W. Bottcher (eds.) *Livestock Environment VI: Proceedings of the 6th International Symposium (21–23 May 2001, Louisville, Kentucky, USA)* ASAE Publication Number 701P0201: 1–4.

Baier, A. (1986) "Poisoning the Wells," in D. MacLean (ed.) *Values at Risk*, Totowa, NJ: Rowman and Allenheld, 49–74.

Barkin, D. (1998) "Sustainability: The Political Economy of Autonomous Development," *Organization and Environment* 11: 5–32.

Bartley, T. (2003) "Certifying Forests and Factories: States, Social Movements, and the Rise of Private Regulation in the Apparel and Forest Products Fields," *Politics and Society* 31: 433–464.

Bell, S. and Morse, S. (1999) *Sustainability Indicators: Measuring the Immeasurable*, London: Earthscan.

Bentham, J. (1789 [1948]) *The Principles of Morals and Legislation*, New York: Hafner Press.

Bromley, D. W. (1998) "Searching for Sustainability: The Poverty of Spontaneous Order," *Ecological Economics* 24: 231–240.

Buttel, F. H. (1993) "The Production of Agricultural Sustainability: Observations from the Sociology of Science and Technology," in P. Allen (ed.) *Food For the Future*, New York: Wiley: 19–46.

Davis, C. and Langham, M. (1995) "Agricultural Industrialization and Sustainable Development: A Global Perspective," *Journal of Agricultural and Applied Economics*, 27: 21–34.

Dewey, J. (1911 [1993]) "The Problem of Truth," in *The Political Writings,* Indianapolis, IN: Hackett Publishing.

Dlott, Jeff W., Altieri, M. and Masomoto, M. (1994) "Exploring The Theory And Practice Of Participatory Research In US Sustainable Agriculture: A Case Study In Insect Pest Management," *Agriculture and Human Values* 11: 126–139.

George, K. P. (1992) "Sustainability and the Moral Community," *Agriculture and Human Values*. Fall, 9(4): 48–57.

Grant, W. E. and Thompson, P. B. (1997) "Integrated Ecological Models: Simulation of Socio-Cultural Constraints on Ecological Dynamics," *Ecological Modeling* 100: 43–59.

Holland, A. (2001) "Sustainability," in D. Jamieson (ed.) *A Companion to Environmental Philosophy*, Cambridge, UK: Cambridge University Press, 390–401.

Howarth, R. B. (1995) "Sustainability Under Uncertainty: A Deontological Approach," *Land Economics* 71(4): 417–427.

Jamieson, D. (1998) "Sustainability and Beyond," *Ecological Economics* 24: 183–192.

James, W. (1904 [2005]) "Lecture II: What Pragmatism Means," in A. Blunden (transcribed) *A Series of Eight Lectures Dedicated to the Memory of John Stuart Mill, a New Name for Some Old Ways of Thinking, in December 1904, from William James, Writings 1902–1920, the Library of America.* Online, available at: www.marxists.org/reference/subject/philosophy/works/us/james.htm.

Moore, S. (2007) *Alternative Routes to the Sustainable City: Austin, Curitiba and Frankfort*, Lanham, MA: Rowman and Littlefield.

Norton, B. G. (1992) "Sustainability, Human Welfare, and Ecosystem Health," *Environmental Values* 1: 97–111.

Norton, B. G. (2005) *Sustainability: A Philosophy of Ecosystem Management,* Chicago, IL: University of Chicago Press.

Pearce, D. (1993) *Economic Value and the Natural World*, London: Earthscan.

Peet, R. and Watts, M. (1996) "Liberation ecology: development, sustainability, and environment in an age of market triumphalism," in R. Peet and M. Watts (eds.) *Liberation Ecologies: Environment, Development and Social Movements*, London: Routledge, 1–45.

Simon, J. L. (1998) "Scarcity or Abundance?" in L. Westra and P. H. Werhane (eds.) *The Business of Consumption*, London: Routledge, 187–193.

Thompson, P. B. (1986) "The Social Goals of Agriculture," *Agriculture and Human Values* 3(4): 32–42.

—— (1992) "The Varieties of Sustainability," *Agriculture and Human Values* 9(4): 11–19.

—— (1995) *The Spirit of the Soil: Agriculture and Environmental Ethics*, London: Routledge.

—— (1997) "Sustainability as a Norm," *Techné: Technology in Culture and Concept* 2(2): 75–94.

—— (2007a) "Agricultural Sustainability: What It Is and What It Is Not," *International Journal of Agricultural Sustainability* 5: 5–16.

—— (2007b) "Norton's *Sustainability:* Some Comments on Risk and Sustainability," *Journal of Agricultural and Environmental Ethics* 20(4).

Thompson, P. B., Matthews, R. and van Ravenswaay, E. (1994) *Ethics, Public Policy and Agriculture*, New York: Macmillan.

Thompson, P. B. and Nardone, A. (1999) "Sustainable Livestock Production: Methodological and Ethical Challenges," *Livestock Production Science* 61: 111–119.

Thrupp, L. A. (1993) "Political Ecology of Sustainable Rural Development: Dynamics of Social and Natural Resource Degradation," in P. Allen (ed.) *Food for the Future: Conditions and Contradictions of Sustainability*, New York: John Wiley and Sons, 47–73.

World Commission on Economic Development (WCED) (1987) *Our Common Future*, Oxford, UK: Oxford University Press.

Editor's Introduction to Chapter 2

As did philosopher Paul B. Thompson in Chapter 1, economist Michael D. Oden struggles with the definition of terms. What is and is not to be included as a dimension of sustainable development? Oden argues that the idea of some form of equity has been routinely affixed to the concept. The canonical model identifies ongoing efforts to balance economic growth, environmental conservation, and equity (the 3Es) as the main project of sustainable development. Nonetheless, a coherent definition of equity has not been seriously considered, nor has the concept been integrated into most sustainable development scholarship and practice. The more refined concept of complex equity offers a compelling way to fashion a more complete normative framework that brings dimensions of social power and exclusion into the heart of sustainable development discourse and practice. If inequalities in one social dimension contribute to inequalities in other social dimensions, exclusion and marginalization can undermine the ability to build the civic culture, mobilize the broader political coalitions and broaden and deepen discourses necessary to advance meaningful sustainable development initiatives. Attention to the concept of complex equity must, it is therefore argued, be at the center rather than the periphery of sustainable development discourse and practice.

In observing that "Business is the order of the day," John Dewey raised his concern that the emerging market economy of 1924 might subvert the very core of our democratic institutions and challenge our ability to regenerate a just society. Better than eighty years later, Oden has articulated terms that will be helpful in challenging the rationale behind that order.

Chapter 2

Equity

The Forgotten E in Sustainable Development

Michael D. Oden

It has been two decades since the Brundtland Commission Report elevated the concept of sustainable development to a prominent position in public policy discourse. As academic and policy discussions flourished around this seminal topic, definitions of sustainability centered on resource conservation as a requirement for ecosystem regeneration through time – a resource concept of continuing without lessening. From the beginning some idea of equity (economic, social, and political), as part of what has been called the "triple bottom line," has been affixed to the ecological foundation of the sustainable development framework.

This chapter argues that a meaningful concept of equity has not, in fact, been seriously integrated into most sustainable development scholarship and practice. Constantly bandied about, but rarely defined or made operational, equity is at best a subsidiary concern in the sustainable development discourse and at worst a politically correct totem to be bowed to when advancing the main agenda. Different ideas of simple economic equity have, by and large, been embroidered onto the broader economic growth/environmental sustainability tapestry.

The central premise here is that significant progress toward social and environmental development processes that dramatically reduce the consumption of natural resources and damage to the natural world depends upon a strong normative position on equity and social justice. The claim that equity should be at the center of sustainable development theory and practice embodies ethical propositions, but the main support advanced in this chapter rests on two pragmatic arguments. First, unless sustainable development proponents incorporate equity into their core agenda, natural capital consumption and environmental degradation will always be "cheap" in certain domains, undermining efforts to radically improve environmental outcomes. The struggle against environmental racism is only one dimension of complex inequality. Unless resources and power are more widely distributed, a firm floor limiting unsustainable environmental practices will not exist on certain lands, in certain settlements or in certain workplaces. Second, unless a clear concept of equity moves to the center of sustainable development practice the political discourse and coalitions necessary to achieve substantial progress cannot be built. This is both a political question and a question of theory. Unless environmental advocates join in new and durable collaborations with groups organized to advance social and political equity concerns, there will be a persistent power deficit vis-à-vis large entrenched interests engaged in unsustainable status quo practices.

Such alternative coalitions will simply not emerge unless a well-defined and well-articulated concept of equity is at the heart of the sustainability discourse. But also unless the voice, influence and knowledge of people and groups currently excluded from effective participation are more fully incorporated into the sustainability discourse, we will not have the information and social basis to deal with the complex adaptive processes highlighted by McDaniel and Lanham or to renew democratic social institutions to maintain what Thompson identifies as functional integrity of whole systems (McDaniel and Lanham, Chapter 3, this volume; Thompson, Chapter 1, this volume).

In the first section of the chapter, I delineate why concepts of economic and political equity have remained on the periphery of much sustainable development scholarship and practice. In the second part, several theoretical constructs of equity are analyzed from traditions of neoclassical economics and moral philosophy. I argue that Michael Walzer's concept of complex equity offers a compelling way to construct a more complete normative framework that brings various dimensions of social power or exclusion to the fore. I then build an empirical case that growing economic inequality in the US is shaping distributions in other social spheres including educational opportunities, political access and power, and protection from environmental hazards. This, in turn, undermines the ability to change the civic culture, draw upon a broader base of information and mobilize political coalitions necessary to advance meaningful sustainable development initiatives.

Based on the case of US urban regions, the chapter concludes by examining the strong complementarities between specific equity concerns (e.g., living wage, affordable housing, and transportation access campaigns) and key urban environmental problems (point and non-point source pollution and excessive energy consumption). The construction of coalitions with the requisite political power to challenge typical urban growth regimes can only be formed when environmental and social justice interests are joined in a more complete normative framework of sustainability.

Avoiding equity

There are very good reasons why full and serious consideration of equity has not generally been embedded in sustainability scholarship and practice. From the environmental side, it is not obvious how more equal distributions of wealth or power relate the central problem of ecosystem regeneration. There are those who argue the essential focus on ecological and biodiversity issues will wane in favor of human needs and desires when social concerns and goals are drawn into the middle of the environmental conservation project (Newton and Freyfogle 2005). Critiques of "anthropocentric" views are common in the sustainability discourse, but not typically directed to equity issues per se. Yet many do not accept the Brundtland Commission's claim that sustainable development is contingent upon or intrinsically consistent with economic growth (Rees 2003). Reducing resource consumption may be so crucial for environmental sustainability that increasing opportunities for poor people or poor countries to climb the ladder of economic wealth must fall to a secondary priority. Blame must also be directed to equity advocates who have failed to demonstrate how more equitable distributions of income or wealth translate into superior economic growth/environmental conservation tradeoffs.

Perhaps a more fundamental reason why equity is an underdeveloped component of the sustainability discourse is the deep conceptual and ideological divides that make serious discussions of equity highly charged and politically problematic. At least in the US context, one could assert that discussions of equity or existing inequality entail more trying ideological resistance than calls for environmental improvement. The popularity of sustainable development as a policy and planning goal is in some measure related to the presumption that it is "in everyone's interests." There are many who believe that sustainable development precepts, rationally discussed, will tend to naturally generate social consensus and action (Gunder 2006). However, easy consensus often unravels when equity issues are seriously engaged.

Discussions of economic and social equity typically run up against deeply held beliefs about the intrinsic fairness of market resource allocations. In Economics 101 we learn a theory of income distribution based upon diminishing returns – the marginal productivity theory of distribution. In a market economy the story goes, private firms hire labor up to the point where the wage of the last worker equals the value of their marginal product. So if the last worker hired added 10 units an hour to output which sold for $1 per unit, they would be hired if their wages were $10 per hour or less. This model could be said to be branded into the minds of many US citizens; workers in the market fairly receive what they contribute at the margin to production or economic wealth.

It doesn't matter that the marginal productivity theory is at best a heuristic, flawed in its specific application to complex private firms producing complex products and services, it tells a compelling tale. If an individual wants higher wages (more economic wealth), they simply choose to become more productive by investing in human capital (education and training). High-income individuals make wise choices to sacrifice immediate work and income to augment their human capital in ways that the market values highly. Low-income individuals, by deduction, simply choose to work for immediate consumption or limit their work, avoiding the sacrifices necessary to become more productive and affluent.

A tiny percentage of US citizens would likely be able to recount the marginal productivity theory of distribution, but an idea of market fairness in distribution dominates public discourse. Highly unequal market outcomes for individuals are viewed as just, or at least acceptable. High income and wealth result from prudent choices and sacrifice, low income and poverty from poor choices or lack of character and discipline. Market distribution is hence aligned with meritocracy and just desserts. This can extend further in accepting that the wealthy have disproportionate political influence due to the prudence and wisdom that their economic position reflects, while the poor are excluded from power because of their lack of virtue or pathological behaviors (Hayes 1995: 27).

While environmental stewardship can be framed as a potentially wise investment in a kind of "capital stock" in pecuniary cost–benefit terms, serious demands to redress inequality strike at the legitimacy of market outcomes and very sensitive social arrangements and systems of belief (or faith). Convincing members of the local chamber of commerce to shut down a nearby coal-powered plant, substituting various energy-saving demand management initiatives might be a hard sell. But one could allude to overall efficiency gains, improvements in local amenities from better air quality and so on. Imagine instead arguing for the need to significantly increase a local minimum wage or to force developers to build affordable housing as part of their residential projects. It is not surprising that consensus-seeking environmentalists may steer clear of basic equity issues or allude to equity in general terms that require little engagement with specific issues.

Most symptomatic of the marginal position of equity in the sustainability discourse is that the term is typically not even defined with care or precision. In much of the sustainable development cannon it is not at all clear what we should be concerned with equalizing. So if we are even going to consider equity as an essential element of sustainability, what do we mean by the term and why is equity essential to the movement toward more sustainable development?

The status and importance of equity

Consideration of equity and social justice has always been a central theme in political and moral philosophy (Jones 1957). Embedded in the social contact theories of Hobbs, Rousseau and Kant are ideals of equity and fairness. The benefits of submitting to the laws of a state are seen as flowing from security, equal treatment of similar cases (lack of arbitrary rule) and a degree of guaranteed personal freedom (Graham 2007).

Equity is misconstrued in some contemporary ideological accounts as a demand for everyone being exactly equal in all material and social dimensions – some idea of leveling to sameness. No one, including Marx, has ever argued this; evolution and the fabric of human society are based upon differentiation and division of activity. Yet all theories of politics and ethics argue that individuals be treated equally across some social or cultural dimension. Libertarians call for equal and unassailable rights over personal property, neoclassical economists argue that all should be treated equally in market exchanges of goods and labor, liberal political theorists view one person – one vote – as an essential foundation for democracy. However, more comprehensive claims for economic and social equity remain controversial and theoretically problematic.

Many contemporary theories and debates focus around concepts and conditions of economic equity. Hausman and McPherson offer a masterful outline and assessment of contemporary debates about economic equity (Hausman and McPherson 1996: 139–144). Beginning with the common distinction between concepts of equity based upon equality of welfare versus equality of resources, they note that striving for equality of welfare between individuals achieves neither equity nor social justice equity (Hausman and McPherson 1996: 139).[1] Organizing our institutions to ensure that everyone feels equally well off or satisfied in the terms of neoclassical welfare measures is impossible because individuals have different preferences for consumption, work, play, and so on. Hence, systematic comparisons and adjustments of welfare across numerous individuals are not achievable. In addition, striving to equalize individual welfare would imply organizing things to make someone cruel and slothful just as happy as someone who was kind and hardworking.

More plausible constructs of economic equity can be derived from theories that argue that resources (versus welfare) should be the subject of redistribution. The resources or means to welfare improvement are what should be the subject of equity concerns; once individuals have access to equivalent resources the welfare they obtain is the outcome of their own free choices. Economists have devised elaborate models to evaluate conditions under which more equal access to resources would lead to more equitable outcomes. All such constructs could be said to have very serious problems. If, for example, all goods and services were divided into equal bundles and distributed to all "community members," the bundles would not be equally valuable due to different individual tastes (Dworkin 2000).[2]

The deeper challenge for resource-based conceptions is the remaining inequality of internal resources, including personal capacities and talents. When internal resources – mental and physical abilities, stamina, proclivity to work, etc. – are unequal, an equal distribution of external resources will lead over time to highly unequal outcomes. Many would view a redistribution of rewards to natural ability as unfair and inefficient (a disincentive to productivity). But distributions of physical and mental abilities (e.g., deafness or photographic memory) may be just as arbitrary as material resources. A lot of logical gymnastics have been carried out to try to distinguish between internal differences that deserve compensation to achieve equity and those that do not (Hausman and McPherson 1996; Cohen 1989; Okin 1989). Physical handicaps are obvious, but what about a person's willingness to work or hardships suffered from undertaking religious prohibitions?

Since very general conditions of economic equity based on either welfare or resource redistribution are both highly abstract and theoretically problematic, a number of less restrictive and comprehensive frameworks have been proposed. A more limited concept of economic equity is the famous difference principle proposed by John Rawls. His goal is to derive a theory whereby rational agents in a liberal market society would consensually agree on a definition of distributive justice and the rules by which it could be achieved. To derive these principles Rawls imposes a veil of ignorance on all citizens in what he terms "an original position" (Rawls 1972). Behind the veil of ignorance agents are completely ignorant of their social position or past (status, race, gender, family background). In this original position, rational agents would seek to minimize the potential harms of ending up at the low end of economic resource distributions. Specifically in the "original position" rational agents would agree on three basic principles: (1) each person has the same claim to the most extensive basic liberties, compatible with the same scheme of liberties for all; (2) social and economic inequalities are to be attached to offices and positions open to all under conditions of fair equality of opportunity; and (3) social and economic inequalities are justified if they provide the greatest benefit to the least-advantaged members of society (Rawls 2001).

The third "difference" principle can be interpreted as a socially compelling choice that "the prospects of each class of individual should be improved so long as the position of the worst off is maximized" (Graham 2007: 61). Everyone can get more so long as those at the bottom get a bit more than everyone else. A number of the above noted difficulties, including how to parse between advantages that are natural versus inherited or involuntary, apply to the Rawlsian framework. However, some idea of a difference principle could offer more practical and convincing justifications for policies limiting hereditary wealth transfer, equalizing educational opportunities and various social safety net measures. Moreover, while it is the third principle that has received the most attention in discussions of economic equity, the first two principles (actually priors in Rawls' broader theory) suggest a broader, more complex idea of equity that encompasses political equity, equal opportunity for participation, equal protection from environmental hazards and so forth.

This brings us to a distinctly different approach that may be more theoretically compelling and practically relevant to the sustainable development project, Michael Walzer's theory of complex equity. Walzer does not believe there is any "right" or intrinsically equitable distribution of resources, but instead argues that each sphere of social life is subject to unique distributive standards (Walzer 1983). For instance, the political realm in liberal democracies should be governed by free political rights (to vote, participate, etc.), while leadership and power are granted to those who can persuade, encourage, and manage public affairs. Inequalities in the economic realm are shaped by self-interest, work, innovativeness, and competitiveness. Because social meanings and standards of operation are different in the distinct spheres of social activity, distributions in each sphere must be autonomous. It is not inequalities within individual spheres that constitute the principle problem of equity, rather it is inequalities in one sphere spilling over and shaping distributions in another sphere with different intrinsic meanings and standards of distribution. In the contemporary US setting, for example, the problem of equity is not economic inequality per se, but the fact that highly unequal wealth distribution strongly influences distributions of educational opportunity, political access and power, exposure to environmental costs and outcomes in other domains. In other countries or cultures the problem may be more that political inequality or inequalities in religious status shape economic or political distributions. The overriding equity concern is preserving the relative autonomy of the major spheres of social life so that inequalities do not corrupt reasonable distributive standards or over-determine broad social outcomes.

Why then should equity concerns, specifically the principle of complex equity, be brought in from the periphery of the sustainable development discourse? Severe violations of complex equity imply that there is exclusion of a significant number of citizens from power and meaningful participation in society. Widespread exclusion can stifle meaningful progress toward a more sustainable model of social and environmental development. First, complex inequalities undermine the habitus of mutual respect between citizens of a liberal democracy (Rorty 1989). The human capacities and potential of those excluded from economic, educational and other spheres are not respected because their exclusion across social spheres itself implies the absence of such capacities. When habits of mutual respect are not pervasive it becomes more likely, for example, that respect for rights of certain people, classes and communities to a clean and healthy environment is diminished. If, on the other hand, different distributive processes were allowed to fully operate in different social spheres this would lead to different outcomes for a broader spectrum of the citizenry. In these circumstances, evidence of capacity and potential would be more widespread, mutual respect would be more prominent, and fewer would be the places where environmental and other rights were not respected.

Second, if complex equality obscures differences between status and rights among citizens, complex inequality sharpens differences and makes them more durable. The exclusion and marginalization stemming from complex inequality undermines the social trust and solidarity required to affect major social change. When some social classes, groups and individuals are disconnected from influence or even meaningful participation, while a small group retains strong influence, this fragments communities, social movements and interests. Social and psychological distance prevails and inter-group trust or what has been termed "bridging social capital," becomes exceedingly difficult to build. A broad and powerful movement pushing for a meaningful sustainable development can only emerge if trust can be built across groups about the real shared sacrifices and shared benefits of a new course.

Third, exclusion also constitutes a narrowing of perspectives, experiences and knowledge about how to understand, and address through social actions, sustainability challenges. If we do not, in the words of McDaniel and Lanham in this volume, develop and maintain relationships among agents with diverse interests and perspectives, we are severely handicapped in generating approaches to complex and often non-linear challenges of sustainable development (McDaniel and Lanham, Chapter 3, this volume). Exclusion, hence, commonly involves a critical loss of information, insight, and know-how.

This brings us to a final related connection between complex equity and the greater sustainability agenda, political strategy. The broad coalition necessary to rebalance the particular form of complex inequality operative in the US case must draw in elements from a large but very diffused environmental movement and a smaller but significant ensemble of groups focused on social equity issues (unions, civil rights groups, community organizations, etc.). Environmental groups now cross a wide spectrum, but retain some air of elitism (Klingle and Taylor 2006). This poor image is in part rooted in the older historic influence of wilderness preservation and strict population management concerns on the environmental movement. Civil rights and union activist Byard Rustin is famously quoted as saying that leading environmentalists were "self-righteous elitists, neo-Malthusians who call for slow growth or no growth and who would condemn the black underclass to permanent poverty" (quoted in Tucker 1977: 49).

Since Rustin's time, environmental advocates have made great strides in framing environmental issues with sensitivity toward social justice, but the recent "anti immigration" insurgency in the Sierra Club points to residual tensions and troubling social distance. The argument that equity concerns must be at the center of building a powerful coalition for sustainable development will be further elaborated below with the case of workplace and regional sustainability projects. However, the social exclusion associated with severe and worsening complex inequality implies that an inclusionary alternative coalition can only be built by a transformative engagement that builds trust and consensus between environmental groups and interests focused on social equity. This in turn requires a sustainability discourse and action program that understands and is energetically engaged in resistance to growing inequality.

The power of money and resistance to complex inequality

The principle driver of complex inequalities in the US, as Walzer emphasizes, is the power of money. It operates in his theory to corrupt other distributions as wealth/property influence holders of political office, educational access, and other spheres of social life (Walzer 1983: 22). There is indeed ample evidence that growing inequalities in the economic realm are polluting other social spheres, accelerating the fragmentation of civic space.

There is very little debate that economic inequality has worsened as the concentration of wealth has sharply increased over the past thirty-five years. More sophisticated estimates of wealth distribution show that economic distributions have shifted dramatically toward the top one percent of households and are approaching distributions in the pre-welfare state 1920s (Piketty and Saez 2003). Pro-market conservatives have been confined to arguing that social mobility remains high (movement between economic strata over time or generations) and poor people today have higher standards of living than the middle class of fifty years ago. Startling evidence shows that social mobility in the US has gone down and that the income position of current workers increasingly mimics that of their parents (falling intergenerational mobility) (Sawhill and Morton 2007). These findings point to both increasing economic inequality and hardening of class barriers.

The fact that fewer low-income individuals face absolute material deprivation in developed countries is encouraging, but reinforces the premise of complex equity that social exclusion is not as related to unequal material conditions as to how economic inequalities shape other social outcomes.

Evidence that inequalities in wealth increasingly determine political, educational and environmental access or outcomes is strong and on many levels non-controversial. The US system of public education, financed by local property taxes, generates wildly unequal educational opportunities and is experiencing a deepening crisis as higher-income households increasingly flee to private schools. The share of students from low- and middle-income families in the top 150 universities is falling, while the share from the top quartile of family income is shooting up (Bowen *et al.* 2006). Needs-based admissions and affirmative action programs have been swamped by the influence of wealth in giving higher-income youth a leg up in early education and subsequent advantages in the complex process of college admissions (Bowen *et al.* 2006).

Increasingly divergent economic and educational distributions in turn undermine political equality and participation. Tales of special interest lobbyists actually writing legislation relating to their industry to be passed into law by legislators desperate for campaign resources are common. The ability of special interests to directly shape energy legislation, recent changes in EPA wetlands protection, regressive reforms in bankruptcy law, and pharmaceutical-friendly drug benefit legislation are only the most recent examples of corporate power over politics (Weisman and Babcock 2006). Special interest power corresponds to, and influences highly unequal participation in basic political and civic activities. Only about one-third of eligible voters turn out in midterm elections and only a bit over half in presidential elections, making the US 138th in participation among countries that conduct regular elections (Freeman 2004). Individuals in higher-income strata are also much more likely to engage in voluntary associations, contact public officials, or work on a political campaign (Jacobs and Skocpol 2005).

This evidence of complex inequality and marginalization also maps to environmental policies and exposure to environmental hazards in communities and in the workplace. A large body of literature suggests that exposure to various environmental hazards and related health effects are associated to race and income (Morello-Frosch and Jesdale 2006; Downey 2005; Hamilton 1995). Workplace exposure to environmental hazards and injury seem also to be associated with income (Robinson 1991; Dembe *et al.* 2004).

In sum, there is a preponderance of evidence that the problem of complex inequality is serious and is becoming more severe in certain social spheres as income inequality worsens. Yet given the bleak picture painted above, how can an emphasis on complex equity reposition and reinvigorate the sustainable development movement? I would argue that we first need to recognize and articulate in specific terms how equity issues are embedded in almost all environmental issues. I will discuss two important examples below in the urban context: the relationship between equity in the workplace and environmental performance of firms; and equity and the social and spatial challenges of sustainable urban planning. Once the centrality of equity concerns is articulated, new and energetic forms of trust and social capital building are essential to bind fragmented and isolated elements of the social justice and environmental movements into powerful collaborations.

Equity and sustainability: building a strong sustainable development movement in metro regions

The cases that will be used to illustrate the above arguments will be specific sustainable development challenges in US urban regions. This is an important focus for several reasons. The ways that complex inequalities shape sustainable policy and planning challenges are more legible at the local level. Also, the potential for civic engagement and coalition building may be higher in a local urban environment where face-to-face contact and access to political and other leaders is more feasible and where the direct impacts of sustainable development conflicts are easier to understand.

The living wage issue

The first issue where the links between complex equity and sustainable development can be put into relief is local living wage struggles. Efforts to pressure firms to pay a living wage have been widespread and have taken on different forms in different places. Cities such as Baltimore, Los Angeles, Tucson and others have passed living wage ordinances that require contractors, and in some cases subcontractors, doing city business to pay wages and benefits that allow workers to be self-sufficient. All firms doing city business must pay enough so that full-time workers do not need to rely on government subsidies such as Food Stamps, Medicaid or other types of public subsidies. Other cities deny any public subsidies or special regulatory treatment to firms that don't pay a living wage. Living wage campaigns have also been targeted to individual firms such as Wal-Mart in the form of resistance to new store locations or any expenditure of local taxes to facilitate firm expansions. The basic equity argument is that employers that do not pay a living wage should not be given any special encouragement, because they demean their workforce and generate social costs. Inadequate pay is unfair to other firms and the local citizenry who indirectly subsidize the firm by providing public subsides to their workers. Indigent health care, aid to low-income children, and affordable housing provision are examples of local programs in which compensation for low wages will drive up local public sector costs.

The status of the living wage issue in the broader "sustainability" conflict with big box retailers is especially emblematic of the challenges involved in bringing equity into the middle of the sustainability discourse. The big box retail model is distinguished in two ways: the organizational and sales strategy of the merchant; and the nature, size and connectivity of the building itself. Equity advocates critique low-wage, low-service mass retail strategies, while environmentalists focus on the physical attributes that contribute to high-energy consumption, heat, congestion and air pollution, and other dis-amenities. In some places like Chicago and the State of Maryland, equity and environmental advocates have come together to change store parameters and internalize social costs through wage and benefit demands (Milner 2006). Efforts have been less successful where opposition based upon planning and environmental issues is disconnected from economic and social equity advocates.

Indeed Wal-Mart's recent strategy moves can been seen as an explicit effort to split opposition.[3] They have launched a multi-billion dollar effort to "green" the company that includes

Michael D. Oden

green building and alternative energy initiatives for their stores, green product promotion, and other programs (Gunther 2006). Because of the tremendous scale of their operations, a 20–30 percent improvement in some Wal-Mart environmental performance measures must be welcomed. At the same time they have vehemently opposed efforts to upgrade labor standards, pay, and labor management relations. Their stock argument (mimicked by some other big retailers) is that higher wages would lead to higher prices, hurting the very groups that opponents are supposedly advocating for – Wal-Mart critiques are hence really elitist.

In response, some equity advocates have noted that market competition is not, in reality, based upon finding a single optimum cost minimization point (or equilibrium). In fact there are numerous ways to produce competitive products and services that combine low costs and high quality. Some firms operate profitably through "low-road" competitive strategies based on minimizing wage costs, input costs and other costs of doing business. Other firms can operate just as profitably by paying higher wages in exchange for higher productivity and a capacity to produce higher-quality products or services. This has been termed a "high-road" strategy of competition.

If firms could produce low-price, high-quality products and pay relatively high wages and benefits, this would undermine the claim of low-road firms that they were not adversely effecting economic distribution. The following table compares "high-road" Costco to "low-road" Wal-Mart. Costco manages to outperform Wal-Mart by paying living wages and by treating workers better, reaping higher productivity and lower worker turnover as a result.

Table 2.1 **Compensation comparisons Costco and Wal-Mart/Sam's, 2003**

	Costco	Wal-Mart/Sam's
Average hourly wage	$15.97	$11.42
Annual health cost (per worker)	$5,735.00	$3,500.00
Covered by health plan	82%	47%
Annual retirement cost (per worker)	$1,330.00	$747.00
Covered by retirement plan	91%	64%
Employee turnover (per year)	6%	21%
Labor and overhead costs (as % of sales)	10%	17%
Sales per square foot	$795.00	$516.00
Profits per employee	$13,647.00	$11,039.00
Yearly operating income (5 years)	10.1%	9.8%

Source: derived from, Holmes Stanley and Wendy Zelner, "Higher Wages Mean Higher Profits, but Try Telling that to Wall Street," in *Business Week*, April 12, 2004, p. 76.

A basic principle of market economics is that business firms should carry the full costs of producing or selling their products. Violation of this principle damages the operation of competitive markets. If some external costs (either social or environmental) are borne by third parties, this creates an implicit subsidy that unfairly lowers the prices of the subject firm below their true marginal costs. Requiring companies to carry the true costs of their own business operations is a fundamental requirement of the fair and efficient operation of the market.

A broader purchase of equity in the sustainable development agenda could be secured if the high-road competitive strategies could be linked to more generalized tendencies to internalize costs. The case here is not airtight, but a lot of evidence indicates that high-road strategies are associated with higher productivity, better pay and benefits, and more democratic and participatory labor management relations (Dresser 2007; Applebaum *et al.* 2000). And some evidence suggests that strategies that treat labor and material inputs as assets rather than mere inputs correlates with reduced environmental damage, and stronger firm commitments to the health and quality of life in host communities (to attract and keep skilled workers and managers) (Luria and Rogers 1997; Florida *et al.* 2001). It seems logical that firms that seek to externalize social costs will be more likely to externalize environmental costs. Organizations that depend on skilled labor, more participation and learning, and innovation would be more likely to aggressively pursue source reduction strategies to make workplaces safer and more efficient. It is further likely that high-road organizations are more inclined to implement more innovative environmental management systems such as ISO 14000 standards. These links between labor standards and environmental outcomes should persuade environmental sustainability advocates that workplace equity issues are integral to the broader environmental agenda. As shown in the "big box" organizing efforts noted on page 39, it is places where environmental and equity advocates were joined that have had meaningful success at regulating low-road development. This case strongly relates to those in Chapter 15 where social regulation of specific practices (child labor) or technologies (steamboat boilers) generated minor short-term costs but dramatically improved long-term efficiency and safety and actually promoted market growth.

Sustainable urban growth initiatives

The second nexus of environmental and equity issues that illustrates the case is sustainable urban growth management initiatives. These efforts typically involve a push for more contained urban settlement patterns, infill, open space, and reduced auto dependence. Here the relationship runs in the opposite direction from the living wage example. With sustainable growth management, environmental sustainability advocates are typically in the lead and the challenge is to incorporate the concept of complex equity to bring equity advocates into the movement. Community organizations, labor advocates, and low-income citizens often do not see the benefits of more sustainable urban forms and transit networks. Increased density, infill, transit-oriented development and even alternative energy programs may be seen as elements of gentrification or as generating additional cost burdens that low-income households can ill afford. At the same time, environmental advocates need strong and committed support from lower-income communities to successfully push through major urban sustainability projects.

Opposition to serious and systematic urban environmental sustainability initiatives comes from what could be labeled traditional urban growth regimes. In metropolitan areas, dense networks of social relations give corporate and development interests real advantages in setting economic growth agendas and related environmental policies. Urban growth regime theory as it has developed over the past two decades stresses bonds of association and interest among privileged groups in urban regions which tend to align values and norms within and between group members (Imbroscio 1997; Stone 1989; Logan and Molotch 1987). Cities are typically governed by coalitions of interest groups whereby a certain level of group coherence is translated into power over broad strategy and decision-making that is expressed in characteristic ways (Imbroscio 1997).

More traditional regimes are dominated by real estate interests and what might be called local fixed capital – firms whose investments are spatially sticky. These would include utilities, road builders, and other public and private contractors whose investment returns are shaped by local economic performance. Private sector players in the growth regime use highly unequal access to economic resources to shape distributive outcomes in the political realm – violating complex equity and excluding or limiting influence of "outside" groups. Financial resources are used to build individual ties to local political decision-makers (political contributions, revolving door relationships, and social relationships) and private interests can exert structural leverage because city officials depend on a sales and property tax base influenced by regime investment decisions.

Members of the local growth regime do, as Imbroscio states, have a "privileged voice" within the context of liberal democracy; they get the meetings, lunches, fundraisers, backroom access to political decision-makers, while other more diffuse interests groups (environmentalists, social justice advocates) get more limited "front room" access (Imbroscio 1997).

The private sector elements of a traditional regime will oppose or support urban sustainability projects based on bottom-line considerations and how these projects influence their broader freedom to operate. Efforts to encourage infill development or residential development in central business districts often offer attractive opportunities to land-based urban interests. Support for other, more environmentally significant measures such as major expansions of mass transit, greater open space requirements, urban growth boundaries or other limits on suburban development are more likely to be opposed. Equity advocates may join with traditional regime members if they view sustainability initiatives as threatening their neighborhoods, stifling job growth or adding costs onto low-income households.

The traditional urban growth regime

For practices and actions of sustainable development to change fundamental patterns of urban growth, they must influence strategic decision-making at the metro level. Otherwise, significant efforts will be trumped by the traditional regime's power to expand developable land, limit development costs, and provide housing and neighborhood characteristics in forms that will yield high returns with low risks. Concessions will be made around the edges, as developers too will be happy to wear the environmental mantle. But marginal improvements will occur in the context of continued failure of the urban system in fundamental environmental and equity terms.

Figure 2.1
The traditional urban growth regime. Source: derived from Imbroscio (1997), reproduced with the permission of Sage Publications.

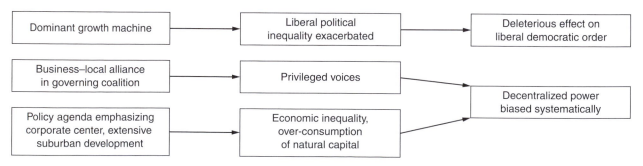

However, an important feature of regime theory that distinguishes it from structuralist accounts is that regimes are contestable; they can be reformed, reconfigured and even overturned by alternative bases of interest and power. In this context, the major changes in investment patterns and regulations needed to forge more sustainable paths of urban development require the formation of an alternative coalition of power based on environmental and social equity interests. Unless, for instance, urban densification, new transit alternatives or alternative energy initiatives are combined with aggressive affordable housing and community job goals the political feasibility of the environmental components is limited. Recognition of complex equity problems must, therefore, be at the center of efforts to build alternative power bases to contest traditional urban regimes. Building and sustaining alternative coalitions requires a radical approach to building social capital in a fragmented urban setting and understanding that change often demands explicit oppositional politics.

The need for social capital building has been a common theme in the sustainability and civic environmentalist discourses. Advocates of various stripes see a profound need to increase interpersonal associations and public participation. Putnam's *Bowling Alone* treatise is accepted with enthusiasm, but his account of the crisis of social capital is problematic for the types of trust building and coalition formation needed to advance a serious sustainability agenda (Putnam 2000). Putnam distinguishes between what he terms "bonding social capital," or associations that solidify links within groups (e.g., neighborhood groups, environmental groups, unions, local real estate councils) and "bridging social capital," his term for between-group association and trust (e.g., environmental–labor coalitions, parent–teacher associations, affordable housing coalitions) (Putnam 2000). What Putnam does not explicitly consider is that in societies with severe complex inequality some may have "surplus" social capital while others have little. Members of a conventional urban growth regime have no dearth of social capital. Large asset owners – land developers, owners and managers of firms, local infrastructure providers – have always had rich associational networks of bonding and bridging social capital.

Community, social justice, and environmental groups are at a real disadvantage. They may have strong within-group associations but very weak between-group ties and/or vertical ties to higher-level representatives (at the state or national levels). These differentials, the direct effects of complex inequality, have a strong influence on the processes and outcomes of public participation. They can lead, through a kind of path dependence toward non-participation and exclusion. The decision of individuals to devote time and energy to participation depends on a clear perception that participation can tangibly affect outcomes (Cleaver 2001; Laurian 2004). It doesn't take most people long to figure out if their participation in a specific activity or action will have any meaningful influence on outcomes. The extent to which the traditional urban regimes retain control over the strategic agenda, limiting the possibilities of alternative outcomes, the more likely broader participation and association will be limited.

Therefore, in conditions of complex inequality the initial impetus for developing new coalitions between groups (e.g., local environmentalists, social justice groups, more progressive elements of the business community) is weak. Unless galvanized by leadership or a particular local crisis, coalition building often cannot, in its early stages, demonstrate that "bridging" participation will tangibly affect outcomes. Furthermore, as much of the literature suggests, the single most important factor for developing the trust needed to build a durable coalition between groups is consistent interaction (Durlauf 2000). So the civic engagement required to build real alternative coalitions of power implies frequent meeting and joining (by those already devoting time to other particular group activities) without the prospect of immediate results.

However, there are notable cases of regime change where formerly marginalized or non-influential groups seized power over strategic decision-making. The overthrow of the traditional growth regime in Chicago by the forces supporting the election of Harold Washington as mayor in 1983 was much more than a "get our share" movement by African American and other communities of color. With an economic and political equity thrust, the agenda of the Washington coalition also featured "buy local" initiatives for city contracting, minority business development, and park and open space improvements across the city. The bridging links that formed and grew from this coalition survived Washington's untimely death in 1987 (Rivlin 1993).

The Communities Organized for Public Services (COPS) initiative in San Antonio was another case of regime overthrow. San Antonio's Anglo elite historically channeled city resources to higher-income neighborhoods on the city's north side, ignoring basic infrastructure and services in the burgeoning Latino and African American communities elsewhere. The economic growth agenda of the traditional regime focused on the promotion of San Antonio as a low-wage/low-cost place to do business. A grassroots organizing campaign was begun in 1974 to address the service, public health, and environmental crisis affecting the city's neglected west and south sides. Based on an Industrial Areas Foundation model of community organizing, COPS built bridging capital among church congregations and community groups. This initiative lead to a new regime structure that extended public services to neglected areas, led to cleanups of blighted areas, stopped a major freeway project, blocked a super mall development that would have adversely affected the aquifer, and forced the adoption of ordinances restricting polluting development (Campbell 1994).

The lessons from these examples for urban environmental sustainability include the need to redeploy social capital especially to more bridging and coalition-building activities. Further, such activities must at times be explicitly oppositional to interests that typically have a privileged voice in setting the strategic agendas of urban areas. The degree of interaction needed to build the foundation of trust for alternative coalitions requires that local environmental groups find ways to be more inclusive within their organizations, but more importantly to actively join and participate in the actions of potential coalition partners. Only when environmentalists actively participate in efforts such as local living wage campaigns will the natural links between equity and environmental improvement emerge (higher wage floors tend to force companies to save on energy and environmental costs, low wages tend to be associated with lax quality control and waste). Only when social justice groups see environmentalists on their front lines, will they fully appreciate natural links and areas of negotiation between their group agendas and efforts to preserve the environment.

The three Es revisited: elements of a coherent sustainability agenda

This account can certainly be criticized as an elite view from the rich developed world as it focuses exclusively on the US context. The problems and effects of complex inequality are certainly more stark and severe at the global level. In this context, it is important to briefly note another important contribution of Michael Walzer from his book *Thick and Thin: Moral Arguments at Home and*

Abroad (Walzer 1994). In this work he notes that moral and ethical values are not, as Kant claimed, some abstract inheritance that we all share, but are rather built out of obligations and trust relationships in direct "local" social relations (families, schools, local communities). When equity concerns are seriously addressed at home, this may prepare us to address international inequality in more meaningful ways (Rorty 2007).

It could be argued that building a sustainable development movement from a critique of market outcomes and a process of social mobilization and oppositional politics will alienate many potential allies and individuals. But the argument here is that severe complex inequality is an elephant in the room that cannot be ignored in a serious sustainable development agenda. Interest group power, stemming from inordinate wealth in limited hands, has distorted market processes and dominated other social and natural realms. This unnatural hegemony of wealth didn't "just happen," it is supported by discrete interests and by a strong ideology of market fairness. Both must be confronted in clear terms if we are to shift to meaningful sustainable development processes.

On the other hand, these positions could be critiqued for not taking the power and hegemony of global capitalism seriously enough. The contemporary market economy, some argue, is hopelessly addicted to unsustainable growth and consumption. Hence, any sustainability project that views economic growth as a central goal is actually only a project for sustainable wealth creation in disguise (Gunder 2006). In my view (consistent with the concept of complex equity), the market is not intrinsically flawed as a mechanism of economic distribution. The problem is fundamentally rebalancing the market and wealth creation with public goods, healthy participation and social solidarity, and true ecological sustainability. This may be an idealistic and naïve project, but certainly not as far-fetched as the overthrow of global capitalism

The cases in this chapter demonstrate a need for a more explicit and coherent value base for inclusion, strenuous bridge building, and formation of active coalitions. Incorporating complex equity into the normative principles of sustainable development can strongly enhance communication and collective action between diverse groups with formally distinct agendas. The 3E framework of sustainable development is a perfectly workable normative framework if equity gains its proper status. This sustainable development paradigm is more than a static agenda of principles and goals as suggested by McDaniel and Lanham. It anticipates and analyzes terrains of conflict and negotiation between, for example, economic growth and environmental improvement, and equity and environmental regulation in dynamic and changing environments. The framework can furthermore accommodate subsidiary or more fine-grained conflicts like those between neighborhood livability (better schools, better neighborhood design and planning, infill densification) and gentrification. I would also argue that the 3E framework can be much more than a "nonsubstantive" banner in the terms put forward in Thompson's chapter (Thompson, Chapter 1, this volume). Tradeoffs and balances can be evaluated empirically and reasonable judgments can be based on substantive information as the living wage and urban sustainability cases suggest.

Sustainable development is a normative framework not a static blueprint, and should appropriately carry on with its own debates and conflicts. However, the basic idea of balancing and progressing along all three dimensions allows those outside the discourse to make basic and essential distinctions about what exactly sustainable development is calling us to do. And with a real concern for equity, the framework can yield legible and compelling principles:

- Sustainable development is based on the activating premise that the natural environment is under grave threat at the local, national and global levels and that future growth and development cannot occur at the expense of the environment.
- Sustainable development is based on a belief that growing inequality of access and outcomes must be reversed to sustain social solidarity, vibrant and inclusive democratic decision-making and environmental balances.
- Sustainable development strives for forms of economic growth that support greater equity and lower levels of natural capital consumption.
- Sustainable development presumes that basic individual rights of property must intrinsically be negotiated in the context of externalities and problems of the commons.

Promulgation of these 3E principles would exclude and alienate – even some who currently march under the banner of sustainability. But gains in clarity of purpose and identification of common ground would far outweigh the fleeting benefits of easy consensus.

Questions for further consideration

1   Those who promote an ecocentric view of sustainability are primarily interested in what Thompson (in Chapter 1) refers to as the "functional integrity" model. Those who promote an anthropocentric model are primarily interested in Thompson's "resource sufficiency" model. In this chapter Oden provides empirical evidence which suggests that a focus on "complex social equity" as a core dimension of sustainability might overcome the disagreement between ecocentric and anthropocentric models of sustainability. Would Thompson agree?

2   It is generally recognized that people living in poverty will, out of short-term necessity, act in ways that may be in their own immediate interest, but contrary to the long-term interests of the ecosystems where they live. If, as Oden and Walzer argue, there is no "'right' or intrinsically equitable distribution of resources," how might we decide what minimum amount of *having* will encourage citizens to *do* the "right thing"?

3   Those of us who live in liberal capitalist democracies like the United States tend to think that it is neutral and natural for wealthy citizens to routinely dominate decision-making in sectors other than banking or industry like education or the arts. Yet, when we are confronted with a theocratic society such as Iran, where spiritual figures dominate decision-making in sectors other than religion we are appalled. Are the values of liberal capitalism more fundamental to sustainable development than those of ecology, politics or religion?

4   If, as Thompson argued in Chapter 1, "solidarity" among citizens is required to achieve sustainable development, how does action toward complex social equity help to promote both "functional integrity" of the ecosystem and "resource sufficiency"?

5   Social justice groups representing the interest of the poor commonly view environmental improvements as desirable, but also as contributing to increased cost in housing or goods that the poor can ill-afford. Although Oden argues that social justice advocates and environmentalists share common interests that are distinct from "traditional growth regimes," how can these groups be brought together in practice?

Notes

1 The following four paragraphs draw heavily from pages 139–144 of their book, *Economic Analysis and Moral Philosophy*. All interpretations of their arguments, however, are the sole responsibility of the author.
2 This problem could, as Dworkin suggests, be remedied by an auction scheme where bundle elements were traded until no one envied another bundle (Dworkin 2000).
3 It should be emphasized that Wal-Mart has become a sort of whipping boy for a "low-road" retail strategy that is common to many large American retailers. While unfair on some level, the company is the largest retailer in the world and is particularly aggressive in maintaining control over its shabby labor–management relations.

Bibliography

Applebaum, Eileen, Thomas Bailey, Peter Berg and Arne Kalleberg. (2000) *Manufacturing Advantage: Why High Performance Work Systems Pay Off*, Ithaca, NY: Cornell University Press.

Bowen, William, Martin Kurzweil and Eugene Tobin. (2006) *Equity and Excellence in American Higher Education*, Charlottesville, VA: University of Virginia Press.

Campbell, Brett. (1994) *Investing in People: The Story of Project Quest*, San Antonio, TX: Communities Organized for Public Service.

Cleaver, Francis. (2001) "Institutions, Agency and the Limitations of Participatory Approaches to Development," in Bill Cooke and Uma Kothari (eds.) *Participation The New Tyranny?*, New York: Zed Press.

Cohen, G. (1989) "On the Currency of Egalitarian Justice," *Ethics*, Vol. 99: 906–944.

Dagger, Richard. (2003). "Stopping Sprawl for the Good of All: The Case for Civic Environmentalism," *Journal of Social Philosophy*, Vol. 32, No. 1, Spring: 28–43.

Dembe, Allard, Bianca Ericson and Rachel Delbos. (2004) "Predictors of Work Related Injuries and Illnesses: National Survey Findings," *Journal of Occupational and Environmental Hygiene*, Vol. 1, No. 8: 542–550.

Downey, Liam. (2005) "The Unintended Significance of Race: Environmental Racial Inequality in Detroit," *Social Forces*, Vol. 81: 305–341.

Dresser, Laura. (2007) "Stronger Ladders, Stronger Floors: The Need for Both Supply and Demand Strategies to Improve Worker Opportunities," Madison, WI, Center on Wisconsin Strategy, February: 1–8.

Durlauf, Steven. (2000) "Bowling Alone: A Review Essay," manuscript, Madison, WI, University of Wisconsin, Department of Economics.

Dworkin, Ronald. (2000) *Sovereign Virtue: the Theory and Practice of Equality*, Cambridge, MA: Harvard University Press.

Florida, Richard, Mark Atlas and Matt Clime. (2001) "What Makes Companies Green? Organizational and Geographic Factors in the Adoption of Environmental Practices," *Economic Geography* 77.3, July: 209–221.

Freeman, Richard. (2004) "What Me Vote," in Kathryn M. Neckerman (ed.) *Social Inequality*, New York: Russell Sage Foundation.

Graham, Paul. (2007) *Rawls*, Oxford, UK: Oneworld Publications.

Gunder, Michael. (2006) "Sustainability: Planning Saving Grace or Road to Perdition?" *Journal of Planning Education and Research*, Winter 2006, Vol. 26, No. 2: 208–221.

Gunther, Marc. (2006) "The Green Machine," *Fortune*, August 7: 21.

Hamilton, J. T. (1995) "Testing for Environmental Racism: Prejudice, Profits, Political Power?" *Journal of Policy Analysis and Management*, Vol. 14: 107–132.

Hausman, Daniel and Michael McPherson. (1996) "Equality and Egalitarianism", in *Economic Analysis and Moral Philosophy*, Cambridge, UK: Cambridge University Press, 135–149.

Hayes, Allen. (1995) *The Federal Government and Urban Housing*, Albany, NY: State University of New York Press.

Imbroscio, David. (1997) *Reconstructing City Politics*, Thousand Oaks, CA: Sage Publications.

Jacobs Lawrence and Theda Skocpol (eds.). (2005) *Inequality and American Democracy, What We Know and What We Need to Learn,* New York: Russell Sage Foundation.

Jones A. H. (1957) *Athenian Democracy,* Oxford, UK: Blackwell.

Klingle, Matthew and Joseph Taylor. (2006) "Caste from the Past, Environmentalism's Elitist Tinge has Roots in the Movements History," *Grist Magazine*, March.

Laurian, Lucie. (2004) "Public Participation in Environmental Decision Making," *Journal of the American Planning Association*, Vol. 70, No. 1 (winter): 53–65.

Logan, John and Harvey Molotch. (1987) *Urban Fortunes*, Berkeley, CA: University of California Press.

Luria, Daniel and Joel Rogers. (1997) "A New Urban Agenda," *Boston Review*, February–March.

Milner, Cowan. (2006) "South Side Chicago Wal-Mart Opens Despite City Council Opposition," *Chicago Epic Times*, February 2: 1.

Morello-Frosch R. and B. Jesdale (2006) "Separate and Unequal: Residential Segregation and Estimated Cancer Risks Associated with Ambient Air Toxics In US Metropolitan Areas," *Environmental Health Perspectives*, Vol. 114: 1–8.

Newton, Julianne and Eric Freyfogle. (2005) "Sustainability: a Dissent," *Conservation Biology*, February, Vol. 19, Issue 1: 23–32.

Okin, Susan. (1989) *Justice, Gender and Family*, New York: Basic Books.

Piketty, Thomas and Emmanuel Saez. (2003) "Income Inequality in the United States: 1913–1998," *Quarterly Journal of Economics*, February.

Putnam, Robert. (2000) *Bowling Alone: The Collapse and Revival of American Community*, New York: Simon and Schuster.

——, Robert Leonardi and Rafaella Nanetti. (1993) *Making Democracy Work: Civic Tradition in Modern Italy*, Princeton, NJ: Princeton University Press.

Rawls, John. (1972) *A Theory of Justice*, Oxford, UK: Oxford University Press.

——. (2001) *Justice as Fairness: A Restatement*, Erin Kelly (ed.), Cambridge, MA: Harvard University Press.

Rees, W. (2003) "Economic Development and Environmental Protection: An Ecological Economics Perspective," *Environmental Monitoring and Assessment*, Vol. 86, No. 1: 29–45.

Rivlin, Gray. (1993) *Fire on the Prairie: Chicago's Harold Washington and the Politics of Race*, New York: Henry Holt and Company.

Robinson, James. (1991) *Toil and Toxins*, Berkeley, CA: University of California Press.

Rorty, Richard. (1989) *Contingency, Irony and Solidarity*, Cambridge, UK: Cambridge University Press.

——. (2007) *Philosophy as Cultural Politics*, Cambridge, UK: Cambridge University Press.

Sawhill, Isabel and John Morton. (2007) *Economic Mobility: Is the American Dream Alive and Well?* Washington, DC: Pew Charitable Trust.

Skocpol, Theda and Morris Fiorina (eds.). (1999) *Civic Engagement in American Democracy*, Washington, DC: The Brookings Institution Press.

Stone, Charles. (1989) *Regime Politics: Governing Atlanta, 1946–1988*, Lawrence, KS: University of Kansas Press.

Tucker, William. (1977) "Environmentalism and the Leisure Class," *Harpers*: 49–80.

Walzer, Michael. (1983) *Spheres of Justice: A Defense of Pluralism and Equality*, New York: Basic Books.

——. (1994) *Thick and Thin: Moral Arguments at Home and Abroad*, Notre Dame: Notre Dame University Press.

Weisman, Jonathan and Charles Babcock. (2006). "K-Street's New Ways Spawn More Pork," *Washington Post*, January 27: p. AD-1.

Editor's Introduction to Chapter 3

Although he is critical of its implementation, in the previous chapter, Michael D. Oden adopts the planner's triangle, or the 3Es, as the most viable model of sustainable development. This model is characterized by the achievement of system balance through the negotiation of competing agent interests. In this chapter, by McDaniel and Lanham, readers will find an alternative perspective. By viewing the systems in which sustainability is sought as always complex and adaptive, the outcomes of any action are rendered fundamentally uncertain and unpredictable. In such an uncertain world it is not static outcome-driven approaches that emerge, but dynamic process-driven ones. McDaniel and Lanham employ the concept of a "fitness landscape" to reframe the striving to achieve sustainability and in the process construct significant links between the assumptions of complexity science and those of pragmatism. In both arenas, "adequate environmental policies would be the ones best able to 'take new information into account and thereby provide for adaptation and change'" (Light and Katz 1996: 12).

Chapter 3

Sustainable Development

Complexity and the Problem of Balance

Reuben R. McDaniel Jr. and Holly Jordan Lanham

Modern urban planners face a challenge of designing and developing appealing spaces for people to live, work, and play in the short- and medium-term while meeting the long-term goal of sustainability. Sustainability is a concern facing the world, and as we continue to see both increases in population levels and advancements in technology, we are likely to see increases in the consumption of resources. The planner's triangle, a model of sustainable development designed by planner Scott Campbell, depicts the concepts of sustainability put forth in the Brundtland Report *Our Common Future* (World Commission on Environment and Development 1987). This triangulated model, based on three pillars: ecology, economy and equity, encourages urban developers to strive toward sustainability, and suggests that the achievement of "balance" through conflict resolution and negotiation among competing pillar interests will result in sustainability (Campbell 1996).

In this chapter, we step back a level of abstraction from the work of Oden in Chapter 2 of this volume. We consider, in a general way, the characteristics of complex adaptive systems (CAS) in terms of how they shape understandings of sustainability and, in particular, how they shape understandings of sustainability as developed in the planner's triangle. We suggest that process-oriented approaches to viewing and managing sustainability are fundamental when one recognizes that systems seeking sustainability are CAS. Key among the characteristics of CAS are the interdependence among agents, nonlinearity in the relationships among agents, and the dynamic nature of the landscapes on which sustainability is typically sought. Oden suggests that the interdependence of equity with economy and ecology has been overlooked and that this has contributed to failure in sustainability efforts. Oden also seems to recognize that the relationships among equity, economy, and ecology are nonlinear as he suggests that effort and results may not always be proportional. We believe that the concept of complex equity, as Oden develops it, is closely aligned with the notion of fitness landscapes, an idea we explore in this chapter.

We use ideas from complexity science and CAS theories to view the problem of sustainable development. Sustainability can be analyzed at many levels – i.e., global, national, regional, municipal, communal, organizational, and individual. In this chapter, we view the systems in which sustainability is sought as CAS and primarily approach sustainability from the municipal, community, and organizational perspectives. Previous research on environmental systems has examined the systems in which sustainable development is sought as CAS (see Norberg 2004; Olsson *et al.* 2004; Chu *et al.* 2003; Janssen 2002). The agents in these CAS – the pillars of ecology, economy, and equity and the individuals that make up these pillars – are diverse, interact nonlinearly, self-organize, contribute to the development of emergent properties, and co-evolve with their environments over time. Rather than striving for system balance, or equilibrium, complexity science informs us that systems can operate more effectively at points far from equilibrium (see Prigogine 1996; Goldberger 1997; Bettis and Prahalad 1995; Waldrop 1992). Campbell's model of sustainable development, which emphasizes the achievement of balance, seems to imply that sustainability is the desired outcome of a single-level, closed system. However, this chapter views the systems in which sustainable development is sought as open systems both affecting and being affected by their environment.

Using ideas from complexity science helps one view sustainable development not as a goal that can be reached through the achievement of balance, but as a dynamic process of continuous evaluation, action, and re-evaluation. A fitness landscape is one way to visualize this process of continuous co-evolution. Complexity science as a framework for sustainable development draws our attention to (1) the importance of relationships among agents, (2) the possibility that operating at points far from equilibrium might be better for sustainability than operating near equilibrium, and (3) our inability to predict and control system outcomes, i.e., future levels of sustainability.

The purpose of this chapter is to develop and share new insights, informed by complexity science, on the challenges of sustainable development. The next section of this chapter provides a brief description of complexity science and CAS as they relate to the ideas of the planner's triangle and sustainable development. This section is followed by a discussion of traditional approaches to sustainability, including a brief description of the planner's triangle. The final sections of this chapter reframe sustainable development using ideas from complexity science and CAS thinking and share key insights that emerge at the theoretical intersection of complexity science and sustainable development. Self-organization is suggested as an alternative approach to traditional regulatory mechanisms for fostering patterns of sustainability. Sustainable development is presented in another alternative perspective – as an emergent property resulting from the quality and pattern of relationships within the systems of sustainability.

Complexity science and complex adaptive systems

> Humanity is at the beginning of a new scientific era. We are observing the birth of a science that is no longer limited to idealized and simplified situations but reflects the complexity of the real world.
>
> (Prigogine 1996 – Nobel Prize winner in Chemistry)

Complexity science is a set of ideas aimed at understanding two questions grounded in chaos and complexity theories (McDaniel 2004). The first question asks how simple systems create complex behaviors (Gleick 1987). The second question asks how complex systems create simple, ordered patterns (Waldrop 1992). Science has historically suggested that complex systems interact to create complex patterns, and simple systems interact to create simple patterns. However, complexity science offers new insights into relationships and patterns created by interactions within both simple and complex systems (Ford 1989).

Complexity science is composed of several areas of study. Because of parallels observed between ideas of sustainable development and CAS thinking and previous research categorizing ecological systems as CAS, this chapter focuses on the application of complexity science in the area of CAS (see Norberg 2004; Olsson *et al.* 2004; Chu *et al.* 2003; Janssen 2002). In addition to ecological studies, CAS have been studied in many fields including biology (Camazine *et al.* 2001), economics (Arthur 1999), and organizations (Stacey 1995; Boisot and Child 1999; Anderson 1999; McDaniel and Driebe 2001).

CAS are generally described through five main characteristics. First, CAS are composed of diverse agents with the ability to learn as new information becomes available (Cilliars 1998). The learning mentioned in the previous statement is not simply aimed at uncertainty reduction. Complexity science views uncertainty as fundamental to CAS – i.e., CAS face uncertainty that cannot be reduced with more information or better information processing. Rather than focusing on uncertainty reduction, complexity science encourages us to direct energy toward dealing with an uncertain world by paying attention to the world as it unfolds and by using strategies such as learning from samples of one, experiencing history richly, and simulating experiences (March *et al.* 1991). Second, many relationships between agents in CAS are nonlinear (Capra 2002; Kauffman 1995). In nonlinear relationships, small inputs can produce large outcomes, and large inputs can produce small outcomes. Thus, in CAS the system outputs may not be proportional to its inputs. Furthermore, the nonlinearity of relationships in CAS implies that future system behaviors may be dependent upon small changes in initial conditions and that future system outcomes are unpredictable. Third, agents in CAS exhibit patterns of self-organization (Camazine *et al.* 2001). Self-organization is the development of dynamic social structures and patterns through local interactions among agents. Agents of a system naturally self-organize. Because systems self-organize, one must recognize the limits of imposed structures, such as formal organizational hierarchies and regulatory control mechanisms, and shift focus on ways to foster beneficial patterns of communication and relationships that can emerge through self-organization. Fourth, CAS display emergent properties. Emergent properties are characteristics of a system that cannot be explained through analysis and understanding of its parts (Agar 2004; Holland 1998). Examples of emergent properties are patterns in recycling behaviors, attitudes toward energy conservation, and as suggested in this chapter, levels of system sustainability. Fifth, CAS co-evolve with their environment (Capra 1996; Holland 1995). Co-evolution occurs when a system's reaction to an environmental stimulus alters the environment; thus, making the original reaction by the system no longer optimal, or even correct, and causing change within the system yet again. The concept of co-evolution has also been applied in science and technology studies with specific regard to sustainable technology development. The logic used in this case is that technology and societies simultaneously co-evolve, rather than favor either technological or social determinism (Rohracher 2001).

Traditional approach to sustainable development

Sustainable is often defined as the ability of an entity to maintain itself, or keep itself in existence, over time. Sustainability, a truly broad concept, has been referred to as a new philosophy in which beliefs about the future, global environmentalism, equity, and biodiversity serve as a guide to decision-making (Basiago 1995). Biologists tend to associate sustainability with the protection of biodiversity and emphasize the preservation of natural resources for future generations (Light and Katz 1996). In economics, ideas about sustainability are discussed in the context of accounting for natural resources, and economists argue that markets have historically failed to protect the environment (Daly 1973). Planners view sustainability as the process of urban revitalization where the goal of design integrates ideas from urbanization and the protection of nature (Steiner 2000, and in this volume). Sustainability in environmental ethics means preservation, conservation, and the sustainable use of natural resources (Light 1996, and in this volume).

A widely used definition of sustainable development taken from the Brundtland Report describes sustainable development as "development which meets the needs of the present without compromising the ability of future generations to meet their own needs." Since the issuance of this report, a dominant approach to sustainability has been through the goal of conflict resolution among competing social, economic, and environmental interests. The planner's triangle articulates these forces and competing perspectives of sustainable development, and this model has been influential in recent thinking and theorizing on the topic of sustainable development.

Campbell illustrated the idea of sustainable development through his planner's triangle model anchored by three pillars: economy, environment, and equity (Campbell 1996). The model

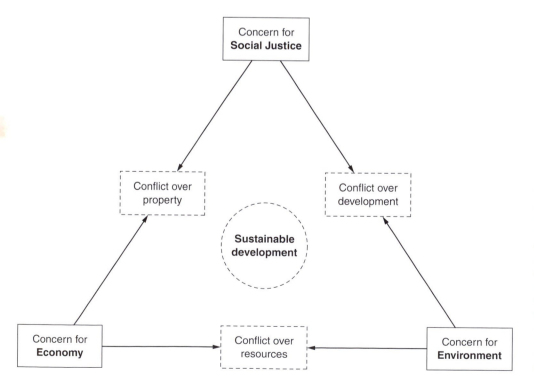

Figure 3.1
The planner's triangle. Adapted from Scott Campbell, "Green cities, growing cities, just cities? Urban planning and the contradictions of sustainable development," *Journal of the American Planning Association* (1996) 62, 3: 468.

suggests that agents in each of these pillars share similar interests, goals, and a common perspective on the world. Planners focused on economic development view production, consumption, distribution, and innovation as critical elements to the system. Economic planners are tuned in to internal and external systemic competition for markets and new economic opportunities. Planners primarily focused on the environment perceive the system as a consumer of resources and a producer of wastes. According to the ecological perspective, system competition resides in the conflict between nature and the system for scarce resources and land, and nature is constantly threatened by changes in the system. Planners who focus on the issues of social equity view the system as a source of conflict over the distribution of resources, services, and opportunities. According to social equity planners, competition is located within the system and results from the conflict among diverse social groups. For instance, competing interests among communities, neighborhoods, and business units create systemic tension (Campbell 1996).

Divergence in interests and perspectives of agents in each domain of the triangle generates conflict at their respective intersections. The planner's triangle suggests these tensions are created by the differences in perspectives among agents in the system and that through negotiation these conflicts can be resolved. The *property conflict* arises at the intersection of economic growth and social equity. Disagreement over topics such as property use between management and labor, landlords and tenants, or urban developers and long-time residents are typical examples of property conflict (Campbell 1996). The *resource conflict* is the tension between business and the environment. A primary source of conflict between agents in these two domains is embedded in the ways in which they view the role of natural resources – economic utility versus ecological utility. The *development conflict* resides at the intersection of social equity and the environment. This tension results from the system's attempts to simultaneously resolve the other two conflicts – how to increase social equity and protect the environment at the same time. Resolving this conflict, for example, might mean restricting rapid development in developing countries to improve global environmental conditions (Campbell 1996).

Sustainable development and complex adaptive systems

> Prevention of perturbations is often a major goal of ecosystem management, not surprisingly. This is unfortunate, not only because disturbance is a natural component of ecosystems that promotes diversity and renewal processes, but also because it distracts attention from the underlying structural problem of resilience.
>
> (Scheffer *et al.* 2001)

Before we can effectively change a system, we must first improve our understanding of the system. By striving to better understand the systems in which sustainability is sought, one can begin to uncover fundamental system characteristics, identify previously unrecognized patterns in relationships, and discover new insights into solving the challenges it presents. This chapter argues that viewing sustainable development in the context of a CAS will improve our understanding of sustainability and the factors that influence it. This new understanding will lead to improvements in policy development, perceptions regarding the role of regulations, and perspectives on decision-making related to environmental, economic, and social equity issues.

Sustainable development can be analyzed at many levels and each level can be described as a CAS. In the global domain, the earth is the system and is composed of geologic, oceanic, and atmospheric agents. In the national domain, a country assumes the role of system and its states, regions, political groups, etc., are agents within this system. In the municipal domain, a city is the system composed of communities, businesses, civic organizations, etc., as agents. This comparison can be continued with systems of communities, households, and individuals. Each of these domains is a CAS interacting nonlinearly with and unpredictably impacting CAS at other levels – i.e., cities and local jurisdictions are CAS within a state which is also a CAS, and each level influences other levels. When the systems in which sustainability is sought are recognized as CAS at all levels of analysis, we can begin to better understand the issues that emerge in trying to improve sustainability and develop alternative methods for facing the challenges they present.

Diverse learning agents

The systems in which sustainability is sought are made up of diverse agents that learn. Each pillar of the planner's triangle is composed of a diverse set of agents interacting with agents in other pillars as well as interacting among themselves – adding to the complexity of the relationships within the system. For example, not all business leaders, environmentalists, or social engineers have the same experiences, perspectives, or interests as other agents (professionals) in their pillar. The interaction of agents within each pillar adds to the dynamic nature of the system through learning, adaptation, and the continual adjustments in the ideas and perspectives in each pillar over time. Thus, a dynamic set of relationships exists within each pillar before, during, and after interactions with agents from other pillars.

Nonlinear relationships

Many of the relationships among agents in CAS are nonlinear. In nonlinear relationships, cause and effect are not necessarily proportional; small events can result in major disruptions, and conversely, large events can result in small disruptions. An example of nonlinearity in the context of sustainability is illustrated through the accidental importation of an invasive species that significantly impacts the ecosystem. Because relationships in CAS are nonlinear, system outcomes based on interactions between agents cannot be accurately predicted. We repeatedly observe this fact as people try, and fail, to predict the level of impact expected to result from catastrophic events.

Efforts to predict and control system outcomes may actually inflict more harm than good. Even though counterintuitive to traditional views and approaches toward protecting the ecosystem, using this logic might lead one to conclude that allowing a species to evolve into extinction may be one responsible way to enhance system performance as a whole.

Self-organization

Self-organization is a decentralized process through which local interactions create order without necessarily receiving guidance from formal structures. A classic example of self-organization is illustrated by the challenge of getting food into the city of Manhattan. When one looks closely at this problem, it becomes clear that traditional management tactics are not responsible for successful completion of this task. No formal managers exist to direct or oversee the process; yet food arrives, is distributed, and is consumed every day by millions of people. The people involved in the planning, purchasing, and delivering food self-organize in a way that meets system requirements without a formal set of control mechanisms.

Emergent properties

CAS display emergent properties. Emergent properties are dynamic characteristics of a system that are created through the interactions among agents over time. Because of the way in which these properties emerge over time, they cannot be explained through analysis and understanding of its parts (Agar 2004; Holland 1998; Camazine *et al.* 2001). Examples of emergent properties relevant to systems of sustainable development are patterns in recycling behaviors, attitudes toward energy conservation, and levels of sustainability.

Co-evolution and fitness landscapes

As nonlinear interdependencies, self-organization, and emergent properties contribute to the unpredictability of system outcomes, so does the co-evolution of agents and systems with their environments. Co-evolution is a continuous and dynamic process in CAS. The concept of system co-evolution can be visualized through the idea of a fitness landscape. The process of trying to achieve sustainability is similar to the process of trying to continuously improve your position on a fitness landscape, or improve your position in the world.

Fitness landscapes were first introduced in the fields of genetics and biology to describe the processes of natural selection (Kauffman 1995). Since then, they have been used to describe the ways in which agents of CAS interact with other agents and contribute to agent/system co-evolution (Allen *et al.* 2005; Rivkin and Siggelkow 2002; Levinthal and Warglien 1999; Santiago and Sanjuan 2003). As agents in a CAS interact to optimize their positions on the landscape, the landscape changes. As the landscape changes over time, agents must continuously evaluate their decisions and take new action based upon these evaluations. This cycle of evaluation and re-evaluation of the system and its environment leads to agent/system learning, which also contributes to the dynamics of the fitness landscape.

A fitness landscape relevant to sustainable development could be described by the following scenario. Think for a moment about the city in which you currently live. This city is likely to be made up of political organizations, educational institutions, medical centers, community organizations, business entities, law enforcement agencies, neighborhoods, social activist groups, financial institutions, animals, natural resources, etc. Each of the organizations is composed of individuals with a range of education levels, financial resources, and attitudes, values and knowledge pertaining to sustainable development. Each element of the city (system) dynamically interacts with other elements in a continuous cycle of co-evolution. This perpetual co-evolution generates the patterns of movement a system experiences along its fitness landscape.

Fitness landscapes can help us visualize and understand the nature of system movement. Fitness landscapes are covered with "peaks" and "valleys" – some large and some small. Systems can only observe their local environment; thus, they often cannot see distant peaks and valleys or judge what actions must be taken in order to reach more optimal points on the landscape. Because systems can only know their current location and immediate surroundings, it might not be possible for systems to experience continuous improvement. In order for a system to reach a higher peak on its landscape, it may be necessary for them to first move down. Moreover, every move a system makes changes the nature of the landscape and affects other aspects in the system in unanticipated ways (Chu *et al.* 2003).

Trying to achieve sustainability is, in fact, a process of trying to improve a position on a fitness landscape. As one recognizes that at all levels of analysis sustainable development can be viewed as a CAS, the idea of co-evolution on a dynamic fitness landscape and its application to sustainable development becomes particularly relevant. The "not in my backyard" (NIMBY) syndrome illustrates an often expressed response by one agent on a fitness landscape to proposed actions of other agents in the system. For example, the addition of a large retail center in a city may provide economic benefit for many communities. On the other hand, the addition of this center may also decrease the perceived attractiveness of some of the communities because of the resultant changes in traffic patterns, destruction of natural resources, or other unintended consequences that might result. People in communities who perceive the center will harm their community will likely try to stop this action, and neighboring communities who seek the forecasted economic benefits from the center will then have to re-evaluate and react based on their new position on the fitness landscape. This perpetual striving and interaction among agents alters the fitness landscape and leads to system co-evolution. Thus, actions taken to improve landscape position change the fitness landscape resulting in the emergence of new and different challenges (Rivkin 2002; Levinthal and Warglien 1999; Santiago and Sanjuan 2003).

Discussion: implications of complexity science for sustainability

Complexity science provides an alternative perspective for understanding sustainable development and suggests that (1) CAS operate more effectively at points far from equilibrium than at points near equilibrium, and (2) the environments in which CAS operate are characterized by fundamental uncertainty and unfold in unpredictable ways over time. These two suggestions lead us to the problem of balance and the impact of unpredictability on control.

The problem of balance

The framework of complexity science informs us that sustainability is not something that can be achieved through attaining balance among competing system interests. Rather, if one views the systems in which sustainable development is sought as CAS, then system equilibrium is equivalent to death, and the system could operate most effectively at points far from equilibrium (Waldrop 1992). Systems that operate far from equilibrium are better able to learn, make sense of their environments, and generate new, creative solutions to difficult challenges (Bettis and Prahalad 1995). By striving for balance, or equilibrium, CAS limit their ability to reach levels of success (represented by "peaks") on the fitness landscape not previously envisioned by individuals in the system. Operating far from equilibrium continuously introduces the system to new, diverse points of view and enables more active and effective navigation of the fitness landscape (Bettis and Prahalad 1995; Capra 1996). Having such a view of one's landscape including the interactions on the landscape and the potential for learning that results provides an evolutionary advantage for those systems able to adopt such a view.

The goal of sustainability in a CAS is impossible to achieve in equilibrium because the system in which sustainability is a part exists on a dynamic fitness landscape. For example, a city (as a system) cannot reach sustainability (equilibrium) because it exists on a fitness landscape that is constantly changing in unexpected ways over time. Because all CAS exist and co-evolve on a fitness landscape, it is impossible to accurately predict future system states. For example, leaders of cities are not able to predict how the development of new industries will ultimately affect the city as a whole. As another example, a community may discover the presence of unanticipated water shortages due to a drought not forecast at the beginning of plans to design and implement municipal sustainable development policies.

The framework provided by complexity science also leads one to recognize sustainable development as many interdependent levels of CAS interacting with each other in meaningful, but unpredictable ways. This suggests that tactics aimed at regulation or gaining control of a CAS will often be ineffective. Systems striving toward sustainability (i.e., families, communities, cities, states, etc.) are all CAS. Because the evolution of CAS is unpredictable and system balance cannot be maintained, efforts to control sustainability will not likely be effective.

Traditional approaches to sustainable development focus on the achievement of sustainability and typically assume that once sustainability is reached, the problem is solved. Ideas from complexity science imply that this type of approach will not work. Rather, sustainable development will require dynamic, process-oriented approaches that emphasize the ability of systems to continuously solve and re-solve problems. Because the agents within the systems in which sustainability is sought are dynamic, the environments in which these systems operate are dynamic, and the problem of sustainability is itself dynamic, we cannot determine how these systems of sustainability will unfold. Because of this unpredictability, to effectively address the challenges of sustainable development we must seek to develop relationship-focused strategies that maximize a system's ability to detect and respond to challenges. Because of the dynamic nature of the systems in which sustainability is sought, it is impossible to "get it right." To foster sustainable development we must instead focus attention on getting the processes for making sense (Weick 1979), for making decisions (March *et al.* 1991), and for taking action, right (Baker 2004).

Such processes will involve paying attention to the system as it unfolds and continuous negotiation and re-negotiation of challenges as they emerge.

Unpredictability and its impact on control

Traditional approaches to sustainable development rely on the ability of individuals to accurately predict and control systems. Complexity science argues that sustainability is not likely to be achieved through acts of prediction and control through laws and other forms of regulation. Nor will sustainability be achieved by making an uncertain world certain. Rather, sustainability can best be enabled through fostering patterns of relationships within the systems in which sustainability is sought and the ongoing negotiation of interests based on demands at the time. Nonlinear interdependencies and self-organization are two key reasons why traditional control mechanisms such as regulation might not be effective in the long term. Because outcomes of systems characterized by nonlinear relationships cannot be accurately predicted, they cannot be controlled. Rather, in CAS outcomes are the unpredictable emergent results of interactions among agents; and traditional methods, such as forecasting, are considerably less helpful in evaluating attempts at sustainability. Recognizing the inability to accurately forecast and control system outcomes alters the way in which one views the roles of sensemaking, decision-making, and taking action toward sustainability.

Research studying traffic patterns and regulations aimed at controlling interaction between motorists, cyclists, and pedestrians at particular intersections illustrates this point by positing that formal procedures designed to reduce the number of accidents by controlling the mechanisms through which individuals relate to each other may actually have the opposite effect (Baker 2004; McNichol 2004). In Holland and Denmark, traffic designers have been experimenting with traffic conditions by removing all formal forms of overt traffic regulation (i.e., stop signs, traffic lights, speed bumps, road markings, crosswalks, etc.) at certain intersections. The removal of legislated traffic control mechanisms resulted in a decreased number of traffic-related deaths and accidents, not an increase (Baker 2004). These results were attributed to the changes in patterns and the increased richness of interactions among motorists, cyclists, and pedestrians at affected intersections. One could argue that traffic control mechanisms often create conditions that encourage people to turn off their minds and operate on "auto pilot" – a condition that occasionally results in fatal outcomes. With traditional traffic controls, motorists learn to rely on lights, signs, and other signals to supply advanced warning of potential danger instead of improving their skills at recognizing potential hazards through interactions with other participants on the road. Self-organized enabled interaction, specifically eye contact between motorists, cyclists, and pedestrians may have allowed for increased environmental awareness and sensemaking during uncertain events.

In many cases, organizations can benefit from similar insights recognizing the importance of processes for sensemaking, decision-making, and action that can be used to deal with uncertainty and unpredictability. For example, businesses need processes for continuous exploration of issues such as who are the customers and what are their current needs; what are the impacts of technological developments for distribution systems and how might these impact other aspects of business; and how might changes in the competitive environment alter the strategic direction of the firm. When nonlinear interdependencies are recognized, decisions will not be made without consideration for, rather than prediction of, unintended consequences on other elements of the system. Instead of designing organizations around the characteristics of agents, we should design organizations around the interactions between agents that create meaning and allow solutions to emerge and re-emerge. Weick suggests effectuation (learning from "prodding"), triangulation (learning from the application of several measures), affiliation (learning by comparing what one person sees with what another person sees and agreeing upon a mutually acceptable version of what happened), deliberation (learning through reasoning), and consolidation (learning from putting experiences into context) as procedures for making sense of the world as it unfolds (Weick 1985).

A key problem with many large information technology (IT) system implementations in businesses is that the systems are often designed in fundamentally flawed ways. They generally assume that once the system is installed, it is *right* and the problem is *solved*. This static view of problem-solving may be an important reason why these systems often fail. Moreover, IT systems are traditionally designed to increase organizational stability, which over time causes organizations to become desensitized to variations in their environments (Hedberg and Jonsson 1978). Not only are IT systems often not designed to fit the dynamic nature of organizations, but their impacts on the organization as a whole are typically overlooked. The mere introduction of an IT system changes the way in which people relate to each other. IT is typically used as a tool for increasing information processing capacity in organizations; however, IT information processing capacity can quickly surpass human information processing capacity. As this happens, organizations will need to adopt new perspectives that allow people to create context-specific meanings and find alternative ways to make sense of their environments (Weick 1985).

This same approach can be applied to a city searching for the right key to unlock the door to sustainability. Instead of searching for the right key, attention should be placed on the continual process of trying to positively influence the relationship systems and the ongoing dynamics involved in addressing these problems. It is the characteristics of the *relationships* within systems that determine system outcomes – not the characteristics of the agents. Changes in the patterns of relationships that emerge over time, the ability of agents to learn, and continuous behavior adjustments also contribute to the unpredictability of system outcomes. For these reasons, it may be beneficial to think about designing processes modeled on the idea of a "recipe" rather than a "blueprint" (Weick 1985). Blueprints are rigid representations, designed at a single point in time, and are developed based on static mental models. On the other hand, recipes are dynamic plans, designed for multiple points in time, and are developed through an evolutionary, iterative process. This metaphor is particularly helpful in illustrating how one might view the process of designing systems for fostering sustainable development.

Peter Allen addresses the issue of sustainability in a recent paper on the topic of evolution of CAS (Allen *et al*. 2005). Allen defines sustainability as the "result of the existence of a capacity to explore and change." He also points out that as systems explore and evolve over time, high-performing systems emerge as levels of internal competition decrease and cooperation increase. As people interested in fostering sustainability search for new beneficial ways to influence interaction between agents in this system, approaching negotiation as a collaborative instead of a competitive relationship can increase the range of negotiated outcomes. The following quote from Allen's paper aptly summarizes the key points from this section:

> Complex systems thinking is telling us that we are forever at risk of evolving into an unknown future, with sometimes interesting, sometimes painful consequences. Though we construct edifices of routine and regularity into our system, the need to innovate and change will always assert itself at some point in time, and we shall be forced to move to a new, temporary set of routines and regularities.
>
> (Allen *et al.* 2005)

Conclusions

Traditional approaches to sustainable development, such as Campbell's planner's triangle, are characterized by the achievement of system balance through the negotiation of competing agent interests. Complexity science offers an alternative perspective for planners and developers to use in thinking about and developing solutions to challenges in the search for sustainability. By viewing the systems in which sustainability is sought as CAS characterized by fundamental uncertainty and unpredictability, dynamic process-oriented approaches toward sustainability rather than static outcome-driven approaches emerge. A particularly salient insight, the role of fitness landscapes in CAS, helps to illustrate the process of striving toward sustainability. Fitness landscapes also serve as an effective integrator of key issues that emerge at the intersection of sustainable development and complexity science. These key issues: the problem of balance, the importance of relationships, and the recognition of our inability to control system outcomes emerged at the intersection of complexity science and sustainable development. The role of nonlinear interdependencies, self-organization, emergent properties, and co-evolution are important characteristics of CAS in improving our understanding of and generating new insights into the challenges of sustainable development. In summary, using a complexity science perspective, systems seeking sustainable development should strive to (1) operate at points on the fitness landscape that are far from equilibrium, (2) foster the development and maintenance of relationships among agents with diverse interests and perspectives, and (3) develop ways for dealing with fundamental uncertainty without simply relying on traditional strategies based on prediction and control.

In addition to building on current models of sustainability, this chapter opens the door to several areas of future research integrating ideas from complexity science and sustainable development. One such area involves studying in greater depth the characteristics of relationships among agents that impact sustainability. Suggestions of potentially significant characteristics of relationships should include those characteristics that significantly impact the way agents in the system of sustainable development relate to one another. A possible topic for study is the role of strong and weak ties between agents and further investigation into the impact of tie strength on the level of effective collaboration between agents.

Researchers and policy-makers should further investigate the roles of self-organization and emergent properties as they relate to sustainability. Additional research in these areas could continue to examine self-organization as an alternative approach to traditional regulatory mechanisms in fostering patterns of sustainability. This research should consider self-organization as dynamic over time and recognize the possibility that the pattern of relationships among agents might not respond to policy initiatives, such as regulation, in a knowable way.

Approaching sustainability as an emergent property resulting from the quality and pattern of relationships within the system would logically extend many of the suggestions made in this paper. Systems develop properties that are emergent and dynamic over time, and some of these properties contribute to sustainability while others do not. For example, a city can be both resistant to new industries because of environmental concerns and at the same time open to new industries because of the expected future economic benefits. The case of Holland's traffic regulation discussed in this chapter demonstrates a goal as an emergent property of a system. In this case, the goal of safe passage becomes an emergent property resulting from changes in the way motorists, cyclists, and pedestrians interact at intersections. Instead of imposed rules and regulations, more stable (safe) behaviors resulted because of the changes in the patterns of relationships that emerged from the different ways in which people interacted in traffic without traditional control mechanisms. Using this perspective, the level of sustainability is dynamic and emerges from the pattern of interactions among system elements over time. An important question continuing this line of thought becomes, "How should a system be designed so that sustainability is more likely to emerge?" Regardless of whether sustainable development is approached as a goal or an emergent property, the systems in which sustainability is sought are CAS that exist on fitness landscapes and the properties of these landscapes affect their ability to reach desirable levels of sustainability.

Complexity science and CAS thinking allow us to recognize our inherent inability to predict and control system outcomes because of nonlinear relationships, self-organization, emergent properties, and co-evolution. As one accepts the presence of fundamental uncertainty in CAS, attention is freed from attempts at uncertainty avoidance and can subsequently be redirected toward recognizing and embracing uncertainty. If one assumes the core of sustainable development really occurs in the interactions among many CAS at many levels, one must also accept the fact that sustainability is not something that can be achieved through balance. Rather, sustainable development is something toward which we must continuously strive. As we strive toward sustainability, we change the world.

Questions for further consideration

1   In the previous chapter, Oden argued for balancing the competing interests of "complex equity" across sectors of society. In this chapter McDaniel and Lanham argue that the condition of "balance" is impossible to achieve in conditions like our own where systems are rapidly evolving. And in Chapter 6, Allen *et al.* hold that the choice between rapidly evolving and durable systems must be made on a case by case basis. Is there a common ground between these authors?

2   Does the concept of complex adaptive systems (CAS), including the idea that systems "self-organize," suggest that government regulation should be avoided because it artificially hinders system evolution?

3   In Chapter 11 Steiner sets out a "sustainable" regional planning process with prescribed steps of information gathering, analysis, policy-making, implementation, and reflection. If city-regions, like frog ponds, are CAS, should we abandon long-term planning processes in favor of short-term fixes?

4   In a CAS there are "diverse learning agents" with competing interests, all hoping to reduce the uncertainty of the situation in which they find themselves. Does this observation support the tenets of Social Darwinism – survival of the fittest?

5   The concept of CAS suggests that we should engage in "dynamic process-oriented" designs (likened to a recipe) rather than static outcome-oriented designs (likened to a blueprint). How will such a proposal influence the worlds of architecture and engineering in which blueprints drawn at a distance from the site and time of construction hope to control the outcome in every detail?

Bibliography

Agar, M. (2004) "We have met the other and we're not all nonlinear: ethnography as a nonlinear dynamic system," *Complexity* 10, 2: 16–24.

Allen, P. M., Strathern, M. and Baldwin, J. S. (2005) "The evolutionary complexity of social economic systems: the inevitability of uncertainty and surprise," in R. R. McDaniel, Jr., and D. J. Driebe (eds.) *Uncertainty and Surprise in Complex Systems*, Berlin: Springer-Verlag.

Anderson, P. (1999) "Complexity theory and organization science," *Organization Science* 10, 3: 216–232.

Arthur, B. W. (1999) "Complexity and the economy," *Science* 284: 107–109.

Baker, L. (2004) "Why don't we do it in the road?" May 20. Online, available at: www.salon.com/tech/feature/2004/05/20/traffic_design/index.

Basiago, A. D. (1995) "Methods of defining sustainability," *Sustainable Development* 3, 3: 109–129.

Bettis, R. A. and Prahalad, C. K. (1995) "The dominant logic: retrospective and extension," *Strategic Management Journal* 16, 1: 5–14.

Boisot, M. and Child, J. (1999) "Organizations as adaptive systems in complex environments: the case of china," *Organization Science* 10, 3: 237–252.

Camazine, S., Deneubourg, J., Franks, N. R., Sneyd, J., Theraulaz, G. and Bonabeau, E. (2001) *Self-Organization in Biological Systems*, Princeton, NJ: Princeton University Press.

Campbell, S. (1996) "Green cities, growing cities, just cities? Urban planning and the contradictions of sustainable development" *Journal of the American Planning Association* 62, 3: 296–314.

Capra, F. (1996) *The Web of Life: A New Scientific Understanding of Living Systems*, New York: Anchor Books.

—— (2002) *The Hidden Connections*, New York: Doubleday.

Chu, D., Strand, R. and Fjelland, R. (2003) "Theories of complexity: common denominators of complex systems," *Complexity* 8, 3: 19–30.

Cilliars, P. (1998) *Complexity and Postmodernism: Understanding Complex Systems*, New York: Routledge.

Daly, H. (1973) *Toward a Steady-State Economy*, San Francisco, CA: W.H. Freeman and Company.

Dewey, J. (1910). "The influence of Darwinism on philosophy," in *The Influence of Darwin on Philosophy and Other Essays*, New York: Henry Holt and Company.

Ford, J. (1989) "What is chaos, that we should be mindful of it?", in P. Davies (ed.) *The New Physics*, Cambridge, MA: Cambridge University Press.

Gleick, J. (1987) *Chaos: Making a New Science*, New York: Penguin Books.

Goldberger, A. (1997) "Fractal variability versus pathologic periodicity: complexity loss and stereotypy in disease," *Perspectives in Biology and Medicine* 40, 4: 543–562.

Hedberg, B. and Jonsson, S. (1978) "Designing semi-confusing information systems for organizations in changing environments," *Accounting, Organizations and Society* 3, 3: 47–64.

Holland, J. (1995) *Hidden Order: How Adaptation Builds Complexity*, Reading, MA: Perseus Books.

—— (1998) *Emergence: From Chaos to Order*, New York: Addison-Wesley.

Janssen, M. (2002) *Complexity and Ecosystem Management*, Cheltenham, UK: Edward Elgar.

Kauffman, S. (1995) "The origins of life," in *At Home in the Universe: The Search for the Laws of Self-organization and Complexity*, Oxford, UK: Oxford University Press.

Levinthal, D. A. and Warglien, M. (1999) "Landscape design: designing for local action in complex worlds," *Organization Science* 10, 3: 342–357.

Light, A. (1996) "Towards ethics guidelines for environmental epidemiologists," *Science of the Total Environment* 184, 1–2: 137–147.

—— and Katz, E. (eds.) (1996) *Environmental Pragmatism*, London and New York: Routledge.

McDaniel, R. R. Jr. (2004) "Chaos and complexity in a bioterrorism future," in J. Blair *et al.* (eds.) *Advances in Health Care Management: Bioterrorism, Preparedness, Attack and Response*, Oxford, UK: Elsevier.

—— and Driebe, D. J. (2001) "Complexity science and health care management," in J. D. Blair, M. D. Fottler and G. T. Savage (eds.) *Advances in Health Care Management*, 2: 11–36.

McNichol, T. (2004) "Roads gone wild," *Wired* 12, December 12.

March, J. G., Sproull, L. S. and Tamuz, M. (1991) "Learning from samples of one of fewer," *Organization Science* 2, 1: 1–13.

Norberg, J. (2004) "Biodiversity and ecosystem functioning: a complex adaptive systems approach," *Limnology and Oceanography* 49, 4: 1269–1277.

Olsson, P., Folke, C. and Berkes, F. (2004) "Adaptive co-management for building resilience in social-ecological systems," *Environmental Management* 34, 1: 75–90.

Prigogine, I. (1996) *The End of Certainty*, New York: Free Press.

Rivkin, J. W. and Siggelkow, N. (2002) "Organizational sticking points on NK landscapes," *Complexity*, 7(5), 31–43.

Rohracher, H. (2001) "Between innovation and diffusion: the importance of users in the shaping of environmental technologies," in *Proceedings of the International Summer Academy on Technology Studies: User Involvement in Technological Innovation*: 223–234.

Santiago, E. F. and Sanjuan, R. (2003) "Climb every mountain?" *Science* 302: 2074–2075.

Scheffer, M., Carpenter, S., Foley, J. A., Folke, C. and Walker, B. (2001) "Catastrophic shifts in ecosystems," *Nature* 413: 591–596.

Stacey, R. D. (1995) "The science of complexity: an alternative perspective for strategic change processes," *Strategic Management Journal* 16, 6: 477–495.

Steiner, F. (2000) "Land suitability analysis for the upper Gila river watershed," *Landscape and Urban Planning* 50, 4: 199–214.

Waldrop, M. M. (1992) *Complexity: The Emerging Science at the Edge of Order and Chaos*, New York: Simon & Schuster.

Weick, K. E. (1979) *Social Psychology of Organizing*, Reading, MA: Addison-Wesley.

—— (1985) "Cosmos vs. chaos: sense and nonsense in electronic contexts," *Organizational Dynamics* 14, 2: 51–64.

—— (1993) "Organizational redesign as improvisation," in G. P. Huber and W. H. Glick (eds.) *Redesigning Organizations*, New York: Oxford University Press.

World Commission on Environment and Development. (1987) *The Brundtland Report, Our Common Future*.

Editor's Introduction to Chapter 4

In this chapter by Andrew Jamison, the struggle to define terms becomes even more basic than trying to pin down the elusive meaning of sustainability, equity, or balance. Jamison seems to be asking, what do we mean by "research"? In the classical definition of the term, research is the interpretation of worldly phenomena, usually through the use of the scientific method, which we understand to be objective. Jamison's essay is, however, a highly subjective one in that its interpretation of historical events is written in the first person – a technique usually reserved for literary rather than scholarly texts. No less unusual is the author's proposal that his research is "change-oriented" – a direct challenge to the modern doctrines of objectivity which hold the purpose of research to be the production of new knowledge independent of the researcher's interests or hopes for the future. Over the past half century there has, of course, been a series of challenges to the epistemological assumptions of modern science, many of which begin with William James who held that,

> Rationalism sticks to logic and the empyrean. Empiricism sticks to the external senses. Pragmatism is willing to take anything, to follow either logic or the senses and to count the humblest and most personal experiences. Her only test of probable truth is what works best in the way of leading us...

> (James 1987: 522)

Jamison's contribution is an attempt to go beyond the traditional forms of academic analysis and provide a narrative representation of change-oriented research as pragmatic sustainability.

Chapter 4

In Search of Green Knowledge

A Cognitive Approach to Sustainable Development

Andrew Jamison

> Looking for an expression that could capture the change that has occurred in the last century and a half in the relation between science and society, I can find no better way than to say that we have shifted from Science to Research. Science is certainty; Research is uncertainty. Science is supposed to be cold, straight and detached; Research is warm, involving and risky. Science puts an end to the vagaries of human disputes; Research fuels controversies by more controversies. Science produces objectivity by escaping as much as possible from the shackles of ideology, passions and emotions; Research feeds on all of those as so many handles to render familiar new objects of enquiry.
>
> (Latour 1998: 208)

It all started with steam cars

There was a brief moment in the early spring of 1968 when it seemed not only possible but actually quite likely that the war in Vietnam would soon come to an end – and largely because of the mobilization of youthful idealism. After Eugene McCarthy, the poetic senator from Minnesota, with his band of student supporters, including yours truly, had nearly beaten the incumbent president in the New Hampshire primary in February, President Lyndon Johnson declared that he would not seek, nor would he accept his party's nomination to run for reelection in the upcoming fall election. Soon thereafter, Robert Kennedy had joined the race, taking on McCarthy in a series of primaries that began in Indiana in early April and would conclude with the final showdown in California in June, when Kennedy would win – but then be murdered, leading to the chaos in the streets of Chicago (I was also there), the election of Nixon in November and the prolongation of the war for seven more years – which drove me to Sweden, where I have lived ever since.

It was in that brief hopeful moment so many years ago that I began my lifelong search for green knowledge. I had gone off to Indiana to campaign for McCarthy against Kennedy, and I can still remember that heady feeling of empowerment from those days in New Hampshire when I had taken part in something truly significant. We had brought down Johnson, and now we were going to stop the war. Whatever else got destroyed that year, in me as in so many others, I have always retained a healthy respect for the power of idealism – and collective action – to change things, or at least to shake things up. I felt it, even though the feeling at the same time was soon gone.

I was nineteen, a particularly impressionable age to be sure, in my sophomore year at Harvard and a budding journalist, serving as science editor of the *Crimson*, the student newspaper. In my studies, I had just begun an undergraduate concentration in history and science, taking courses in both of what C.P. Snow had termed the two cultures – the literary and the scientific – with "tutorials" in history of science to try to bring out the hidden connections between them. I had gone to Harvard to become a scientist – my Dad was an industrial chemist and math had been my favorite subject in high school, and we were taught at the time that ours was the age of science (on TV there was the jovial "Mr Wizard" in his lab coat and his infinite wisdom, showing us between commercials all of the wonderful things that science could do: I loved it). But when I got to Harvard I found it hard to deal with the involvement of scientists in the war effort, and the way in which the military seemed to dominate the sciences, and so I wandered into the woolly world of interdisciplinarity where I have remained ever since.

It must have been shortly after my return from Indiana that I received a phone call from Bryce Nelson, who worked for the news and comment section of *Science* magazine in Washington. He asked if I would like to spend the summer serving as a student intern, and without really knowing what I was getting into – namely signing up for life in the not yet existing environmental movement – I said sure, be happy to, sounds like a wonderful opportunity. And so it was that in June – between the murders of Martin Luther King and Robert Kennedy, when the mood of the country was beginning to change considerably – I arrived in Washington to begin my internship.

I should say that I had been aware of the environmental debate that had been going on for several years by then, but like many, if not most student "activists" at the time, I had tended to disregard it. Compared to the destruction in Vietnam, the problems that were discussed in the environmental debate seemed to be of relatively minor importance. And even worse, the environmental debaters seemed to be challenging the very idea of progress and science-based innovation that was so central to modern civilization – and to my own belief system. Many of the environmental debaters seemed to be politically naïve, even downright reactionary in their concern with population growth and protecting nature when there was a dreadful war to stop. How dare they complain of dead birds when people were getting killed every day in a far-off land by our own government?

It was thus with some trepidation that I took on my first assignment for *Science*. A Senate committee had recently held hearings on alternatives to the internal combustion engine, and I was asked to do a story. I remember talking to one of the staff members at the Senate office building and wondering how he could get so excited about automotive air pollution. But gradually, as I worked my way through the hearings and the background reports that had been prepared, I found myself getting intrigued. For I soon realized that there was a perfectly good alternative to the internal combustion engine that didn't pollute the air, namely, the steam-powered automobile, and the only reason that there weren't such things available was the opposition of the auto companies.

Steam cars had been the main kind of car back at the turn of the century, and it had not been due to any overriding technical drawbacks that they had disappeared from the "market." Apparently, they had never been inferior to gas cars on purely technical grounds (if such grounds actually ever exist); rather, as the automotive industry had developed, by exploiting the methods of mass production initiated by Henry Ford, steam-powered automobiles had become outmoded, antiquated symbols of a bygone age. It was their cultural meaning that had buried them, not their technical capacities. Over the years, there had been a few attempts to revive them, but they had never been able to shake off that stigma of premodernity, even though it was known fairly early on (I later found an article in *Scientific American* from the 1920s pointing to the fact) that they didn't pollute the air the way gas cars did.

In the late 1960s, when it had become ever more obvious that automotive air pollution was dangerous to the natural environment and to human health, steam cars were thus staging something of a comeback. A handful of idealistic automotive mechanics and professional engineers – and, not least, officials in California who were trying to do something about the smog that was afflicting Los Angeles – were giving them some attention, and the Senate was about to take the unusual step of passing a bill to support funding for some of the development work.

When I returned to college in the fall, I received a letter from Indiana University Press, wondering if I would like to turn my article into a book – and it was then that I started my lifelong exploration of what I later came to call green knowledge. In doing the research for my book, I realized that far from being opposed to science and technology, the people I interviewed – the engineers and politicians and businessmen who were trying to revive steam cars – were simply trying to make a different kind of science and technology than the scientists and engineers and businessmen who had produced the environmental crisis; they were trying to bring an environmental concern, however vaguely defined it was at the time, directly into the process of making facts and artifacts, that is, knowledge. They were trying to turn knowledge green.

In the following years, as the war in Vietnam intensified, and spread to Laos and Cambodia, and the antiwar movement grew more extreme and embittered, it was hard to find a place for my burgeoning environmental interest in the American political scene. And so I took my search for green knowledge to Scandinavia, where environmentalism had apparently been combined with support for the Vietnamese, and where I found a "redder" shade of green, infused with a touch of socialism, pragmatic and reformist to be sure, but socialism nonetheless. I joined in the environmental movements that developed in the 1970s in Sweden where I lived and Denmark where I worked and, for another brief moment, I experienced something similar to that feeling I had had back in the spring of 1968.

In both countries, the environmental movements of the 1970s were primarily antinuclear movements, and they had a major impact on society, splitting the population but also fashioning new sorts of political and cultural processes. In Sweden, anti-nuclear opposition brought down the social democratic government that had held power since the 1930s and forced a referendum in 1980 in which some 80 percent of the population voted to phase out nuclear energy within twenty-five years. It revitalized the tradition of public education through self-organized "study circles" that had been developed in the early days of social democracy, but which had become institutionalized into the Swedish model of the postwar years and lost much of its radical flavor as a result. I took part in many a study circle, trying to bring my American variety of environmental politics into discussions with biologists and nature-lovers, which I continued to do for many years thereafter in editing a journal of socialist environmentalism, as well as with friends on the left who did not always share my environmental interest.

In Denmark, anti-nuclear opposition was even more successful than in Sweden, stopping the government's plans to build nuclear plants altogether, and nurturing the emergence of the wind energy industry, which now provides some 20 percent of the country's electricity, the highest percentage in the world. The people's high schools in the countryside, which had grown out of the farmers' movements of the nineteenth century, provided a base for much of the movement's activity, and I was at the Tvind schools in 1978, when the second wing on what was to become the largest wind power plant in the world was brought out of the workshop by its amateur builders in ceremonial fashion to show what the people could really accomplish if they set their mind to it.

As in 1968, my involvement in the anti-nuclear movement gave me opportunities to learn things together with other people that I could never have learned in a classroom on my own: it was a kind of collective learning. As with the attempted revival of steam cars in the 1960s, the anti-nuclear movement provided a meeting place for people from different backgrounds to make knowledge together: engineering students who wanted to show that energy could be produced in an ecological way, biologists who were concerned about the risks of nuclear radiation on their beloved nature, socialists who didn't like the power relations in the nuclear industry, and ordinary citizens who wanted to make their voice heard and take a little power back from the politicians. The human energy that was mobilized in the anti-nuclear movement impressed me, and I have spent much of my subsequent academic career trying to understand where it came from, what it meant, and what happened to the knowledge that was produced in the process: how it came to be culturally appropriated (Hård and Jamison 2005). As I have tried to understand green knowledge, I have had to transgress disciplinary boundaries, and assume what I have come to think of as a hybrid research identity, combining the engagement of the activist with the intellectual ambition of the academic, and, for that matter, the abstractions of the theorist with the details of the empiricist.

Change-oriented research

The kind of research I have done is part of a much broader transformation of knowledge-making that has taken place since the 1960s when so many of the assumptions that had traditionally governed scientific research were fundamentally questioned and began to be overhauled. In our time, the boundaries that, for some three hundred years, had separated science and technology, and knowledge-making in general, from the surrounding society have largely been broken down. The relative autonomy of academic institutions and the "academic freedom" that were once considered essential for the health and vitality of scientific research have been almost entirely eliminated, and, even though many of those who work at universities continue to bemoan their passing, there seems to be little value in wishing that they could suddenly be brought back to life.

The integration of science and technology into society was already well underway in many branches of industry, and, of course, in the military before the 1960s, but it was accentuated enormously by the technological innovations that emerged in the 1970s: in particular, personal computers and genetic engineering. What have come to be called information technologies and biotechnologies essentially mix what had long been characterized as the separate spheres of science and engineering, and their ensuing development and societal significance have largely been based on an ever closer collaboration between academics working in universities and people working in commercial business enterprises. Indeed, in many cases, due to the various attractions and not least the wealth that can be accumulated in the commercial marketplace many academics have largely become "entrepreneurs" in their attitudes, behavior, and way of life – and many universities have come to resemble business firms in their underlying modes of operation, as well as in the values and norms by which they are administered and organized.

At the same time, scientists have also been interacting ever more intimately with government, or the world of politics. Again, there are many scientists who refuse to recognize the increasing role of politics in academic life, but there can be little denying that the boundaries between science and politics have become substantially blurred. In the United States, this had become obvious already in the 1960s, with many academics serving as key advisers in the war and therefore being subjected to student protest activity (I remember when I came to Harvard people joked about Professor Kissinger spending more time in Washington than he did in Cambridge). But in Europe, as well, as science and technology, in the course of the 1960s, became ever more central to social and political life, not least because of their environmental "consequences," and as new government agencies and departments were established to take charge of these new areas, scientists became more and more involved in politics. Thus while in many, if not most branches of industry, the borders between science and business were becoming increasingly transgressed, and in many areas of social science, the traditional boundary between science and policy-making was increasingly crossed, in the humanities, or human sciences, academics like me have been ever more doing something new, as well: namely, carrying out research in closer cooperation with "activists" or other concerned members of the public who are trying to change things. I call it change-oriented research.

In different areas of social life and in different fields of research, it is referred to by different names – action research, advocacy, participatory planning, public education, technology assessment are all synonyms and reasonable descriptions for the kind of work I do – but what they all have in common is an ambition on the part of the researcher to engage in various processes of social or cultural change. Such research is problem-driven rather than disciplinary-driven, and it involves a range of methods that are different from the traditional methods of the sciences. Much of the research I have done draws on experiences from the progressive movement in the United States in the early part of the twentieth century, when "muck-raking" journalists, social workers, and public health experts, and pragmatic philosophers like John Dewey, carried out projects in urban reform and human ecology, in occupational medicine and regional development, and not least in public education. Revived in the 1960s, these examples of change-oriented research were complemented by the forms of consciousness-raising that were initiated by Paolo Friere in Brazil and by many of the "movement intellectuals" who took part in the environmental movements and in the movements of women's liberation that formed such an important part of the politics of the 1970s.

In Denmark and a few other countries in Europe, this kind of research was directly stimulated by the energy debates of the 1970s, which led to the creation of state-supported research programs in technology assessment, and new methods of interaction between citizens and experts in relation to science and technology. One of the more widely used methods has been the consensus conference developed by the Danish Board of Technology, in which a group of laypeople are brought together in an organized way to question experts on a particular topic of interest and are then given the opportunity to prepare a report where they can propose changes in the established ways of doing things.

The aim of such research is obviously not the same as traditional science. There is little interest in "proving" an assertion or justifying a truth claim, or in explaining causal relations among different variables. There is also little interest in grand, or abstract theorizing, or in what might be called philosophical speculation. Instead, the aim is to intervene creatively and constructively in an ongoing social or political process: to contribute to change. Rather than the traditional notion of enlightenment, by which is usually meant that the role of the scientist is to provide insights for the broader society, derived from a "disinterested" pursuit of the truth, change-oriented research is about empowerment, by which the researcher applies knowledge gained from experience to processes of social learning, carried out together with those being "studied."

In connecting knowledge-making to political action, change-oriented research is similar to the kind of pragmatic philosophy that has been developed in recent decades by Jürgen Habermas and Richard Rorty. Habermas and Rorty have both drawn on the pragmatic tradition of James and Dewey to challenge the dominance of positivism – or technological rationality – in the humanities and social sciences. To a large extent, my search for green knowledge has been an attempt to combine a pragmatic epistemology, or theory of knowledge with a holistic, or ecological worldview, or ontology, such as the complexity theory that was discussed in the previous chapter. More specifically, it has represented an effort to combine the philosophical critique of technological rationality of Habermas and Rorty and others with the environmental, or ecological critique of reductionist science that has formed what I have termed the cosmological dimension of the environmental movement's cognitive praxis (Eyerman and Jamison 1991).

Already as an undergraduate, I had begun to realize that science and technology, and the roles that they played in society, were in the midst of fundamental change. There had been an enormous expansion of science and technology in the period after World War II, both for military purposes, as well as for other "missions" – such as landing a man on the moon. Science, which had previously been considered "pure" by many, if not all of its practitioners – that is, free from outside influence in terms of substance and organization – had become ever more applied to particular social tasks, and ever more subservient to interests and values other than the purely academic. As could be seen in relation to the war in Vietnam, social and human scientists were also subjected to these new conditions; the rise of what John Kenneth Galbraith (1968) termed the "new industrial state" had brought about major changes in the interaction between the public and private sectors in the development of new technology. Technological development, derived directly from scientific research, had become a key factor of production and one of the main contributors to economic competitiveness. And in the course of the 1960s, these transformations had led to changes in the ways in which scientific knowledge was thought about by philosophers and scientists themselves.

In accordance with the language that was presented in the influential *The Structure of Scientific Revolutions* by Thomas Kuhn (1962) knowledge-making had become normalized, or, as Jerome Ravetz (1971) called it, "industrialized"; social, or external interests had come to steer the cognitive frameworks, or paradigms by which scientists organized their research. Rather than choosing for themselves the topics that they would investigate, scientists had become enmeshed in elaborate systems of research and development, or "R&D" by which scientists at universities were connected to business firms and government departments in various programs of "big science." Universities, in turn, had largely become factories for producing knowledge workers who served to bring the ideas generated at research laboratories as quickly as possible to the commercial marketplace. The process of innovation was coming to be recognized as a central topic for economists and business managers, and, the relations between science, technology and society were beginning to be investigated by academic experts, as well as by new cadres of science politicians and policy-makers.

By the 1970s, programs had begun to spring up at universities, and it was at one such place – the Research Policy Program at the University of Lund – where I started to carve out my particular approach to research. The first few years were primarily a continuation of the journalism that I had carried out at college, but gradually, I was introduced to the emerging field of science, technology and society studies, or STS, which served as a meeting place for what had previously been an abstract philosophizing about science and empirical investigations of what Bruno Latour (1987) later termed "science in action." From the outset, I combined my "expertise" in STS with an interest in environmental politics, and through the years, I have mixed my two "subjects" in various ways. What has remained central has been the "cognitive approach" to reality, a focus on the knowledge-making that goes on in society, and, in particular, the making of knowledge within the world of environmental politics.

The cognitive approach

It was never my intention to become an "expert" in environmental movements, but for both internal and external reasons (it was both what interested me and what I could get funded), my post-doctoral research career began with a project in the 1980s on the relations between political strategy and knowledge interests in the environmental movements in Sweden, Denmark, and the Netherlands. We were a group of former activists who brought different kinds of competence into the project: Ron Eyerman, a fellow American émigré, was a social theorist, who had written about ideology and intellectuals; Jacqueline Cramer was a biologist and STSer, who had written about ecologists in the Netherlands; Jeppe Læssøe was a social psychologist, who had studied the cultural dynamics in NOAH, a Danish environmental organization in which he was active; and I was a doctor in theory of science, which was a field that had broken away from philosophy in the 1960s to connect philosophy to empirical research. The project led to a comparative history of the movements (Jamison *et al.* 1990), as well as to a new approach to social movements: the cognitive approach, which combined theory of science and social theory in a kind of hybrid combination (Eyerman and Jamison 1991).

Ron and I had both read *Knowledge and Human Interests*, by Jürgen Habermas, in which he discussed the different human motivations for knowledge-making. Where the technical–natural sciences were interested in instrumental knowledge, and the social sciences were interested in administrative knowledge, the human sciences were interested in reflective or emancipatory knowledge. Habermas was updating in his book the categorization of knowledge into three types that had been a part of the theory of science at least since Aristotle, and for us it provided a framework for deconstructing the knowledge that was made in environmental movements. We rephrased the categories into three dimensions of what we came to call "cognitive praxis": a cosmological dimension, a technical dimension, and an organizational dimension. And we then went on to use these categories to analyze the ways in which knowledge had been made in the environmental movements in Sweden, Denmark, and the Netherlands.

On the basis of our analysis, we argued that the environmental movements throughout the industrialized world had provided a space, or context in which an ecological cosmology, or worldview, derived from systems thinking and, in particular ecosystems ecology, had been combined with particular technical and practical activities that were organized in newly formed public spaces (here again, we "operationalized" the abstract Habermasian public sphere to researchable public spaces). As expressed in a number of programmatic works that were published in the early 1970s, there was a kind of "systemic holism" in the air that provided a shared discursive framework, or cosmological knowledge interest. In books, such as Barry Commoner's *The Closing Circle*, Barbara Ward's and Rene Dubos' *Only One Earth*, Edward Goldsmith's *A Blueprint for Survival*, and, perhaps most influentially, *Limits to Growth*, the report to the Club of Rome, ecological ideas were translated into a program for social action. Another kind of literature – E.F. Schumacher's *Small is Beautiful*, Ivan Illich's *Tools for Conviviality*, the Whole Earth Catalogs, and journals such as *Mother Earth News* in the US and *Undercurrents* in England – were offering perspectives on what David Dickson (1974) called "utopian technologies" showing how the ecological ideas could be put into practice in the development of alternative technologies, especially renewable energy technologies and organic agriculture. In the movement organizations, there was a very open anti-elitist structure, which, as in many other social movements before or since, made it possible for anyone who identified with the movement's aims to take part in what we came to call "cognitive praxis": the integration of the three dimensions into a collective learning process.

For those of us who were active in the environmental movements of the 1970s, it was apparent that the knowledge we were making was based on a new "paradigm" which was different from what was to be found in the established sciences. The concept of cognitive praxis was an attempt to clarify the nature of that new paradigm – and to recognize that there had been – and continued to be – serious differences of opinion about what that new paradigm consists of, both in terms of theory, method, and forms of organization. There were those who wanted to change as little as possible in relation to the established ways of carrying out research, merely add an environmental concern into science and technology, much like the steam car enthusiasts I had written about in the 1960s. At the other extreme, there were those who posited the need for an entirely new kind of science and technology, seeing in the environmental "crisis" a fundamental turning point in human history which required a totally new approach to knowledge and to society. But whether reformist or revolutionary – what Murray Bookchin termed environmentalist or ecologist, and Arne Naess termed shallow or deep ecology – certain features distinguish what I have come to call green knowledge from traditional forms of knowledge-making.

For one thing, environmental knowledge is inherently interdisciplinary. In order to understand environmental problems, it was necessary to combine knowledge from different fields of science and technology, and especially to transgress the boundaries between the natural sciences and the social and human sciences. This was, of course, easier said than done. Then as now, it was difficult for many environmentalists with a natural science education to give up their privileged position, to accept the fact that environmental problems transcended their intellectual terrain, indeed that the very concept of the "environment" was a kind of borderland, a place in between the natural and the social, the human and the non-human. It was a place where nature was affected by society, but also where humanity was affected by nature. It was a place – or perhaps more accurately, a cognitive space – where humans interacted with, had relations to, or, to wax philosophically, took part in the co-construction of reality with non-humans. And how could all that be investigated and conceptualized?

Obviously, there could not be one method that would suit all purposes. And this has meant that green knowledge must be referred to in *pluralis*. As in many, if not most areas of research today, there is no one universally recognized form of green knowledge. The knowledge that is produced in order to understand environmental problems and to deal creatively with their resolution is highly dependent on context, or on the specific contingencies in which the problem emerged. Green knowledge is thus a situated form of knowledge-making, or collective learning, in that the particular combination of insights and techniques is contingent on setting, on the particular site in which the learning takes place. This means that the ways in which lessons are learned, the ways in which knowledge is exchanged, is different from what is involved in the traditional sciences. In many respects, it is more like the pragmatic "learning by doing" that has long characterized engineering knowledge, with the important difference that the knowledge that is learned is never replicable – because the context, in significant ways, is never the same. The particular mix of culture and nature, of the human and the non-human will never be able to generate the exact same response.

Green knowledge is exchanged by example rather than by replication. But the example cannot be slavishly, dogmatically followed the way an experimental method can be repeated in a laboratory. In the "laboratory" of the real world, where environmental problems are to be found and dealt with, the example has to be recounted; it is by telling stories about what has been done in a particular place that green knowledge can be disseminated and eventually exchanged. And those stories require a particular kind of story-telling, an ecological, or holistic kind of story-telling, an attempt to grasp the whole.

The exemplar remains *Silent Spring*. It is a book of science, but it is also, and even more importantly, a book of ecological story-telling. The facts that are presented – about the effects on human and non-human health of chemical pesticides – are mixed with presentations of the fact-finders, and the cultural history of the environmental problems is told along with the natural history of the landscapes in which the problems are situated. The example is presented not as a particular "case" that has been studied in all of its myriad details, but for its exemplariness, its capacity to awaken other researchers to investigate other examples and tell other stories about the human war on nature, as Rachel Carson called it.

My own modest attempts to follow in her footsteps can further illustrate some of the features of ecological story-telling. In the steam car book, I outlined the problem of automotive air pollution, sketched the political background, recounted the history of steam automobiles and gave a general overview of different examples before narrowing in on one detailed "case": William Lear, who had set up shop in Reno, Nevada, to spend some of his many millions of dollars developing a commercially viable steam car (which he eventually did do, but the auto companies were

In Search of Green Knowledge

not interested). The examples were meant to illustrate the more general points, not to "stand alone" or serve as a microcosm for the whole. As such, the general needs to be presented along with the specific, and it is in the mixing, the combining, that the story unfolds.

More recently, in *The Making of Green Knowledge*, I tried to tell a different kind of story, a theoretical story, framed by a cultural theory derived from the writings of Raymond Williams. It was the story of an emerging cultural formation, an ecological culture, and I tried to tell it as a kind of ongoing struggle between environmentalists and the surrounding society. The story-line was of a multifaceted process of cultural transformation, by which environmental ideas and practices had been appropriated by the surrounding culture, first by providing new words, things and activities, and gradually by transforming institutional, laws and routines, and, not least, forms of knowledge-making.

The plot was of a series of tensions, or conflicts that, in their resolution, led to the emergence of new conflicts and tensions – and what I called dilemmas and ambiguities. I attempted to recount the "dialectics of environmentalism." In the 1970s, the conflict over nuclear energy had led to a differentiation of environmentalism between the practical-minded and the theoretically-minded that was resolved at the end of the 1980s by the articulation of a new discursive framework – sustainable development – that served to spread the environmental consciousness much more broadly through the society. By the end of the 1990s, however, sustainable development had also led to a tension between what I have termed "green business," on the one hand, and "critical ecology," on the other, the one articulating discourses of ecological modernization and natural capitalism, and the other linking sustainable development to other discourses of global justice and sustainable community. As such, the emerging ecological culture has been waging a struggle on two fronts: against the dominant commercial culture which attempts to incorporate what Raymond Williams (1977) termed its "structure of feeling" into established business, on the one hand, and against residual cultures of traditional ideologies and scientific disciplines, which attempt to capture sustainable development in outmoded discursive frameworks, organizational forms and personal identities. In recent years, I have come to see possibilities for resolving the tension both by redefining sustainability – as science, as community, as "just sustainability" – but also by producing new examples that combine in new hybrid combinations, something of the seriousness of the business people with the passion of the critics (Jamison 2008).

The hybrid imagination

It might be helpful by way of conclusion to attempt to characterize the tensions that have developed in the quest for sustainable development – and how they might be resolved – in terms of research identities. In this regard, it seems to me that there is a substantive difference between interdisciplinary and transdisciplinary approaches to green knowledge. Both are attempts to transcend the traditional disciplinary identities that were so important to scientists and engineers in the past, but which have become increasingly difficult to sustain, because of the external pressures that scientists and engineers and all other knowledge makers are increasingly subjected to. Thus, while there is a fairly widespread promulgation of a "hybrid imagination" and a general recognition of the importance of flexibility and mixing and the combination of skills and knowledge, there are very different forms in which the hybrid imagination is being put into practice.

As ideal types, we can distinguish between interdisciplinarity, which, at least for me, is something that emerged in the 1970s as a goal for many scientists, who were interested in contributing actively to the social challenges of the time, and, not least, to the social movements that emerged at the time, and transdisciplinarity, which started to be used in the 1980s as a term to characterize those working in the ever more commercialized and globalized world of "high-tech" knowledge-making. Where the one signals a primarily internally generated process of knowledge integration, the other signals a largely externally generated process of knowledge combination.

Within interdisciplinarity there is a further distinction between what might be termed as collaboration – in which a real synthesis of different knowledges takes place (as in my books with Ron Eyerman) – and cooperation – in which people with different disciplinary backgrounds work together on a common project (as in the first volume that Ron and I wrote with Jacqueline Cramer and Jeppe Læssøe). Both are internally generated and involve integration of knowledge into something more comprehensive or collectively shared, but whereas the one involves the making of a true hybrid, or joint work, the weaker form, cooperation often results in a collection, a group work, usually an anthology of some kind that is more or less integrated.

Similarly, within transdisciplinarity, it is possible to draw a distinction between a stronger form – which can be characterized as explicit nondisciplinarity, or even antidisciplinarity – by which the research identity is derived from expertise in a particular technique or concept or method, that has little connection to any particular academic field, but which is widely applicable in combination with other specialized competencies – environmental impact assessment is perhaps a good example of what I mean – and what might be termed subdisciplinarity, by which the researcher largely retains a disciplinary identity but transcends downward, so to speak, specializing within a disciplinary matrix or framework in order to have an expertise that is combinable with other subdisciplinary competencies. The various environmental subdisciplines, such as environmental sociology, environmental chemistry, environmental engineering, can illustrate what I mean. In all four types, disciplinarity has been transgressed, but in very different ways. In cultural terms, interdisciplinarity is a highly personal process, or series of processes of self-transformation, while transdisciplinarity involves the seeking of niches in a competitive market, in a process or series of processes of furthering self-interest.

Obviously, in the contemporary world, there is a need for all four types of hybridization, but what is perhaps most important to emphasize is that one type should not, and indeed must not, be favored at the expense of the others. There needs to be room – and acceptance – of plurality and of the crucial importance of both personal engagement and what might be termed enlightened self-interest. In some contexts, where it is primarily public participation and cultural change that need to be fostered, there must be opportunities for what I have termed interdisciplinary research, and, in particular, for research in which academics and laypeople collaborate in efforts that are organized "from below" in relation to local needs and concerns. But in other contexts – in relation to global problems like climate change and biodiversity – there is a need for transdisciplinarity, by which different types of experts with different forms of specialized skills and knowledge, provide new sorts of technological solutions, or "fixes," to particular problems.

The challenge for the future, for science and society alike, is in finding a proper balance between personal engagement and specialized expertise – or, in other words, between sustainable communities and sustainable growth. What is involved are two rather different cultural value systems, or structures of feeling. On the one hand, there is the democratic, or political motivation to provide opportunities for people to take part in dealing with the challenges that confront them, and, on the other hand, there is the instrumental, or economic motivation to provide real solutions to real problems. Much will depend on how well we as academics and as citizens manage to combine those two ambitions or motivations in the years ahead.

Questions for further consideration

1   In this chapter Jamison begins by sounding the same note that McDaniel and Lanham did in the last – arguing that the uncertainty of both history and science should be embraced rather than avoided. Jamison proposes that where "science" is the search for "disinterested truth," "research" is "to engage in various processes of social or cultural change." A question that derives naturally from such claims is, how do we know what change is desirable if we give up the quest for "truth"?

2   What Jamison refers to as "cognitive praxis" has "a cosmological dimension, a technical dimension, and an organizational dimension" which he holds to be a superior approach in the making of "green knowledge" than that conducted in traditional, or "positivist" science. Does this suggest that we should give up traditional science as we know it?

3   Jamison's account of the history of science in his lifetime is highly personal. Does his personal experience make his account more or less reliable?

4   If, as Jamison holds, "environmental knowledge is inherently interdisciplinary," does it follow that disciplinary knowledge (that which comes from a single discipline like chemistry or architecture) is not knowledge at all because it lacks an understanding of how it can be applied outside its own view of reality?

5   In lieu of "pure science" Jamison argues in favor of the "hybrid imagination" – an activity in which citizens find "a proper balance between personal engagement and specialized expertise." Will engineers and scientists find it difficult to accept this challenge to their disengaged objectivity?

Bibliography

Dickson, D. (1974) *Alternative Technology and the Politics of Technical Change*, London: Fontana.

Eyerman, R. and Jamison, A. (1991) *Social Movements: a Cognitive Approach*, Cambridge, UK: Polity Press in association with Basil Blackwell.

Galbraith, J. K. (1968) *The New Industrial State*, New York: The New America Library.

Hård, M. and Jamison, A. (2005) *Hubris and Hybrids. A Cultural History of Technology and Science*, New York: Routledge.

James, W. (1987) *William James: Writings 1902–1910*, Bruce Kucklic (ed.), New York: The Library of America.

Jamison, A. (2001) *The Making of Green Knowledge. Environmental Politics and Cultural Transformation*, Cambridge, UK: Cambridge University Press.

—— (2008) "Greening the City: Urban Environmentalism from Mumford to Malmö," in M. Hård and T. Misa (eds.) *Urban Machinery*, Cambridge, MA: MIT Press.

——, Eyerman, R., Cramer, J. and Læssøe J. (1990) *The Making of the New Environmental Consciousness*, Edinburgh: Edinburgh University Press.

Kuhn, T. (1962) *The Structure of Scientific Revolutions*, Chicago, IL: University of Chicago Press.

Latour, B. (1987) *Science in Action*, Philadelphia, PA: Open University Press.

—— (1998) "From the world of science to the world of research?" *Science* 280, 5361: 208.

Ravetz, J. (1971) *Scientific Knowledge and its Social Problems*, Oxford, UK: Clarendon Press.

Williams, R. (1977) *Marxism and Literature*, Oxford, UK and New York: Oxford University Press.

Technological Cultures

Editor's Introduction to Chapter 5

Political theorist Langdon Winner offers in this chapter the sort of "change-oriented research" that is advocated by Andrew Jamison in the previous one. Winner holds that a central conflict in contemporary efforts to imagine and build a sustainable economy often arises as the plans of global corporations disrupt ongoing processes of reform in local communities. An early twenty-first-century encounter of this kind took place in upstate New York when a transnational firm proposed building a massive cement plant on the banks of the Hudson River, sparking widespread regional opposition by those who were quietly charting a green future. As a participant observer in the fracas that ensued, Winner charts the visions and strategies of the major players in the story, especially ordinary citizens who crafted ways of knowing far more flexible and resourceful than the engineers and businessmen they eventually defeated.

It is through the comparison of local and technological cultures in this story that we understand the power of local languages, of people who "talk like us" without reference to the abstractions that motivate corporate action. Richard Rorty argues that "what binds societies together are common vocabularies and common hope" that things will get better (Rorty 1989: 86). In the case chronicled by Winner, the local talk invented by citizens prevailed because it more accurately described the consequences of proposed corporate action.

Chapter 5

Renewal and Resistance

The Quest for Sustainability in the Hudson River Valley

Langdon Winner

Flashpoints for social conflict in the early twenty-first century often arise as insistent forces of globalization clash with organized efforts to create a sustainable, local economy. Among citizens and politicians a common concern is that corporations are "going South," moving capital and jobs to the world's developing countries in search of low-cost labor, access to natural resources and more favorable conditions in taxation and environmental regulation. For working people in the North this spells the "outsourcing" and "offshoring" of jobs, declining incomes and diminishing economic horizons for the present generation, and bleak prospects for their children as well.[1] While these problems are highly significant ones, in recent years an equally troubling set of issues has become starkly apparent. In fact, many transnational firms are willing to build new facilities and expand their operations in developed countries of the North, creating jobs in the process. But following the logic of global economics, they often treat the towns and cities targeted for new "development" as if they were districts in a newly colonized Third World. Yes, costly projects in mining, chemicals, energy production, real estate, and mass retailing promise to bring new dollars to the locality. But they often do so at the expense of environmental quality, public health and the long-term vitality of the communities affected.

As a community learns it has been selected as a site for expansion by a transnational giant, one of the most difficult questions it confronts is how to interpret the promotional bombast that accompanies the news. In a typical case, the corporation announces that "we are going to build" – build a new energy plant, factory, big box store, shopping mall, real estate complex, or other major facility. At a well-staged inaugural event the firm shows lovely drawings and scale models that depict the project in the most attractive light. Expecting that any infusion of money is bound to serve their interests, local business leaders welcome the initiative with open arms. In turn, politicians, eager to show a forward-looking, results-oriented vision of the area's future, praise the project as solid evidence of the economic growth they promised during the last election. Similarly, the local press, always happy to cover upbeat news, offer their readers glowing reports about wonderful changes on the horizon. As the story unfolds in the days and weeks that follow, an aura of momentum and inevitability quickly surrounds the project. Especially if the development involves technology of any kind, the impression of high-tech dynamism and innovation often enters the mix. Soon people begin to accept the pending transformation as something beyond their power to influence. People on the street say, "I hear that Global Dynamics is building a big new (fill in the blank) just outside of town."

In the summer of 1998 a situation of this kind suddenly confronted the citizens of Columbia County in upstate New York. Saint Lawrence Cement, a division of Holcim, Inc., a Swiss-owned transnational company, the world's second largest cement producer and listed among the Fortune "Global 500," announced that it would build an enormous $320 million cement factory and mining complex on Beecraft Mountain just east of the City of Hudson on the banks of the Hudson River. Said to be "a done deal" by many businessmen and local politicians, described as a welcome boost for the economy by the most prominent local newspaper, "the plant," as it came to be called, was at first greeted with stunned amazement by much of the populace in the surrounding region. People asked quietly: Would it be good to have such a huge, coal-burning plant as one's next door neighbor? What would the benefits to the community actually be? But faced with a glowing public relations blitz touting new jobs and economic growth as its obvious contributions, many accepted the plant's coming as a given.

During the next several years, however, a growing number of people did begin to ask questions and, eventually, to organize spirited opposition to the plant. Calling attention to the considerable harm the factory's construction and operation would have upon environment, economy and social life in the city and region, the "Stop the Plant" movement eventually attracted thousands of supporters. Although widely regarded as a losing cause by political "insiders" in the know, the opponents surprisingly won. In the spring of 2005, the State Department of New York denied Saint Lawrence a crucial permit needed to begin construction. Shortly thereafter, Holcim announced that it had withdrawn any further plans to build on the site.

The story of the defeat of the Greenport mega-project offers an illuminating case study of how a broadly based, well-organized, ingenious grassroots mobilization can succeed against even the most powerful of global giants. But the underlying story has less to do with organization of surprisingly effective opposition, than it has to do with underlying conditions in the town, county and region that made this victory possible. The movement drew upon the vitality of localism and the vision of an environmentally sustainable economy that began long before "the plant" entered the picture. While the story in many ways mirrors the arguments Andrew Jamison outlines in his discussion of change-oriented research, the particular blend of local knowledge, expert knowledge and political strategy seen in the "Stop the Plant" struggle contains some important, perhaps even transportable, lessons for those who would promote local sustainability against what seem to be insurmountable, global odds.

Columbia County is a rural section of upstate New York on the east bank of the Hudson River, a two and a half hour drive from Manhattan. Its population of 63,000 is scattered among several towns and villages across a landscape of green fields and rolling hills. From one point of view, it is a county in economic decline, part of the "rust belt" that covers much of the US Northeast. The small industrial factories that were once a key source of employment long since closed. For the most part, the dairy and grain farms that once provided a decent living for many countryside families have ceased operation. Today the main sources of work in the county are in retail trade, professional services, tourism and recreation (including restaurants), and some light manufacturing. According to the 2000 US Census, the median family income is $41,915, a little below the national level.

During the past quarter century, as "stagnation" has become endemic in the upper Hudson River Valley, a fairly common response has been to propose strategies for economic and ecological renewal. Despite the abuse its land suffered during the industrial era, the region still has great natural beauty and places of deep historical significance, features identified as good opportunities for community development. Hence there have been a good many initiatives to protect the lands, forests and marshes through the projects of The Nature Conservancy and other environmental groups. The acreage purchased or donated is usually open to the public for walking and cross-country skiing. Similar impulses are at work in efforts to restore the old houses, shops, and public buildings that give the towns their appeal. Several old railroad stations in Columbia County, for example, have been restored and put to new uses. On main street districts of several towns, as the old shops, department stores and hotels have gone out of business, new owners have refurbished them as restaurants, antique shops, clothing stores, book stores, and the like. Builders and craftsmen in the county are kept busy restoring old houses, many of them bought by weekend and summer residents from New York City and New Jersey, some of whom eventually move their homes and businesses to the locale. Since the middle 1990s it has become fairly common for people to use digital communications to relocate all or part of their small businesses in advertising, media, and financial services to refurbished buildings in the area. A benefit of this version of the reuse and restore model has been that the region has so far been spared many of the bulldozer manias that have generated strip malls, housing tracts, big box blight seen in other parts of the country, although "developers" still circle overhead, like vultures, imagining "unused" parcels of land as carcasses to be devoured.

A growing movement in Columbia County and the Hudson River Valley more generally seeks a sensible balance between the economic and ecological value of the land. A number of farms specialize in organically grown vegetables and meats. Innovative orchards in the area use integrated pest management and natural nitrogen in growing their fruit rather than using chemical intensive methods. Especially promising are several farms organized as community supported agriculture (CSA) enterprises in which a strong connection between healthy land and strong community is an important goal.[2]

Whether in the countryside or in the town, Columbia County has become a place in which changes associated with a sustainable economy are welcome. Several restaurants in the area feature locally grown, organic vegetables and meats on their menus. A successful manufacturer of magnetic products has launched a project in Chatham, Solaqua Power and Art, to reclaim the buildings of a defunct cardboard box factory, using them as a hotel, artists' workspace, and home of a start-up business in renewable energy products.[3] Both non-profit organizations of business people in the towns and villages continually look for opportunities to set aside forests, wet lands, and other green spaces that might otherwise be paved over. Most towns in the county have instituted long-term land use planning and zoning in hopes of avoiding the chaotic, often stifling patchwork of commercial and residential development encouraged by other upstate communities in earlier times. Several organizations in the region foster both theoretical and practical deliberations about ways to transform society in ways that reflect concerns for environment, peace, and social justice. In discussions about both the entrepreneurial and policy aspects of these matters, the language of "sustainability" has become an accepted part of public speech, enough so that some chamber of commerce old timers have been heard to say, "Why can't we get back to no-nonsense concerns about economic growth?"

The renewed attention to relationships among ecological, historic, and economic features of the region builds upon a deep history. In the works of early American writers – Washington Irving, James Fenimore Cooper, Nathaniel Hawthorne, Herman Melville, and others – the Hudson River Valley is a place that defines the nation's relationship to the wilderness. During America's industrial revolution of the nineteenth century, the Valley was home to one of the nation's most famous group of artists, the Hudson River school of landscape painters. In vividly colorful, romantic scenes they depicted highly idealized visions of the natural realm and of humanity's involvement in it. The underlying impression in many of the canvasses is that of nature in peril as signs of roads, factories and locomotives suggest that the Eden of American dreams is being transformed by industrial progress.[4] In that light it is ironic that the leaders of the school, Thomas Cole and Frederick E. Church, lived and painted within easy view of the site that Holcim chose a century later as the location of its mammoth cement plant. Cole's house was on a scenic overlook in Catskill, just across the river from Columbia County. Church designed and built an elaborate Turkish style home at the top of a small mountain just south of the City of Hudson.

Contemporary efforts to create a sustainable economy in the region also bear the legacy of the Valley's role in spawning the modern environmental movement. In 1963 Scenic Hudson, a small group of citizens led by lawyer Stephen Duggan and his wife Beatrice "Smokey" Duggan, astonished the economic and political elites of New York by opposing a decision by Consolidated Edison to build an electric power plant on Storm King Mountain overlooking the Hudson River. The ensuing protests and law suits lasted more than a decade, but eventually Consolidated Edison dropped its plans to conquer Storm King. As both a legal victory and model for later environmental movements, the campaign showed what can happen if a handful of concerned citizens take a stand.[5]

It is against the background of both historical and contemporary efforts to cherish the Hudson River Valley and renew its economy in imaginative ways that the controversy about Saint Lawrence Cement should be seen. Many of those who eventually decided to oppose "the plant" were already engaged in wide-ranging attempts to start new businesses, restore old buildings, keep farms in production, establish arts centers, and, in general, to move their communities forward within a post-rust belt economy already taking shape. Some of these were long-time residents of the region interested in building new enterprises and institutions based upon what they saw as the region's distinctive strengths. Others were newcomers who had moved from large East Coast cities, attracted by the greener, quieter way of life in Columbia County. These hopeful, forward-looking efforts were aided by several waves of national attention to the Hudson River Valley and its importance. In the late 1990s Congress designated the Valley as one of twenty-seven National Heritage Areas in the US and the Environmental Protection Agency (EPA) listed the Hudson as an American Heritage River Area. In 2000 the National Trust for Historic Preservation listed the Valley as one of America's "most endangered places."

The sources of endangerment are substantial. Throughout much of its history the waters and lands of the Hudson Valley had been a vast waste dump for the residues of industrial production. Among the most significant of these were millions of pounds of toxic PCBs used in the production of electrical equipment, dumped into the Hudson watershed by General Electric from the late 1940s well into the 1970s. Although the EPA has ordered dredging of the affected areas to remove the chemicals, actual work on the project has been slow in coming. New problems for air and water quality are posed by projects of "reindustrialization" – the construction of large energy plants and industrial factories – promoted since the 1980s as economic revitalization by many New York business leaders and politicians. In stark contrast to plans to create a sustainable economy, visions of this kind point to a revival of ham-fisted, backwards-looking nineteenth-century industrialism in which the river is used to transport coal and other raw materials and as a convenient source of water for cooling industrial processes.

Indeed, there are many, even in Columbia County, who support a return to large-scale smokestack industry. As the news spread that there would be a new, modern cement factory on the outskirts of town (but before full details of its construction and operation became available), some businessmen and blue-collar workers in Greenport and Hudson offered nostalgic arguments of the following sort: times were good when the old plants were here; things got bad when the plants shut down; the good times will return when new plants are built. Often sentiments of this kind were tinged with feelings of nostalgia. For working families of the Northeast it was once common for their children to take jobs in the same factories where their parents had worked. For the most part, that comforting option has vanished as manufacturing jobs have moved down south or out of the USA altogether.

Opposition to the plant was far from a knee-jerk reaction. In fact, during the several months that followed the Saint Lawrence Cement (SLC) announcement, there was little resistance at all. Among those who were aware of the issue there was much perplexity and a desire for information. In January 1999 a handful of people came together to form Friends of Hudson (FOH), an organization dedicated to enhancing quality of life in the City of Hudson and the Hudson River Valley. Leaders of the organization Sam Pratt, a Yale-educated writer, and Peter Jung, proprietor of an antique shop in Hudson, gathered a small but devoted volunteer staff and soon proved to be a formidable team. Their first project was a successful effort to rally opposition to a chemical processing plant that an entrepreneur wanted to establish at a site near downtown Hudson. Then, without taking a stand for or against, the group took up the SLC proposal as a matter for study and debate. In firehouses, churches and other gathering places in the county, the group arranged a series of evening meetings to explain what was known about the plant and to listen to citizen comments. With soft-spoken moderators Sam Pratt and Peter Jung leading the discussion, the meetings helped, presenting general information about the technology, economics and environmental effects of cement manufacturing and about SLC's "track record" at its existing facilities in Canada and the US. As interest in the issue grew, the organization's membership increased steadily and soon numbered in the hundreds.[6] By the summer of 2000, the board of directors of FOH decided that it knew enough about the situation to declare its opposition. At that point the "Stop the Plant" campaign officially began.

A disadvantage the group had to face was that, in fact, problems of cement production had been not been emphasized by the environmental movement previously. No extensive knowledge base on this global industry, its practices and local consequences had ever been assembled for public use. There were no widely recognized strategies for countering the penchant of today's cement corporations to build large, coal-burning factories. While there were scattered movements around the US and the rest of the world trying to stop particular mining and cement production projects, there was nothing that faintly resembled an organized global network to share information and ideas. Hence, FOH was faced with the daunting task of gathering new data and forging new methods to achieve its goal. As the new millennium began, the "smart money" in upstate New York, including several established environmental organizations, thought the little movement had embarked on a fool's errand; the plant was a "done deal," 100 percent certain to be constructed within three or four years.

A surprising break for the opponents came in April 2001 with the publication of the "Draft Environmental Impact Statement" (DEIS) for the Saint Lawrence plant. Under New York State law the Department of Environment and Conservation requires a report of this kind for all building projects that may have significant environmental effects, a step crucial in the process of granting the permits needed to begin construction. The SLC document, more than a thousand pages long, was written by the company's management and technical staff and spelled out basic facts of the plant's design, construction, operation, and expected impacts. Although the report's bureaucratic prose makes for dry reading, the DEIS gave FOH and other opponents more than enough ammunition to carry the battle forward. Read carefully, much of the data in the report tended to contradict the firm's glowing claims about jobs, the economy and environmental impact touted in its well-financed advertising campaign. Equally important, crucial gaps in the study, e.g., the distinct possibility that the plant would burn tires and hazardous wastes, opened the door for wide-ranging research by FOH and others, called attention to aspects of the project that SLC was not eager to publicize.

For many residents of Columbia County and the surrounding region, the most important realization to emerge from the SLC impact statement was the plant's staggering size. The $320 million facility would be built on 1,800 acres, an area much larger than the entire City of Hudson. Its 1,200 acre mine would blast and extract 6,700,000 tons of limestone each year. Running twenty-four hours a day, 365 days a year, the SLC factory would crush and grind the limestone, feeding it in to an enormous kiln burning 250,000 metric tons of coal to achieve temperatures of 2,650 degrees Fahrenheit with the "clinker" issuing from the kiln finally mixed with gypsum to produce 2,600,000 metric tons of cement yearly. The process would require building an enormous complex: a 406-foot tall main stack, 372-foot preheater, eight cement silos twenty-three stories high, and two clinker silos nineteen stories tall and nearly the same width. Also required would be a 2.5 mile long conveyor tube to carry coal and other raw materials from a steady stream of massive "Hudson Max" barges (754 foot by 80 foot) parked at a docking complex on the town's waterfront, and to transport finished materials from the plant to the barges. In addition, an estimated 400,000 tons of cement would be shipped each year by truck, an estimated 265 trips per day, one trip every two and a half minutes over Columbia County's predominantly two-lane roads (Saint Lawrence Cement Company 2001).

While the statistics on the SLC plant were impressive, many local citizens found it difficult to imagine how large the plant would be. A mistaken impression stemmed from memories of the old, very much smaller Atlas Cement factory, the remains of which can be seen on where SLC hoped to build. To help people visualize the proposed facility, FOH produced drawings and a scale model showing the breathtaking dimensions of the plant's smokestack, kiln and other structure as compared to the seemingly minuscule size of the Statue of Liberty, the old Atlas plant, and several Hudson landmarks. "Oh, my God, it's enormous!" many exclaimed when they finally saw the visual replica. The growing sentiment that the plant was simply out of proportion to anything reasonable for the location was strengthened by balloon tests on the SLC site showing how high its structures would be, how they would overshadow much of their surroundings, including Frederick Church's home, Olana.

Concerns about the sheer scale of the SLC plant prompted many in Hudson and the surrounding region to study its environmental consequences more carefully. At the top of the list were worries about the 19,730,740 pounds of pollution, roughly twenty-seven tons everyday, that would, according to the company's own estimates, belch from the forty-story smokestack each year. The plume of smoke would include fine particulate matter, sulfur dioxide (SO_2), nitrogen oxide (NOX), carbon monoxide (CO), and volatile organics, as well as a lengthy catalog of toxic substances – dioxins, furans, arsenic, benzene, cadmium, mercury and others – produced by cement kilns everywhere.[7] Saint Lawrence managers argued that the new factory would actually be cleaner than the old, obsolete plant just across the river in Catskill, one to be dismantled when the modern, efficient "replacement plant" opened. Critics countered that improved technology or not, the Greenport factory would, according to the company's own application, pump 43 percent more pollution into the air because it was much larger than the one in Catskill. In this discussion, especially telling were reports about local places where increased air pollution would pose a danger. Within a mile of the stack were an elementary school, nursing home, a cancer treatment center, city reservoirs, and residential neighborhoods, places not mentioned in SLC's optimistic application. At one of the places affected, Columbia Memorial Hospital, the medical staff voted 35–1 to oppose the plant, citing their concerns for patient health.

Other concerns about the SLC plans covered a wide range. Among the ones commonly mentioned were:

- airborne dust produced at each stage in cement production, dust that typically settles on homes, automobiles and everything else in a plant's vicinity;
- destruction of plants, animals and natural habitats on the plant's site;
- high decibel noise from mine blasting, as well as the operation of the kiln, crushers, and other machinery;
- high levels of truck traffic on local roads;
- destruction of the Hudson waterfront as a place for recreation and other water-dependent activities by the SLC's large dock and steady stream of barges that would off-load and on-load thousands of tons of material;
- physical and visual insult to the historic and esthetic qualities of the natural and human-made features of the Hudson Valley near the plant;
- increase in greenhouse gases from the burning of coal at the very moment when curtailing such emissions is needed to stem the advance of global warming.

Other persistent worries had to do with issues not addressed in the firm's environmental impact statement, especially the record of Holcim/Saint Lawrence at its other North American plants. Resourceful spade work by FOH turned up detailed, documentary evidence of government fines for excess air pollution, fines for polluting wetlands, the burning of tires and hazardous wastes in some of the company's kilns, refusal of clean-up responsibilities for a plant it had closed, and other suspect practices. The strong suggestion from these findings was that the mass of data supplied in SLC's account of likely environmental impacts did not tell the whole story. Of particular relevance was the company's silence on the question of whether or not the Greenport facility would eventually burn tires and other hazardous wastes. Since discarded tires are virtually a free source of fuel for cement plants, they are strongly favored by companies in the industry. But using cement kilns as incinerators brings a host of pollution problems, given the range of substances, including steel and industrial chemicals, that go into their production.

To soften these worries and build public support, SLC launched a vigorous program of television, radio, and newspaper advertising. The TV spots showed children running through green meadows and birds flying through clear, sunny skies. A comforting voice explained that the "replacement plant" would protect the environment, provide new jobs for the community, be "a good neighbor," and contribute millions to the region's economy. The company's ad campaign referred derisively to the opponents as "alarmists" and insisted that most local folks "overwhelmingly" supported construction of the plant. On another front, an organization calling itself Hudson Valley Environmental Economic Coalition (HVEEC), probably funded by SLC, sent out a mass mailing that warned, "Don't let a group of millionaires from New York City deny Columbia County good paying jobs and a stronger economy" (quoted in Gardner 2002). The organization was a casebook example of the phenomenon of "astroturf" (as opposed to grassroots) politics in which corporate interests feign concern for a widely beloved social cause. Showing how little it understood environmental values, the HVEEC web page showed a smiling little cartoon pig holding a shovel, standing next to SLC's familiar yard sign: "Support the Plan(e)t."

FOH's strategy for neutralizing SLC's costly but poorly tuned propaganda was to build a broadly based network of support along with a deep reservoir of local knowledge. Sam Pratt, Peter Jung, FOH staff, and enthusiastic members of the organization offered to meet with anyone interested in the SLC controversy, to explain FOH's position and to listen to what people had to say. Over a several year period they met with hundreds of small groups of people in living rooms throughout Columbia County and surrounding areas, including communities in Massachusetts, Connecticut and Maine. Their plea was that each person should study the situation and contribute whatever knowledge and skill they had to a process in which local communities would choose their own destinies, not a large corporation in Geneva, Switzerland. The message had enormous appeal; FOH grew steadily from a couple of dozen to approximately 4,000 dues-paying members by the struggle's end. Donations from the members, along with a substantial grant from the Open Space Institute, paid for the lawyers and engineering consultants needed for the more specialized aspects of what became a well-organized, highly professional campaign. At town meetings, county fairs, barbecues, and other public gatherings, FOH distributed information and collected thousands of signatures on petitions to "Stop the Plant."

Perhaps the single most persuasive point in Friends of Hudson's case was one that even the plant's most enthusiastic local supporters could not refute. Citing figures from SLC's own Draft Environmental Impact Statement, FOH noted that the plant would create only *one new permanent job*. The reason was evident in the fact that the operation would need only 155 employees of which 154 would be transferred from the SLC factory across the river in Catskill, one that would close when the new facility opened. Yes, hundreds of temporary jobs that would be available during the twenty-two month period of the plant's construction, most of them filled by workers from outside the region. After that there would be just one additional job in the new, highly automated facility. Although one would not have known it from SLC's advertisements, the company's own DEIS candidly admitted that building the plant would bring little continuing economic benefit to the surrounding region.

From the outset, FOH saw the battle against SLC as a sidetrack, a necessary task that deflected people from the true goal – using the area's scenic, historic, and natural resources to achieve "smart and balanced development" in towns and villages that were already well along the path of economic, social, and cultural renewal. As the campaign continued, however, it was increasingly apparent that the two objectives were entirely compatible. Ironically, SLC had done the region a favor, reminding a great many residents why they had decided to live in Hudson River Valley in the first place and what kinds of ingenuity and initiative would be needed to secure its future.

The extent of this reawakening surfaced at hearings held at Columbia Green Community College in June 2001 by the New York Department of Environmental Conservation. Open to all members of the public with thoughts to share on the proposed SLC plant, the event attracted several hundreds citizens on all sides of the issue, dozens of whom presented personal views and/or the positions of their organizations. Moderating the discussion was Helene G. Goldberger, administrative law judge for the DEC, who patiently listened and took notes from 10:00 in the morning to 12:40 a.m. that night. The presentations were passionate and usually well reasoned, often accompanied by loud cheers and jeers from the audience. For those who worry about the health of American democracy, the gathering showed that when given a chance to express their views in public, many people will and intelligently and enthusiastically take part.

Speaking in favor were a number of SLC managers and employees along with several everyday working people, all of whom emphasized the economic growth they anticipated from the plant's coming. Some praised the caring, responsible way the company did business. While proponents acknowledged that there might be environmental and social costs, they argued that the overall effects would be favorable. As one longtime resident of Greenport told the judge, "I have three children who live in the town with me, and I would like to see them have a good future. They won't have a decent future in Columbia County if we don't have the cement plant built here. It will be better for the environment. It will be cleaner, and I believe that my children will be able to work here in Columbia County as opposed to driving out of the county to work like I had to do."[8]

As one might expect, the majority of those who testified in opposition zeroed in on pollution and its effects upon children, the elderly and others in the region. Several doctors spoke about the danger to patients with asthma and other respiratory illnesses as well as cancers associated with cement plant pollution. A teacher in the Hudson Middle School commented, "Many children in my school have asthma already, visiting the school nurse for a puff of medicine from an inhaler helps them to breathe a little bit easier. We know the affects of PM 2.5. Why in the world would we want to put our children at further risk?"

Expanding on this topic, one young man, Warner Johnson, argued that additional pollution would aggravate the asthma epidemic in his Hudson neighborhood. "This is a threat to the well-being of the citizens here, and especially the African American community. And I'm not going to tolerate it." Johnson's comment reflected some of the concerns of the city's several hundred black residents whose voices in the controversy – both for the plant and against – suggest that the controversy was never simply a "Not in My Backyard" (NIMBY) matter instigated by white, middle-class people alone. Indeed, the hearings unearthed concerns of low-income people, both black and white, that have to do with questions of environmental justice.[9]

Several speakers noted that beyond the health effects were matters of severe environmental damage, especially to Hudson River wetlands, that the factory's construction and operation would bring. One old-timer scoffed at SLC's newly professed care for the environment, noting that it did match local cement industry practice. "Take a look at the three abandoned plants that the industry has stuck us with," he complained. "We have Lone Star. We have Atlas, and we have the old Alston Plant all within five miles of where we're standing now. The industry has walked away from the mess and left them standing for decades."

In a similar vein, several people testified that the outsized plan would clash with the historic and scenic qualities of the region. One woman, a local resident and member of an international organization of art critics, spoke of the aesthetic injuries the plant would inflict. "Everyone who is involved in the arts understands the unique value of the Hudson River, of the Hudson River Valley and the particular area where we stand tonight. This is the birthplace of American art. And I am here today to remind you of the devastation St. Lawrence will bring to that landscape.... Our cultural health and our cultural survival is also incredibly important. We have a legacy to guard."

Among the issues that caused most ire at the hearing was a sense that St. Lawrence and the HVEEC had consistently misinterpreted the concerns of those who had raised valid questions about the company's plans. The idea that a handful of outsiders, "millionaires from New York," were the only ones worried about the plant was consistently derided. Several speakers proudly noted how deeply rooted their families were in Hudson and other Columbia County communities. One man who had lived in the area for nearly a half century exclaimed, "I'm against the plant, and I deeply, deeply resent being called a New Yorker. I have lived in this county; you can ask my wife, you can ask my kids, if they were still alive you could even ask my parents." Many openly expressed doubt that the managers of the Swiss firm had any understanding of the needs of everyday people in the region. "SLC ... is the real outsider," one speaker concluded, "a real corporate giant looking to make tons of money from tons of cement, caring nothing about the local residents, only taking advantage of us and our weaknesses and trying to divide us more in their own interest."

As the afternoon and evening sessions moved along, many speakers argued that the plant's size and conditions of operation made it incompatible with recent social and economic trends in the region. According to Kate Korin, the executive director of a non-profit organization, Hudson River Heritage, "The regional economy has grown slowly but steadily as people, drawn by the incomparable scenic character, have made their way here for a day or a lifetime. This type of growth in Columbia County is a state-wide model for sustainable development.... The St. Lawrence Cement Plant would not be an economic boon, but a bust, eroding the sustainable framework for progress now in place." Some testified that, in fact, the beginning of progress toward the new economy of the region could be precisely dated: the moment twenty-five years earlier when the last of the old cement plants ceased production. Others commented that because the Hudson River Valley offers a green, healthful, convivial environment, they had been able to launch new businesses – farms, garden supply centers, building contracting firms, restaurants, pubs, and shops of interest to tourists. Of particular note, some observed, has been the astonishing revival of downtown Hudson during the 1990s. "Restaurants, gift shops, home furnishing stores, clothing stores and even a high-fashion cosmetic store have opened on Warren Street. Why? Because people have moved out of urban areas for the refreshing beauty, clean air and overall quality of life they see here."

One business woman from the town of Philmont, ten miles east of Hudson, described her success in growing medicinal herbs of the sort previously available only from growers in China. "Just to let you know that medicinal herb production is not an airy fairy fantasy," she explained, "since we started High Falls Gardens in 1993 the number of licenses issued to practitioners of acupuncture and oriental medicine in the US has tripled, making it the fastest growing health profession in the US... I am telling you all of this because I see new jobs in the future for Columbia County. Many thousands of new practitioner jobs have been created already nationally. In addition, I see excellent potential from medicinal plant production, including new cash crops for existing farms and on-farm and local value added processing." The speaker suggested that one advantage the county would have is that China has become a place in which the massive presence of coal-burning plants, industrial wastes in the groundwater and use of pesticides and herbicides creates doubt about the quality of its medicinal herbs.

The overall drift of comments at the June 2001 hearing revealed a serious flaw in SLC's presentation of its scheme: the company's study of environmental impacts had done a poor job of estimating some important economic consequences the development would likely involve. Equally important, the preliminary judgment of the staff of the New York State Department of Environmental Conservation "that all statutory and regulatory criteria can be met through the imposition of special conditions" now seemed hasty and ill-conceived. In a series of brief, well-grounded statements, citizens of the surrounding communities explained what they knew about the matter, especially the ways in which the emerging, fairly prosperous, local economy in which they were involved would likely be wrecked by the coming of an oversized, heavily polluting industrial city. As a spokesperson from a small organization, Community Action Now, observed, "the DEIS ignores the connection between the demise of the cement industry and the development of this new economy, which is based on national beauty, ecological appeal of the area, a revival of home-based businesses, and thriving retail sector, a mixture of light industry, real estate, tourism."

In the months that followed the hearings it became increasingly clear that the plant was anything but "inevitable" or "a done deal." A growing list of community groups and environmental organizations in the locality, region and nation joined the opposition and found ways to make their voices heard.[10] Echoing the concerns of the medical staff of Columbia Memorial Hospital (55–0 opposed in its second vote), the American Lung Association warned about the health effects of the plant's emission on those downwind. Leading the way, FOH continued to attract support and eventually enrolled approximately 4,000 dues-paying members. In its public events – community forums, lectures, picnics, potlucks, benefit concerts, and the like – FOH combined celebrations of community with the fundraising needed to pay for the organization's lawyers and technical consultants. Some notable figures from the arts, including rock legend Patti Smith, actor/playwright Kaiulani Lee, and composer Philip Glass, gave benefit performances to help the cause. An arts center in Hudson, Time and Space Limited, opened its doors for an ongoing series of gatherings in which issues related to the SLC were publicized and debated. Eventually the mouse that roared in Hudson began to attract widespread attention in political circles. Richard Blumenthal,

Attorney General of Connecticut, one of the states downwind from the SLC plant, announced his worries about airborne emissions, as did Angus King, governor of Maine. Many residents of Western Massachusetts chimed in, saying that the new pollution scheduled to waft over the border from New York was cause for legal action. To the surprise of a great many, the editorial page of the *New York Times* declared its strong opposition on three occasions from 2002 to 2004, urging Governor Pataki to take decisive action. "We called nearly a year ago – and a year before that – for Mr. Pataki to find the political courage to put an end to this proposal. He has a rare opportunity to prevent serious environmental and scenic degradation of the Hudson River Valley. He should seize it before it's too late" ("Here We Are Again" 2004).

The reaction of Saint Lawrence/Holcim to growing criticism was at first to intensify its costly public relations and advertising blitz. According to its own yearly financial report for 2004, the firm had spent nearly $58 million in its efforts to win public support and the required permits to build the plant. In December 2003 the company abruptly replaced project manager, Philip Lochbrunner, with another administrator. Obviously stung by widespread criticism of its plans, SLC boldly announced a redesign of the proposed facility, one supposed to reduce its visual affront to the surrounding terrain and viewshed. The factory would be moved to a lower elevation on the site and its smokestack shortened by forty-five feet. But, as the *New York Times* pointed out, this was little improvement since the stack would still be visible, nearly six hundred feet above the Hudson River. Opponents also scoffed, arguing that the new design meant that more pollution would simply be redistributed, descending on nearby communities. As indicated by its flailing tactical maneuvers, SLC was rapidly losing control of the rhetoric and imagery crucial to a decision in its favor.

In contrast, FOH and its allies were, by and large, pursuing a low-cost but highly effective strategy to advance their cause. It was signaled clearly in a campaign Sam Pratt, Peter Jung and the FOH staff unveiled in late 2001. On yard signs, bumper stickers and other pieces of publicity, the organization pleaded: "Tell the truth. Stop the Plant." In fact, many in the organization at first thought this was too awkward and ill-tuned to be a good, fighting slogan. But as more and more people in the area focused on it, the slogan had a corrosive effect upon SLC's attempt to frame the central issues.

But what was "the truth" in actual practice? Much of it, as we've seen, was simply a matter of loading up the information in SLC's impact statement and shooting it back at them. Thus, the phrase "only one new job" became a watchword in letters, editorials, and everyday speech. In more detailed legal presentations, FOH hammered away at SLC's permit application (the DEIS), charging that it did "not appear to be organized in any meaningful way" and did not explain how "the facility is being regulated with respect to each contaminant" (Friends of the Hudson 2001). By simply bearing witness to what the company itself had said or, significantly, left unsaid, FOH and other community groups let "the truth" emerge as a major embarrassment.

Other dimensions of "the truth" arrived as expert knowledge obtained from highly paid engineering consultants. Here FOH hired one of America's largest and most prestigious engineering firms, Camp Dresser McKee (CDM), a company whose business is building large, expensive industrial facilities and public works. Faced with technical details about cement production, technologies of pollution control and other arcane topics, FOH turned to the engineers for information and advice. For example, were SLC's claims about the length of the smokestack's plume accurate? The CDM consultants looked at the data and determined that SLC's estimates were based on outdated assumptions and that "the plumes created by this project are likely to be significantly greater than represented" (quoted in Scenic Hudson 2005). Was the Greenport plant going to use state-of-the-art equipment in pollution abatement, as SLC claimed? The CDM consultants studied the matter and concluded that this was not the case; SLC's designs called for less sophisticated technology that was currently available. CDM recommended "Selective Catalytic Reduction" as "not only significantly better in the control of NOx, but also has greatly reduced potential for plume formation."[11]

Equipped with first rate technical advice of this kind, FOH was able to make ingenious recommendations about alternative designs that SLC might choose. For example, it proposed that the company consider building a much smaller factory on Beecraft Mountain, one with a capacity of one million metric tons per year. A second alternative was to construct a new high-tech, natural gas-fired plant at the existing facility in nearby Catskill (Friends of the Hudson 2003). Such use of engineering expertise enabled FOH to appear reasonable and flexible while showing that SLC had not done sufficient analysis of the full range of possibilities. Rigidly committed to its two million metric tons per year model, the company was never happy with the state-of-the-art improvements that Sam Pratt, FOH lawyer Jeff Baker and their colleagues so helpfully suggested.

Another domain of "truth" powerfully tapped by the opposition was the local knowledge distributed among hundreds of citizens in Columbia County. Knowledge of this kind proved to be perhaps even more important to the struggle's outcome than the gems of expert knowledge offered by credentialed technocrats. Very wisely, the leaders of FOH encouraged literally everyone with something to say about "the plant" to explore issues, do their own research, write letters, talk with friends, speak at hearings, contribute whatever the person thought would be useful. This approach produced a rich and highly varied collection of contributions at various stages in the process. We have already noted this in public statements at the June 2001 DEC hearing, a practice that continued during later opportunities for "public comment." No one could have predicted in advance where possibly relevant inquiries and findings would materialize.

One citizen with an interest in history looked deeply through the archives of property records and cast doubt on SLC's property claims on the City of Hudson waterfront. A local woman with a detailed interest in coastal wetlands and the regulations governing them, suggested that SLC's plans could face strong challenge in that area of law and policy. This piece of advice proved decisive, as we will see. There were other pieces of information about local ecologies, economic conditions, new small industries, historical backgrounds, and even the relationship between nature and art in the Hudson River Valley, that strengthened the case against the plant and the increasingly strong case in favor of the emerging, environmentally sustainable economy.

At a decisive moment, early 2005, some of the best information and insight in this vast storehouse of local knowledge was written down in letters by ordinary citizens, addressed to the coastal zone management program in the New York Department of State. At issue was whether or not a key permit, "Certificate of Coastal Consistency," would be granted, a decision that both sides knew would determine whether or not SLC's plans could move forward. The Department of State received more than 13,000 letters, 87 percent of which were opposed to granting the permit. According to staff members in the Department of State's Albany office, the letters were not just scanned and then filed away; they were carefully read. The decision eventually announced by the agency strongly suggests that the ideas, observations, pieces of evidence, and arguments in the letters offered were taken seriously.

The judgment that denied SLC a key permit needed to begin building the plant was delivered by New York Secretary of State, Randy A. Daniels in April 2005. Daniels' letter to the company states flatly, "the proposed activities are inconsistent with New York's federally approved Coastal Management Program's enforceable policies..."[12] His strongly worded, point-by-point judgment left little room for legal appeal. Recognizing how untenable its position had become, the company announced shortly thereafter that it had withdrawn its application and had no further intention to build on the Greenport site. As the news got out there were shouts of joy and some dancing in the streets of Hudson and widespread celebration in Columbia County, Western Massachusetts and up and down the Hudson River Valley. In the evening of the same day, the Hudson Common Council voted to reject a "Host Agreement" that would have given SLC plans favorable consideration in return for a cash inducement. Thus, what had once seemed a sure win for one of *Fortune Magazine*'s "Global 500," had turned into an extraordinary rout.

Daniels' decision identifies numerous specific features of the plant that are "inconsistent" with New York coastal policies. These include the physical size of the plant and the scale of industrial activity involved; the widely visible plume rising from its smokestack; the high decibel noise of its factory and shipping operations; the "fugitive dust" that would drift into surrounding areas; the disruption of scenic views; and adverse effects upon sites with historic, architectural, and cultural significance. Of particular importance, in the Secretary of State's view, would be the stretch of the Hudson River where SLC hoped to build its dock, park its enormous barges and Hudson Max vessels and large piles of raw materials before they were taken to the plant by the conveyor system. The company's use of the waterfront in this way is, he finds, "inconsistent" with a range of valuable "water-dependent" uses – boating, tourism, commercial, and other uses – that are affirmed in state policies.

As Daniels lays out the particulars of the Department of State position, he offers a grand overview of the situation in the City of Hudson, Columbia County and the Hudson River Valley that give these "inconsistencies" their force. His description is relevant here for the way it echoes key arguments in public hearings and letter-writing campaigns about the economic, social, and cultural revitalization of local communities in the region. In recent years, he notes, the Hudson River Valley has undergone a profound change. "By the mid-20th century industrial activity along the river, especially in urban centers, was in decline. The result was outdated industrial structures, brownfields, as well as derelict land fronting a severely polluted river." Fortunately, he notes, both state government and local communities began "a dramatic shift, moving from industrial uses and brownfields to mix use redevelopment, recreation, cultural activities, and, increasingly, to high-tech businesses." An important dimension of this shift was that "communities began to rediscover their waterfronts" and to emphasize the environmental, scenic, and historic virtues of the Valley as a stimulus for positive economic change. "This shift in land use," he continues, "coincides with a shift in the Valley's economic engine from industrial uses to tourism, office, high-tech, and retail activities. These new uses have generated spin-off businesses and a wide range of stable and growing employment and revenues, including significant public revenues that include property, sales, business and other taxes."

While Daniels' portrait of the situation tends to downplay aspects of renewal that people in Columbia County explicitly associate with an environmentally sustainable economy, his description emphasizes evidence of locally based economic and cultural vitality, finding them strong enough to discredit any suggestion that the Hudson River Valley return to outmoded patterns of nineteenth-century industrialism of the kind SLC openly prescribes. Worthy of particular praise, in his view, is the City of Hudson for "a significant revitalization of its waterfront and community." In what seems to be a paraphrase of hundreds of letters sent from the little city, he concludes, "It relies on a diversified economy in which tourism, commercial, retail, recreation, and second home purchases play a large role. Hudson relies on the area's high quality of life, contributed to by the visual appeal of the area, its historic fabric and texture, its pastoral setting, and attractions such as its waterfront park and Olana as the basis for continued economic growth."

Such glowing sentiments are definitely not what St. Lawrence/Holcim hoped to read in a legally binding decision issued by the Republican appointee in a state agency overseen by the no-nonsense, business-friendly governor George Pataki. Indeed, it seems that if Pataki had wanted to do so, he could have intervened in the decision in ways favorable to the Swiss corporation. The New York Department of State *could* have found the SLC plant "consistent" with state policies, perhaps if certain cosmetic changes had been included in its design. SLC's own steps in 2004 to alter its plans in ways responsive to public objections seemed to signal movement in that direction. Why Governor Pataki did not move in this direction, to "expedite" the decision, remains a mystery. Over the years he had taken some environmentally progressive steps, agreeing to EPA proposals to dredge the upper Hudson River to remove the PCBs left behind by General Electric, for example. In other respects, however, his administration was far from enthusiastic about other measures that place environmental protection over the profit-seeking activities of business. It is possible that as the end of his third and final term drew near, Pataki's often professed view that preserving the Hudson River Valley would be his "legacy" took on more than just rhetorical significance. Faced with a personal and policy choice about New York's future it appears that he did, at least, give Randy Daniels and the State Department staff leeway to decide in favor of arguments favoring environmental protection over big money and heavy industry.

What general lessons can be drawn from the success of the "Stop the Plant" crusade? In retrospect there are several elements of the story that stand out.

Here was a contest between a large, multinational corporation with vast financial resources, extensive experience in the industry, and a wealth of expert knowledge at its disposal – on the one hand – and a scattered bunch of local citizens that, in the beginning, had little knowledge of the industry and its technology. But in the last analysis, the opponents were able to demonstrate that in important respects they actually *knew more* about cement production and its consequences than the managers and technical experts employed by the firm. Within a relatively short period of time, the opponents had crafted a blend of local and expert knowledge far more extensive, well grounded, and persuasive than the studies, facts, and conclusions repeatedly emphasized by SLC. On crucial questions about jobs, economic effects, health, environmental impacts, and quality of life within the region as a whole, the opponents seemed eminently well informed while the Swiss firm seemed helplessly out of touch. As the company spent tens of millions of dollars for slick but increasingly vacuous television ads, its presentations merely underscored how thin and callous its grasp of the real situation was. Hence, an important lesson in the struggle is that people in localities – perhaps seen from the outside as mere rubes and bumpkins who can be easily rolled or bought off with trinkets – often understand enough implicitly to build a foundation of explicit, well-organized knowledge to counter the highly paid but often woefully disconnected expertise of global managers. Yes, it requires much hard work and strong focus, but prospects for a strong mix of local knowledge, aided by good science and engineering, are well within reach.

Another lesson that the story suggests is that what may seem to be undeniable evidence of material and social decline can mask underlying signs of vitality. This is certainly the case in the City of Hudson, Columbia County, and much of the Hudson River Valley. Many of the buildings look ramshackled and the towns rundown; the old dairy farms have closed and, yes, many young people have moved away. But a closer look shows that apparent economic malaise can be an occasion for creative re-appropriation, refurbishing and new enterprise. In fact, people were busily restoring the old buildings and starting new enterprises, reclaiming the land for new kinds of farming, finding opportunities in places where "rundown" can also mean "low cost." From their offices in far-off Geneva it may have seemed to the Holcim moguls that a region clearly down on its luck and on its back would welcome a nice jolt of heavy industry. But for many of those who lived in the region, a turnaround was well underway, one based upon an obvious virtue of the place – that the countryside is beautiful and the towns and cities, while down on their luck, still offer appealing settings for the restoration of economy and community. An old warehouse can become a center for the arts and community. An old factory and its brownfields can be cleaned up to become a research center on solar energy technology. Look again; even the most gloomy appearance can contain lively possibilities.

A feature in the politics of the conflict is also worth noting. It was clear from the outset that many of those in the "Stop the Plant" movement were political progressives involved with causes on the left end of the political spectrum. But, for the most part, key organizations in the campaign remained scrupulously non-partisan, welcoming supporters from the Democratic, Republican, Conservative, Green, and other parties in New York. As Sam Pratt commented months after the final decision came down, "The pitch we made was that ... all we're asking for here is a level playing field. Give us the opportunity to make our case, to be heard objectively and we're confident we can prevail" (Pratt 2005). This proved a wise strategy because, as we have seen, the key decisions would ultimately be made by the Republican governor and his administration in power in Albany. As events unfolded, many pro-business Republicans came to feel that the Holcim/St. Lawrence model of economic development was far from the best model for business in the region to pursue. Regardless of political affiliation, people from the various parties found much upon which they agreed, especially the belief that the Hudson River Valley is a place worth preserving from a new wave of industrial blight. Their explicitly non-partisan, welcoming stance made it possible for organizations opposed to the plant to attract thousands of people with widely different political views and to help them to move, step by step, onto a broad patch of common ground.

While qualities of openness and inclusiveness characterized the "Stop the Plant" movement as a whole, there was another, seemingly contradictory political feature crucial to its success, especially in the inner workings of the organization that spearheaded the drive – FOH. As we have noted, FOH steadily built a large grassroots membership and worked tirelessly to find ways to involve its members in a variety of activities – living-room meetings, dinners, fundraisers, marches, concerts, letter-writing campaigns, and the like. At the same time, however, its leaders – Peter Jung and, especially, Sam Pratt – retained tight (some FOH members thought too tight) control of the organization's day-to-day, indeed minute-to-minute decisions and actions. They crafted strategies with the organization's lawyer, conducted extensive research on worldwide cement plant operations, looked for points of SLC vulnerability in information from their engineering consultants, chose the bullet points to be emphasized as they hammered away at the corporation's central claims. Using the internet email as the basis for communication with the organization's more intense and committed members, they organized "rapid response" methods used to counter SLC's various moves. One fine morning, for example, the company dispatched a bulldozer to gouge a new road on its land. Immediately, messages went out across the internet for anyone with a digital camera to go to the scene to document the damage. Late that afternoon, FOH filed a complaint with the New York Department of Environment and Conservation demanding a halt to the project because it intruded upon protected wet lands. The agency soon ordered the road-building experiment to be stopped.

A final lesson that can be taken from this episode is subtle but nonetheless crucial; one that concerns the language and imagery employed in making social decisions. In retrospect, the very first step taken by those who opposed "The Plant" proved to be the one most decisive – refusing to accept the rhetorical frame that depicted the project as "inevitable" – a "done deal." What they offered instead was the idea that people in the region were facing a serious choice, one that had not yet been made. From that standpoint the goal was to expand the range of voices and perspectives that might be gathered for public activities of information gathering, deliberation, debate, and political mobilization to shape the final outcome. Perhaps without realizing it, the people of Hudson and the surrounding region stumbled upon what is often the real meaning of the phrase, "This is inevitable!" If one listens carefully, those words often mean, "Your role in the negotiations is not needed. Just go away. We'll take care of everything." By refusing that offensive conclusion at the outset, by refusing to accept the passivity it involves, the proponents of an environmentally sustainable future replied: "The future has not been foreclosed. We're still here. And we insist upon having a voice!"

During the years that followed the successful attempt to "Stop the Plant" the central players in the drama moved on to new pursuits. A progressive coalition in City of Hudson politics won an election that threw out the old guard politicians who had supported SLC. An excellent documentary film, "Two Square Miles," exploring the town's troubled social divisions as well as creative attempts at reconciliation, was shown in theaters across America and broadcast on PBS television.[13] Surprisingly, a town recently down on its luck and mired in political torpor, had risen to become a model for reviving local democracy. Several key figures in the film went on the road to share their strategies with communities. Continuing the effort to create a sustainable economy in the region, a chapter of the Business Alliance for Local Living Economy as well as a Sustainable Business Network were organized in the Hudson Valley, offering assistance to green, socially responsible entrepreneurs. Meanwhile, fresh from its debacle in upstate New York, Holcim Corporation fought off a coalition of environmental and community groups to build a much larger – $905 million and four million metric tons per year – cement factory on the Mississippi River in Ste. Genevieve County, Missouri. More than a few residents of Columbia County agonized over the news, worried that their victory had simply shifted the company's mischief elsewhere.

Today there is little time for musing about the unfortunate ramifications of successful community struggles, because the landscape of the County itself remains under continual threat. Several tacky, oversized projects of questionable worth, including an enormous shopping mall the size of twelve football fields, are regularly proposed by aggressive, bottom-feeding "developers." Indeed, the very success of the anti-plant struggle seems to have made the upper Hudson River Valley attractive for hasty, ill-conceived real estate schemes. In response to these pressures, some towns and villages in the area have begun to view zoning and land use regulation much more seriously than in earlier times. But hopes to transform the triumph of "Stop the Plant" into an energetic effort to "Start the Plan" has fallen on its face. The coalition of environmental and community groups so resolute in its battle with a global colossus, now finds itself fragmented and beset by debilitating small town squabbles. A thoughtful observer might well ask: will the successful experience of resistance and renewal of recent times be refocused within a continuing movement for positive, forward-looking change? Or will it unravel into a familiar, dreary pattern in American life – division, isolation, and torpor?

Questions for further consideration

1   In the case chronicled by Winner, can the local resistance to industrial development be described in any way other than a progressive version of "NIMBY," not-in-my-back-yard?

2   Winner's documentation of the struggle against industrial redevelopment by a transnational corporation clearly rested on the shoulders of a very few energized and talented people. Does this scenario contradict the need for broadly-based democratic coalition-building described by Oden in Chapter 2?

3   Winner argues that the knowledge of locals who chose to fight "the plant" was more accurate and more convincing – at least to other locals and politicians – than was the knowledge of the scientists and engineers employed by Holcim Inc. How might we characterize the difference between these two kinds of knowledge?

4   In the author's analysis of the case he finds that the distant and abstract view of the Hudson Valley calculated by Holcim Inc. failed to see the cultural richness actually lived by locals. In lieu of cultural richness, Holcim Inc. saw only economic deterioration and an investment opportunity. What methods, if any, are available to assess both kinds of value?

5   Winner holds that one reason that the "Stop the Plant" coalition succeeded was that they were able to counter the "rhetorical frame" used by developers – that the plant was "inevitable." Does the redescription of the future help to make it so?

Notes

1   A good summary of the issues can be found in Dorgan, B. L. (2006) *Take this Job and Ship It: How Corporate Greed and Brain-Dead Politics Are Selling Out America*, New York: Thomas Dunne Books. Dorgan is US Senator from the State of North Dakota.

2   As of January 2005 there were 1,500 CSAs in the United States: www.localharvest.org/csa.jsp One successful example in Columbia County is Roxbury Farm run by Jean Paul Courtens and

Jody Bolluyt whose website, www.roxburyfam.com, includes archives of its weekly newsletter as well as farm manuals that describe how the work is done.

3 More information on Solaqua is available online at www.solaqua.org/

4 A good introduction to the Hudson River School and its significance is Kornhauser, E. M. *et al.* (2003) *Hudson River School: Masterworks from the Wadsworth Atheneum Museum of Art*, New Haven: Yale University Press.

5 A brief history of the Storm King battle is given in National Resources Defense Council (2000) "E-law: What Started It All?" Online, available at www.nrdc.org/legislation/helaw.asp

6 The author of this article, Langdon Winner, was a member of FOH during this period.

7 A comprehensive summary of the critics' concerns are presented in Citizens for a Healthy Environment, a Project of the Native Forest Council (2002) *The Proposed St. Lawrence Cement Plant in Greenport and Hudson: Understanding the Impact*, Philmont, New York.

8 All comments from the meeting quoted here are taken from the record of the State of New York Department of Environmental Conservation (2001) *In the Matter of the Application of St. Lawrence Cement Co., LLC, DEC Application # 4-1040-0001/00001: Issues Conference before Administrative Law Judge Helene G. Goldberger*, June 21, Greenport: New York. Online, available at: www.friendsofhudson.com/research/hearing.html.

9 It is possible that one reason why SLC believed the City of Hudson would be ripe for a cement plant was that the low-income neighborhoods of Hudson, both white and black, would welcome the project as an economic boon and not worry about its consequences for their health and the environment.

10 The list includes Scenic Hudson, Preservation League of New York, Scenic America, The Natural Resources Defense Council, Concerned Women of Claverack, Friends of Clean Air (Mass.), Berkshire Regional Planning Commission, Berkshire Natural Resources Council, Citizens for a Healthy Environment (CHE), H.A.D.A., S.T.O.P.P., Columbia Action Now (CAN), Historic Hudson, The National Trust for Historic Preservation, The Olana Partnership (TOP), Citizens for the Hudson Valley, Massachusetts Department of Environmental Protection (DEP), The Olana Partnership, Hudson Valley Preservation Coalition, and River Keeper, and others.

11 Quoted in Scenic Hudson 2005. During its campaign against SLC FOH raised nearly $2 million, most of which paid for engineering and legal advice.

12 All quotes from Secretary Daniels here are taken from Daniels, R. A. (2005) "Letter from Randy A. Daniels, Secretary of the State of New York, to Mr. David Loomes, Director of the Greenport Project, Saint Lawrence Cement Company, LLC," April 19. Online, available at www.nyswaterfronts.com/news_pressreleasedisplay.asp?ID=38.

13 Produced and directed by Barbara Ettinger, "Two Square Miles" is now available on DVD. www.twosquaremiles.com/

Bibliography

Citizens for a Healthy Environment, a Project of the Native Forest Council (2002) *The Proposed St. Lawrence Cement Plant in Greenport and Hudson: Understanding the Impact*, Philmont, New York.

Daniels, R. A. (2005) "Letter from Randy A. Daniels, Secretary of the State of New York, to Mr. David Loomes, Director of the Greenport Project, Saint Lawrence Cement Company, LLC," April 19. Online, available at: www.nyswaterfronts.com/news_pressreleasedisplay.asp?ID=38.

Friends of Hudson (2001) *Comments on the Draft Environmental Impact Statement and NYSDEC Permits Applications for the St. Lawrence Cement-Greenport Project*, July 2.

Friends of Hudson (2003) *Comments on the Draft Joint Permit Application to the Army Corps of Engineers for the St. Lawrence Cement-Greenport: comments prepared by Jeffrey S.*

Baker, Esq. and James Muscator, Esq., Young, Sommer, Ward, Ritzenberg, Baker & Moore, LLC, April 21.

Gardner, R. (2002) "Cry Them a River," *New York Magazine*, June 10. Online, available at: http://nymag.com/nymetro/realestate/urbandev/features/6098/

"Here We Are Again" (2004) *New York Times*, September 5.

Pratt, S. (2005) "No Such Thing as a Done Deal: How Ordinary Citizens Beat A Global Giant," Lecture at Rensselaer Polytechnic Institute, September 27.

Rorty, R. (1989) *Contingency, Irony, and Solidarity*, New York: Cambridge University Press, 86.

Saint Lawrence Cement Company (2001) *Saint Lawrence Cement Greenport Project, Draft Environmental Impact Statement: Town of Greenport, Columbia County, New York*, April 27.

Scenic Hudson (2005) *Groups Call on State to End SLC Proposal: press release,* March 22. Online, available at: www.scenichudson.org/press/announcements/details.cfm?ID=152&topic=all&type=REL.

State of New York Department of Environmental Conservation (2001) *In the Matter of the Application of St. Lawrence Cement Co., LLC, DEC Application # 4-1040-0001/00001: Issues Conference before Administrative Law Judge Helene G. Goldberger*, June 21, Greenport: New York. Online, available at: www.friendsofhudson.com/research/hearing.html.

Editor's Introduction to Chapter 6

In documenting the struggle against the siting of a large cement facility in Columbia County, New York, Langdon Winner notes in the previous chapter that,

> Holcim Corporation fought off a coalition of environmental and community groups to build a much larger – $905 million and four million metric tons per year – cement factory on the Mississippi River in Ste. Genevieve County, Missouri. More than a few residents of Columbia County agonized over the news, worried that their victory had simply shifted the company's mischief as well as the burdens of environmental injustice to another community in another part of the country.

Will demand for ever more materials and energy mean that the sustainability of one area comes only at the expense of another? If Americans continue to make and use 100 million tons of cement per year[1] will one community's struggle against a cement plant mean that the plant will simply be moved to another community?

Such perplexing questions require engineers to consider how we might design a sustainable built environment for a single locale, but for ten billion people? Within the next fifty years, world populations are projected to reach this level, and this growing world population is achieving ever greater levels of affluence. If our world population increases to ten billion over the next fifty years, and if average per capita affluence increases by 5 percent per year over this period, the world gross economic product will increase by roughly a factor of 10–20. This means that if our engineered environment operates in the same way, with the same efficiencies, consumption of resources and environmental impacts would increase ten-fold.

Can our technologies, our engineered systems, adapt to this challenge? Can we reduce resource consumption per unit of economic output by a factor of ten or more? The common response to such challenges, in engineering design, is to modify existing designs using simple heuristics. Use less material. Use less energy. Design longer-lasting products. But simple heuristics are not always effective design approaches. Two case studies examined in this chapter, mobility systems and information storage, illustrate the difficulties in using simple heuristics. Achieving sustainable systems will require a robust range of design solutions.

This chapter by Allen *et al.* quantifies our demand for materials, and the magnitude of change that will likely be required in our engineered systems, if global change is to be accomplished. They argue that the challenges, both technical and societal, will be great and far from simple, involving both rapid and long-term changes. Yet in responding to such need for massive change, the authors argue that "simple rules will not be universally applicable." In this respect, Allen and his colleagues adopt a classically pragmatist attitude toward the desire to achieve engineering certainty – there are no universal solutions. They argue that successful solutions depend upon the social as well as ecological context in which they are applied. Or as Dewey argued: "any sentence isolated from place and function in inquiry is logically indeterminate."[2]

Notes

1   US Geological Survey, Commodity Report for Cement, available at http://minerals.usgs.gov/minerals/pubs/commodity/cement/cemenmcs07.pdf, accessed December 15, 2007.
2   John Dewey, *Logic: The Theory of Inquiry* (Carbondale, IL: Southern Illinois University Press, 1991 [1938], 138).

Chapter 6

Engineering Sustainable Technologies

David Allen, Cynthia Folsom Murphy, Braden R. Allenby, and Cliff I. Davidson

Background

Can improvements in engineered technologies protect the environment, and preserve natural resources, even as populations grow and societies demand more materials and energy? The challenges are enormous. To grasp the magnitude of the challenges, it is useful to invoke a conceptual equation that is generally attributed to Ehrlich and Holdren.[1] The equation relates impact (I), which can represent energy consumption, materials use, environmental emissions, or other types of impacts, to population (P), affluence (A), and technology (T).

$$I = P * A * T$$

This conceptual relationship, often referred to as the IPAT equation, suggests that impacts are the product of the population (number of people), the affluence of the population (generally expressed as gross domestic product of a nation or region, divided by the number of people in the nation or region), and the impacts associated with the technologies used in the delivery of the affluence (impact per unit of gross domestic product). If the IPAT equation was used to describe energy use in the United States, then I would represent energy use per year, P would represent the population of the United States, A would represent the annual GDP per capita, and T would represent the energy use per dollar of GDP.

The form of the IPAT equation suggests a quantitative relationship, but the relationship is not nearly so simple. Returning to the example of energy use in the United States, if affluence doubled, it is not immediately clear that energy use would precisely double. A population twice as affluent might choose to spend their additional income on goods and services that are either more or less energy intensive than the goods and services they used before their incomes doubled. A more affluent population might choose to spend a greater fraction of its income on air travel, for example, thus changing the average value for T, the energy consumed per dollar of GDP. So, the IPAT equation is not a mathematical identity; rather, it describes a conceptual relationship between impacts, population, affluence and technology.

While the IPAT equation should not be viewed as a mathematical identity, it can be used to assess the magnitude of the challenges that our societies face in material use, energy use, and environmental impacts. What will be the impacts of expanding population and affluence over the next several decades, if our technologies remain static? Estimates from the United Nations[2] suggest that world population will increase at the rate of 1–2 percent per year until peaking at somewhere near ten billion, over the next century. Gross domestic product is growing in some regions of the world by approximately 8–10 percent per year.[3] World economic output is growing somewhere in the range of 5 percent per year. If these trends continue for several decades then world economic output (P*A) will increase by 60 percent in ten years, by 300 percent in twenty-five years, and by more than a factor of ten in fifty years.

Invoking the IPAT equation, the implications of world economic growth are that, if technology remains static, energy use, material use, and environmental impacts will grow ten-fold over the next fifty years. Is it reasonable to expect that impacts, like energy use, will increase in proportion with global economic activity? Figure 6.1 shows that in many of the world's economies, petroleum use per capita is proportional to economic activity per capita, so it is not unreasonable to expect that a ten-fold increase in economic activity will result in increases in impacts approaching a factor of ten, if technologies remain static.

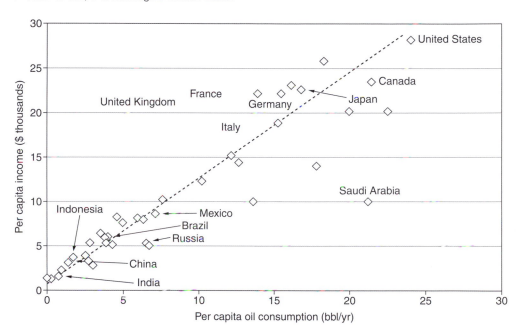

Figure 6.1
Oil consumption as a function of per capita income (adapted from JPT 2001).

Returning to the question that opened this chapter, can improvements in engineered technologies protect the environment, and preserve natural resources, even as populations grow and societies demand more materials and energy? Certainly, improving technology is not the only approach to reducing the footprint of human populations, but it is also certainly an important part of the solution. The IPAT equation suggests that a factor of ten decrease in impact per economic output is necessary.

Design heuristics

Can our technologies, our engineered systems, reduce resource consumption per unit of economic output by a factor of ten or more? The common response to such challenges, in engineering design, is to identify heuristics. Use less material. Use less energy. Design longer-lasting products. But is the use of such simple heuristics an effective design approach?

In order to address this question, this chapter will characterize how technologies respond to change and the engineering goal of ever greater efficiencies. Then, an example of how the application of a simple design heuristic – design long-lasting products – might interact with that evolution will be described. Finally, a more structured approach to applying simple design rules will be proposed.

The patterns of technological evolution

Can factor of ten improvements in the footprints of our technologies be achieved? How rapidly can such improvements be achieved? The data are mixed. Consider engine efficiencies and the efficiencies of lighting, shown in Figure 6.2.[4] The data shown in Figure 6.2 show the energy efficiency of lighting technologies from the time of candles and the earliest incandescent bulbs, to the use of fluorescent lighting and light-emitting diodes. As an example, between 1900 and 1950,

Figure 6.2
A measure of energy efficiency. Fraction (f) of the limit of efficiency that the devices can reach is plotted over time for lighting systems and for systems for producing mechanical energy; efficiency increases at about 5% per year for lighting and 1–2% per year for mechanical engines (adapted from Ausubel 2000).

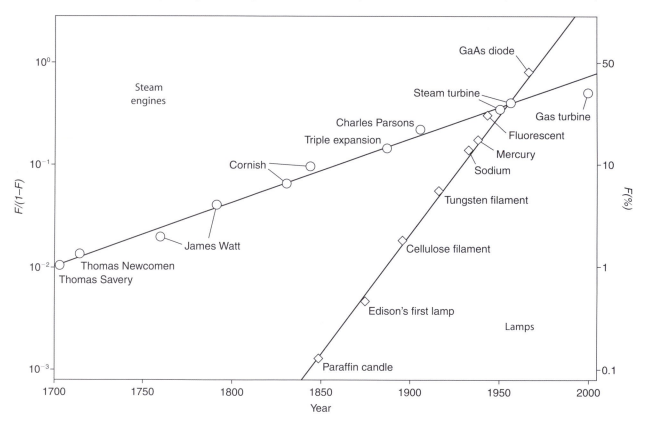

the energy efficiency of lighting increased by a factor of ten, an improvement of about 5 percent per year. In contrast, the energy efficiency of converting heat into mechanical or electrical energy (steam engines) has increased by a factor of two or three over twenty years, an average of 1–2 percent per year.

Figure 6.2 suggests that, for some but not all technologies, factor of ten improvements are possible over fifty-year time scales. This may, however, be an overly simplistic view of the potential contributions of technology development. Figure 6.2 implicitly paints technological evolution as a linear progression, but a more detailed examination reveals changes that are more disruptive. A clearer way of viewing the disruptive nature of technological change is through the use of a logistic curve. Figure 6.3 shows one such logistic curve, contrasted with a time series curve, for the patterns of energy use in the United States. In the upper portion of Figure 6.3 are data showing the amount of various fuel sources used in the United States, while the lower portion shows the ratio of the fraction of total energy provided by a specific type of fuel. The representation of the data in the lower part of the Figure, as a logistic curve, much more clearly illustrates a consistent pattern in the data. Wood was the primary energy source in the United States until the middle of the nineteenth century, but was then replaced, in roughly 50–100 year cycles, by coal, then oil and natural gas. Each new dominant technology sequentially disrupted the previous dominant technology.

This pattern of emergence of dominant technologies repeats itself in many technological systems. Figure 6.4 shows the same type of pattern, on the same time scales, for transportation infrastructures. Canals were replaced by rail lines, which were replaced by highways systems, which were replaced by air travel. Each technology dominated for approximately fifty-year periods. An interesting contrast is provided by the evolution of information storage devices. Figure 6.5 shows the evolution of dynamic random access memory. The pattern is once again an example of one dominant technology replacing another, but in this case, over much shorter time periods. The well-known Moore's law is an observation that every two years, the speed of computation and the degree of miniaturization doubles. Clearly this technological system is evolving far more rapidly than mobility systems.

Collectively, these data indicate that changes in technological systems can be disruptive, not just linear and evolutionary. Further, different technological systems have different rates of change, ranging from years to multiple decades. Finally, although Figures 6.3 to 6.5 do not represent this, technologies are interdependent. A change in transportation systems is not independent of changes in the types of energy.

In this context, it is instructive to ask whether a simple heuristic – design long-lasting products – promotes the development of sustainable systems. If, for example, the muscle cars of the 1960s had been designed for forty-year lifetimes, we would not be seeing the benefits of new automotive designs that reduce tailpipe emissions by 95 percent or more. On the other hand, short lifetimes of electronic products are leading to accumulations of electronic wastes.

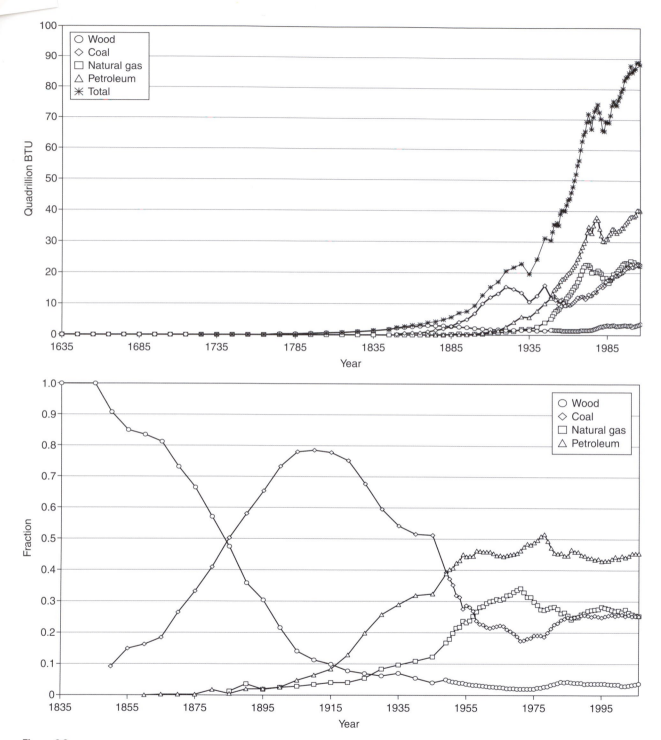

Figure 6.3
Evolution of energy use in the United States: (upper) Time series of energy source utilization; quadrillion BTU of energy use from 1650 to 2000; (lower) Time series of the fraction, f, of total energy use provided by major sources (adapted from EIA, 2007 and Ausubel *et al.* 1988).

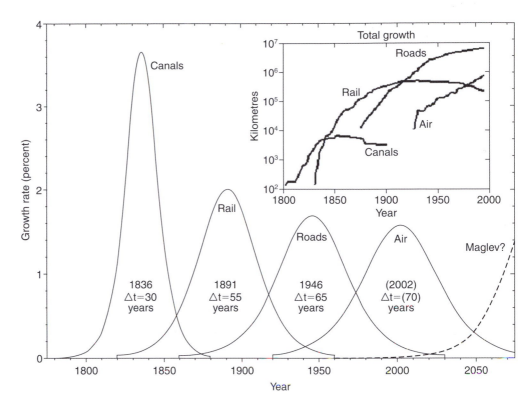

Figure 6.4
Evolution of the growth rate of transportation types (adapted from Ausubel 2002).

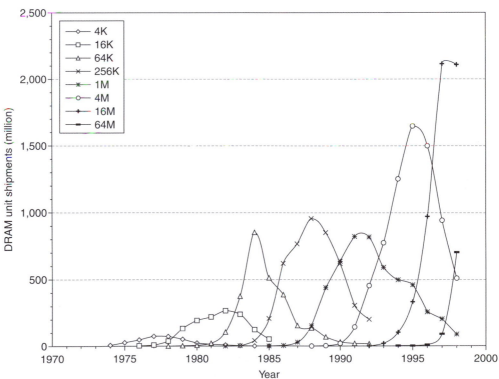

Figure 6.5
Evolution of Dynamic Random Access Memory (DRAM) devices (adapted from Victor and Ausubel 2002).

Design for long life or rapid evolution: implications for engineering design

Mobility and information technologies provide contrasting patterns in the design and evolution of technological systems. Both are ubiquitous in developed economies. Both are pervasive in their influence on the daily pattern of lives. Yet information technologies, in the past several decades, have experienced a rate of evolution that is unprecedented in mobility systems. Technologies are updated and replaced every few years instead of over multiple decades. Is more rapid technological evolution preferable to greater stability?

It could be argued that nature provides a model of continual change and evolution, and therefore favors design for rapid evolution. But, nature also performs its changes with living organisms that live for periods ranging from days to decades. DRAMs can be viewed as simply the fruit fly or the marine algae of technological evolution,[5] while mobility is the elephant. Both life spans have their place in the webs of natural systems and industrial ecologies.

Of course, simple categorizations of technologies as monolithically rapidly or slowly evolving are overly simplistic. While dependence on automobiles for personal mobility in North America has been a constant for decades, the technologies to deal with the smog-forming emissions have evolved much more quickly. Similarly, while personal information devices have changed significantly from year to year, the infrastructure over which information is transmitted – electrical wires, optical wires, and wireless networks – have changed much more slowly.

If both long-lived and quickly evolving technologies have a place in industrial ecologies, and if simple rules do not distinguish each niche, how should engineers think about their designs?

Simple heuristics may fail, so the engineer must learn to examine the multi-tiered levels of their designs as a matter of routine. These levels of impact, associated with mobility decisions, are shown conceptually in Figure 6.6.[6] Design considerations that can evolve rapidly (represented by the innermost layer of Figure 6.6) are the choices faced by a designer of a personal use device, such as a part of an automobile or a personal communication device. In selecting the materials for a bumper/front end, for example, the engineer could select a material that lowers the ecological footprint of the automobile (for example by reducing weight and providing greater fuel economy). This feature of the design can evolve rapidly, and is only moderately influenced by other parts of the industrial ecosystem. The next level of design considerations, represented by the second layer from the center in Figure 6.6, involves the lifecycle of the personal device. An example of how supply chains can influence the time scale of design evolution is provided by the selection of a material used for electrical interconnections (solder) in a personal communications device. In considering the replacement of the element lead (Pb) in solders, AT&T concluded that use of a replacement solder containing iridium would rapidly consume all available world supplies of iridium.[7] Although the replacement material worked, it could not be provided at the scale needed through the supply chain. So, in this case, the evolution away from the use of Pb in solders was slowed by limitations in the choices of materials available through the supply chain.

A third level associated with the design of mobility systems involves much more long-lived infrastructures. For example, the replacement of the existing infrastructure that delivers high-energy density liquid fuels, like gasoline, for powering personal vehicles, with systems that could

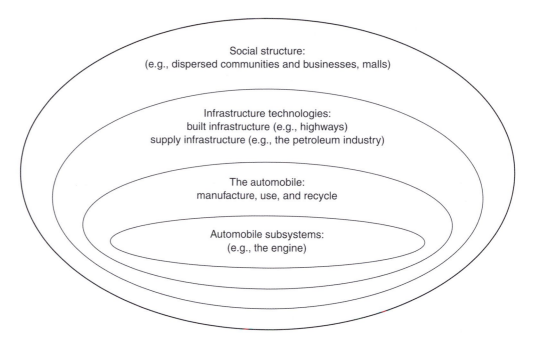

Figure 6.6
The technological–social system of the automobile. The system exists in multiple layers and design decisions made in any of the layers shown influence decisions in all other layers (adapted from Graedel and Allenby, "Industrial Ecology of the Automobile," 1998).

provide a fuel like hydrogen, will take a decade or more to change. This limits the design choices that are available for the power train components of the vehicle.

Finally, there are clearly societal and cultural implications of mobility that influence design decisions. For example, an interesting feature of mobility is that throughout the world, the fraction of time spent and the fraction of income spent on mobility are relatively invariant.[8] The fraction of time dedicated to mobility is not only spatially invariant, it has remained relatively constant for centuries. This may never change, so designers of personal mobility devices may never be able to change their designs to forms that require much greater amounts of time to use.

So, as engineers and other designers consider how to adapt their designs to promote sustainability, seeking factor of ten or more improvements, simple design rules will not be universally applicable. Designers will be faced with a web of different time scales, with neither long-lived designs nor quickly evolving technologies completely becoming universally preferable. Both long-lived and rapidly evolving designs, like the fruit fly and the elephant, will have their place in sustainable industrial ecosystems.

Questions for further consideration

1   In their assessment of population expansion, increasing global affluence and environmental degradation, Allen *et al.* hold that it is necessary to improve industrial efficiency by a factor of ten or twenty in order to achieve what some refer to as "hyper-efficiency." Philosophers warn us, however, that efficiency in itself has "no independent moral ground." They ask, for example, is an efficient Nazi, or an efficient cancer, a good thing? Should we, then, pursue

hyper-efficiency before we pursue radical reduction in human demand or more clearly articulate the ends to which increased efficiency is aimed?

2   On the basis of history, the authors argue that "factor of ten improvements are possible over fifty-year time scales." They do not, however, enter the discussion concerning how such innovations occur. In other words, who decides if we will make technology "X" or technology "Y" more efficient? Should such decisions be left to the marketplace or citizen groups?

3   In the debate regarding "long-lasting" vs "rapidly evolving" technologies, how should we make choices? How does this dilemma relate to the case of the cement plant studied by Winner in the last chapter?

4   If, as Allen *et al.* argue, "simple design rules will not be universally applicable," how will corporate and public entities create public policies and technological codes designed to implement sustainable development?

5   In their analysis of "personal mobility devices," Allen *et al.* hold that some patterns of human behavior "may never change." What are the implications of this claim for the design disciplines like engineering, architecture, or industrial design?

Notes

1   See, Ehrlich and Holdren 1971; Ehrlich and Holdren 1972; Chertow 2001.
2   United Nations 2005.
3   IMF 2003.
4   Ausubel 2000.
5   Victor and Ausubel 2002.
6   Graedel and Allenby 1998.
7   Allenby 1992.
8   WBCSD 2001.

Bibliography

Allenby, B. R. (1992) "Design for environment: Implementing industrial ecology," Ph.D. dissertation, Rutgers University, New Brunswick, NJ.

Ausubel, J. H. (2000) "Where is Energy Going?" *The Industrial Physicist*, 6(1): 16–19.

—— (2002) "Maglevs and the Vision of St. Hubert or The Great Restoration of Nature: Why and How," Chapter 33 in *Challenges of a Changing Earth*, W. Steffen, J. Jaeger, and D. Carson (eds.), Heidelberg: Springer.

——, A. Grubler and N. Nakicenovic (1988) "Carbon Dioxide Emissions in a Methane Economy," *Climatic Change*, 12: 245–263.

Chertow, M. R. (2001) "The IPAT Equation and Its Variants: Changing Views of Technology and Environmental Impact," *Journal of Industrial Ecology*, 4(4): 13–29.

Ehrlich, P. and J. Holdren (1971) "Impact of population growth," *Science* 171: 1212–1217.

—— (1972) "Impact of population growth," in R. G. Riker (ed.) *Population, Resources, and the Environment*, Washington, DC: US Government Printing Office, 365–377.

Energy Information Administration (EIA) (2007) "Energy in the United States." Online, available at: www.eia.doe.gov/emeu/aer/eh/frame.html.

Graedel, T. E. and B. R. Allenby (1998) *Industrial ecology and the automobile*, Upper Saddle River, NJ: Prentice Hall.

International Monetary Fund (2003) "World Economic Outlook." Online, available at: www.imf. org/External/Pubs/FT/weo/2003/01/ Journal of Petroleum Technology (May 2001), 53

United Nations (2005) "World Population Prospects: The 2004 Revision." Online, available at: www.un.org/esa/population/publictions/WPP2004/wpp. 2004.htm.

Victor, N. M. and Ausubel, J. H. (2002) "DRAMs as Model Organisms for Study of Technological Evolution," *Technological Forecasting and Social Change*, 69(3): 243–262.

World Business Council for Sustainable Development (WBCSD) (2001) *Mobility 2001: World mobility at the end of the twentieth century and its sustainability*. Online, available at: www.wbcsd.org, www.wbcsd.org/web/projects/mobility/english_full_report.pdf.

Editor's Introduction to Chapter 7

Sociologist Simon Guy argues in this chapter that there is a "pragmatic" quality to Japanese urbanism. His reasoning raises an interesting question: how can a tradition of rational problem-solving so associated with American culture as is pragmatism be associated with such a distinct and ancient technological culture as Japan? Guy's argument is not that the Japanese have consciously appropriated pragmatism as a theory, which has in turn influenced local practices, or that pragmatism is a system of reasoning common to all humans across cultural lines. Rather, Guy argues that informal improvization and experimentation have simply shown up as a part of modern Japanese everyday urbanism.

As Westerners who imagine that we can "read" the meaning of our own architecture visually – by deeply contemplating its form, order, proportion and materials – it is hardly surprising that we would presume to apprehend meaning in the architectures of other cultures in the same way. As did Frank Lloyd Wright a century ago, we continue to gaze upon ancient Japanese gardens and pagodas in search of oriental harmony and nature. Guy, however, argues – at least indirectly – that we are looking in the wrong place, not only in Japan, but also at home. Sustainability, or harmony with nature, is less likely to be visually manifested in *what* we build than it is in our material habits – how we build.

Chapter 7

Beyond Japonisme

The Adaptive Pragmatism of Japanese Urbanism

Simon Guy

> A piece of architecture, in its nature, ought to be fickle, and a momentary phenomenon. I find it unbearable how a building is able to stay on earth for hundreds of years, displaying its unchanging appearance. The form of a piece of architecture should be non-completing, non-central, and synchronized with nature and urban spaces.
>
> (Japanese architect Toyo Ito (quoted in Berwick 1997))

The search for the essence of "natural" building has led many commentators to go both back in time and across international and cultural borders. Typical has been a pilgrimage to Japan where, it is often claimed, a different relationship to nature than that which underpins Western industrialization (and industrialized architecture) exists. As the celebrated Japanese architect Tadao Ando has put it, "When you look at Japanese traditional architecture, you have to look at Japanese culture and its relationship with nature. You can actually live in a harmonious, close contact with nature – this is very unique to Japan" (Ando 2007). But there is another Japan, that of the teeming metropolis of Tokyo, a rather less environmentally celebrated icon of modernization where perhaps more than any other city in the world, all that is solid melts into rather polluted air. In this chapter, I want to offer some critical reflections on this search for essences of sustainable architecture based upon my own journey to Japan in spring 2005 and on critical readings about Japanese urbanism. In doing so I want to argue that we may indeed have much to learn from Japanese architecture and urbanism, but that we may hitherto have been looking in the wrong places. For rather than finding a timeless relationship to a stable nature expressed in and through buildings and cities, it is rather in the processes and practices of adaptive design and (re)development that we might locate some lessons for sustainability. By contrasting the search for an exotic essence, the "other" of Western rational planning, with an exploration of more situated, pragmatic strategies of Japanese urban design, we might usefully identify some transferable tactics in the search for sustainable urban futures.

Searching for signs of nature in Japan

> At first the Western observer in Japan is struck by contradictory impressions: aesthetically arranged food, a love of perfection in packaging and the tea ceremony on the one hand, set against the chaos of the cities, the teeming millions in the metropolises and the legendary discipline of the population.
>
> (Schittich 2002: 9)

Sitting in a coffee bar on a hot day in Kyoto contemplating the lack of cafés in Japan and enjoying rare direct access to the river and a cool breeze, my reverie was disturbed by the waitress who was keen to close the generous glass doors and cut off my connection to nature. The ladies, she explained, were disturbed by the insects. When I suggested that this would make us all very hot, she reassured me that she was also turning on the air conditioning. Such an experience seemed a little incongruous in a city world-famous for its traditional architecture, Zen gardens, and monasteries, all celebrated for their empathy with nature. Like many before me, I had come to Japan drawn by a timeless image of Japanese architecture as representing a very different relationship to nature than that found in the West. Eschewing the defensive, industrialized, energy-intensive models of Western modernism, Japanese architecture was supposed to represent a more permeable, craft-based, naturally ventilated approach, which embraced nature rather than resisted it. As Ando further suggests, "Far from the characteristic Western vision of nature as something to subdue and curb, the Japanese realized they were part of it, and from their love and understanding of nature they made it their ideal to act in harmony with it" (Ando 1991: 10). For Ando, "the essence of Japanese architecture is inseparable from nature" and according to Christian Schittich, this essence is still present: "Without an appreciation of traditional Japanese values, the Japanese relationship to simplicity and understanding of form, and how these differ from the west, there can be little understanding of today's architecture in Japan" (Schittich 2002: 9). Livio Sacchi has similarly written that "the ancient respect for nature is also at the centre of contemporary architectural sensibility" (Sacchi 2005: 121) while Fumihiko Maki suggests that "Japanese architecture has always been characterized by the confluence and simultaneous expression of beauty and technology" (Maki 2001: xiii).

There is a long tradition of searching for nature in Japanese architecture and design. In his review of Western interest in the Japanese city, Barrie Shelton identifies architectural luminaries such as Frank Lloyd Wright, Bruno Taut, and Walter Gropius as early explorers and celebrants of the apparent simplicity, beauty, and pragmatism of Japanese design and construction (Shelton 1999: 5). In particular, Wright was impressed by the insulated roofs, the underfloor ventilation, and the continuous space between garden and home, arguing that "the question of modern architecture seemed more involved with Japanese architecture in native principle than with any other architecture" (quoted in Shelton 1999: 7). Dana Buntrock's celebration of Japanese architecture as a collaborative practice continues this tradition of distinguishing Japanese architectural practice as crafts based even within a high-tech construction context (Buntrock 2001). However, Shelton also notes that responses to the Japanese city were almost polar opposite in tone, with Tokyo routinely described as a city synonymous with chaos and confusion. Shelton quotes an Australian playwright Hal Porter's description of Tokyo as "makeshift and confused, a freak weed

Figure 7.1
Tokyo. © Simon Guy.

sprung from a crack in history, and drenched by a fertilizer that makes it monstrous but not mighty, immense but immoral, over-grown and uncivilized" (quoted in Shelton 1999: 8). More recent travelogues of Japan have also echoed with a very different image of Japan's relationship to nature. For example, Alex Kerr has argued that Japan has become arguably the world's ugliest country:

> The native forest cover has been clear-cut and replaced by industrial cedar, rivers are dammed and the seashore lined with cement, hills have been leveled to provide gravel fill for bays and harbors, mountains are honeycombed with destructive and useless roads, and rural villages have been submerged in a sea of industrial waste.
>
> (Kerr 2001: 14)

Certainly, traveling around Tokyo and Japan more widely there is plenty of evidence of environmental destruction. The widespread planting of industrial cedar trees Kerr notes on p. 52 has been instrumental in what the *Japan Times* has described as a "national ailment," that of hay fever and other respiratory ailments that lead to the sometimes disturbing (for visitors) sight of so many Japanese people wearing protective face masks. What's more, the *Japan Times* blames "concrete addicted urban planners" for creating cityscapes that accelerate the mobility of pollen (McCurry 2005: 18). Anyone seeking out the refined Japanese design which celebrates links to an idealized nature has to search keenly, wandering across four-lane highways, passing industrial building structures draped in infrastructure and electronic signage. As the travel writer Jan Morris has put it, the Buddhist temples and traditional architecture of the picture books are

Figure 7.2
**A tea house tree
accommodated.
© Simon Guy.**

"scattered across the city like gems in mud" (quoted in Shelton 1999: 9). Instead, the Western traveler finds nature celebrated in the cracks of the city, in isolated plant boxes on the pavement, in a café where a tree is accommodated with a roughly cut hole in the roof, in artificial flowers in a glass box at the entrance to the subway station, on a color-saturated loop video of changing landscapes on a huge plasma screen on a restaurant wall, in countless reproductions of Mount Fuji on hotel bedroom walls and so on. This is second nature, disciplined but disorganized and part of a pervasive landscape of consumption that is an organizing principle of the Japanese city. As the long-term resident American writer Donald Ritchie has put it:

> Nature has been presented. Tidied up, stylized, it has been made, as the old garden manuals have it – to express nature better than nature itself does. It is assumed that the integrity of any original does not exist. As in any dramatic presentation, the only integrity is that of the performance.
>
> (Ritchie 1999: 108)

This play of nature through abstract "signs" echoes the celebration of Japan by another Western visitor, Roland Barthes, who identifies "in many aspects of Japanese life, a certain regime of meaning," an "ethic of the empty sign," a "utopia of a world both strictly semantic and strictly atheistic" (Barthes 1982: 83). Barthes presents Japan to us in a series of "flashes," a discontinuous order of fragments – chopsticks, packaging, stationery, landscapes such as the station and city center, and activities such as bowling and eating. For example, the Japanese poetic form of Haiku highlights and celebrates the semantic fluidity of Japanese culture:

> The number and dispersion of Haikus on the one hand, the brevity and closure of each of them on the other, seem to show an infinite division and classification of the world and to set forth a space of pure fragments, a swarm of events which owing to a sort of disintegration of signification, neither can nor should coagulate, construct, direct, terminate.
>
> (Barthes 1982: 78)

For Barthes, Haikus, like nature, act as an empty sign which "means nothing" and therefore is "open to meaning in a particularly available, serviceable way – the way of a polite host who lets you make yourself at home with all your preferences, your values, your symbols intact" (Barthes 1982: 69). But as Susan Sontag has pointed out, "Barthes was hardly the first Western observer for whom Japan has meant an aesthete's utopia, the place where one finds aesthete views everywhere and exercises one's own at liberty" (Sontag 1982: xxv). As Edward Said has famously argued, writing about the East from the standpoint of the West is more often than not less the discovery of any "natural essence" than a product of particular "communities of interpretation" which in effect position the Orient as the West's "silent other" (Said 1985: 2). Said was specifically talking of the Middle East in his work on Orientalism, but Zhang Longxi believes the critique can be extended to the far east of China and Japan. Longxi points to the use made of the Far East by Western writers to signify a utopian "other," a "reservoir for its dreams, fantasies, and utopias" (Longxi 1988: 110). Susan Hyman has highlighted the importance of "Japanisme" for European culture, suggesting that it "profoundly altered the course of French nineteenth century painting, and by extension the art of the Western world" (Hyman 1992: 22) while Toshio Yokoyama, in a study of the stereotypes of Japan in the Victorian mind, points to the persistence of the idea of Japan as a "strange and singular country" (Yokoyama 1987: 2). Oscar Wilde famously suggested that, "In fact, the whole of Japan is a pure invention. There is no country, there are no such people" (Wilde 1990: 927). Kevin Robins and David Morley further point out that the "otherness" of Japan has been "contained in the idea of some mysterious ambiguity. It is this ambiguity in the image of Japan that has given it a particular resonance in Western phantasy" (Robins and Morley 1991: 33). This is not to suggest that those early architectural explorers were deluded or ideologically motivated. There is indeed much beauty, craft and celebration of nature in Japan. But in directing our gaze through a veil of "Japonisme" it is arguable that a powerful interpretive frame has been placed around Japanese architecture and cities, one that encourages a search for meaning that is fundamentally frustrating when faced with the material practices of Japanese urbanism. Hence the dualism of delight and dismay we can both read about and experience for ourselves in encountering Japanese urban design. If we are to learn something from Japan, it seems we must engage a very different interpretive frame.

Pragmatism and the Japanese city

> The great appeal of pragmatist aesthetics for anyone interested in architecture, is that it takes everyday experience as the basis from which to extrapolate ... most often what we need from a building is for it to give an appropriate frame and support for our everyday habits
>
> (Ballantyne 2004: 33)

There is growing interest in the application of philosophical pragmatism to architecture and urbanism (as this edited collection exemplifies). For urbanists seeking to escape the semantic and material rigidities of modernism, but resisting the free-play of meaning and style advocated by postmodernism, a theory which "for certainty and invariable method, substitutes experimentation and belief in the world" and which focus on "things in the making" is very appealing (Rajchman 2000: 7). Gary Bridge has argued that an urbanism inspired by pragmatism posits "not the modernist city where rationality is sameness, nor the postmodern city where rationality is abandoned to an endless play of difference" (Bridge 2005: x). For Ballantyne, a pragmatic aesthetics implies "a move away from trying to determine the 'real' innermost significance of an object by trying to contemplate it in isolation, but seeing it always in relation to other things (involved in processes) which can in turn generate a plurality of interpretations and experience" (Ballantyne 2004: 34). As John Dewey has famously argued, art is not the same as the art-object:

> In order to understand the aesthetic in its ultimate and approved forms, one must begin with it in the raw; in the events that hold the attentive ear and eye of man, arousing his interest and affording him the enjoyment as he looks and listens: the sights that hold the crowd – the fire-engine rushing by; the machines excavating enormous holes in the earth; the human fly climbing the steeple-side; the men perched high in the air on girders, throwing and catching red-hot bolts.
>
> (Dewey 1934: 4)

For Dewey, we need to shift identities from that of the "cold spectator" to an impassioned participant in the drama of urbanism. As Dewey put it, productive pragmatism calls not so much for a

Figure 7.3
In such tight quarters, form adapts to context. © Simon Guy.

"planned" society as for one that is continually "planning" (quoted in Hickman 2001: 139). From this pragmatic perspective, a focus on timeless essences distracts from the urgent need to tackle immediate challenges in particular circumstances. Similarly, focusing on the identification of cultural absolutes (such as a unique Japanese design sensibility rooted in tradition) tends to result in strategic intransigence and a lack of tactical flexibility in design responses. For Dewey, technology (or for our purposes, design) is a rich blend of theory and practice that eventuates in new and improved tools for living and out of which new norms develop (Hickman 2001: 183). As Hickman points out, such an approach "dictates strategies of design and implementation that remain flexible by maximizing options and creating redundancies wherever possible" (Hickman 2001: 62).

Such a perspective finds strong resonance with the Japanese architect and urbanist Arata Isozaki, who has argued that, "the city is not a work of art" (quoted in Hajime 1992: 87). For Isozaki, "Architecture is not the fixing of images; in the design process we have to realize that architecture is always growing or decaying" (Isozaki 1999: 112). The emphasis on flexibility and change is a strong meme within debates about Japanese architecture. Critics point to factors as various as the vulnerability of Japanese cities to natural disasters, financial factors such as the notoriously expensive property market in Tokyo, and to the Buddhist emphasis on impermanence and fragility (Bognar 1997). The history of Japanese cities can be read as a litany of catastrophes; climatic, political, and financial. The result is a dramatically different relationship to durability than that found in Western cities. Pick up any book about Tokyo and the opening paragraphs are likely to focus on the rapid turnover of building stock to the degree that almost all of Tokyo's buildings have been replaced in the last thirty or forty years. This is not confined to poorly designed, outdated buildings. Bognar points out the fate of a number of iconic buildings by well-known Japanese architects including Toyo Ito, Kazuo Shinohara, and Kenzo Tange whose buildings have been routinely demolished to make way for the new with little regard to questions of heritage or preservation (Bognar 1997). A good example is Frank Lloyd Wright's famous Imperial Hotel which survived the devastating 1923 Kanto earthquake but had to make way for a high-rise hotel in a wave of 1960s redevelopment. Seen this way, Tokyo can be re-read less as a chaotic mess and more productively as a restless landscape of experimentation in which architects accept, even celebrate their fate of impermanence, and are freed to explore new design solutions in a variety of stylistic genres. As Donald Ritchie observes:

> In this most pragmatic of nations, everything must be for immediate use. Architecturally, this means that a pure style (if there is any such) would be too limiting (in terms of space, time and energy) for domestic use. How much more practical to miniaturize, to diversify, to combine. That any original integrity has been lost is no-one's concern, nor is the fact that the result is often kitschy. Indeed, the Japanese language has no word for kitsch. Nor would one expect it to. To quote an old Japanese proverb, "Fish have no word for water".

> (Ritchie 1999: 67)

Barrie Shelton has noted a slow process of rediscovery of the virtue of Japanese urbanism, one that escapes what Isozaki has termed "Japan-ness," either in its celebratory or condemnatory forms (Isozaki 1999). Shelton points to the landmark work of Gunther Nitschke who condemned what he saw as a superficial reading of traditional Japanese architecture which he argued was read into Japanese aesthetics by Western architects in pursuit of their modernist ends (Nitschke 1966). Instead, he saw in Japanese urbanism not compositional values but rather a vague space defined by "human activities" (quoted in Shelton 1999: 10). Nitschke's work has been picked up and applied by contemporary scholars of Japanese architecture such as Botond Bognar, who contrasts the "predominant reliance on visual perception" of Western urbanists which "tends to objectify and to instill feelings of mastery over the environment," with that of Japanese urbanists who comprehend the city as "created, perceived and understood as an additive texture of its parts or places" (Bognar 1985: 67). Shelton points to another Japanese architect, Fumihiko Maki to exemplify this view, highlighting Maki's view that "everything from signs (and) vending machines . . . to infrastructures participate equally with buildings in the imagery of urban Japan" (Maki 1988: 8, also quoted in Shelton 1999: 15). For Maki, these characteristics result in an amorphous and more collage-like surface in Japan "that favors fluctuations, fluidity and lightness" (Maki 1988: 8). Sarah Chaplin describes this as a "makeshift aesthetic" that refuses to acknowledge the Western definition of the term as limited and compromised and instead celebrates "the fleeting, the temporary, the impermanent, the imperfect, the irregular, the perishable" (Chaplin 2005, p. 79). As Bognar puts it:

> In Japan today we find an ephemerality that, at its best, can paradoxically yield "lasting" or enduring achievements in urban as well as architectural design – regardless of how short their material existence may be.
>
> (Bognar 1997: 7)

While coffee table books of "recent Japanese architecture" tend to focus on the latest offering from the superstar elite of global designers, there is growing interest in a less glamorous manifestation of this tactical architecture. Avoiding the iconic statements of grand projects, the focus here

Figure 7.4
Available space is unceremoniously filled. © Simon Guy.

is on street-level urbanism, on what Nicolas Boyarsky terms "dirty cities," "inclusive, fluid and responsive to small actions" (Boyarsky 2003: 5). Boyarsky finds in Tokyo a "system of disorder" which is not synonymous with "chaos," but with a "constantly changing value structure" and a "fascination for the ephemeral" (Boyarsky 2003: 6). Refusing the Western obsession with visual order and purity, this design approach is "pragmatic and concerned with close readings of the existing fabric and behavioral patterns" (Boyarsky 2003: 6).

Dirty cities/da-me buildings

> Shamelessness can become useful. So let's start by considering that these shameless buildings are not collapsible into the concept of "chaos", but are in fact an intricate reporting of the concrete urban situation.
>
> (Kajima *et al.* 2001: 8)

The Hong Kong architect Gary Chang argues that efficiency and intensity of urban use results through improvization rather than more structured planning and while the "three-dimensional cityscape is breathtaking, it is the non-visual-based pragmatism behind that affects such realization" (Chang 2003: 59). This non-visual pragmatism "favors adaptation instead of imposition, reuse instead of erasure, diversity instead of homogeneity" (Chang 2003: 59). Viewing Tokyo through this lens refocuses our attention away from the search for visual order and encourages us to look again at the strange and unfamiliar juxtaposition of styles and uses that make up the city. Here we have to abandon the conventional architectural guidebooks and histories that frame debate about Japanese urbanism and attempt to decipher a more unfamiliar landscape. Leaving behind the "good taste" encouraged by architectural criticism, we must learn to engage with the "disgusting" buildings that dominate Tokyo and other Japanese cities according to Momoyo Kajima and Yoshiharu Tsukamoto who make up the architectural practice Atelier Bow-Wow, whose work focuses on the narrow, in-between spaces of Tokyo where uses are continually shifting (Kajima *et al.* 2001: 8). Most cities, they argue, are a medley of anonymous buildings that are neither beautiful nor acclaimed by the current culture of architecture, yet reveal the essence of a city better than anything designed by architects or urban planners (Kajima *et al.* 2001). These buildings they affectionately describe as "da-me architecture" (no-good architecture). In two alternative guide books to Tokyo, *Made in Tokyo* and *Pet Architecture Guide Book*, Atelier Bow-Wow have made a study of what they term Tokyo's "Pet Architecture," buildings which appear monstrous in their rejection of standardized design and purpose and which instead celebrate wild juxtapositions of use: temples and shops, laundries and saunas, shrines and restaurants, pachinko parlours and banks, taxi companies at golf driving ranges, supermarkets with driving schools on the roof (Atelier Bow-Wow 2001; Kajima *et al.* 2001). Why Pet Architecture? Pets, for Atelier Bow-Wow, are "companion animals of the people ... usually small, humorous and charming" (Atelier Bow-Wow 2001: 1). Such Pet Architecture appears in the most unexpected places within the city. Atelier Bow-Wow define Pet Architecture as typically occupying marginal spaces, "areas such as a 1-meter width space among many closely placed buildings, a small and subdivided piece of land, or a long and slender city block sandwiched between the road and the railroad" (Atelier Bow-Wow 2001: 1). These are non-standard spaces, the leftover, awkward spaces of urban development and are abundant in Tokyo:

> The buildings of *Made in Tokyo* are not beautiful. They are not perfect examples of architectural planning. They are not A-grade cultural building types, such as libraries and museums. They are B-grade building types, such as car parking, batting centers, or hybrid containers and include both architectural and civil engineering works. They are not "pieces" designed by famous architects.
>
> (Kajima *et al.* 2001: 12)

For Atelier Bow-Wow, da-me buildings "don't have a speck of fat," they are "practical" and "highly economically efficient" and "utilize whatever is at hand" (Kajima *et al.* 2001: 12). Turning the pages of these guide books is to be taken on a journey through an endlessly varied landscape of buildings squeezed on impossibly narrow plots, pulled in, up and across whatever space has been left over from adjacent office buildings, railway lines, storage facilities, car parks, and so on. These are hybrid structures, a combination of industrial construction and self-build, mixing up public and private spaces, combining work, leisure, services, shopping and domestic activities, often reversing front and back orientations, open to radical reprogramming of use, connecting openly to all available infrastructure, adapting to need and available resources through a "desperate response to the here and now" (Kajima *et al.* 2001: 13). These are buildings as infrastructures of everyday life and demonstrate a remarkable fluidity of program and purpose, which presents the city as rather less obdurate than is often portrayed in urban studies. Atelier Bow-Wow rejects

Figure 7.5
An urban infill project by Atelier Bow-Wow. © Heide Imai.

the semiotic analysis of cities as images, which they argue is the root of urban analysis which represents Tokyo as visually cluttered and chaotic. Instead, Tokyo pictured from above will always evade interpretation or simply result in confusion and criticism. To understand Tokyo, they claim, the researcher must come down to street level and travel across the city experiencing it as a piece of theater in which distinctions between architecture and engineering become meaningless.

Atelier Bow-Wow use these Pet Architectures as inspiration for their own design practice, which is characterized by strategic interventions into the existing fabric, responding to new demands through creative conversion and adaptation of the built fabric of Tokyo earning them the label "architectural pragmatists" (Dauerer 2007). In a 2006 exhibition at the Netherlands Architectural Institute, they set out their design philosophy:

> Our process starts by observing the city at the smallest scale: we look at very small structures, spontaneous urban phenomena like the gap space between buildings, hybrids born of different programs, and public behavior and ritual.
>
> From our observations we have extracted a series of principles that allow us to generate site-specific spatial practices. The city of Tokyo, for example, is a treasure trove of solutions developed as a result of its very special urban regulations. Law prohibiting party walls and requiring "one building, one site" have stimulated ingenious thinking around gap spaces.
>
> A landscape of urban phenomena embedded in daily life – a profuse anthology of urban tactics from which we can draw a set of principles. These principles are then applied to a specific context and made to interact with each other.
>
> The very act of recording spaces in a given framework triggers ideas for new tactics and further spatial practices. And so the whole process starts again: observation, mapping, induction, collection, deduction, observation provides the principles underlying the project, which in turn feeds into new research.
>
> (de Baan *et al.* 2006)

Atelier Bow-Wow draw upon this research in their own design work, focusing on creating individual housing solutions (including the award-winning "Mini-house") in highly constrained sites. They also design more experimental architectural interventions for exhibition such as an outdoor bath that takes advantage of the underutilized space atop a large incinerator smokestack; the "Manga Pod," a structure for relaxation made of recycled Manga comic books and a flexible shelving structure, its rotating joints flex to adapt to the movement of its users; and the "Furnicycle," mobile food tricycles that allowed people in Shanghai to meet, eat, and relax where such activities are discouraged in public places. In each case, the traditional architectural object is reinvented and reinserted into a new urban context to better match new needs and uses. Yoshiharu Tsukamoto and Momoyo Kajima point to the influence of Henri Lefebvre's theory of the "Production of Space," in which the clash between the representation of space (that of architects and planners) and the space of representation (that of the users of space), as strongly influencing the work of Atelier Bow-Wow by highlighting the ongoing tension between the visions of designers and the experience of users. However, there are also strong resonances here with the emphasis of Dewey and other pragmatists on the importance of experimentalism, what they termed "fallibalism," the commitment to the continual review and revision of projects. As Hickman explains,

Dewey thought that the "history of human progress is a history of men and women coming together to form communities of discussion, inquiry, and activity and then constructing new tools: new ideas and new habits of action that are based upon careful experimentation" (Hickman 2001: 52). It is this emphasis on the experiential process of making buildings and cities as opposed to absorbing timeless and universal design truths that may have import for wider debates about sustainable urbanism.

Conclusions – Japan in the making

> In a world of ordinary cities, ways of being urban and ways of making new kinds of urban futures are diverse and are the product of the inventiveness of people in cities everywhere.
>
> (Robinson 2006: 1)

Returning from Japan, I am left with conflicting memories and impressions. I took great pleasure from battling through Kyoto to visit famous Zen gardens and sitting silently, even for a moment alone, contemplating the deeply satisfying aesthetic qualities of traditional Japanese garden and building design. But the stronger impression is of the equally, if differently, pleasurable dynamism of Tokyo and the senses of a city constantly being remade. But what might we learn from all this about sustainable architecture?

Perhaps first we need to look beyond the architectural object in glorious isolation. Atelier Bow-Wow are critical of the way Japanese architects always design buildings as one single concrete piece of architecture: "They talk about the relationship between street and building but in fact they are about the adjacent environment. And if that environment seems bad they close the building with a very hard concrete wall to create an abstract nature inside" (McGuirk 2005). Nature here becomes a second-hand and second-best nature, a commodified experience providing scant consolation for a poor urban environment.

Second, we might helpfully develop a more critical position on the issue of durability. For despite huge uncertainty and contestation around the meaning of environmentalism to Western architecture, the notion of longevity as a core quality has endured as integral to notions of sustainability. Here the lifecycle durability of materials fuses with ideas of traditional knowledge and enduring cultural heritage. This is not to suggest a quasi-romantic avocation of a Buddhist cosmology for all building design and development, but rather to encourage once again some caution in the commitment to universal values either of permanence and stability, or of impermanence and flexibility. As Allen *et al.* argue in Chapter 6 of this volume, "Both long-lived and rapidly evolving designs, like the fruit fly and the elephant, will have their place in sustainable industrial ecosystems." A contextual and critical consideration of these issues should always be prioritized.

Third, a "flexibility" to a range of design options – whether high-tech or low-tech – and an appetite to mix these where it makes sense. Equally, looking beyond contested tables of environmental performance in terms of materials (wood vs concrete), height (skyscrapers vs groundscrapers vs underground architecture), location (cities vs suburbs vs rural villages), and a willingness to be open to heterogeneous combinations of purpose and program, from "mixed" to "mixed-up" uses. Echoing the emphasis on "interpretive flexibility" found in Science and Techno-logy Studies, the point here is not to abandon judgment but to avoid closing down the evaluative process prematurely, to always be open to other design possibilities (Bijker 1995).

The danger of course is to replace one version of Japanisme with another, from celebrating timeless beauty to advocating restless adaptation. The question is less whether such pragmatic urbanism provides a universal blueprint (by definition it will not), but more how it might contribute to meeting specific environmental challenges. Seen this way, we might begin to take some inspiration from the "fluid urbanism" identified in this chapter in order to frame diverse sustainable design approaches which may aspire to be flexible, situated, pragmatic, and participative (Guy 2009). While not overtly a "green" practice, the work of Atelier Bow-Wow is dedicated to satisfying changing human needs, intensifying use of urban space with great economy and efficiency, and focusing on recycling and reusing space. If there are some resources of hope to be gathered here it is in this focus on meeting diverse human need through inventiveness and the challenge of making this the ordinary work of urbanism.

Questions for further consideration

1   If, as Guy claims, Westerners have routinely misunderstood the Japanese relationship to nature by projecting onto an idealized version of our own conception, should we accept the existence of multiple "natures" as a setting for multiple cultures?

2   As does Langdon Winner in Chapter 5, Guy argues that places can be understood through competing "interpretive frame[s]." Does such relativism make the concrete engineering concerns of Allen *et al.* in Chapter 6 seem less threatening?

3   In Chapter 4, Andrew Jamison argues that "green knowledge" is never abstract, but always engaged in personal and local conditions. In this chapter Guy, like Jamison and John Dewey before him, argues that we must "shift identities from that of the 'cold spectator' to an impassioned participant in the drama of urbanism." Does this logic undercut the more abstract reasoning found in the IPAT equation promoted by Allen *et al.* in Chapter 6?

4   Guy, contradicting most art historians, but corresponding to McDaniel and Lanham in Chapter 3 and Allen *et al.* in Chapter 6, sees great potential in the constantly adapting visual chaos of Tokyo – "a restless landscape of experimentation." On the other hand he is disenchanted with the idyllic beauty of Kyoto as a model for sustainable development. Is he suggesting that classical Western ideas about eternal beauty should be rejected in favor of temporary ad hoc experimentalism?

5   Guy suggests that we add " 'flexibility' to a range of design options." Does this proposition suggest that there are no permanent rules, as Vitruvius held, for "firmness, commodity, delight?"

Bibliography

Ando, T. (1991) "Traces of Architectural Intentions," in Y. Futasawa (ed.) *Taido Ando Details 1*, Tokyo: A.D.A Edita.

—— (2007) Quotation from BrainyQuote.com. Online, available at: www.brainyquote.com/quotes/authors/t/tadao_ando.html (June 20 2007).

Atelier Bow-Wow (2001) *Pet Architecture Guide Book (Living Spheres Vol. 2)*, Tokyo: World Press Photo.

de Baan, C., Guldemond, J., van Pinxteren, G. and Vlassenrood, L. (2006) *China Contemporary: Architecture, Art, Visual Culture*, Rotterdam: NAI Publishers.

Ballantyne, A. (2004) *Architecture Theory: A Reader in Philosophy and Culture*, London: Continuum.

Barthes, R. (1982) *The Grain of the Voice: Interviews 1962–1980*, Berkeley, CA: University of California Press.

Berwick, C. (1997) "An Interview with Toyo Ito: Tower of Winds and the Architecture of Sound," *The Take*. Online, available at: www.thetake.com/take05/take04/html/42ndst.html (June 18 2007).

Bijker, W. E. (1995) *Of Bicycles, Bakelites and Bulbs. Toward a Theory of Sociotechnical Change*, Cambridge, MA: MIT Press.

Bognar, B. (1985) *Contemporary Japanese Architecture: Its Development and Challenge*, New York: Van Nostrand Reinhold.

—— (1997) "What Goes Up, Must Come Down," *Harvard Design Magazine*. 3: 1–8. Online, available at: www.gsd.harvard.edu/research/publications/hdm/back/3bognar.html (June 7 2007).

Boyarsky, N. (2003) "Introduction: Dirty Cities," in N. Boyarsky and P. Lang (eds.) *Urban Flashes Asia: New Architecture and Urbanism in Asia*, West Sussex: Wiley-Academy.

Bridge, G. (2005) *Reason in the City of Difference: Pragmatism, Communicative Action and Contemporary Urbanism*, London: Routledge.

Buntrock, D. (2001) *Japanese Architecture as a Collaborative Practice: Opportunities in a Flexible Construction Culture*, London: Spon.

Chang, G. (2003) "In the Age of Indeterminancy: Towards a Non-Visual Pragmatism," in N. Boyarsky and P. Lang (eds.) *Urban Flashes Asia: New Architecture and Urbanism in Asia*, West Sussex: Wiley-Academy.

Chaplin, S. (2005) "Makeshift: Some Reflections on Japanese Design Sensibility," in B. Sheil (ed.) *Design Through Making*, Chichester: Wiley-Academy.

Dauerer, V. (2007) "Atelier Bow-Wow: Architectural Pragmatism," *PingMag*, March 5. Online, available at: http://pingmag.jp/2007/03/05/atelier-bow-wow-architectural-pragmatism/ (June 7 2007).

Dewey, J. (1934) *Art as Experience*, New York: Putnam.

Guy, S. (2009) "Fluid Architectures: Ecologies of Hybrid Urbanism," in D. White and C. Wilbert (eds.) *TECHNONATURES: Environments, Technologies, Spaces and Places in the Twenty First Century*, Waterloo, ON: Wilfred Laurier University Press.

Hajime, Y. (1992) "Between West and East – Part III," *Telescope* 8: 87.

Hickman, L. A. (2001) *Philosophical Tools for Technological Culture: Putting Pragmatism to Work*, Bloomington, IN: Indiana University Press.

Hyman, S. (1992) "Turning Japarisian," *Guardian*, April 11, p. 22.

Isozaki, A. (1999) Interview in C. Knabe and J. R. Noennig (eds.) *Shaking the Foundations: Japanese Architects in Dialogue*, Munich: Prestel.

Kajima, M., Kuroda, J., and Tsukamoto, Y. (2001) *Made in Tokyo*, Tokyo: Kajima Institute Publishing Ltd.

Kerr, A. (2001) *Dogs and Demons: Tales from the Dark Side of Japan*, New York: Hill and Wang.

Longxi, Z. (1988) "The Myth of the Other: China in the Eyes of the West," *Critical Inquiry* 15, 1: 109–131.

McCurry, J. (2005) "The View from Tokyo," *Guardian*, March 11, p. 9.

McGuirk, J. (2005) "Atelier Bow-Wow," *Icon Magazine* 22. Online, available at: www.icon-magazine.co.uk/issues/022/bowwow.htm (June 7 2007).

Maki, F. (1988) "City, Image and Materiality," in S. Salat (ed.) *Fumihiko Maki: An Aesthetic of Fragmentation*, New York: Rizzoli.

—— (2001) "Making Architecture in Japan," Foreword in D. Buntrock, *Japanese Architecture as a Collaborative Practice: Opportunities in a Flexible Construction Culture*, London: Spon.

Nitschke, G. (1966) "'Ma': The Japanese Sense of 'Place' in Old and New Architecture and Planning," *Architectural Design* 36: 117–130.

Rajchman, J. (2000) "General Introduction," in J. Ockman (ed.) *The Pragmatist Imagination: Thinking About "Things in the Making,"* New York: Princeton Architectural Press.

Ritchie, D. (1999) *Tokyo: A View of the City*, London: Reaktion Books Ltd.

Robins, K. and Morley, D. (1991) "Japan Panic," *Marxism Today*, September, 32–35.

Robinson, J. (2006) *Ordinary Cities: Between Modernity and Development*, London: Routledge.

Sacchi, L. (2005) *Tokyo: City and Architecture*, New York: Universe.

Said, E. (1985) "Orientalism Reconsidered," *Race and Class* 27, 2: 1–15.

Schittich, C. (2002) "Japan – A Land of Contradictions?" in C. Schittich (ed.) *In Detail Japan: Architects, Construction, Ambience*, Munich: Birkhauser.

Shelton, B. (1999) *Learning from the Japanese City: West Meets East in Urban Design*, London: E&FN Spon.

Sontag, S. (1982) "Introduction," in S. Sontag (ed.) *Barthes: Selected Writings*, London: Fontana.

Wilde, O. (1990) *The Complete Works*, Leicester: Blitz Editions.

Yokoyama, T. (1987) *Japan in the Victorian Mind: A Study of Stereotyped Images of a Nation 1950–80*, London: Macmillan.

Sustainability and Place

Editor's Introduction to Chapter 8

Written in the first person, this chapter is both historical and philosophical in scope. As history, Andrew Light summarizes the transformation of North American environmentalism through three stages of development – each stage is described as part of the moral journey moving toward crisis. The historical crisis is so severe, Light argues, that it has prompted some to announce "the end of environmentalism." As a philosopher, the author responds to these historical conditions in two parts: first, he argues that by idealizing wilderness as external to human values and relationships we have unintentionally emptied the landscape of information that makes nature relevant to our everyday lives – we have made it abstract and thus more, not less vulnerable to the abstraction of human economics. And second, he holds, that this unfortunate turn of history might be countered by replacing the old focus on wilderness with a new substantive notion of "place." If, as Light suggests, the value of place is to be found in its importance to valuers like us, then we might create intentional communities of people dedicated to the places around us as an extension of themselves.

In his critique of the environmental movement Light redirects Dewey's critique of conventional science, that "analysis is but a process of abstraction, leaving us ... know[ing] almost nothing about the actual activities and processes..." Taken together Light and Dewey hold that abstraction by "idealizing wilderness" or by scientific "analysis" amounts to the same thing – it tragically distances natural processes from everyday life (Dewey 1975: 39).

Chapter 8

The Moral Journey of Environmentalism

From Wilderness to Place

Andrew Light

Like many environmentalists I am sometimes asked why I am an environmentalist. I find such questions annoying. They are particularly troubling when put in terms like this: "What were the experiences of your youth that led you to become an environmentalist?" The problem is that such questions seem too often premised on a set of assumptions about what it means to be an environmentalist. My specific worry is that those asking such questions presuppose that environmentalism is a kind of identity that one discovers about oneself that is supposed to come through some experience, usually an experience of connection to a wild, natural, other. Unlike similar questions that one might ask about a chosen career path – "At what point did you *know* that you wanted to become a doctor?" – the formidable experiences of the environmentalist are to be found in the realm of feeling or emotion rather than rational thought.

Now, certainly, one could answer the question about when one knew they wanted to become a doctor by pointing to a set of experiences that inspired feelings of wanting to care for others. And I, at least, would not endorse a distinction between the passions and reason which would deny rationality to the emotions. Still, there is something, especially in North America and other new world countries, to the worry that a draw to environmentalism is seen as a calling not unlike the ministry. We answer in this case not to a holy spirit but to nature itself and thus come to embrace our commitment to our connection to the world. And when we make that commitment we ally ourselves with nature, and others like ourselves who have also answered the calling, against the unenlightened masses who are only concerned either with themselves, their families, or human social issues. So, not unreasonably, when a relative of mine who would not call themselves an environmentalist asks me the question with which I started I hear it as, "What made *you* one of *them*?"

To my mind we environmentalists brought this sad state of affairs on ourselves. For surely, concern for the environment is a concern that we should all have and that concern cannot be easily (if ever) divorced from concern for one's self, one's family, and the welfare of humanity. The environmental literature, however, is rife with the myth of the environmentalist as the person who goes out into the world to connect with nature and thus has the experience that allows admission to the tribe.

Thoreau had his hut where he went to distance himself from his fellows. And even though readers quickly learn that Walden wasn't really that far removed we can take solace in his overly excitable experience on Mt. Katahdin ("Contact! Contact!").[1] More recently that Norwegian environmental export, deep ecology, was spread by some of its American adherents as practically requiring a conversion experience of sublime proportions:

> Most people in Deep Ecology have had the feelings – usually, but not always in nature – that they are connected with something greater than their ego, greater than their home, their family, their special attributes as an individual – a feeling that is often called oceanic because many have it on the ocean. Without that identification, one is not easily drawn to become involved in Deep Ecology.
>
> (Devall and Sessions 1985: 76)

While the influence of deep ecology has waned in the last ten years, many would still embrace those such as Julia Butterfly Hill, sitting in her redwood Luna for 738 days to save the 1,000-year-old tree and a three-acre buffer zone around it, as an example that should be seen as exemplary. Describing her initial view of these trees, Hill says, "When I entered the majestic cathedral of the redwood forest for the first time, my spirit knew it had found what it was searching for. I dropped to my knees and began to cry because I was so overwhelmed by the wisdom, energy and spirituality housed in this holiest of temples."[2] No emphasis is necessary.

I am not alone in maintaining that environmentalism needs a new set of faces and a new ethos if it is to survive as anything more than a special, clubby, somewhat anti-social interest.[3] To expect environmentalists to be, quite literally, converts baptized through wilderness experience, is to exclude many from the beginning, including myself. For, by those standards, I am an aberration. I never had a profound wilderness experience. I didn't take my path after reading a Muir or Leopold who did. And while I would maintain in the end that what is needed is a model of environmentalism, or at least a motivation for better environmental regulation, which is not premised on any particular kind of experience, what experiences I can recall that made me care about the non-human world were much more prosaic. As a child I spent just about every afternoon playing at a place called Flat Rock Creek in the little town that I grew up in outside of Atlanta. It ran behind a row of suburban houses wedged between old farmland which would eventually become a golf course after my family moved away. Though a place like this certainly can be huge for a little person, in my case it didn't take me outside of myself but rather became the first place that I ever cared about. And while some of that caring came through moments of solitude more of it came through recognition that it was the place that knitted together my community of pre-teen friends. Flat Rock Creek was as much a part of our circle as any one of us was. It was not soul satisfying but rather an integral part of community building.

While I am loathe to make predictions there are signs that North American environmentalism is leaving its romantic experiential idealizations of the wild behind in favor of a focus on encouraging a more common, local, attachment to place. I believe that such local connections, be they rural, suburban, or urban, are a necessary first step to building the critical mass of those across ideological lines which will be necessary to get traction on the global environmental challenges that we currently face. My reasoning is simple. An attachment to place is not only an attachment to a nature external to us but to the people with whom we inhabit those places. If environmentalism is to avoid becoming a special interest then environmental concern must not only be about our connection with the natural world but our connection with people, and hence based in our understanding that environmental problems go hand in hand with human social problems rather than representing a moral realm outside of those problems. By way of making an argument that this should indeed be our path I will first offer a very brief tutorial on American environmentalism. I will then consider the question of how recent critiques of the very idea of wilderness have changed our understanding of the appropriate limits of what we consider when we want to make a contribution to environmental protection or restoration. It is in this new domain of an expanded understanding of the environment of interest for environmentalists where we will see a growing chorus of others claiming that concern for the environment can never be isolated from other human concerns if it is to be meaningful and effective.

What is environmentalism about?

Imagine opening the front page of your favorite daily paper and seeing a headline announcing a new report by an environmental group critical of some government's environmental policies. Before reading further, what do you expect the report to be about? Who do you expect it to be from? If it was about Friends of Wildlife bemoaning the lack of collaboration between the governments of three Western states on the reintroduction of wolves into Yellowstone would you be surprised? If it was about Greenpeace's condemnation of an emissions trading plan for power producers would it meet your expectations? If it was a local group called More Gardens! demanding municipal protection of community gardens would it seem more appropriate for the city section? Historically, environmentalists have gone back and forth in understanding their priorities and even the scope of their labor as embracing one, two, or all three of these sorts of issues. With these shifts in focus over the years it is no surprise that those not seeing themselves as environmentalists have also changed their expectations on what counts as an environmental issue.

The first wave of American environmentalism is often marked at the beginning of the twentieth century as the "conservation wave." This is the period dominated by figures such as Theodore Roosevelt, John Muir, Gifford Pinchot and later Aldo Leopold (Dowie 1996; Nash 1982; Schlosberg 1999). Most of their efforts have been characterized as the work of white Eastern establishment elites calling attention to the critical decisions that would have to be made about the future of the grand wilderness areas of the American West. Leopold, Bob Marshall, and Benton MacKaye founded the Wilderness Society as a small, invitation only organization aimed in part at limiting automobile access to the new national parks (Sutter 2002). According to Paul Sutter's exceptional history of the founding of the Wilderness Society, each of these figures saw very different things in the value of wilderness that needed to be preserved and different opportunities that the preservation of wilderness would create. While Marshall saw the value of wilderness in its potential for solitude and exertion – an alternative to the "effete superstructure of urbanity" – MacKaye saw the wilderness as a buffer from the individualism of the cities and a place where a new form of communal living could be created in quasi-socialist work and art camps (Sutter 2002).[4] What is important for my purposes here is that all of these figures saw wilderness as a thing that actually existed that needed protection. And while some like Aldo Leopold would later revise his view of the relative wildness of some areas (for example, his first forays into northern Mexico convinced him of how domesticated his old stomping grounds in New Mexico actually had become) by the end of this period Leopold's son, A. Starker Leopold, would set in motion an orthodoxy concerning wilderness that would have ramifications to this day.

During the winter of 1962–1963 the National Park Service incurred adverse publicity following a large removal of elk from Yellowstone National Park. After the population in the park had risen to about 10,000, about twice the estimated carrying capacity of the range, and because of projected food shortages that year, the NPS culled 4,283 animals. To justify these actions then Secretary of the Interior, Morris Udall, commissioned Starker Leopold to lead a blue-ribbon panel of scientists to assess the NPS policy. The committee endorsed the action as justified, given the possible degradation that the overpopulated elk would cause to the park, but then went much further.

In order to assess the culling of the elk the committee recommended first a general statement about the goals of ecosystem management in the parks. While extensive, one of the most important claims created a default definition of wilderness: "As a primary goal, we would recommend that the biotic associations within each park be maintained, or where necessary rec-reated, as nearly as possible in the condition that prevailed when the area was first visited by the white man. A national park should present a vignette of primitive America" (Leopold 1962: 32).[5] Wilderness could now be historically located as the thing that existed in the new world prior to white contact. The environmental community enthusiastically endorsed the report and on May 2, 1963 Secretary Udall ordered the NPS to incorporate its philosophy and findings to the administration of the parks and "maintain or create the mood of wild America" (National Research Council 1992: 44). What would this mean? A number of things including maintaining successional communities in the parks, removing exotic species, minimizing observable artificiality, rationing tourists, and, perhaps most importantly, resumption of fire suppression practices, all designed to get the parks back to their "natural" state. Unfortunately, as we will see later, what counted as the natural state of the parks, or at least their pre-Columbian state, was severely limited given the lack of accurate information on the conditions of the pre-Columbian Americas.

The second wave of environmentalism symbolically begins with the first Earth Day on April 22, 1970, though its origins certainly precede this date. The focus of much of the activity at this time, up to the 1980s, was on the creation of a series of legal protections for the environment aimed at insuring greater provision for clean air and water, and the reduction of the human and larger ecological health effects of toxic chemicals and radioactive materials. In addition to figures like Rachel Carson, whose landmark *Silent Spring* helped to shape this movement, other important intellectual leadership was provided by Paul and Ann Ehrlich, Barry Commoner, and David Brower, though these figures, especially Commoner and the Ehrlichs, differed sharply on their interpretations of the causes of environmental problems and their appropriate resolution.[6] What is most striking about this period of environmental activity is the sheer amount of important federal legislation passed: twenty-three acts in ten years. These included the Wilderness Act (1964), the Clean Water Act (1965), the Clean Air Act (1967), the Wild and Scenic Rivers Act (1968), the National Environmental Policy Act (1970), the Water Pollution Control Act (1972), the Endangered Species Act (1973), and perhaps the biggest and most far-reaching, the "Superfund" Act (1980).

The lasting effect of all of this activity continues to be debated in the US today, and since the end of the presidential administration of Jimmy Carter many of these laws have suffered the winds and tides of the various presidential administrations which have inherited their enforcement. Still, in 1970 an impressive 53 percent of Americans viewed "reduction of air and water pollution as a national priority," and environmentalism successfully overcame its earlier, turn-of-the-century incarnation as the purview of select wealthy citizens to become a public social movement in its own right (Dowie 1996: 32). At this time we see the creation and flourishing of many of today's major environmental NGOs, including the Environmental Defense Fund, the Natural Resources Defense Council, the legal arm of the Sierra Club, as well as more radical environmental groups such as Greenpeace.

Depending on one's views though, environmentalism remained a fairly narrow movement even as its intellectual horizons expanded. One reason is that the dominant focus of much work in this area, even with the variety of issues represented in the environmental legislation of the 1970s, was on questions concerning wilderness, now understood as those vast untrammeled swaths of what is presumed to be original nature (Light 2001). Here we see a constant return to the first wave of the movement with its roots in nineteenth-century romantic thought, including Thoreau (though there is reason to believe that he is misunderstood as a wilderness advocate), and later John Muir. We ought not to be surprised by this focus. The North American environmental movement has long been dominated by concerns over wilderness, and even given the diversity of issues addressed by the movement in its second wave, the focus on less controversial issues of wilderness advocacy re-emerged to dominate the agendas of many environmental organizations after the election of Ronald Reagan. A new third wave of "beltway" environmentalism emerged in the 1980s in response to an antagonistic White House intent on rolling back the legislative successes of the 1970s. The so-called "Big 10" mainstream environmental organizations at this time abandoned most controversial environmental issues involving regulation of industry to focus on cute and fuzzy animal preservation priorities and those bits of land that looked best on Sierra Club wall calendars (Dowie 1996).

But why is this focus on wilderness controversial, let alone distressing? Before getting into the conceptual problems with defining what wilderness is, one answer is that the resulting lack of attention to human communities, especially cities and postindustrial landscapes, and the unique environmental challenges and possibilities they face in achieving sustainability, created a disastrously incomplete picture of the scope and complexity of environmental problems. Politically, an answer to these concerns came with the rise of various environmental justice movements in the 1990s, which argued that mainstream environmentalism had left behind people of color and people in general, no matter where they lived, in its focus on natural resource conservation and the value of nature outside of its human cultural context. One charge was that even though environmentalism had become a social movement in its own right, it had too narrow an agenda, and hence too homogeneous a constituency. Criticism of this sort is exemplified in Dorceta Taylor's remark that:

> If it is discovered that birds have lost their nesting sites, environmentalists go to great expense to erect nesting boxes and find alternative breeding sites for them. When whales are stranded, enormous sums are spent to provide them with food ... But we have yet to see an environmental group champion human homelessness or joblessness as issues on which they will spend vast resources. It is a strange paradox that a

> movement that exhorts the harmonious coexistence of people and nature, and worries about the continued survival of nature ... somehow forgets about the survival of humans...

(Taylor 1990)

As a result of this retreat from the problems of the human-made environment we have lost sight of the fact that some of the most pressing ecological issues also raise questions of distributive and participatory justice (Figueroa and Mills 2001). In October 1991 when the First National People of Color Environmental Leadership Summit passed its "Principles of Environmental Justice," it was based on a variety of claims that the burdens of environmental pollution were inequitably distributed. According to Mark Dowie's history of North American environmentalism such claims included arguments that: 57 percent of whites reside in counties with federally substandard air quality while 65 percent of blacks and 80 percent of Hispanics live in communities with worse conditions; enforcement of the Clean Air act may benefit 78.7 percent of white communities and only 14.2 percent of black communities; 50 percent of all African-American infants tested for lead contamination have higher levels than tolerated by US standards; three out of four toxic waste dumps not in compliance with federal regulations are in black or Hispanic neighborhoods; and more than 200 million tons of radioactive waste lie in tailings piles on Indian reservations (Dowie 1996: 145).

While the research behind such figures has been called into question, the rise of the movement for environmental justice and the debates over its legitimacy had a good effect on the environmental movement. While there is still a good deal of work to be done there is at least a firm foundation now established for criticizing environmental organizations that do not address questions of environmental justice. On February 11, 1994, President Clinton signed an executive order requiring the EPA and other federal agencies to make "achieving environmental justice part of its mission by identifying and addressing, as appropriate, disproportionately high and adverse human health or environmental effects of its programs, policies, and activities on minority populations and low income populations" in the US and its territories. The impact of this executive order and its successful implementation (even during the Clinton administration) is, of course, in question.

From nature to place

This redirection of environmentalism, encouraging a greater integration of social and environmental concerns, has, nonetheless, been incomplete. Against the backdrop of the environmental movement's focus on wilderness the activities of these organizations is still the exception rather than the rule. As the environmental justice movement became stronger it became tempting to react against it by insisting on the separation of two realms of environmental problems: those in cities and other areas which involved humans, or at least specific human communities, and what many persisted in claiming were the "real" environmental issues involving the wild places unsullied by human intervention, which deserved an unassailable priority as the core focus of the movement (see, for example, Rees 1999: 1). The former leads us closer to the kinds of concerns raised in the previous chapter by Simon Guy. The later locates the environments of most concern outside of cities.

Such a distinction, however, had its own challenge from those who had long insisted that such a dualism between nature and culture was unwarranted. This position achieved its most eloquent rendition in and outside of environmental circles through the publication of William Cronon's landmark 1995 essay "The Trouble with Wilderness; or, Getting Back to the Wrong Nature" in the *New York Times Magazine*. There, Cronon, one of the most important contemporary environmental historians, argued that wilderness was a myth that not only rested on an unsupportable metaphysical distinction between culture and nature, but also had led to very bad management policies. The historical argument was straightforward enough – wilderness was an ethnocentric concept which Europeans had mistakenly used to describe North America, a land that appeared wild and "untrammeled," but which was in fact highly cultivated by Native Americans before European settlers ever arrived. For example, the enormous prairie ecosystem that dominated the middle of the continent was the size it was due to intentional burning. Aboriginal peoples actively burned the prairie in order to get young succulent plants to grow, thus attracting buffalo to new feeding grounds. Other agricultural practices created similar ecosystems and so what many regarded as the rich variety of biomes in North America was evidence not of the lack of human habitation and use but of its presence. The only true wilderness in 1492, Cronon argued, was Antarctica. When we fail to recognize this history we embrace the false hope that it is possible to escape from responsibility for what we have done, "to," as Cronon put it, "somehow wipe clean the slate of our past and return to the *tabula rasa* that supposedly existed before we began to leave our marks on the world."

Even further, if we accept the arguments of those such as archaeologist Henry Dobyns and geographer William Denevan, that the native population of the Americas prior to 1492 may have been as high as 115 million (higher than the population of Europe) rather than the previously accepted figure of 8.4 million, with only about 1.75 million in North America, the existence of pre-Columbian wilderness gets even more complicated. Very persuasive arguments that smallpox, hepatitis, tuberculosis and other deadly diseases had wiped out as many as 80–100 million Indians prior to the larger European settlements and incursions of the seventeenth century means that the first significant wave of European immigrants would have not seen the civilization that actually existed here (Mann 2006). Hence they would have bequeathed to us a legacy prime for misidentifying the pre-settlement landscape as "wild" if by that we mean untrammeled. Thus, if we really want a pre-Columbian Yellowstone, we may well have to move permanent Indian residents into it rather than restrict the activities of visitors.

In terms of management policies, the idea of wilderness, as understood in the Leopold Report, has been unhelpful because it has led to a policy of preservation tantamount to freezing a swath of nature in time. Rather than allowing ecosystems to grow and evolve it picked one moment and anointed it as the time at which a particular landscape would stand as a museum piece for future generations to enjoy as wild. This led to disastrous decisions, especially the resumption of fire suppression in national parks mentioned on p. 139, thereby stopping a natural ecological process which keeps some forests healthy and immune to catastrophic burning which can happen when too much organic ground litter builds up over time. Cronon and others argued that this policy in part led to the devastating western fires of 1988 and 1997 that destroyed enormous parts of these parks.

Many more details could be added to make this history more complete, for certainly, in each of these waves of the history of environmentalism there were minority voices arguing for something different, but the reverberations of what some of my colleagues termed "the great new wilderness debate" created something of a crisis in the environmental movement. If wilderness was really a myth, a cultural construction amenable to deconstruction, then what would environmentalism focus on? One could answer by simply saying "nature," but such a term seemed as difficult to define as wilderness. If true, then how could environmentalism change, evolve and adapt so as to make a stronger contribution to the fashioning of a more environmentally sustainable world?

While debates among academics can easily fall on deaf ears, especially when their terms are mired in the obscure *lingua franca* of the ivory tower, this one did not quickly go away. Cronon and his allies published the highly regarded volume *Uncommon Ground* (1995) continuing to challenge the sacred cows of traditional environmentalism. The founder of the field of conservation biology, Michael Soulé answered with other anti-constructivists in *Reinventing Nature? Responses to Postmodern Deconstruction* (1995) (see Cronon 1995a: 69–90; Cronon 1995b). The poet Gary Snyder joined Earth First! founder Dave Foreman and others in answering Cronon in the pages of the popular magazine *Wild Earth*. Park Service employees and rank and file members of Greenpeace joined others on one or another side of a growing divide and wondered about the effects of these positions on their own work. The debate eventually made it to the front page of the *New York Times* in April 1999. Cronon's intention was surely not to undercut the ground for all environmental protection, but the effect of his argument was to demolish the accepted claim that the environments of importance to environmentalists could conveniently be delimited by the rough and convenient boundaries of city and countryside. Or, at least, the effect was that one could not make this distinction without defending it.

I remind us of this debate because it shows how environmentalists, in their recent history, were faced with the challenge of either thinking of the scope of their concerns as limited by what one would consider as "nature" or "the natural" or else expanding it to encompass broader human social arenas which could be better captured in other language. If we could not easily designate a landscape as worthy of environmental protection merely by labeling it "wild," "pristine," or even "natural" then we needed some language that was less controversial, more meaningful, and flexible enough to refer to the variety of environments that environmentalists had historically been engaged with. The goal of such a task is not to take a position for or against Cronon or his critics but simply to recognize that we cannot expect to make much progress on any particular environmental issue in isolation from others. We cannot preserve the Grand Canyon without considering urban growth in Arizona. Nor can we take up the issue of asthma hotspots in inner city Chicago without attending to land use patterns in the counties surrounding Lake Michigan. But doing this is not easy. Cronon himself commented in one of the stories on the controversy surrounding his work that even though he loved Manhattan and Yosemite, when he is in either of these places "it's hard to see how Manhattan is implicated in Yosemite or how Yosemite is implicated in Manhattan."

One possible alternative can be found in the language of place: not simply the sense of place as mere location, but a more psychologically robust and even morally loaded conception of location imbued with a storied relationship between people and the things around them. Discussions of the importance of place have long been evident in the environmental literature, and if there is any common thread to them it is that the description of the importance of a place is always presented from the perspective of a specific individual or a community of valuers. As opposed to the more abstract language of wildernesss, wildness, or natural value, when we say that a place is important in this context we cannot divorce it from an understanding of how it is valuable to some people. Such a view is intrinsically pragmatic in the sense evoked by Guy in Chapter 8. It does not valorize an abstract notion of nature or the natural but rather speaks to the deep but shifting cultural connections between a specific people and their surroundings.

Writers such as William Whyte had long advocated the importance of architecture, planning, and land management in strengthening the quality of the ties between people and their local communities (Whyte 2002). In Whyte's vision, and that of other regional planners such as Lewis Mumford, clear connections could be made between the local public park, the wilderness area out of town, and the private plots of land in between. Even the smallest woodlot or roadside patch could be a "tremendous trifle," as Whyte put it, worthy of protection because it could anchor an individual or communities' devotion to a place. The small stream running near my childhood home was not wild, nor probably natural to many people, but it was a place that I cared for, and in caring for it I came to shape an identity as someone concerned about the care of other places. But, again, since Whyte focused in part at least on the environments of cities and suburbs, which he saw as increasingly threatened by bad planning and sprawl, his work on the value of place is rarely if ever included among the canonical works of environmentalism.

Cronon's thesis, the rise of the environmental justice movement, and other landmarks of recent environmental history which could also be mentioned, encourage us to not only recover the work of people like Whyte, but also to return to those environments which have been at the periphery of environmental concern. Some more traditional environmentalists may find fault with my reasoning here and see little by way of force of argument to convince them to reassess their priorities. But surely those who took such a position would not claim that more humanized environments are unimportant in the search for a more sustainable society. In the rare instance where protection of a relatively pristine area conflicts with that of a more settled landscape we may need to go back to these debates, but in most cases we should be able to agree that there are more than enough environments, more than enough places, and more than enough connections between them, to warrant some active struggle for protection. In the end too we can assume that any expansion of environmental concern to refer to more places can only help to broaden the fold of those who would call themselves environmentalists. If I can get my neighbors to consider the importance of volunteering in the renovation of our local park, to facilitate the delivery of some critical ecosystem service, then I am more likely to be able to convince them that other, broader environmental concerns are important as well.[7]

How to achieve such attention to the importance of our local places will require new skills for the environmental community. It is not simply a matter of lobbying, writing letters, or living in a tree for several years, but of community building toward the goal of helping people to understand that their future is dependent on that of their local environment. One brief example of such a project is New York City's Bronx River Alliance, a project of the City of New York Parks and Recreation Department and the non-profit City Parks Foundation. The Alliance is organized by paid city employees who have brought together and coordinate sixty voluntary community groups, schools and businesses in direct projects to clean up the twenty-three miles of the Bronx River.

The focus is not only on the environmental priorities of the area, but also the opportunities afforded by it to create concrete links between the communities along the river by giving them a common project on which to focus their civic priorities. In the words of the alliance, the project is to "restore the Bronx River to a Healthy Community, Ecological, Economic and Recreational Resource." The activities of the Alliance are thus jointly civic and environmental and the scale of the environmental problem, crossing several distinct communities, helps to create a common interest between them. The environment in this case becomes a place, or perhaps civic space, which glues together various local publics.

Like the creek I fell in love with as a boy, the Bronx River is not wild and it is far from pristine. But both are places that have been lived in, worked, and made into a home, a source of both economic and social capital. Recent trends in environmental art may also provide alternatives which highlight the importance of place in ways not limited to the traditional tools of resource management, such as biological surveys, and the concomitant arguments that something should be preserved because it is rare. Artists and designers may be uniquely suited for this kind of project. Artists are mediators between the realms of subjective experience (even when that experience is purely conceptual) and techniques for representing that experience to others. At bottom, the same is true of an expression of the importance of a place. To tell you why some place is important to me I must find some way of expressing it that can, in the end, be meaningful to you. As John O'Neill, Allan Holland and I argue in a recent book, all landscapes are landscapes rich in human narrative, either as a place that has been inhabited or one that has been set aside and preserved (O'Neill *et al.* 2008). It is these narratives that need to be revived and revisited in order to make these places important for the people who inhabit them now.

If a new focus for environmentalism is to get beyond the debates of the past and develop a more comprehensive notion of place then it must not repeat the mistakes of the older focus on wilderness. As the importance of place is tied to the stories we can tell about it then our understanding of the importance of place must change with new experiences. Again, following the intuitions of Guy concerning the Japanese experience, place cannot become static. It is ever changing and malleable as new experiences are garnered and as our own experience of places change as we are drawn into the discussion of its importance with others. When we value a place because it is important to us, and not simply because an argument can be made about its environmental value in the traditional sense, then we must accept that the ground for that value can change. We may be called to the task of its preservation using the resources at hand, but must accept that our claims about the importance of any place are only as good as the arguments we can mobilize in support of them at a given time. We all pass on and can only hope that we have left a mark for others that is vivid enough to last as an impression of why we think something is important.

This is all by way of saying that if the value of place is to be found in its importance to valuers like us then its importance is also as impermanent as we are. I learned this lesson most clearly in May of 1997 when I was traveling through the west coast of Newfoundland and had the pleasure of spending an evening with the people of a small fishing village working to preserve their sense of place. This place, like many small fishing communities in Newfoundland, was dying. With the collapse of the cod industry, people were leaving the community to seek work elsewhere. To try to articulate the importance of their community to others, the remaining people of the village put together a video with the help of local environmental activists which tried to "map" the values of the community, focusing on the land and sea around them and the role that it had played in giving them a home and a source of work and leisure. One thing was clear: these people deeply cared about the place that they had made their own. They wanted to preserve it, protect it, and insure that it would be a living community into the future. The stories they told were profound. They did not consist of a list of traditional environmental amenities suitable for ecotourism, but rather, of an account of experiences – a first kiss and then a marriage proposal at a small inlet; a spot favored by a deceased loved one that had become a burial ground.

But at the same meeting where I saw the video I also learned that recently, when a huge nickel deposit was discovered in Labrador and a competition was announced for the location of a nickel smelter in the area, the people of this village stepped forward to make a bid on putting the smelter in their community. They knew that placing the smelter there would seriously jeopardize the natural and communal values that they had articulated in their video, but they also knew that without new jobs for the community, their village would die. They knew that even if the smelter could be made safe, using the best available environmental science and technology, it would certainly have a negative effect on the natural and community values of the place. It would make their village less special and potentially destroy the traces of the important moments of their lives that had made that place so valuable to them. The choice to make a bid on the smelter was nothing less than tragic, and the people of this village knew it. But the creative act of helping this community articulate the importance of this place to them in terms of the stories that they had to tell about the place was perhaps the best way for them to fully understand the depths of the tragedy unfolding before them and, perhaps, to keep it from happening. And in creating the tools to understand the importance of the place to them they also created a tool that could convey the importance of this place to me. In turn, I came to care about their small community and was motivated to help to protect and preserve it. But perhaps most importantly, because they had shown me how important this place was to them, I was now in a position to ask them why they would put it in jeopardy? At the very least they now had to defend this decision to an outsider as uncomfortable as it might be to do so. The conversation of the future of this place had been broadened by its own inhabitants and so a focus on locality had not made this decision more insular, but actually less so. For a community to open themselves up to the outside in this way was more inspiring to me than any number of lone people having a transcendent experience of humility on an empty ocean, or anywhere else for that matter.

We cannot live in most places and "leave only footprints," as we are advised to do when entering a national park. Whether we destroy or merely transform our places into something different, possibly something better, is a choice that we have to make every day. We make these choices in the best way, however, when we have visions of alternative possibilities of how the future can relate to what has gone before. Many will see this vision of environmentalism as fundamentally flawed. If we base our claims to preservation or restoration of a place on human desires and preferences, then will we not always in the end choose short-term development over long-term protection? We have ample examples of the successes of the new integrated environmentalism not to worry overly much at such a hasty conclusion. But we should also remember that even when such failures occur we have something larger to gain: not just the preservation of bits of nature on the periphery of civilization but the creation of an intentional community of people dedicated to the places around us as an extension of themselves.

Questions for further consideration

1   As did Guy in the previous chapter, Light argues against abstraction in this one. But, are the chaotic urban landscapes preferred by Guy at all sympathetic to the legible and coherent places described by Light? What do they have in common?

2   In his preferences for "everyday" places, does Light fail to recognize how exceptional places like Kyoto, the Vietnam Memorial, or the Versailles Gardens inspire new possibilities?

3   If we adopt the trajectory of history in the relationship of humans to wilderness that Light documents – which takes us from the love of "nature" to the love of "places" – does it mean that the endangered American Bald Eagle is no more "valuable" than the millions of fan-tailed grackles that have colonized southern cities?

4   Light holds that "the value of place is to be found in its importance to valuers like us." This kind of value, he recognizes, is no more permanent than are we and it suggests that we give up the kind of permanent or foundational values that bind together communities as diverse as Earth First! and the Roman Catholic Church. In relinquishing claims to permanent or even enduring values don't we give up the very idea of sustainability?

5   In his conclusion Light opens the door to human "transformation of places" in a positive, rather than only in a negative way. In doing so he may also open the door to the loss of "wilderness" as an operative concept. Is this other than a semantic problem?

Notes

1   In full the quote is: "What is this Titan that has taken possession of me? Talk of mysteries – Think of our life in nature – daily to be shown matter, to come in contact with it – rocks, trees, wind on our cheeks! the solid earth! the actual world! the common sense! Contact! Contact! Who are we? where are we?" (Thoreau 1974: 5).

2   See www.circleoflife.org/inspiration/julia/. See also Hill's book (2000).

3   Michael Schellenberger and Ted Nordhaus (2005) have made one of the most damning cases for this sentiment. While I do not endorse all of the sentiments of their paper I found it a welcome wake-up call to the problems environmentalists face in order to get traction on critical issues like global warming. The two are currently finishing a book extending the argument of this chapter that I hope will be similarly enlightening and am sure will instill some healthy debate.

4   The apparent anti-urbanism of Marshall here is troubling as he was also a keen advocate for bringing together environmental interests with social justice concerns. Many commentators, including Dowie (1996) have argued that had Marshall not died very young his legacy might have been to anticipate the turn to environmental justice in the last two decades.

5   In addition to Leopold the report's other authors were Stanley A. Cain, Clarence M. Cottam, Ira A. Gabrielson and Thomas L. Kimball.

6   For a discussion, see Feenberg (1999), chapter three.

7   The literature in place on geography, and increasingly on philosophy, is immense. I won't attempt here to summarize it all. For starters though one could look at Hiss (1991), and Light and Smith (1999). Also see my journal, co-edited with Jonathan Smith, *Ethics, Place, and Environment*.

Bibliography

Cronon, W. (1995a) "The Trouble with Wilderness," in W. Cronon (ed.) *Uncommon Ground: Toward Reinventing Nature*, New York: W.W. Norton and Company.

—— (1995b) *Reinventing Nature? Responses to Postmodern Deconstruction*, M. Soulé and G. Lease (eds.), Washington, DC: Island Press.

Devall, B. and Sessions, G. (1985) *Deep Ecology: Living as if Nature Mattered*, Salt Lake City, UT: Peregrine Smith Books.

Dewey, J. (1975) *The Early Works of John Dewey, Volume 2, 1882–1898: Psychology, 1887*, Carbondale, IL: University of Southern Illinois Press.

Dowie, M. (1996) *Losing Ground: American Environmentalism at the Close of the Twentieth Century*, Cambridge, MA: MIT Press.

Feenberg, A. (1999) *Questioning Technology*, London: Routledge.

Figueroa, R. and Mills, C. (2001) "Environmental Justice," in *A Companion to Environmental Philosophy*, D. Jamieson (ed.), Malden, MA: Blackwell Publishers: 426–438.

Hill, J. B. (2000) *The Legacy of Luna*, New York: HarperCollins Publishers.

Hiss, T. (1991) *The Experience of Place*, New York: Vintage Books.

Leopold, S. (1962) "Wildlife Management in the National Parks," U.S. National Park Service. Online, available at: www.cr.nps.gov/history/online_books/leopold/leopold.htm.

Light, A. (2001) "The Urban Blind Spot in Environmental Ethics," *Environmental Politics* no. 10, vol. 1: 7–35.

Light, A. and Smith, J. M. (eds.) (1998) *Ethics, Place, and Environment*, London, Routledge.

—— (eds.) (1999) *Philosophies of Place*, Lanham, MD: Rowman & Littlefield Publishers.

Mann, C. (2006) *1491: New Revelations of the Americas Before Columbus*, New York: Vintage Books.

Nash, R. (1982) *Wilderness and the American Mind*, New Haven, CT: Yale University Press.

National Research Council (1992) *Science and the National Parks*, Washington, DC: National Academy Press.

O'Neill, J., Holland, A. and Light, A. (2008) *Environmental Values*, London: Routledge.

Rees, W. E. (1999) "Life in the Lap of Luxury as Ecosystems Collapse," *The Chronicle of Higher Education*, July 30: 1.

Schellenberger, M. and Nordhaus, T. (2005) "The Death of Environmentalism," *The Sun* no. 350. Online, available through the Breakthrough Institute website at: www.thebreakthrough. org.

Schlosberg, D. (1999) *Environmental Justice and the New Pluralism*, Oxford, UK: Oxford University Press.

Sutter, P. (2002) *Driven Wild*, Seattle, WA: University of Washington Press.

Taylor, D. (1990) *Proceedings of the Michigan Conference on Race and the Incidence of Environmental Hazards*. Cited in Dowie, M. (1996) *Losing Ground: American Environmentalism at the Close of the Twentieth Century*, Cambridge, MA: MIT Press.

Thoreau, H. D. (1974) *The Maine Woods*, Joseph Moldenhauer (ed.) Princeton, NJ: Princeton University Press.

Whyte, W. H. (2002) *The Last Landscape*, Philadelphia, PA: University of Pennsylvania Press.

Editor's Introduction to Chapter 9

As in the previous chapter by philosopher Andrew Light, architect Vincent B. Canizaro is concerned in this chapter with the concrete qualities of "place." He presents an historical and polemical account of four regionalist discourses that precede and inform sustainability in architecture and planning. Each of these is an attempt to secularize the romantic notion that geographic regions are somehow sacred, and that they determine the characters of the peoples that inhabit them. As an extension of this secular tradition in regionalism, he presents the possibility of a fifth discourse, *civic environmentalism*, which might serve as a fruitful direction for the future development of regionalism and sustainability. Canizaro argues that that by reconsidering the contemporary assumptions that support sustainability in architectural design and planning, it is possible to redirect its future trajectory away from the technocratic impulse that now dominates the field toward a pragmatic foundation for a better way of life.

In characterizing regionalist thinking about community life as *a posteriori* rather than *a priori*, Canizaro weems to recall Richard Rorty's critique of high modernism, which proposed that,

> If we give up this hope (of finding *a priori* structures), we shall lose what Nietzsche called "metaphysical comfort," but we may gain a renewed sense of community. Our identification with our community – our society, or political tradition, our intellectual heritage – is heightened when we see this community as *ours* rather than *nature's*, *shaped* rather than *found*, one among many which we have made. In the end, pragmatists tell us, what matters is our loyalty to other human beings clinging together against the dark, not our hope of getting things right.[1]

Canizaro's contribution to the tradition of radical empiricism is to recognize that regionalism in architecture and planning can be the literal building of life-enhancing and secular communities.

Note

1   Rorty, Richard. *Consequences of Pragmatism*. (Minneapolis: University of Minnesota Press, 1982), 166.

Chapter 9

Regionalism, Place, Specificity, and Sustainable Design

Vincent B. Canizaro

> Regionalism suggests a cure for many current ills. Focused in the region, sharpened for the more definite enhancement of life, every activity, cultural or practical, menial or liberal, becomes necessary and significant; divorced from this context, and dedicated to archaic or abstract schemes of salvation and happiness, even the finest activities seem futile and meaningless; they are lost and swallowed in a vast indefiniteness.
>
> (Lewis Mumford (Mumford 1928: 140))

New developments, devices, and ideas, often rely on past associations to affect their widespread acceptance and use. The concepts "iron horse" and "horsepower" for example, helped disturbed citizens of the American West adjust to the radical change from animal to mechanical power. Theorists constructing the discourse of sustainability in architecture, however, have rarely built such bridges between ideas and practices from "before."[1] Like many developments in the modern era, sustainability has been seen and promoted primarily as something new, progressive, and future-oriented – a set of practices, mostly technical, that have come into fashion only recently. A fuller account of architectural sustainability would reveal *at least* three related discourses – work spurred by the energy-efficiency movement of the 1970s (a reaction to the 1973 OPEC oil embargo), the sustainable development discourse catalyzed by the Brundtland Report of 1987, *Our Common Future* (World Commission on Environment and Development 1987), and the long tradition of regionalism that dates at least to the seventeenth century.

The "hyper-efficient" projects of Amory Lovins and the Rocky Mountain Institute represent one tendency within the first discourse. The other tendency are those architects and planners who have looked to the past for answers to the environmental and social dilemmas of our time. The romantic "earthships" constructed by Mike Reynolds are the result of such thinking. Both tendencies are representative of the unimaginative yet energy-conscious work of what we now refer to as the "passive solar" movement.[2]

But no matter whether we search the future or the past for inspiration, my view is that architectural sustainability is too often portrayed in idealized or utopian terms. If, however, we reject utopias of the future as technocratic fantasies, and reject utopias of the past as historical ones, a fuller account of architectural sustainability would reveal *at least* two other substantive discourses that compete for our attention and allegiance. These are the sustainable development discourse catalyzed by the Brundtland Commission Report of 1987, and the long tradition of regionalism that dates at least to the seventeenth century. It is this second discourse – regionalism – that I will consider at length.

The first and more recent discourse derives from the cogent yet vague directive captured in the Brundtland Commission Report of 1987. This seminal text gave us the most widely referenced definition of sustainable development as that which is able to meet "the needs of the present without compromising the ability of future generations to meet their own needs" (United Nations General Assembly 1987). It gained much currency at the beginning of the twenty-first century, as awareness of global climate change and the political instability of the worldwide energy supply (chiefly oil) has grown. The result is a discourse and practice dominated by technical solutions to mostly technologically framed problems. The Brundtland discourse differs from the earlier passive solar tradition in that it is explicitly concerned with the balance between what is generally referred to as the 3Es – economic development, environmental protection, and social equity. But as Michael D. Oden's chapter in this volume demonstrates, the third E – equity – has largely been lost to the quantitative impulses of technocracy. The result is a highly reductive, even impoverished understanding of the built world, but one which uses less active and embodied energy, collects rainwater for local use, and involves some sort of recycling in the use of materials. To some these strategies alone are enough to inspire celebration. And as green products and organic foods have become more stylish, such tactics are increasingly sought after. But in itself popularity, especially in modern liberal capitalist societies, is inherently a temporary condition. Soon enough other tactics, likely stimulated by aesthetic concerns, will clamor for everyone's attention. More sustainable are those tactics and forms of inspiration that tend to stick around. This view is shared with preservationist Jeffrey M. Chusid, also a contributor to this volume. But rather than focus on the preservation of the built world, as does Chusid, this criteria leads me to the second discourse mentioned above, regionalism.

Regionalism is a more subtle, and more substantial practice that has been carried forward by architects and theorists concerned with the manifest realness of places and the people who live there. Regionalist architects have a long history of resisting fads, technophilia, and "new" architectural design trends based mostly in aesthetic concerns. Some have emphasized craft and the importance of local labor and materials. Others emphasized the specificity of site, climate, and situation or place in their development of settings for everyday life. In the twentieth century, they resisted the classic modernism (International Style) proffered by Hitchcock and Johnson and the Museum of Modern Art, the techno-rationality and behaviorism of the 1960s, and the post-modern historicism of the 1980s. Within this architectural history, there lies a common thread of concern that leads to the possibility of a more environmentally responsive architectural practice than the technocratic and fashionable practice we see today.[3] That thread, regionalism, is attention, awareness, and thinking in terms of local places (or regions) experientially, ecologically, and in terms of their social and cultural construction.

Applying these sensibilities to architectural production is to materialize the relationship between human and nonhuman communities that Andrew Light articulated in the previous chapter. It is to physically construct the life-enhancing settings required by communities in the broadest sense of the term.

So, as I contend here, sustainability is not an idea that suddenly sprang up in the 1970s (and again in the late 1980s). Nor was it thrust upon a resistant and anti-nature modern architecture. Rather, it is an extension of the long-term discourse concerning regionalism that is deeply embedded within modernism itself. As such, regionalism prefigures sustainability and can provide it a still fertile and sound basis for its future development. This chapter considers, then, how regionalism, in its various manifestations, can support and promote a more viable environmental architecture. By linking regionalism and sustainability, the latter may be understood as part of the wider cultural project of architecture.

At its base, progressive regionalist practitioners and theorists seek respect for a contemporary vernacular. They demonstrate a secular view of the natural world, not a transcendental experience of nature received from the past or imagined in the future. Architectural regionalism focuses on design in terms of particularity and locale, and has, in certain formulations, reframed architectural production as a specific variety of socially just environmental action. Variations of the regionalist impulse that apply most cogently here include at least four distinct discourses: regional planning, referential regionalism, regional modernism, and bioregionalism (a movement eclipsed by the ecological and sustainable design movements it fostered). A fifth discourse, much newer, is that of civic environmentalism (CE). It shares much in terms of its basic assumptions with regionalist concerns. Like the regionalism of Lewis Mumford and the Regional Planning Association of America (RPAA), it is a serious ethical and practical challenge to architectural and planning professionals from the disciplines of social science and philosophy: to be more socially and ecologically engaged as citizen-architects who care for the environmental quality of the communities in which they build and less concerned with the self-reflexive design of aestheticized objects divorced from the crucial immediacy of their places.

In what follows, I will present regionalism through a brief account of each of these five discourses. My intention is to demonstrate that the regionalist attitude, focused as it is on place specificity, is a stronger foundation upon which to build the discourse of sustainability than is the desire to reduce greenhouse gas emissions or save money on your electric bill. By providing a pragmatic, intimate, culturally enriching, participatory, and everyday relationship with their local or regional environment, the abstractions of sustainability and sustainable techniques are made direct and personal. Once one's energy consumption is connected to the pollution of a particular place, or one experiences natural places that demonstrate negative environmental effects, we are motivated to act in the way that hunters and fishermen do, as they make some of the most avid environmentalists, because their pastime puts them in a position to experience shrinking habitats due to unplanned growth or pollution (LiveScience Staff 2006, and O'Connell 2004). So too can architects and planners act to design in a way that link people to place, culturally and experientially. They can provide experiences that may foster the environmental concern that can serve as the foundation for sustainability. They do this through planning cities with parks, cities that support wildlife, buildings with natural ventilation and lighting that connect people to the outdoor environment, buildings and gardens that use rainwater and thereby participate in local climatic cycles, buildings that produce their own power and buildings that participate in and extend the local historical heritage.

Regions and regionalism

Regionalism can be generally characterized as a discourse about connectedness to place and within this discourse are distinct conversations about contextualism, site-specificity in art and design, landscape urbanism, and planning. Regionalism is also allied with other disciplines, which take account of spatial phenomena such as cultural geography, cartography, anthropology, and folklore and historical studies, *all of which deal with the effects of modernization and modernity, globalization, and technological development on individuals and society.* How it differs from these is both a function of scale and application. By utilizing the scale of a region many issues not available to studies of the immediate site or context or even the city (even as these are, in some cases, becoming as large as regions) are made available. Thinking in terms of a region grounds these other settings within a physical and natural situation. It is sufficiently large enough to be understood as a spatial area capable of supporting a diversity of human and non-human life via agriculture, naturally available resources, and with provision for adequate recreation. Watersheds, topographical difference, areas of distinctive land use, climatological difference, and consistencies of architectural, cultural, linguistic, and political organization are criteria available to the regionalist to consider in the design of environments for those places. Thinking in terms of regions, rather than the immediate "property" being developed affords architects, planners, economists, and others to make specific and local choices in a wider cultural and environmental perspective. The varying viewpoints from which this wider perspective derives is what differentiates the plural regional discourses of regional planning, referential regionalism, regional modernism, bioregionalism, and civic environmentalism. In what follows I will consider each of these in turn.

Regional planning

The discourse of regional planning is central to that of architectural regionalism. During the early twentieth century, regionalism was understood as an interdisciplinary affair that implicated any and all environmentally-based fields including architecture, planning, landscape, engineering, and forestry. This inclusive view is showing signs of a re-emergence as environmental practitioners are confronted with a new generation of environmental threats. The real concerns usually taken up by planning come squarely into play once the insufficiency of the singular site is understood. Most environmental concerns span across much larger domains if the satisfaction of resource needs and "habitats" can rarely be confined to any single, economically defined, site of development. Further, it is doubtful that a single family home or office building could ever be reasonably defined as sustainable in itself. Pliny Fisk III has shown clearly that in fact it requires, in most measures, a neighborhood and ultimately a region for the appropriate access to materials, skills, and energy required to live within one's means, and productively so (Fisk 2000). It is an issue of scale. And for architectural regionalism, the embrace of planning is primarily about thinking within the larger context of the region.

Regional planning, as framed by Lewis Mumford and the RPAA, was about revising the logic by which we develop our settings, including whole regions, cities, neighborhoods, and streets. The RPAA intended a socially progressive practice that set out to establish a regionally relevant order, which would prioritize the possibility for a healthy and balanced quality of life.

Theirs was a pragmatic vision, which respected and secularized nature as a source of a productive economy and locus of social life. Carl Sussman has framed the collective goals of the group as wanting "to replace the existing centralized and profit-oriented metropolitan society with a decentralized and more socialized one made up of environmentally balanced regions" (Sussman 1976: 1). Many of its members were influenced by the social critiques of Thorstein Veblen, and as a whole their focus was on improving the quality of life through design, legislation, and advocacy. Specific achievements included the pioneering of low-cost housing, community planning, statewide planning, economic planning, design which considered the conservation of energy and resources for the general good, and such radical ideas as increasing productivity through increasing the comfort of workers (Sussman 1976: 7).

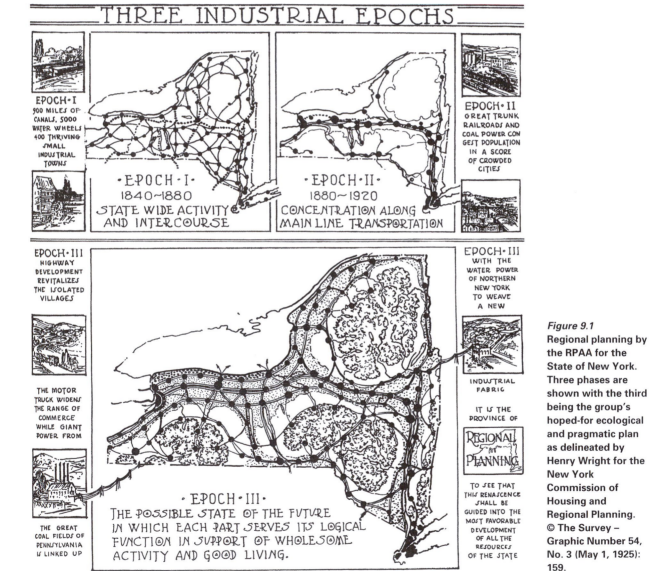

Figure 9.1
Regional planning by the RPAA for the State of New York. Three phases are shown with the third being the group's hoped-for ecological and pragmatic plan as delineated by Henry Wright for the New York Commission of Housing and Regional Planning. © The Survey – Graphic Number 54, No. 3 (May 1, 1925): 159.

Among planners it is widely acknowledged that the soul of their discipline is claimed by both economists and place-makers. Mumford and his colleagues supported the latter claim – they were against prevailing tendencies in instrumental metropolitan planning (which are still with us), through which development and growth are designed for effective administration and profit (which is an economic abstraction), rather than a response to the underlying social and ecological conditions of regions (which are real) (see Figure 9.1). Instrumental economic planning has been driven primarily by the logic of free-market capitalism, or its opposite, Soviet-style communism. In both, development is "planned" according to abstract notions of profit or productivity – which amount to the same thing. Under such logic, the well-being of locals (and local ecologies) is often secondary to the "revenue generation" of individuals. Accepted, are negative social effects such as gentrification, which often results in unintended evictions and resulting lack of diversity (income, age, vocation) among residents. Stephen Wheeler contends that in recent years regional planning has begun to return to its socially progressive roots and to deal with the changed setting of the modern metropolis – unprecedented size realized through sprawl, political fragmentation, and the need to re-urbanize the city center, yet again (Wheeler 2002). An example of this return is Scott Campbell's proposal for planning to be guided by a tripartite consideration of the local economy, environment, and issues of social equity. Overall, we can hope, this represents a return to planning in which the ecological region serves as the source of balance between the abstractions of modern market interests and ecological reality. Richard Dorman has described those pursuing this "new regionalism" as:

> ... a small and "informal coalition of local government leaders, college researchers, environmentalists, and volunteers," as well as landscape architects and urban planners, who called themselves "regionalists," ... seeking to find some middle way between the extreme but futile tactics and life-styles of the radicals, the inertia and complacency of most of the rest of the public-at-large, and the remote and unaccountable policies of distant regulators and powerful developers ... The key, they believed, lay in instilling the public, a local public, with a sense of "connectedness" – aesthetic, historical, and personal – to the place *where they lived*.
>
> (Dorman 1993: 325)

In short, the regionalist planning discourse sparked by Mumford and his contemporary allies is a two-sided project: It seeks to secularize the negative tendency towards the mythification of place and the economic abstraction of places. Both practices, I hold, conceal the accumulation of power by elites behind false claims to represent a higher authority. By secularizing both nature and economics, regionalist planners look toward the democratic construction of sustainable places.

Referential regionalism

As I argued above, the abstract impulse of early twentieth-century modern design was less dominant than is commonly assumed. The regionalist architecture and theory of the 1920s and 1930s was rooted in a popular American regionalist movement generally. While the cultural production of this time appeared to focus on the stylistic or aesthetic aspects of regions, its intentions were no less politically progressive, yet distinct from international modernism.

In the United States, the mid-century regionalists sought a cultural reconstruction of American life through the revitalization in regional literature, dialect, art, craft, food ways, land use, and social life. It was a progressive, pragmatic, and pluralistic movement based on learning enough about a place and its past to provide lessons for the future. On the whole the regionalists did not intend a return to mythical regional pasts (as the Nazis in Germany did). Nor did they have provincial or chauvinistic intentions, in which a region might celebrate its attributes as an expression of superiority over others. Rather, the veneration of the local was to serve as a source of creativity and uniqueness – a celebration of the potential for a rich and modern life "here." It was a secularization and celebration of the vernacular, liberated from the social hierarchies of premodern life. It was also a reaction to the post-World War I influence of European ideas and the increasing regimentation and centralization of modern life generally. As a response to modernizing forces that bore down on regional and local differences it was a movement that supported cultural identity through productive respect for the local.

Despite the strong linkage to these socially-oriented regionalist movements, the architectural work of this period is recognizable due to its referential nature. For this it has been labeled by some as scenographic, romantic, and commercial in various attempts to locate its meaning. Those critics have focused on the outward appearance of buildings and not on the reason for the references, which was intended to be both culturally and physically performative. Important figures of the time (who built and wrote about building) such as David Williams, Mary Colter, and John Gaw Meem, while attentive to issues of appearance, evidence this deeper approach.

David Williams' writing reveals the motivations and methods behind his own search for a sincere and satisfying Southwestern architecture for Texas (Williams 1931). He finds this captured in the preexisting architecture of settlers throughout Texas who wholly transformed the architectures of inheritance they brought with them, to fit with local climatic and material conditions. His central conviction was that within pioneer buildings lay valuable lessons regarding adaptation to local climate, the best use of local materials, and the aesthetic sensibilities of a region's residents (Figure 9.2). Similarly, John Gaw Meem, in his "Old Forms for New Buildings"

Figure 9.2
Vallejo Adobe, near Petaluma, CA. In a 1954 article William Wurster uses this building as an example of the origins of a uniquely Californian architecture that is distinguished by its "sense of fitness to site and purpose." Further it is a building, which exemplifies both material traditions of California's history, adobe and wood construction. © Library of Congress, Prints & Photographs Division, #HABS, CAL, 49-PET.V, 1–3), Roger Sturtevant, Photographer.

makes a claim common at the time that the "regional is modern" (Meem 1934). In the indigenous work of the southwest he finds an example of a "well adapted type of architecture" that would serve well as a regional and modernist architecture. "Old traditional forms" of pueblo architecture exemplify a logical, clean, honest, and performative architecture within a local material tradition and climatic setting.

In Europe, around the same time, similar efforts were underway to reinvigorate regional traditions and, as a part, regional architectures. Lewis Mumford summarizes them this way:

> In France regionalism has meant a protest against excessive centralization in politics and culture.... In Denmark regionalism has meant the adaptation of Danish agriculture ... in Czecho-Slovakia it has resulted in the formation of a new political state; in England regionalism has worked out a characteristic theory of civilization enriched by a harmony of local cultures ... and has created a movement, the Garden City movement, whose purpose is to ... colonise the country itself with new cities, fully equipped for industry and culture.
>
> (Mumford 1927: 279–280)

In the shadow of World War I, referential regionalists in both Europe and North America sought to redescribe the many patterns of local life in progressive rather than overtly romantic terms. Those aesthetic modernists who tend to paint them as otherwise generally fail to see the political, social, and ecological content of this work.

Regional modernism

From the 1930s to the late 1950s, another discourse began to emerge in response to the emergence of European modernism and referential regionalism in the 1920s and 1930s, culminating in the 1932 exhibition or works later referred to as the "International Style" at the Museum of Modern Art (MoMA).[4] The exhibition was touted as an event that through its influence would "save American architecture from languishing any longer in the dark period of eclecticism" and served to polarize the discourse of modernism in America between two processes: *conflict* and *maturation* (Germany 1991: 102).

With regard to conflict, a number of battles can be mapped. Wayne Andrews, a mid-century architectural critic, pitted Veblenites (modernists) against Jacobites (regionalists and humanists) while historian David Gebhard developed descriptive distinctions between soft and hard modernism (Gebhard 1995). Key in the debate was abstraction and dogmatism that appeared to surround the emergence of an "international" style.[5] Rather than foster local relevance, internationalism presumed to be a formula relevant to anywhere, and specific to nowhere in particular. As described in Hitchcock and Johnson's influential catalogue, which invented the concept, the "International Style" was based primarily in aesthetic principles. It was an abstract and aesthetic style against which modernist Rudolph Schindler said: "the classical mode of set forms for columns, architraves, and cornices is [merely being] replaced by a stereotyped vocabulary of steel columns, horizontal parapets and corner windows, to be used ... both in jungles and on the glaciers" (Schindler 1935: 19). Lewis Mumford, also a prominent architectural critic, was highly critical of the stylistic focus of the international style. He held that it did not adequately address human comfort or local social patterns. He failed to see how importation of European practices would lead to an architecture suited to regional differences.

With regard to the process of maturation, a number of modern architects gradually inflected the abstractions of the international style toward regional conditions. It is this hybrid work that I refer to as regional modernism (Dussel 2004). In time, critics would begin to recognize as regionalist the work of many early European modernists. Le Corbusier's "Post-purism" phase of the 1930s, for example, employed local materials and climatic responsiveness was a central theme. Similarly, Alvar Aalto's work gradually became understood as regionally modern architecture due to his embrace of regional materials and construction techniques.[6] Even Walter Gropius, former director of the Bauhaus, would argue by 1943 that modernism serves as an armature for regionalism (Figure 9.3). His logic was that the modern elements afforded by new technology, would provide a foundation "with which regionally different architectural manifestations can be created." Gropius ultimately criticized the "International Style" by arguing that, "It is not a style, because it is still in flux, nor is it international, because its tendency is the opposite – namely, to find regional, indigenous expression derived from the environment, the climate, the landscape, the habits of the people" (Gropius 1962: 14). And among all the Europeans it was Richard Neutra's work that exemplifies the maturity of regional modernism.

American architects and critics of the early to mid-twentieth century such as William Wurster, Pietro Belluschi, John Yeon, Harwell Hamilton Harris, O'Neil Ford, Paul Rudolph, Hugh Morrison, and Katherine Ford achieved a regional modernism through the secularization of both nature and the vernacular. These architects had concern for the environment and people's relation

Figure 9.3
Walter and Ise Gropius, Gropius House, Lincoln, MA, 1937, serves as an example of a project that is both modern and regional. Regional by virtue of its siting, exterior materials, and spatial form (esp. porch) that makes possible unique climatic experiences.
© Library of Congress, Prints & Photographs Division, #HABS, MASS, 9-LIN, 16–20.

to it, but did not ascribe to the natural world the spiritual value that it held for earlier American environmentalists such as John Muir. Rather, the natural world provided for these designers a situation that demanded response and, in turn, offered opportunities for new experiences made possible by technological advances. Similarly, the vernacular gave them a source for material use, details, and spatial forms that had local relevance. Often it exemplified a more honest use of materials than practiced by the modernists who highly valued the concept. By secularizing the vernacular in this way they found it could not only serve as a source for meaning and distinctiveness, but also of time-tested performance.

In 1944 the MoMA redirected itself with "America Builds," an all-American exhibition of American regional and modern architecture curated by Elizabeth Mock. It is a critique of the International Style. In a 1945 review Hugh Morrison states:

> Mrs. Mock has so clearly indicated the nature of the essential style developments of the past ten years that it is worth summarizing them. There has been first, a renewed interest in the vernacular – in the old stone barns of Pennsylvania, in the shingled or clapboarded houses of New England, and the ranch houses of the West. The straightforward use of material in the native folk architecture, and its adaptation to climate and topography, have been emulated in modern buildings, and have produced "a friendly, more differentiated contemporary architecture." With new emphasis on wood, in its natural texture and in new structural uses, there has come a tendency to "lose that insistence on machine-like precision of finish" so much desired a decade ago. The modern architect welcomes the challenge of climatic difficulties as a basis of design, and the modern house "becomes ever more intimately related to the ground and the surrounding landscape." This I believe is an accurate picture of the trend of development of the modern style during the past decade.
>
> (Morrison 1945: 163)

Regional modernism is, then, very much as its name implies – a hybrid practice that developed out of the conflict experienced by design practitioners who struggled to make sense out of the Cartesian tendencies of orthodox modernism. It was this day-to-day struggle to build in the concrete conditions of real communities and places that led to a process of maturation in which a regionally inflected modern architecture emerged.

Bioregionalism

Leading most directly to the contemporary discourse of sustainability is bioregionalism – a way of reasoning that has been eclipsed by the movement it has fostered. Bioregionalism emerged in the Pacific northwest of North America as part of the counter-cultural movement of the 1960s. Defining bioregionalism, like regionalism, has been a work in progress that continues today.[7] But generally it is best characterized as a political movement aimed at decentralization and the realignment of arbitrary political boundaries to coincide with ecologically defined regions determined via climatology, geomorphology, plant and animal geography, and natural history. Human history is considered, but remains secondary. Exemplary buildings are "vernacular," and secularized as a facet of "natural history." They demonstrate local and environmentally sensitive adaptation to places reflective of local resources, climate, and a part of a local culture more closely connected to the land. Bioregionalists argue that present political boundaries do not relate sensibly to "people's sense of natural associations and relationships with place."[8] The aim of its protagonists is to integrate ecological with cultural affiliations creating a place-based sensibility – informed by in-depth knowledge of the local natural landscape (as an ecosystem or watershed), climate, geography, indigenous cultures, and their environmental history (Figure 9.4). In this context, bioregionalism is an "ecocentric" rather than an anthropocentric discourse.

Texts such as Peter Berg and Raymond Dasmann's "Reinhabiting California" are key (Berg and Dasmann 1977). Its central metaphors, "Living-in-place" and "reinhabitation" describe both the ecological and political goals of bioregionalism and have become its central tenets

Figure 9.4
Map of the Columbia River Bioregion demonstrating an alternative manner by which to divide up geographical space when adhering to bioregional principles. © Vincent B. Canizaro from a Map by the Columbia River Bioregional Education Project.

(Aberley 1999: 23). Further, their collaboration is unique in that it combines both Dasmann's career in science and Berg's career as an activist. In the 1950s Dasmann, a field biologist, had been active in environmental conservation issues since the mid-1950s. Based on his studies of the ecological habitats, in the mid-seventies, he was commissioned by the United Nations to map the world in terms of bioregions and describe the interlocking structural relations that exist between them. Berg meanwhile, co-founded the Planet Drum Society, a non-profit organization aimed at the promotion of bioregional ideas, attitudes, strategies through publication, education, and the staging of events.

The work of Pliny Fisk III and Gail Vittori of the Center for Maximum Potential Building Systems (CMPBS), Robert and Brenda Vale, Sim Van der Ryn, and John and Nancy Todd are central to the bioregionalist discourse within architecture. Particular cases that embody the values of this discourse include the Advanced Green Builder Demonstration House built in Austin, Texas by CMPBS (Figure 9.5) and the Ark on Prince Edward Island, Canada by Solsearch Architects.

Figure 9.5
The Center for Maximum Potential Building Systems, The Advanced Green Builder Demonstration House, Austin, Texas. House demonstrates many of the concepts described by Fisk. Shown here is the "green form" framing system (recycled content post and beam), adobe block infill, and the rainwater-harvesting system.
© Vincent B. Canizaro

Both are prototype residential projects that employ unique means to achieve ecological and performative integration with their immediate and regional context. The latter, self-described as a "bioshelter" integrates heating, cooling, and food production in an off-the-grid complex in a cold northern climate. The former integrates energy, water, waste, and material cycles (using lifecycle analysis) within a unique modular off-the-grid building in hot-humid central Texas.

Civic environmentalism

Providing what may be a new and fruitful direction for both regionalism and sustainable development is the emerging discourse of civic environmentalism (CE) (Light and Wellman 2003). As a planning and design-oriented discourse, CE focuses on the production of ecologically functional and socially just cities through democratic and participatory means. It pays special attention to these concerns in the context of the expanding urban–suburban realm, updating the concerns of regionalist architects and planners such as Lewis Mumford for the twenty-first century. Unlike the forms of regionalism that preceded CE, it redescribes the role to be played by both professionals and citizens as well as the means by and through which they conceive of "projects."

The term civic environmentalism was coined by Dewitt John in 1993 (John 1993). It has been, however, environmental author/activist, William Shutkin, who has popularized the term. Shutkin defines CE as *"the idea that members (stakeholders) of a particular geographic and political community – residents, businesses, government agencies, and non-profits – should engage in planning and organizing activities to ensure a future that is environmentally healthy and economically and socially vibrant at the local and regional levels"* (Shutkin 2000: 14). Andrew Light, an environmental philosopher and contributor to this volume, has built upon Shutkin's proposal to argue that environmental virtues might become the governing factor in relationships between persons in a community (the civic dimension), and non-humans in that same community (the ecology dimension).[9] In sum, Shutkin and Light suggest revived dimensions of civic life that prioritizes the protection of the environment for all.

Collectively, CE scholarship suggests that architects and planners need to consider six propositions in their work: first, social justice for both human and non-human populations including the equal dispensation of rights, representation, and physical space. Second, the creation of better places, defined mostly in terms of the maintenance of diversity and enhancement of community through such notions as enhancing street life and battling gentrification. Third, the conservation and maintenance of local ecologies. Fourth, the importance of local knowledge. Fifth, the power of participatory activity in every project and place. And finally, *fidelity to* and respect for the *particularity* of places. As a group, these propositions rest on the importance of direct sensory experience for the care and renewal of concern for places (Light 2003).

How do these propositions pose important challenges to design professionals? Overall they reframe the practice of architecture and planning as a specific variety of regionally informed environmental action. In lieu of acting as distanced experts, design professionals, architects and planners must begin to serve as citizen/designers who care for the social, cultural, and environmental quality of the communities in which they build. Prior regionalist discourses suggest three innovative ways of reframing design practice that are required to become practitioners of civic environmental design (CED): First, the built environment must be understood as an agent for the benefit of both humans and non-humans, and as such, designers must work to preserve and enhance the environment aesthetically, ecologically, functionally, and with respect to history and the specificity of local or regional cultures. Second, project "sites" must be understood as always already social, political, and ecological entities such that any project is and conceptually treated as a local renovation. And third, "programs" must be understood not as free-floating abstract descriptions of economic needs in search of real estate to appropriate, but as responses developed in consultation with regard to the specific conditions of the place. Or by extension, that places (sites) may serve as the catalyst for the development of programs most suitable to that place.

These last two ways of reframing practice are derived from a unique attribute that regionalism, sustainable design, and CED practices share – that is the attention to local social and physical conditions. By prioritizing the region, neighborhood, or building site, a designer is more effectively able to produce work that is respectful and responsive to the place. My own study of CED process in action revealed two distinct conceptual approaches that are very helpful here – *a priori* or *conventional* and *a posteriori* or *emergent*. In philosophical terms, *a priori* justifications are fashioned through reason alone and rely on correspondence between culturally accepted "facts" and a world reduced and simplified to a few manageable variables.[10] Likewise, an *a priori* design process is one in which the inquiry, range of solutions, and sites for possible projects correspond to the structures and logic found within conventional practice. It is to operate within the normative limits of accepted procedure and *apply* solutions to a place, as is done in many New Urbanist proposals.[11] *A priori* work finds its basis in the known and circumscribed – the expected.

In contrast, *a posteriori* justifications are contingent and rely on local experience.[12] An *a posteriori* design process is one in which the kinds of sites, projects, and order of process are developed in direct response to the context of a *possible* project. Possible solutions are open-ended in scale, type, duration, and purpose and can lie outside of the specific disciplinary domain of architectural or planning practice. *A posteriori* work is exploratory and emerges from the problem itself, resulting at times in the unexpected.

To be more concrete, I will use an example from my own region. In San Antonio, Texas the city's water supply emerges from a single source, the Edwards aquifer. It is a highly porous series of underground karst limestone chambers, which provide little filtration to the rainwater that recharges (or fills) it. The political and geological conditions that have made San Antonio the unique place that it is have also made it vulnerable to ecological disaster. A few years ago, developers who owned land on the "recharge zone" sought to develop the land and proposed a PGA golf resort as its "highest and best use." This particular kind of development, however, threatened the quality of the aquifer due to increased run-off from paving, irrigation requirements to keep courses green, and use of nitrate fertilizers and pesticides. This development decision is an example of *a priori* thinking as it was not made in consultation with the interests present at the site, but was made based only on the external interests of the developers. First came ownership of land that was likely perceived as devoid of intrinsic value. Second was the application of the abstract idea of a golf course to that land. In contrast, an *a posteriori* example would have played out differently. It would demand that we privilege the site first, as an ecological entity and resource for the city. In turn this ethical virtue would suggest that with its fragile ecology, the site could only serve purposes that preserved the integrity of ecological services provided to the community. Perhaps, its development as a city park or nature preserve would be reasonable options. Were society to privilege equally all of the interests present at the site it would suggest that the golf course developer "seek" an appropriate location for an otherwise benign activity – his or her judgment would be influenced by the consequences of action rather than abstract possibilities.

While it is an example from planning, the process relates equally to the work of the architect. It suggests site development and design as an *emergent* practice – one marked by discovery and sensitive response – that can result in unique programming and/or unique spatial forms. Both can be responsive to place and region, but utilize different means. With *a priori*, the primary source for a program was the designer's ideas informed more by architectural discourse, and typically, only later conditioned to local circumstances. With *a posteriori*, the source is the place itself, for which ideas from architectural discourse act as interpreter. Howard Davis provides a partial description of what the *work* of civic environmentalist designers might look like (to which we must add a concern for ecological integrity):

> Some deliberately take on work with a strong community orientation: low-income housing, work for minority communities, active participation in local planning issues, design of community centers... These architects recognize that for the built environment to be in good health, a diverse population must have decent places to live, and issues of land use and downtown planning must be appropriately solved for everyone.
>
> (Davis 1999: 311)

Provisional conclusions – the goods

In sum, I must stress that CE remains more a hope for the future than a present reality. Full implementation will require consideration of ideas I have summarized and a fuller scrutiny of the possibilities latent with this emerging discourse and informed by the successes and failures associated with regional and sustainable discourses. The foundation of CED practice is the merger of civic and ecological concern, which must be based upon a renewed attention to the specificity of places, experientially, performatively, and critically. Examples that might be found in practice, whether they are referred to as regionalist or sustainable, would benefit from a fuller synthesis of their civic or environmental commitments. Those practices whose focus is the civic/social dimension, like architect Michael Pyatok, would benefit from a more thorough embrace of the ecological dimension. And, those focused on the ecological dimension, like architect Edward Mazria, would find balance through greater concern for social justice and cultural meaning. CED is inherently democratic, socially-engaged, ecologically-informed (including care for non-human populations), and aesthetically-skilled. The objects of its production are likewise socially-beneficial, ecologically-sound, and capable of being understood as beautiful by all within a local community. Moreover, it relies on processes, which are in sync with these goals.

In pursuit of CED, I have posited the *a priori* and *a posteriori* as dialectically interrelated concepts – each serving to balance the weakness of the other. A process characterized by *a priori* consideration is weak in that it tends to result in applied or conventional solutions but strong in that it embodies collective cultural knowledge. A process characterized by *a posteriori* consideration is weak in the reliance on local circumstances for solutions (i.e., ecological concerns may be ignored unless requested by the community), but is strong by its responsiveness to those local conditions. Further, *a priori* judgments can guard against naive localism (prejudice, narrow-mindedness, provincialism) by maintaining codes and norms that emerge from outside of the particulars. And, *a posteriori*, by focusing on specific sites as the source of "programs" favors a "closer" or more well-matched renovation.

Certainly any good practice derives its robustness from an appropriate blend of considerations. But I will maintain that at present *a priori* justification, process, and agency remains dominant in contemporary practice limiting the full potential of a civically environmental, regionalist, or sustainable practice. And, further, that for CED abstract principles must always be tempered and conditioned by local opportunities. The benefits of *a posteriori* process is that it can foster connections between citizens and their local environment, while *a priori* holds open the possibility of distance – of decisions liberated from the burden of particular circumstances. *A posteriori* process can encourage ecological citizenship and link locals and professionals in a dialogue.[13] From there the possibility of creating ecologically functional places is realized. But, I must reiterate, we need to first construct or build a discourse that enables shared participation and care. I have shown above how regionalism suggests the promotion of thoughtful reference, participation, and responsiveness in order to, in its own way, achieve places of social and ecological betterment. Further, regionalism should be understood as supportive of a progressive and high-performance sustainable architecture through its secularization of both nature and the vernacular – theorists and practitioners of which view both as sources for pragmatic action rather than subjects of sanctification. It also promotes design that can re-embed us within the reality and diversity of our local places and allows awareness of local climate and the changing of seasons. Taken together, regionalism not only shares assumptions, but also provides a firmer and long-term foundation for sustainable design. It supports the construction of an ecological discourse through the creation of an experiential relation to place. Through local sensitivity tempered with knowledge and skills from the outside, we increase the potential for design to yield the "goods" promised by regionalism, regional planning, sustainability, and CE – places of ecological and economical integrity, community, justice, and beauty.

Questions for further consideration

1   Canizaro is skeptical of popular topics, including the technocratic interpretation of "sustainability" as being synonymous with the concept of "hyper-efficiency," as was promoted by Allen *et al.* in Chapter 6. Canizaro prefers, rather, topics "that tend to stick around," like architectural regionalism, because they tend to resist aesthetic and technological solutions of the moment. If Allen *et al.* are correct, however, in holding that historic patterns are more a part of the problem than the solution, it becomes necessary to ask: are regional traditions any longer relevant?

2   In Chapter 7 Guy argues for a cultural approach to architecture and in Chapter 8 Light argues for a cultural approach to nature. Is Canizaro's proposal for "critical regionalism" a synthesis of these two views or are there substantive differences?

3   Although the regional planning movement sparked by Mumford and others in the US is championed by Canizaro, most historians recognize that it has been successfully implemented only in a few places, like the Pacific Northwest. What reasoning does Canizaro present to suggest that it might succeed elsewhere in the future?

4   Canizaro demonstrates that modern architecture, far from being anti-place, has often inflected its abstract tendencies toward local conditions and embraced the kind of local knowledge advocated by Jamison in Chapter 4 and Winner in Chapter 5. How does Canizaro's civic environmentalism correlate to Jamison's "hybrid imagination?"

5   As have several other contributors to this volume, Canizaro rejects the modern tendency toward abstraction, or *a priori* valuation as in the case reported by Winner in Chapter 5. His proposal for "*a posteriori* design process is one in which the kinds of sites, projects, and order of process are developed in direct response to the context of a *possible* project." In the context of our discussion his proposal makes perfect sense. What consequences, however, would derive from this model of sustainable development for bankers, developers, and cities?

Notes

1   There have been a few, but they have not been a part of the dominant discourse. See Steele (2005); Farmer (1996); Porteus (2002).
2   See examples in Kachadorian (1997) and Wright (1984).
3   This argument is of the central concepts documented in my recent book: Canizaro 2007.
4   The exhibition was neither well attended nor widely praised at the time, but has since achieved a cult status (Clausen 1994).
5   Lisa Germany (1991) documents the increasingly negative reception of emigrating European modernists in the US (Germany 1991: 102–105).
6   Works making this point are many. See Giedion (1954); Golan (1995); Helfrich (1997); McLeod (1985); Passanti (1997).
7   The term bioregionalism was coined by Allen Van Newkirk in 1975. See Aberley (1999).
8   Snyder as cited in Aberley (1999).
9   Light's point is that environmentalists have neglected the city, calling it a "blind spot in environmental thought." See Light and Wellman (2003).
10   For example the equation $2 + 2 = 4$ can be known to be true or justified based on the logic of the equation itself. Nothing outside need be known to justify one's claim that the statement is true.
11   Many New Urbanist proposals rely on a standard ensemble of "responses" to a place.
12   For example, the claim "gravity causes all things to fall to the earth" can only be known by observation of falling things and the supposition that "gravity" is responsible. Rationalization requires experience.
13   CED can fulfill the promise captured by the Bronx River Alliance. See Light (2003b).

Bibliography

Aberley, Doug. (1999) "Interpreting Bioregionalism: a Story from Many Voices," in McGinnis, Michael Vincent (ed.) *Bioregionalism*, London: Routledge.
Berg, Peter and Raymond Dasmann. (1977) "Reinhabiting California," *Ecologist* 7, 10: 399–401.

Bramwell, Anna. (1989) *Ecology in the Twentieth Century: A History of Ecology in the Twentieth Century: A History*, New Haven, CT: Yale University Press.

Canizaro, Vincent B. (ed.) (2007) *Architectural Regionalism: Collected Writings on Place, Identity, Modernity and Tradition*, New York: Princeton Architectural Press.

Clausen, Meredith. (1994) *Pietro Belluschi: Modern American Architect*, Cambridge, MA: MIT Press.

Davis, Howard. (1999) *The Culture of Building*, New York: Oxford University Press.

Dewitt, John. (1993) *Civic Environmentalism: Alternatives to Regulation in States and Communities*, Washington, DC: CQ Press.

Dorman, Robert L. (1993) *Revolt of the Provinces: The Regionalist Movement in America, 1920–1945*, Chapel Hill, NC: University of North Carolina Press.

Dussel, Susanne. (2004) "The 'Own' and the 'Foreign': Cultural Identity in Contemporary Architecture in Mexico (1980–2000)," Architecture and Identity Research Project, Research paper/Baseline Paper, 9.

Farmer, John. (1996) *Green Shift: Towards a Green Sensibility in Architecture*, London: Architectural Press.

Fisk, Pliny. (2000) "Eco-Dynamic Architecture and Planning," Austin, TX: Center for Maximum Potential Building Systems.

Gebhard, David. (1995) "William Wurster and His California Contemporaries," in Treib (ed.) *An Everyday Modernism: The Houses of William Wurster*, Berkeley, CA: University of California Press: 164–183.

Germany, Lisa. (1991) *Harwell Hamilton Harris*, Austin, TX: University of Texas Press.

Giedion, Sigfried. (1954) "The State of Contemporary Architecture: I – The Regional Approach," *Architectural Record* (January): 132–137.

Golan, Romy. (1995) *Modernity and Nostalgia: Art and Politics in France Between the Wars*, New Haven, CT: Yale University Press.

Gropius, Walter. (1962) *The Scope of Total Architecture*, New York: Collier Books.

Helfrich, Kurt. (1997) "Building The Contemporary House: Modernity, Regionalism and The Ideal of Japan in Antonin Raymond's Residential Designs, 1921–1952," Ph.D. dissertation, University of Virginia.

Kachadorian, James. (1997) *The Passive Solar House*, White River Junction, VT: Chelsea Green Publishing Company.

Light, Andrew. (2003a). "Summary," address given at *Designing for Civic Environmentalism Workshop*, University of Texas School of Architecture, Austin, TX (November 14–15, 2003).

—— (2003b) "Urban Ecological Citizenship," *Journal of Social Philosophy* 34, 1: 44–63.

—— and Christopher Wellman. (2003) "Introduction: Urban Environmental Ethics," *Journal of Social Philosophy* 34, 1: 1–2.

LiveScience Staff. (2006) "Hunters and Fishermen Want Action on Global Warming." Online, available at: www.netscape.com/viewstory/2006/06/07/hunters-and-environmentalists-on-the-same-page-re-global-warming (June 15 2007).

McLeod, Mary C. (1985) "Urbanism and Utopia: Le Corbusier from Regional Syndicalism to Vichy," Ph.D. dissertation, Princeton University.

Meem, John Gaw. (1934) "Old Forms for New Buildings," *American Architect* 145: 10–20.

Morrison, Hugh. (1945) "Review of *Built in USA, 1932–1944*, edited by Elizabeth Mock," *The Art Bulletin* 27, 2: 163.

Mumford, Lewis. (1927) "Regionalism and Irregionalism: The Regional Outlook," *The Sociological Review* 19: 279–280.

——. (1928) "The Theory and Practice of Regionalism," *The Sociological Review* 20: 140.

O'Connell, Emmett. (2004) "Hunters are environmentalists." Online, available at: www.westerndemocrat.com/2004/12/hunters_are_env.html (June 15, 2007).

Passanti, Francesco. (1997) "The Vernacular, Modernism, and Le Corbusier," *Journal of the Society of Architectural Historians* 56, 4: 438–451.

Porteus, Colin. (2002) *The New Eco-Architecture: Alternatives from the Modern Movement*, London: Taylor & Francis.

Rorty, Richard. (1982) *Consequences of Pragmatism*, Minneapolis: University of Minnesota Press.

Schindler, Rudolph. (1935) "Space Architecture," *California Arts & Architecture* 47: 19.

Shutkin, William. (2000) *The Land That Could Be: Environmentalism and Democracy in the 21st Century*, Cambridge, MA: MIT Press.

Steele, James. (2005) *Ecological Architecture: A Critical History*, New York, NY: Thames & Hudson.

Sussman, Carl (ed.) (1976) *Planning the Fourth Migration: The Neglected Vision of the Regional Planning Association of America*, Cambridge, MA: MIT Press.

Treib, Marc. (ed.) (1995) *An Everyday Modernism: The Houses of William Wurster*, Berkeley, CA: University of California Press.

United Nations General Assembly. (1987) "Report of the World Commission on Environment and Development: Our Common Future," General Assembly Resolution A/43/427.

Wheeler, Stephen M. (2002) "The New Regionalism: Key Characteristics of an Emerging Movement," *Journal of the American Planning Association* 68, 3: 267–278.

Williams, David R. (1931) "Towards a Southwestern Architecture," *The Southwest Review* 16, 3: 301–313.

World Commission on Environment and Development. (1987) *Our Common Future*, Oxford, UK: Oxford University Press.

Wright, David. (1984) *Natural Solar Architecture: The Passive Solar Primer*, New York: Van Nostrand Reinhold.

Editor's Introduction to Chapter 10

Casual observers rationally assume that those who advocate for the preservation of natural resources and those who advocate for the preservation of cultural resources would be natural allies. In practice, however, this has not always been the case. Seen from the perspective of historic preservation professionals their discipline is alternately one of the parents of modern sustainability, a flip side of the same coin, or a parallel endeavor. In any case, preservation affords sustainable development tools, opportunities, methods and experiences that are, arguably, not just techniques of adding value, but ideas that are central to the ultimate success of sustainable design. After all, the reuse of existing buildings and urban infrastructure provides modern society one of its single greatest sources of energy and resource savings. And historic preservation has had centuries of experience with the political, economic and social debates concerning the conservation and re-use of cultural and natural resources, and the creation and meaning of place. In this context, historic preservationist Jeffrey M. Chusid continues to investigate the theme initiated by Light and Canizaro in the preceding chapters. All three authors are skeptical that sustainability will be found in either transcendent nature or transcendent science.

Despite the potential contributions the fields of historic preservation and sustainable design have yet to form the easy, comfortable and familiar relationship of essential collaborators. This discomfort emerges in part from the alien social origins of the two disciplines, but also from the epistemological grounds upon which choices in each field are made. Where building scientists are comfortable with making decisions on the basis of "context-independent knowledge" (tons of carbon sequestered or btu's burned), building preservationists require that which is "context-dependent" (patterns of brick coursing or forestry practices).[1] Still, an increasing number of exemplary "green building" projects from the past few years that have used old or historic structures suggest the artificial walls between the disciplines are breaking down.

Note

1   In *Making Social Science Matter: Why Social Inquiry Fails and How It Can Succeed Again*, Cambridge, UK: Cambridge University Press, 2001, Bent Flyvbjerg draws upon one of Aristotle's principal virtues, *phronesis*, to make the distinction between "context-dependent" and "context-independent knowledge." Many pragmatist thinkers, Charles Sanders Peirce in particular, have used a slightly different vocabulary to make a similar point.

Chapter 10

Natural Allies

Historic Preservation and Sustainable Design

Jeffrey M. Chusid

Introduction

Sometime around AD 500, the Roman Emperor Theodoric the Great appointed Aloisio "architectus publicum," and charged him with the conservation, repair and reuse of all structures of value to the people of Rome. These included such sites as palaces, baths and aqueducts. It is largely thanks to their efforts 1,500 years ago that we have, for example, the Coliseum and Castel Sant'Angelo as monuments of modern Rome (Jokilehto 2002). But even by that early date, historic preservation in Rome was at least 400 years old. Since the first century it was common for ruins marking important cultural and historical sites to be preserved, for other sites in disrepair to be rehabilitated or restored, and for both to receive bronze plaques explaining the sites' significance. In addition, fines and harsher penalties were imposed for vandalism or the destruction of temples, tombs and other structures of value to the community.

The importance of this historical flashback to a discussion of sustainability in the twenty-first century is that the conservation and stewardship of a community's resources has been public policy and practice for at least two millennia. And while the conservation of natural and cultural resources in the form we understand it today is largely a response to the industrial revolution and the Modern Movement, there has long been an understanding that resources are finite, and their loss robs not only the present but the future as well.

Aloisio's work on the aqueducts of Rome is a case in point. These were part of an efficient and sophisticated water system, much of which remains in use today, that brought water to the city where it was used and re-used, making its way through a system of drinking fountains and potable wells, to water sources for animals, baths, laundries and decorative fountains, until finally exiting into the Tiber. Many of these structures in turn became major features in the social and aesthetic construction of the city, and in Rome's ability to function throughout the ages (Rinne 2007).

In other words, there are a number of different ways we value resources. The aqueducts of Rome were not only a system of efficiently and frugally delivering water – a valued and necessary natural resource – but also a symbol of the power and glory of empire and of what it meant to be Roman. As well, the aqueducts were visible manifestations of the labor of thousands of workers over hundreds of years and of the skill and erudition of Roman engineers, and they embodied countless quantities of natural and man-made materials that were too valuable to lose, too expensive to replace. Thus we find an early example of the social calculus inherent in contemporary sustainable practice: how can we act in a way that will allow us to continue to grow and to thrive, in our existing communities, reducing needless waste and expensive new construction while celebrating and nourishing our culture, our identity, our sense of place.

During the Renaissance, preservation was seen to yield yet another economic benefit, heritage tourism, and Rome, for one, worked to accommodate its visitors with both services and places worth seeing. The Grand Tour soon became a staple of educated European life. By the time of the French Revolution, there had been generations of philosophical and aesthetic debate about the meaning and value of cultural resources, and proper ways to treat them. Their role in establishing national character and identity (or subverting revolutionary aspirations) was vigorously argued in the streets of Paris, and in the nascent nations of nineteenth-century Europe. In Austria, particularly, cultural resources were understood to be arrayed along a continuum of things worth understanding and saving, ranging in scale from the small and intimate work of art or piece of furniture to buildings and districts, all the way to broad swaths of the landscape that combined both nature and culture in illustrating and teaching national history and character and establishing identity and place.

As the industrial revolution completed Western man's taming of nature it both placed the natural landscape at risk and made nature's presence increasingly valuable. Hence environmentalism took its place alongside the battles to save the monuments, and cultural ethos, of national identity. Neither environmentalism nor historic preservation was a monolithic entity, however. Each saw (and continue to see) protagonists from often-contradictory positions arguing for or against particular policies and practices. And both movements undergo variations in theory and implementation from place to place, and from one conservation battle to the next. These arguments can be reduced, perhaps a bit simplistically, to a set of four dichotomous and related debates about meaning, product, action and ethics (Ketter 2004). Amplifying on these reveals that the arguments are also central to almost any discussion on sustainability.

The first argument is about meaning: whether resources are valuable because they are useful and necessary or because they inspire, enrich and help place us in the world. This question applies whether we are discussing a southwestern pueblo, a butterfly, or a stream, and raises associated questions of significance to whom, and who decides. The second argument concerns what we are actually trying to save, object or practice. Do we save the pueblo, or the ability to make adobe, or the ceremonies that make the pueblo come alive? Do we save the field, or the family farm?

The third argument is a question of how we see our mission. Are we (not necessarily politically here) progressive or conservative? Do we believe we are more likely to achieve our goals by acting vigorously in pursuit of a radically different future or by fighting change, by slowing or halting the forces that are destroying communities and resources?

The final argument is ethical, and has to do with what we leave behind after we act. In preservation in the nineteenth century, the debate was termed scrape/anti-scrape. It asked whether we seek to reverse history in search of an idealized or purer or more original condition. In our national parks today, it is the question of whether to remove the last fifty years of human accretion and return the land to a wilder, less hospitable state. The issue is whether we seek to restore, not just conserve.

Of course, each of these arguments take place on its own continuum, with our answers dependent on individual circumstances and likely to fall somewhere in the middle. What is perhaps most illuminating about them as they have played out over the past two thousand years, however, is the extent to which contemporary debates have their antecedents not just once, but time and time again.

If we return to the Roman period, for example, restoring a building was understood to be both economically and culturally desirable. Where new construction was appropriate, design codes helped to ensure its compatibility with the existing context. Today, we save buildings for the same reasons, and use the same tools, along with a few new ones developed over the years. The Romans understood that demolishing good and useful structures was unsustainable. The same thing applies today.

Therefore, preservation ought to be at or near the core of sustainable design. Except that it isn't. LEED, the US Green Building Council's commonly adopted standards for evaluating the sustainability of buildings is defined on the organization's website as follows, "The Leadership in Energy and Environmental Design (LEED) Green Building Rating System™ is the nationally accepted benchmark for the design, construction, and operation of high performance green buildings" (US Green Building Council 2007). There is no mention of the reuse or management of existing buildings in that introductory statement. Although a second set of LEED ratings for existing buildings have been developed in the past few years, it neither acknowledges cultural or historical values nor sufficiently credits the full extent of embodied energy in the built environment. An informal survey of sustainability literature and debate suggests that most of the journals, most of the architecture school design studios, most of the texts focus on new construction, or critique the most egregious examples of existing building, such as exurban subdivisions. Even more telling, almost a decade of US construction activity during which buildings could apply for both LEED ratings and certification under the Secretary of the Interior's Standards for Rehabilitation, has yielded exactly two projects that have met both criteria (Buddenborg 2006).[1] Which is essentially all a preamble to asking why it is that today historic preservation and sustainability are not more widely understood to be inextricably linked.

The concept of sustainability is an attempt to be proactive on a battlefield more commonly marked by reaction; an attempt to create a theory and set of values in what is often a game of numbers; and an attempt to transgress the disciplinary barriers and domains of power typically associated with planning and design. It is sufficiently ambiguous to be a big tent, one that includes a number of (often) competing agendas, methods and outcomes. In other words, sustainability shares a lot with its parents, environmentalism and historic preservation. So it is a bit curious that historic preservation and sustainability have been so divorced.

Sustainability's enemy, sprawl, usually means the abandonment of historic downtowns (buildings, streets, infrastructure) along with the destruction of wild or, more likely, (agri-)cultural landscapes. The cost in energy, materials, water, and money required to build suburban Detroit while urban Detroit disappears is one America can ill afford, on numerous levels. And the cost to a community of losing cultural identity, memory and sense of place, is incalculable. Andrew Light ends his chapter in this book with a visit to a town in Newfoundland facing just such a future.

The US is estimated to generate 136 million tons of construction debris annually, which is 2.8 pounds per person of dead buildings every day (compared with 4.3 pounds of Municipal

Waste) (Franklin Associates 1998). That does not include what it takes to clear new land, build roads, etc. In California, construction debris constitutes as much as 30 percent of the state's landfills.

Lifecycle cost analyses demonstrate that it can take thirty years to make up in energy savings what is expended when a new building is constructed to replace an older one, without even taking into account any of the values a community places in a historic site. And if the old building is demolished in the process, then any savings are likely never to be realized, as the IRS depreciation period for new construction runs out first (National Trust for Historic Preservation 1981 and Jackson 2005).

There is one last compelling reason for those involved in sustainable design to pay attention to the existing built environment. Building renovation is a larger industry than new construction in the US, $126 billion annually vs $100 billion (Davis 2003). The potential impact of greening preservation is even greater when one considers that most renovation projects cost less than new construction, hence there are a lot more renovation projects out there than there is new construction. In fact, one author collects all forms of natural and cultural resource reclamation, restoration and rehabilitation projects into what he terms the Restoration Economy, and forecasts for it the greatest growth of any sector of the US (and world) economy (Cunningham 2002).

So why, then, is sustainability such a stranger to preservation? There are a number of possible reasons. These are worth considering before examining what sustainability can learn from a field that has the conservation of natural and cultural resources as its central focus, and what historic preservation can learn from sustainability.[2]

Let me count the ways

The first problem may be that to many of those engaged in sustainable design, historic preservation is seen as archaic both in focus and technique, fixated on the past. I would argue that historic preservation is more accurately described as planning for and managing socially valued and constructed cultural and (increasingly) natural resources. While these resources derive their meaning from historical and contemporary usage and associations, the purpose of preservation is to move these resources forward into the future, making them useful and meaningful to new generations while protecting their essential character and embedded narratives. Preservation is about new uses for existing resources, new audiences for public history and culture, layering new and old to form rich places that resonate through time, and it is even about lessons from the past or from vernacular traditions on how to live more sustainably.

Unfortunately, many in the design professions find dealing with existing buildings, sites and neighborhoods to be constraining at best. This is our second problem. One might argue that an attitude that privileges individuality and novelty over community and conservation is inherently unsustainable. Nonetheless, many if not most designers have difficulty *not* viewing cutting-edge technology and radical design as markers of success. This is partly about the ego of the designer, partly about modernism's positivist attitude towards progress. Both the design and popular press rewards new, expensive and striking projects with coverage. A low-profile, low-cost, low-energy transformation of an existing building that allows it to function efficiently for another 100 years is rarely considered photogenic or newsworthy. And unless the resource is a monument on the scale of Grand Central Station in New York, the self-effacing architect rarely receives the publicity that makes careers in the design professions.

Parenthetically, this complaint about the distortions of press coverage on architectural values and ethics has arisen before, perhaps most noticeably in the 1960s and 1970s in movements such as advocacy planning, when many of the current ideas that inform both preservation and sustainability were being developed and articulated.

Taste and consumerism introduces our third problem: money. The genius of a successful design trend often lies in the way it becomes economically remunerative to developers. New Urbanism took many of the ideas of such anti-capitalist design theorists as Christopher Alexander (Alexander 1977, 1979), and made them not just palatable but marketable. Historic preservation was most successful when the 1976 Bicentennial made older buildings popular, and when federal tax legislation started handing out tax credits to developers. Today, LEED certification is becoming a marketing device in its own stead. Perhaps even more importantly, there are a large number of entrepreneurial businesses springing up around the topic of sustainability, many with the potential to make significant sums of money, who are collectively pushing a national sustainable agenda. This can be a danger to historic sites. Several window manufacturers, for example, put considerable pressure on governments and developers to replace historic windows in the name of energy savings. However, historic windows are among the most significant character-defining features of a building. And while replacing the historic windows will often gain some benefits (most of which also can be achieved through caulking gaps while leaving windows in place), finding energy savings elsewhere is usually easy to do, and much less destructive and costly.

Our fourth problem is that historic preservation can be difficult, complex, ambiguous and slow. It is usually harder to do than clearing a site, or choosing virgin land, and constructing something new. Preservation requires what both Light and Canizaro advocate in their chapters: immersion in place, engagement with stakeholders, an understanding about historic technologies, deep understanding about a particular site and structure through extensive documentation and research, and respect for others, past, present and future. I would argue this is a large part of why preservation is also inherently sustainable; using Donella Meadow's description of sustainability: a symbiotic relationship with complex systems, not just in nature but in relationship to each other (Meadows 2001).

Fifth, preservation can seem – or be – object-fixated, rejecting engagement with processes and institutions that will lead to a healthier, more economically and socially just world. While some aspects of preservation, such as material conservation, may be concerned with keeping an object intact and useful, the field as a whole is concerned with

> not only ... the built and natural environment, but also the fundamental elements of the social environment. In fact, there is increasing agreement on the definition of heritage as a social ensemble of many different, complex and interdependent manifestations reflecting a culture of humanity. Thus the challenges of the conservation field stem, not only from cultural heritage sites themselves, but from the context in which society embeds them.
>
> (Punekar 2006)

This dialogue between object and social construction is one at the heart of sustainable design as well as historic preservation, and the processes developed by preservationists to negotiate a project tlrough the political structures of public life are relevant to both disciplines. In addition, because historic preservation spends so much time examining how buildings perform over time, studying the effects of use and environment on materials and systems, preservationists are quite attuned to process, to seeing a site as a nexus of social and physical forces caught at a moment in time.

The sixth issue is that in recent years historic preservation has become a prime scapegoat in the political, economic and cultural battles associated with gentrification. In 2003 Austin, Texas came close to scrapping its preservation ordinance over this issue, although subsequent studies demonstrated that preservation activity was at best a minor player in the city's unaffordable housing crisis. Still, Austin did drop its Smart Growth program because of accusations of environmental racism. These controversies have made preservation suspect as a mechanism for social equity, which is a stated goal for sustainability. Community conservation remains a difficult issue for preservation, but quick reference to a site such as Policylink.org (the Brookings Institution Gentrification Toolkit) demonstrates that there are many things that need to be done in a coordinated manner to minimize the negative impacts of gentrification. Just as many things came together to create gentrification in the first place, not just the desire to re-use old buildings.

Finally, the poor communication between historic preservation and sustainability derives in large part from their (apparently) disparate forms of discourse. Each seems to operate within its own worldview, knowledge base, skill set and regulatory environment; and these can often be contradictory when combined, as the example of the historic windows demonstrated. The practitioners of each have seldom engaged each other, sharing neither a common language nor places to meet and interact.

This plays out in the processes for certifying projects. Preservation projects are described and evaluated qualitatively, and in terms of cultural values and meanings. Governments use the *Secretary of the Interior's Standards*, a single page of directives, as guidance during the extensive process of site visits, reviews and discussions required to approve or certify preservation work. Sustainability projects are described and evaluated quantitatively, in terms of numerical performance objectives. The LEED standards contain as many as 100 pages, while certification, which is done by an NGO, is relatively straightforward and done completely off site (Buddenbrooks 2006). Perhaps most importantly, the public is deeply involved in the process of identifying, designating and protecting cultural and natural resources; while declaring a project "sustainable" is much more a private decision.

As is the case with preservation and sustainability, preservation and environmentalism were often at odds before realizing their essential common history and values. The first major public historic preservation effort in America, Mt. Vernon, was followed not much more than a decade later, by Yellowstone National Park. In 1891, when Massachusetts established the first state-wide preservation organization, The Trustees of Reservations, its mandate included both wild landscapes and cultural landscapes with historic buildings. The 1966 National Historic Preservation Act was embedded squarely in the middle of a slew of environmental legislation coming out of the Johnson administration and Congress.[3]

In 1963, Stewart L. Udall cited two events that summarized "the plight of modern man." The first was the destruction of Robert Frost's farm for an automobile junkyard, and the second was the air pollution in London that made the poet TS Eliot gravely ill. He wrote that historic preservation and environmental conservation were inextricably entwined, and needed to collaborate in the face of a "society of consumption" (Udall 1963).

The concept of the cultural landscape, which has arisen over the past ten to fifteen years, has allowed historic preservation and environmentalists to work together productively in common purpose, and to place their obvious connections within an intellectual and action-oriented framework. Today, both groups take a more holistic approach to resources, contexts, and uses. Both groups not only look to history but to the future. And both groups understand that "we are losing biological diversity and cultural diversity.... Both our natural and cultural heritage is under siege" (McMahon 1992).

HP and sustainability: the first date

Interestingly, historic preservation and sustainability also have a past. Back in the 1970s, following on the heels of the Arab Oil Embargo, Sim Van der Ryn, a faculty member at the University of California at Berkeley who went on to become the state architect for California under Jerry Brown, focused on adaptive re-use as an energy-efficient practice. He led a campaign to re-use Hamilton Field (a combined military installation in Marin County) as a new town, with affordable housing.[4] Those of us who were his students at the time spent endless hours trying to quantify the built environment, by identifying the embodied energy in all aspects of construction and demolition. How many barrels of oil to build a road? How many to make the truck driving down the road? The goal was to determine how much energy had already been spent building the base, and how much would be saved by reusing the facility instead of building more sprawl? Today, this is still a valid question, and one often ignored to the detriment of the existing built fabric of the United States and at great cost in terms of energy consumption.

Several theoretical and aesthetic streams came together at that time at Berkeley, which helped to form the intellectual basis for sustainability today.[5] The various disciplines of architecture, landscape architect, planning and design had recently been assembled into a School of Environmental Design by its Dean William Wurster, and many of the faculty were involved in groups such as Telesis, a west-coast equivalent of Clarence Stein's Regional Planning Association of America. Besides energy-conscious design as exemplified by Van der Ryn and others, there was active exploration in Appropriate Technology, Vernacular and Traditional Architecture, and Regional Modernism. Even architectural history was being recast as a social and cultural phenomenon rather than a catalogue of styles. Elsewhere in the Bay Area, organic farming and regional cuisine, personal computing and the Whole Earth Catalogue were rising from the counter-culture to shape our future. While historic preservation was only taught at a few East-coast schools at that time, pioneering preservation projects, such as the Cannery and Ghirardelli Square, were taking place in San Francisco, with UC faculty as architects.

The decade ended with the 1978 publication from the National Trust for Historic Preservation entitled Conserving Energy in Historic Buildings (McMahon 1992; Booz 1979), a major

1979 study by The Advisory Council on Historic Preservation of the embodied energy in buildings, and 1980s Preservation Week (another National Trust Program) dedicated to "Preservation: Reusing America's Energy."

Commonalities and lessons

> Both [sustainability and historic preservation] are concerned about resources and their stewardship. Both are concerned with the built environment and its relationship to the natural one.
>
> (Jackson 2005)

Preservation and sustainability share numerous tools, methods and values, despite the issues enumerated earlier. And some of the differences between the fields are not all bad; they can each provide a useful critique of the other or suggest ways that either might change productively. One of these differences is the issue of scale. Sustainability often operates at the building level and/or at the regional level. Preservation operates in those two realms, but also at the neighborhood level, which may be the most useful for discussions that affect social and cultural values. It is the level at which community participation is logically most possible and, traditionally, most effective.

Now let us turn to a few of the reasons why preservation is heuristic for sustainable design. Historic buildings often used indigenous, renewable materials and responded to their local climate and culture. "Sustainable" technologies adopted as a matter of course included operable windows for natural ventilation and daylight, high ceilings, rainwater cisterns, compact building form, siting for light and air, shading with shutters and awnings, vestibules and porticoes, reflective or absorptive roofing, and native plantings. These make many historic buildings energy efficient (Sedovic 2006). Interestingly, rehabilitating an older building continue to reap some of these same benefits. Local labor, materials, skills and values are used and supported by a preservation project. And preservation returns more money and more jobs to the local community than does virtually any other economic activity, including new construction (Rypkema 2005).

In addition to the resources themselves, preservation practice has some approaches that can be of value in the search for sustainability. "The evaluation tools for sustainable design involve many of the same variables that are used to evaluate historic buildings: material performance characteristics, lifecycle studies, and energy efficiency among them." Perhaps more important are "the skills of preservationists in understanding the value and durability of the built environment and their ability to extend a building's future" (Jackson 2006). This is especially true because preservationists have to think beyond the current owner or occupant, and so look to how change can be either reversible or valuable to future generations.

Preservation utilizes a "less is more" approach, as alluded to previously. This is founded in the idea that the more work done to a historic site, the more real and potential loss of integrity or authenticity. Hence preservation favors repair over replacement, and accepts the patina of age. The result of this attitude when applied to sustainable rehabs is what Mike Jackson calls "stealth green" (Jackson 2005). Again, an argument could be made that modest, incremental and largely invisible modifications to a historic site is good sustainable practice as well as good preservation practice.

Finally, the area in which historic preservation may be of most value to sustainability is the question of values: values held by individuals, by neighborhoods and communities, by societies. Sharon Park, of the National Park Service, writes, "...the connection of existing buildings to their communities can bring stability, a sense of pride of place, a scale of livability and interesting craftsmanship; of materials and details often missing in new construction. Historic Buildings, often very durably constructed, have stood the test of time.... What the 'green' movement needs is to get away from the catalog of construction parts that can be used or reused in new construction and consider both the amortized investment found inherent in older buildings and the contributions these buildings make to the cultural, social and historic environments they have helped to shape" (Park 2006). This logic is supported by Light and Canizaro who understand the "usefulness" of things not only in terms of btu's conserved, but in terms of the regenerative bonds created between social and natural systems.

Two consequences of a failure to understand and appreciate this reality are outlined by Zetter and Watson:

> On the one hand, the destruction of the patrimony of indigenously designed and developed urban places and spaces is accelerating: built environments which are culturally rooted, locally produced and technologically adapted in time and space are being rapidly eroded. Their potential responsiveness to the needs of a changing social and functional world is largely ignored. Instead, unique built environments are being removed from their context and replaced by global forms and designs which are often poorly adapted to local needs and conditions.... On the other hand, these pressures are commodifying the place-identity of historic urban spaces and places. At once detaching them from their continuity with locality, space and time, whilst at the same time representing them as uniquely preserved "authentic" artifacts for global cultural consumption. These outcomes question the sustainability of new patterns and processes of urban design and the production of urban space. They question how place identity is created, recreated and sustained.
>
> (Zetter and Watson 2006)

In other words, without comprehending how and why places have been and continue to be created by a community over time, how can we create new places that will survive, that will be themselves "sustainable"? Zetter and Watson continue,

> Vernacular is an adaptive process, not just a style or building type. Communities have historically adapted and changed within their own terms and traditions, even when confronted by outside forces or influences. This is the true meaning of vernacular design. Hence, the sustainable question is "How to recognize design and development of cities defined in terms of their cultural identity, indigenous built resources, the assembly of buildings and their constituents of places, spaces and neighborhoods."
>
> (Zetter and Watson 2006)

Again from Zetter and Watson: "Contrasting community, professional, political and user interests create a nexus, located in time and space, in which sustainable urban design cannot be a pre-defined goal or objective physical end state. Rather, it is an open-ended process of reconciling competing values and priorities in the building, rebuilding and adaptation of livable cities.... Proactive civil society and structures of governance which enable polarities to be debated, articulated, become highly instrumental elements for establishing the constructive co-existence of competing 'urban designs.'... [This approach gives] capacity to local communities to articulate their socio-political needs in sustainable ways."

This may be the greatest critique that preservation, and the design professions, give sustainability. Communities contain numerous competing values, many equally valid and worthwhile, and a transparent process for achieving consensus may challenge a rigid or formulaic quantitative system that is based in a singular worldview. Is a new building with minimal operating expenses really better than the historic site it replaced at great cost? Or worth the open space lost? And who decides?

A few projects

As mentioned earlier in this chapter, LEED rates the "greenness" of building projects. It assigns points to different performance categories, and then ranks the overall project on what percentage was earned of the total points possible. The current structure of categories and points undervalues the embodied energy in existing construction by failing to give enough points for saving building fabric. It also gives no points for saving structures with cultural or social value. The Secretary of the Interior's Standards, as interpreted by some state and local officials, often penalize the kinds of alterations advocated by current green building practice. Despite this, over the last few years a number of important organizations operating in the area of sustainability and resource protection have understood the deep connection between preservation and sustainability, and made the rehabilitation of a historic site central to the search for a new headquarters. These include the Natural Resources Defense Council, The Audubon Society (both in New York City), The School of Natural Resources and Environment at the University of Michigan, Eco-Trust (Portland), and the Thoreau Center for Sustainability in San Francisco.

Two brief examples help to demonstrate the natural relationship between preservation and sustainability, and how well they work together when the agendas and interests of each are respected and supported. The aptly named Thoreau Center for Sustainability is the home to more

Figure 10.1
The Thoreau Center for Sustainability, the former Letterman Hospital at the Presidio, San Francisco. Letterman General Hospital, Presidio, San Francisco in 1920. Today it is the Thoreau Center, a home for non-profit organizations. J. D. Givens, photographer. Library of Congress, Prints and Photographs Division.

than fifty organizations working for "social justice, community education and development, public health and environmental stewardship" in the San Francisco Bay Area. These groups occupy twelve buildings that used to be portions of the Letterman Hospital at the Presidio in San Francisco. A National Historic Landmark, the Presidio is also part of the Golden Gate National Recreation Area, a park with a mandate as a "global center dedicated to addressing the world's most critical environmental, cultural, and social challenges." The reuse of the historic hospital helps fulfill the Presidio vision: "Combining preservation of the park's historic resources with creation of a global center for a sustainable future."

The Presidio was founded by the Spanish in 1776, and served as a military base for Spanish, Mexican and US forces until 1994. Letterman was at one time the largest Army hospital in the United States, and had a number of substantial attractive buildings in its campus. Even today, exhibits on the Presidio and the Hospital can be found at the Thoreau Center and on its website.

The rehabilitation of the facility was done using sustainably harvested wood, recycled building materials, nontoxic paints and energy-efficient designs that maximized sunlight and natural ventilation (Thoreau 2007). Seventy-three percent of the 700 tons of construction debris produced by the project was recycled. Rehabilitation costs for 73,000 square feet of office space came to $5,600,000 (National Trust for Historic Preservation 1996). Even for the time, that was cheap; less than half what new construction would have cost for a lower quality of building. But besides the cost savings during the project, and in its operations today, the project also received awards from the National Trust for Historic Preservation, the AIA California Chapter

Figure 10.2
West Medical Building *c.*1900. Renamed the Samuel T. Dana Building, the structure was extensively renovated into "the greenest building in Michigan" as the new home for the School of Natural Resources at the University of Michigan. Bentley Online Image Bank, Bentley Historical Library, University of Michigan.

and the California Preservation Foundation for its sympathetic treatment of the character and integrity of the site, and for the way in which new and old were celebrated and made mutually supportive.

The structure known today as the Samuel T. Dana Building at the University of Michigan, Ann Arbor, was built in 1903 as the medical school. By the late 1990s, it was clearly in need of rehabilitation, partially for age-related issues, and partially because it was not working adequately for its current occupants, the School of Natural Resources and Environment (McInnes and Tyler 2005). And yet, the building's central location, elegant Beaux-Arts design, and historical importance argued strongly against relocating the School – as did concerns over the loss of open space a new building would require. Over a five-year period, between 1998 and 2003, the building underwent a comprehensive rehabilitation including new structural elements, new mechanical systems, a new roof, etc. The project was designed as a laboratory for learning about sustainability, and how to "modernize" a historic structure so that it operated more efficiently. The result received a LEED Gold certification. Because the building was relatively simple, with a functional, spare interior, there were significant savings achieved by keeping 100 percent of the shell, while altering 50 percent of its interior structural floors and load-bearing walls. Subcontractors on the project were trained to divert demolition debris, wherever possible, to recycling or to salvage and reuse. Low VOC paints and adhesives, all-wool carpeting, an active solar system on a new roof, and new lighting were among other measures utilized in the project. High ceilings were retained and used in the design of the building's performance. A major technical innovation was the use of radiant cooling. Others included waterless urinals, touchless faucets, (some) composting toilets, and the use of rapidly renewable materials (linoleum, bamboo, etc.). The result was a 30 percent reduction in annual energy costs even while providing more usable space, and more sophisticated facilities.

Both the Dana and Thoreau projects are models of sustainable design. Both maintain the historic exterior essentially intact, thus also preserving their neighborhoods, while making considerable change to the interior. Both were building types that accommodated those modifications without suffering a major loss of historic character because they had utilitarian spaces and materials that could be manipulated while keeping to the spirit of the original design and use. However, different projects will require balancing at a different place between the polarities of modernization and sustainability on the one hand and historic character and integrity on the other.

What's next?

There is no question that preservation needs to do a better job addressing lifecycle costs, energy efficiency and the use of safe and renewable materials. Preservation also has some way to go in accepting sustainability as a social goal that justifies change in the way that disabled access, seismic upgrading and affordable housing do. Recent conferences, sustainability task forces of national preservation organizations, and related publications indicate both an awareness and eagerness for preservationists to play their part in making a better world. I am tempted to venture that those practicing in historic preservation are spending more time thinking about issues of sustainability in the operation and rehabilitation of historic sites and neighborhoods than those in sustainability are spending understanding and responding appropriately to the historical and cultural properties of building and place, or to the social construction of significance and value. However, both Light and Canizaro show that there is indeed a debate on these topics among those with an interest in sustainability, with Civic Engagement and increased attention to narratives and other social constructions of place and meaning among the strategies proposed to create "intentional communities dedicated to the places around us."

Preservation, environmentalism and regionalism turn out to be three related fields of inquiry, each with similar histories of repeated redefinition and re-conceptualization. While regionalism is a powerful way of understanding place, community and history, the other two are also professional fields with legislation, government agencies, myriad special interests, and design practitioners. All three can fall heir to the danger of advancing simulacra in the name of authenticity, to borrow from Baudrillard. Light's history of environmentalism gives a good example of this when he describes national park advocates in the 1960s as calling for the restoration of a wilderness condition that was already largely gone, if it ever actually existed. Preservation skirts the precipice of artificiality constantly. And regionalism can easily become nativistic and exclusionary. Nonetheless, the three taken together serve as powerful models for sustainability as a field that strives to be broadly inclusive, interested in the fullness of human existence, in the natural and cultural resources around us, and in the complex histories that make place. Preservation, regionalism and environmentalism also bring a level of transparency and a history of public engagement that needs to be central to sustainability as well.

The concept of the cultural landscape united the skills and concerns of preservationists and environmentalists. We need to develop and support a similar unifying vision of sustainable culture, in which the values and meanings (and dollars) invested by a community in its tangible and intangible resources and identity are also passed along to future generations, enhanced and revitalized.

Questions for further consideration

1   In Chapter 6 Allen *et al.* argued that there is a natural tension between proposals to build for long-term durability and/or for short-term flexibility. Once buildings have endured long periods of use, however, most agree that they should be preserved. A few, however, argue that in times of dramatic change, like our own, even these icons of the past must adapt to emerging conditions. Why should we not continue to modify good and usable structures?

2   In Chapters 8 and 9 both Light and Canizaro argue for the secularization of nature by making it part of everyday life. Why should we not treat iconic buildings and landscapes in the same way?

3   Standards, codes, and rating systems have been developed by both preservationists and sustainability advocates to assess not only buildings, but also the professionals who design and maintain them. When these standards come into conflict, how should we determine which one is "right"?

4   Preservationists tend to be skeptical of new technologies because they have not been tested over time. Sustainability advocates, however, tend to be optimistic about new

technologies because they open new possibilities for solving problems. Behind these differing attitudes toward technology lie differences in education, language, and values. Is this conflict somehow productive, or should we strive to construct a hybrid discipline of "sustainable preservation"?

5   Advocates of sustainable development, such as Oden in Chapter 2, argue that social equity must be a core element in determining the value of any design. On the other hand, the advocates of historic preservation are frequently accused of promoting gentrification and inequitable urban conditions. How might the preservation of buildings and other cultural resources be made more equitable?

Notes

1   Since that study, however, and even since the first draft of this chapter, there has been a substantial increase in preservation projects seeking LEED certification, although many conflicts remain between US GBS and the preservation community.

2   To be fair, it should be noted that preservation is a broad, diverse field; playing out differently regionally and across different audiences. This discussion presupposes a normative model of historic preservation. One could easily, and beneficially, take Light's critical approach to environmentalism and apply it here, exploring a series of issues such as equity concerns and NIMBYism, from which both fields suffer.

3   See Light's chapter for a fuller discussion of this period of legislation, and the underlying attitudes and intentions of environmentalists during the period.

4   While the base was decommissioned in 1974, it wasn't closed and put up for sale until 1988. An Environmental Impact Report for redevelopment of Hamilton Field was finally issued in 1999; the site is still a work in progress.

5   Canizaro does a nice job of describing these in his chapter, although I add to his list the interests in traditional and appropriate architecture of people such as Bernard Rudofsky (allied to Berkeley through his friend Constantino Nivola) and Jesse Reichek.

Bibliography

Alexander, C. (1977) *A Pattern Language*, New York: Oxford University Press.

—— (1979) *The Timeless Way of Building*, New York: Oxford University Press.

Booz, A. and Hamilton, Inc. (1979) *Assessing the Energy Conservation Benefits of Historic Preservation: Methods and Examples*, Washington, DC: The Advisory Council on Historic Preservation.

Buddenborg, J. L. (2006) *Changing Mindsets: Sustainable Design in Historic Preservation*, Unpublished Masters Thesis, Cornell University.

Cunningham, S. (2002) *The Restoration Economy: The Greatest New Growth Frontier*, San Francisco, CA: Berrett-Koehler.

Davis, A. (2003) "Recycling Construction Debris," *Architecture Week*, March: E2.1.26 March 2003. Online, available at: www.architectureweek.com/2003/0326/environment_2–1.html (July 2007).

Franklin Associates (1998) *Characterization Of Building-Related Construction And Demolition Debris In The United States*, Prepared for The US Environmental Protection Agency Municipal and Industrial Solid Waste Division Office of Solid Waste. Report No. EPA530-R-98-010. Online, available at: www.epa.gov/epaoswer/hazwaste/sqg/c&d-rpt.pdf (July 2007).

Jackson, M. (2005) "Introduction," *APT Bulletin (Special Issue on Sustainability and Preservation)* 36, 4.

—— (2006) Cited in "A Natural Connection – Sustainable Design and Historic Preservation," *COTENotes Newsletter of the Committee on the Environment, American Institute of Architects*, Summer 2006. Online, available at: www.aia.org/nwsltr_cote.cfm?pagename=cote%5Fa%5F200608%5Fpreservation (July 2007).

Jokilehto, J. (2002) *A History of Architectural Conservation*, Oxford: Butterworth-Heinemann.

Ketter, P. (2004) "The Parallel Histories of Cultural and Natural Resource Preservation," *Platform*, Winter 2003–2004: 4–5.

McInnes, M. and Tyler, I. R. (2005) "The Greening of the Samuel T. Dana Building: A Classroom and Laboratory for Sustainable Design," *APT Bulletin* 36, 4.

McMahon, E. T. and Watson, A. E. (1992) *In Search of Collaboration: Historic Preservation and the Environmental Movement*, Information Series No. 71, Washington, DC: National Trust for Historic Preservation.

Meadows, D. (2001) "Dancing with Systems," *Whole Earth*, Winter 2001.

Morton III, W. B. *et al.* US Department of the Interior (1992) *The Secretary of the Interior's Standards for Rehabilitation and Illustrated Guidelines for Rehabilitation Historic Buildings*, Washington, DC: US Government Printing Office.

National Trust for Historic Preservation (1981) *New Energy from Old Buildings*, Washington, DC: The Preservation Press.

—— (1996) *New Life for White Elephants: Adapting Historic Buildings for New Uses*, Washington, DC: The Preservation Press.

Park, S. C. (2006) Cited in "A Natural Connection – Sustainable Design and Historic Preservation," *COTENotes Newsletter of the Committee on the Environment, American Institute of Architects*, Summer 2006. Online, available at: www.aia.org/nwsltr_cote.cfm?pagename=cote%5Fa%5F200608%5Fpreservation (July 2007).

Punekar, A. (2006) "Value-led Heritage and Sustainable Development: The Case of Bijapur, India," *Designing Sustainable Cities in the Developing World*, Aldershot: Ashcroft.

Rinne, K. (2009) *Aquae Urbis Romae. The Waters of Rome*. Online, available at: www.iath.virginia.edu/rome/ (July 2007).

Rypkema, D. (2005) *The Economics of Historic Preservation: A Community Leader's Guide*, Washington, DC: National Trust for Historic Preservation.

Sedovic, W. (2006) Cited in "A Natural Connection – Sustainable Design and Historic Preservation," *COTENotes Newsletter of the Committee on the Environment, American Institute of Architects*, Summer 2006. Online, available at: www.aia.org/nwsltr_cote.cfm?pagename=cote%5Fa%5F200608%5Fpreservation (July 2007).

Smith, B. (1978) *Preservation Brief No. 3: Conserving Energy in Historic Buildings*, Washington, DC: US Government Printing Office.

Teutonico, J. M. and Matero, F. (2003) *Managing Change: Sustainable Approaches to the Conservation of the Built Environment*, Los Angeles, CA: The Getty Conservation Institute.

Thoreau Center for Sustainability. Online, available at: www.thoreau.org (July 2007).

Udall, S. L. (1963) *The Quiet Crisis*, New York: Holt, Rinehart and Winston.

US Green Building Council (2004) *Green Building Rating System for Existing Buildings: Upgrades, Operations and Maintenance (LEED-EB) version 2*, Washington, DC: US Green Building Council.

—— (2007) "Leadership in Energy and Environmental Design." Online, available at: www.usgbc.org/DisplayPage.aspx?CategoryID=19 (July 2007).

Von Hagen, B., Kellogg, E. and Frerichs, E. (eds.) (2003) *Rebuilt Green: The Natural Capital Center and the Transformative Power of Building*, Portland, OR: Ecotrust.

Watson, G. B. and Zetter, R. (eds.) (2006) *Designing Sustainable Cities in the Developing World*, Aldershot: Ashcroft.

Sustainability and Cities

Editor's Introduction to Chapter 11

Planning is commonly practiced as the worldly application of science. We imagine that we can apply our assessments of success or failure in place "A" and time "Y" to place "B" and time "Z." But the environmental degradation that has attended so many well-intended actions suggests we need a new or "sustainable" mode of planning the landscapes we inhabit. Planning for sustainability would, then, link action less to the amalgamated past than to its particular environmental and social consequences in the future.

One particular condition for planning in the United States is that, in contrast to European nations, we have a legal tradition of weak rather than strong planning by the state. In the hope of improving the success rate of our efforts to plan our cities at all, Frederick Steiner constructs in this essay a method for planning cities and landscapes that embraces rather than resists that weak tradition. In this way, Steiner reflects John Dewey's famous argument – that it is foolish to make City Plans, yet we should always be planning cities. Their common interest emphasizes the public learning that occurs in the process of planning, not the artifacts that result from it. In the pragmatist tradition, city planners are not technical experts hired to make informed decisions on behalf of citizens, but educators who facilitate methods of adaptive design through which informed decisions are made by citizens.

Steiner sets out his proposal for a fresh approach that might be labeled *applied human ecology*, or simply *ecological planning* – a procedure for studying the biophysical and sociocultural systems of a place to reveal where specific land uses may be best practiced. Following the basic procedures proposed by Ian McHarg in the 1970s and 1980s, Steiner attempts to rebalance the interests of ecological and social systems through a flexible eleven-step process that may occur simultaneously at many scales. Crucial to success of the process is the constant involvement of citizens in setting goals, specifying designs, and administering plans. The result is an ever-changing working plan more analogous to a jazz composition: not a fixed score, but a palette that invites improvization.

Chapter 11
Planning for Sustainability

Frederick Steiner

Planning has been defined as the use of scientific, technical, and other organized knowledge to provide options for decision-making as well as a process for considering and reaching consensus on a range of choices. As John Friedmann (1973) has succinctly put it, planning links knowledge to action. Such a view of planning flows directly from pragmatism. As John Dewey suggested, the public possesses the capacity to learn from the planning process. There is a difference between project planning and comprehensive planning. *Project planning* involves designing a specific object such as a dam, highway, harbor, or an individual building or group of buildings. *Comprehensive planning* involves a broad range of choices relating to all the functions of an area. Resolution of conflicts among often competing social, economic, and environmental interests, frequently through compromises, is the inherent purpose of comprehensive planning.

The use of land has been a principal focus of planning. *Land use* is a self-defining term. One can debate whether a harbor involves land use or water use, but "land" generally refers to all parts of the surface of the earth, wet and dry. The same area of that surface may be used for a variety of human activities. A harbor, for instance, may have commercial, industrial, and recreational purposes. A farm field may be used for speculation and recreation as well as for agriculture. All human activity is in one way or another connected with land.

Landscape is related to land use. A landscape is the composite features of one part of the earth's surface that distinguish it from another. It is, then, a combination of elements – fields, buildings, hills, forests, deserts, water bodies, and settlements. The landscape encompasses the uses of land – housing, transportation, agriculture, recreation, and natural areas – and is a composite of those uses. A landscape is more than a picturesque view; it is the sum of the parts that can be seen, the layers and intersections of time and culture that comprise a place – a natural *and* cultural palimpsest.

The English word *ecology* is derived from the Greek word for house, *oikos*. The expanded definition is the study of the reciprocal relationships of all organisms to each other and to their biotic and physical environments (Ricklefs 1973). Obviously, humans are organisms and thus are engaged in ecological relationships.

The use of ecological information for planning has been a national policy since late 1969, when the US Congress, through the National Environmental Policy Act (NEPA), required all agencies of the federal government to "initiate and utilize ecological information in the planning and development of resource oriented projects." The act, signed into law by President Richard Nixon on January 1, 1970, is a relatively recent development in American planning. In spite of NEPA and other laws, ecological information has not yet been adequately integrated into the planning process. Although much more work will still be necessary to realize an ecological approach to planning, NEPA represents an important step. To begin to understand its importance, it is useful to quickly review the status of American planning.

The traditional framework of planning in the United States

The function of land-use planning in the United States has been the subject of much debate. There are diverse opinions about the purpose of planning; that is, whether it is to achieve a specific physical project, or comprehensive social, economic, or environmental goals. The traditional role of planning in the United States is responsible for many of these divisions. In England, for instance, planning is undertaken as a result of strong statutes. Statutory planning gives English planners considerable authority in the decision-making process. In contrast, American planners generally have more limited statutory power than in England and other European nations.

There are several reasons for the differences between European and American planning. First, land is recognized as a scarce commodity in Europe and in many other parts of the world. In land-hungry Europe over the last century, public officials have been granted increasing planning powers over use of land (and other resources) through the governing process. In Europe, there is much concern about the quality of the environment, both in the older democracies of the European Union and the emerging democracies of Central and Eastern Europe. This concern has resulted in complex systems of planning that address a broad range of issues, including housing, recreation, aesthetics, open space, and transportation.

Another difference emerges from the origins of the United States. Thomas Jefferson and the other founding fathers were influenced strongly by John Locke, who viewed the chief end of establishing a government as the preservation of property. Locke, in his *Two Treatises of Government*, defined property as "lives, liberties, and estates" (Laslett 1988). Elsewhere, Locke wrote of the "pursuit of happiness." It was Jefferson who combined Locke's terms, "life, liberty, and the pursuit of happiness." But it has been the view of property as possession, rather than Locke's predominant version – life, liberty, and estate – that has prevailed. The constitution of the Commonwealth of Pennsylvania states in Article 1, Section 1, that "all ... men have certain inherent and indefensible rights, among which are those of enjoying and defending life and liberty, of acquiring, possessing and protecting property." And the Fifth Amendment of the US Constitution contains this clause: "No person shall ... be deprived of life, liberty, or property, without due process of law; nor shall private property be taken for public use without just compensation." To those in the new republic who had fought against the landed elite of the mother country, property rights were seen as a fundamental freedom.

The Bill of Rights institutionalized the founding fathers' concern about private property rights. Their "Bill of Rights included no fewer than four separate provisions aimed specifically at protecting private interests in property," observes John Humbach (1989: 337). However,

Humbach also notes that "private property exists to serve the public good" (1989: 345). The influential British utilitarian philosopher Jeremy Bentham declared that "before laws were made, there was no property; take away laws and property ceases" (1864: 113). As a result, according to Humbach (and other legal scholars), "Property rights are a creation of laws, and the law of property must, like all other law, serve a public purpose" (1989: 345).

The initial public purpose for the new nation was the settlement, or the resettlement by mostly European immigrants, of the American subcontinent (Opie 1998). However, when Jefferson (who had written the Declaration of Independence) and the others who had authored the Constitution rode to Philadelphia on horseback or in carriages from their Virginia estates, their Pennsylvania farms, or their New England towns, they traveled through a seemingly endless expanse of woodlands, rich farmlands, and rolling pastures graced by fresh, clear creeks and rivers, abundant game, and pristine coastlines. In Philadelphia, they were concerned foremost with protecting human rights and freedoms. Even the most foresighted of the framers of the Constitution could not have envisioned the environmental and social crises that subsequently accompanied the industrialization and urbanization of America or the rest of the planet.

The US Constitution, however, does give the states and their political subdivisions the power of regulation. Police powers, which provide the basis for state and local regulation, were derived by the states from the Tenth Amendment, which reads: "The powers not delegated to the United States by the Constitution, nor prohibited by it to the States, are reserved to the States respectively, or to the people."

The states, in the use of police powers, must consider the Fifth Amendment because the US Supreme Court has held that the "taking clause" is embodied in the due process clause of the Fourteenth Amendment and hence applies to the states. In addition, state constitutions contain taking clauses, some with rather interesting twists. For instance, Article 1, Section 16 (the Ninth Amendment) of the Washington State Constitution states: "No private property shall be taken or *damaged* for public or *private use* without just compensation having first been made" [emphasis added]. A person's private use of property cannot damage the property of another person in Washington State.

Given this constitutional backdrop, the federal and several state legislatures have slowly but steadily increased statutory authority for planning. In addition, the courts have consistently upheld land-use regulations that do not go "too far" and thus constitute a taking. In addition, courts have supported some restrictions on the use of environmentally sensitive areas, such as wetlands, floodplains, and the habitats of endangered species. However, planning remains a fragmented effort in the United States, undertaken primarily by powerful, vested business interests and sometimes by consent. Planning by consent, which depends largely on an individual's persuasive power, has caused several adaptations on the part of American planners. These adaptations can be broken down into two broad categories: *administrative* and *adversary*.

Administrative planners are realists who respond directly to governmental programs either as bureaucrats in a city or regional planning agency or as consultants. Successful administrative planners build political power in the city or metropolitan region where they work. They administer programs for voluntary community organizations and health, education, and welfare associations designed to support the political–economic structure of the nation-state. They may also administer transportation or utility programs deemed necessary by the same structure. By building political power, administrative planners serve the power structure of the city or region. The result is that often the underpowered groups in an area suffer. Poor people suffer the most, bearing the brunt of the social costs, when planners and others administer the programs of the status quo.

Adversary planners are idealists and respond to issues, such as those resulting from social or environmental concerns, often as advocates for a certain position. They usually work outside the power structure, forming new coalitions among the previously unorganized in order to mobilize support for their cause. Often advocacy planners work for veto groups – ad hoc organizations opposed to a controversial project or proposal such as a highway, a high-density housing complex, a factory, or a landfill. Advocacy planners also work for nongovernmental organizations (NGOs), neighborhood planning committees, and community associations.

Equity, the equal rights of all people, has a deep-seated heritage in American history, from the Declaration of Independence, the Constitution, and the Bill of Rights through the Thirteenth and Nineteenth Amendments and to the labor, civil rights, and women's movements. Human rights have been the important issue for one group of advocacy; planners called by various terms, including *community organizers*, *adversary planners*, and *change agents*. In *Reveille for Radicals*, Saul Alinsky (1946) best articulated the philosophy for the latest crest of this movement, which began to ebb when Richard Nixon cut off funding for a variety of programs created during the 1960s. Many of the social programs created during the 1960s were concerned with making basic changes in the urban power structure. The programs were a result of the civil rights movement and the attention brought to the poor living conditions in urban ghettos by the riots that occurred there. The withdrawal of the federal commitment to domestic human rights programs begun by President Nixon continued through most of the 1970s, except during the presidency of Jimmy Carter. During the Ronald Regan administration, the social programs that had been created during the 1960s were almost completely dismantled. The emphasis on "privatization" and "state and local control" for addressing social issues continued during the 1990s in the United States, as well as in some European nations.

With the passage of the NEPA, the Congress of the United States put into motion the machinery for the protection of the environment by setting forth certain general aims of federal activity in the environmental field, establishing the Council on Environmental Quality and instructing all federal agencies to include an impact statement as part of future reports or recommendations on actions significantly affecting the quality of the human environment. Subsequent regional, state, and federal actions – such as state environmental policy acts, land-use legislation, and the Coastal Zone Management Act – have furthered this commitment.

As with the heritage for human rights, these environmental measures are deeply rooted in the American tradition. Laced throughout the social criticism of Henry David Thoreau, the novels of Mark Twain, the poetry of Walt Whitman, the photography of Ansel Adams, the films of John Ford, the art of Georgia O'Keefe, and the music of Woody Guthrie is the love for nature.

Even before the recent governmental action, both administrative and adversary planners had been concerned with degradation of the environment. In the nineteenth century, the young Frederick Law Olmsted traveled to England where he witnessed the efforts of reformers to use techniques of the English landscape garden tradition to relieve the pressures of urban blight brought on by the industrial revolution. The resulting public parks were viewed as natural refuges from the evils of the surrounding industrial city. Public parks in English cities were pastoral retreats and escapes from urban congestion and pollution. Olmsted and American reformers adopted the idea. Their first creation was Central Park in New York City, planned and built between 1857 and 1861. Eventually, these efforts led to the City Beautiful Movement, after the World's Columbian Exposition of 1893 in Chicago. The City Beautiful Movement resulted in numerous parks and public facilities being built in the early twentieth century.

During the late nineteenth and early twentieth centuries, a great national parks system took form and blossomed under the leadership of President Theodore Roosevelt. Also in the late nineteenth century, the use of river drainage basins or watersheds as the basic geographical unit for planning was initiated. The humanist engineer Arthur Morgan, an advocate of the watershed conservancy idea, helped organize the Miami Conservancy District in and around Dayton, Ohio, and later directed the Tennessee Valley Authority. During the New Deal, greenbelt new towns – new satellite communities surrounded by parks and accessible to cities by automobile – were created by economist Rexford Tugwell and other leaders. Urban parks, national parks, watershed conservancies, greenbelt new towns – each was a response designed to maintain some portion of the natural environment during periods of increased human settlement.

Ian McHarg (1969) is Saul Alinsky's environmentalist counterpart and the author of a manifesto for ecological planning similar to the one Alinsky wrote for community advocacy. Although social activism and environmentalism are separate (and sometimes conflicting) American traditions, they share common problems. Environmental programs were as vulnerable in the 1980s as social programs were a decade earlier. Ronald Reagan chose not to enforce many environmental laws enacted during the 1970s. He appointed people to key positions in environmental and natural resource management agencies who were opposed to the conservation missions of those agencies. Legally established environmental goals will not be achieved unless governmental enforcement is supported by the public. In spite of actions of the Reagan administration, the American public has generally continued to favor the protection of water, air, and land resources. In addition, President Reagan's successor, George H. W. Bush, declared himself an environmentalist and, when presenting Ian McHarg with the National Medal of Art in 1992, he stated, "It is my hope that the art of the twenty-first century will be devoted to restoring the Earth" (1997a: 331). Furthermore, former Vice President Al Gore (1992) is an avowed environmentalist. The Clinton–Gore administration established the influential President's Council on Sustainable Development (1969) and generally emphasized more environmentally sensitive policies for the federal government. However, even the Clinton–Gore approach was not as devoted to sustainable development as other nations, and the United States was even less so under the George W. Bush administration.

Neither administrative nor advocacy planners have been totally effective. While administrative planners may be able to get things done, underpowered groups often suffer. While advocacy planners may win important civil rights struggles or stop flagrant abuse of the natural environment, overall problems persist and people remain poor – frequently poorer – and environmental degradation continues, too often at a more rapid rate.

A new approach

There is a need for a common language, a common method among all those concerned about social equity and ecological parity. This method must be able to transcend disciplinary territorialism and be applicable to all levels of government. And it is imperative that this approach incorporates both social and environmental concerns. As the poet Wendell Berry has observed, "The mentality that destroys a watershed and then panics at the threat of flood is the same mentality that gives institutionalized insult to black people [and] then panics at the prospect of race riots" (1972: 73).

What is needed is an approach that can assist planners in analyzing the problems of a region as they relate to each other, to the landscape, and to the national and local political economic structure. This might be called an *applied human ecology*, or simply *ecological planning*. Each problem is linked to the community in one or more specific ways. Banking is related to real estate which is related to development pressure which is related to schools which is related to a rising tax base which is related to retirees organizing against increasing property taxes. This approach identifies how people are affected by these chain reactions and presents options for the future based on those impacts.

Ecological planning method

What is meant by *ecological planning*? *Planning* is a process that uses scientific and technical information for considering and reaching consensus on a range of choices. *Ecology* is the study of the relationship of all living things, including people, to their biological and physical environments. *Ecological planning* then may be defined as the use of biophysical and sociocultural information to suggest opportunities and constraints for decision-making about the use of the landscape. Or, as defined by Ian McHarg, it is the approach "whereby a region is understood as a biophysical and social process comprehensible through the operation of laws and time. This can be reinterpreted as having explicit opportunities and constraints for any particular human use. A survey will reveal the most fit locations and processes" (1997a: 321).

McHarg has summarized a framework for ecological planning in the following way:

> All systems aspire to survival and success. This state can be described as synthropic-fitness-health. Its antithesis is entropic-misfitness-morbidity. To achieve the first state requires systems to find the fittest environment, adapt it and themselves. Fitness of an environment for a system is defined as that requiring the minimum of work and adaptation. Fitness and fitting are indications of health and the process of fitness is health giving. The quest for fitness is entitled adaptation. Of all the instrumentalities available for man for successful adaptation, cultural adaptation in general and planning in particular, appear to be the most direct and efficacious for maintaining and enhancing human health and well-being.
>
> (1981: 112–113)

Arthur Johnson explained the central principle of this theory in the following way: "The fittest environment for any organism, artifact, natural and social ecosystem, is that environment which provides the [energy] needed to sustain the health or well-being of the organism/artifact/ecosystem. Such an approach is not limited by scale. It may be applied to locating plants within a garden as well as to the development of a nation" (Johnson *et al.* 1979: 107).

The ecological planning method is primarily a procedure for studying the biophysical and sociocultural systems of a place to reveal where specific land uses may be best practiced. As Ian McHarg summarized repeatedly in his writings and in many public presentations, "The method defines the best areas for a potential land use at the convergence of all or most of the factors deemed propitious for the use in the absence of all or most detrimental conditions. Areas meeting this standard are deemed intrinsically suitable for the land use under consideration."

In the previous chapter, Jeffrey M. Chusid argues that paying attention to our past is important. An appreciation of our history, as recorded physically by our built environments, helps strengthen the case for sustainability. The process described here depends on an understanding and appreciation of context. Such context includes the cultural and natural attributes of a place as suggested by Chusid.

As presented in Figure 11.1, there are eleven interacting steps. An issue or group of related issues is identified by a community – that is, some collection of people – in Step 1. These issues are problematic or present an opportunity to the people or the environment of an area. A goal (or goals) is then established in Step 2 to address the problem(s). Next, in Steps 3 and 4, inventories and analyses of biophysical and sociocultural processes are conducted, first at a larger level, such as a river drainage basin or an appropriate regional unit of government, and second at a more specific level such as a small watershed or a local government.

In Step 5, detailed studies are made that link the inventory and analysis information to the problem(s) and goal(s). Suitability analyses are one such type of detailed study. Step 6 involves the development of concepts and options. A landscape plan is then derived from these concepts

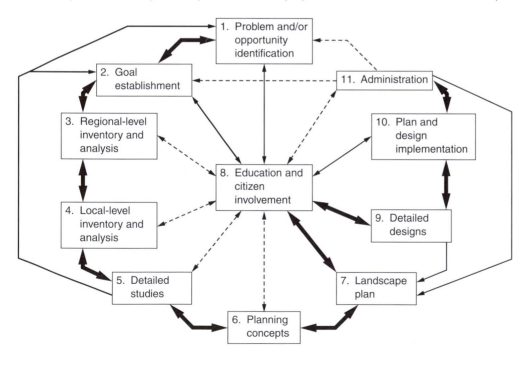

Figure 11.1
The ecological planning model. Source: Steiner, F. (2008) *The Living Landscape* **(2nd edition, paperback), Washington, DC: Island Press.**

in Step 7. Throughout the process, a systematic educational and citizen involvement effort occurs. Such involvement is important in each step but especially so in Step 8, when the plan is explained to the affected public. In Step 9, detailed designs are explored that are specific at the individual land-user or site level. These designs and the plan are implemented in Step 10. In Step 11, the plan is administered.

The heavier arrows in Figure 11.1 indicate the flow from Step 1 to Step 11. Smaller arrows between each step suggest a feedback system whereby each step can modify the previous step and, in turn, change from the subsequent step. The smaller arrows indicate other possible modifications through the process. For instance, detailed studies of a planning area (Step 5) may lead to the identification of new problems or opportunities or the amendment of goals (Steps 1 and 2). Design explorations (Step 9) may change the landscape plan, and so on. Once the process is complete and the plan is being administered and monitored (Step 11), the view of the problems and opportunities facing the region and the goals to address these problems and opportunities may be altered, as is indicated by the dashed lines in Figure 11.1.

This process is adapted from the conventional planning process and its many variations (for example, see Hall 1975 and Stokes *et al.* 1997), as well as those suggested specifically for landscape planning (for example, see Marsh 1998 and Duchhart 2007). Unlike some of these other planning processes, design plays an important role in this method. Each step in the process contributes to and is affected by a plan and implementing measures, which may be the official controls of the planning area. The plan and implementing measures may be viewed as the results of the process, although products may be generated from each step.

The approach to ecological planning developed by Ian McHarg at the University of Pennsylvania differs slightly from the one presented here. The Pennsylvania, or McHarg, model places a greater emphasis on inventory, analysis, and synthesis. This one places more emphasis on the establishment of goals, implementation, administration, and public participation, yet does attempt to do so in an ecologically sound manner.

Ecological planning is fundamental for *sustainable development*. The best-known definition of sustainable development was promulgated by the World Commission on Environment and Development (WCED), known as the Brundtland Commission, as that which "meets the needs of the present without compromising the ability of future generations to meet their own needs" (1987: 8). Another definition was provided by the National Commission on the Environment, which has defined sustainable development as

> a strategy for improving the quality of life while preserving the environmental potential for the future, of living off interest rather than consuming natural capital. Sustainable development mandates that the present generation must not narrow the choices of future generations but must strive to expand them by passing on an environment and an accumulation of resources that will allow its children to live at least as well as, and preferably better than, people today. Sustainable development is premised on living within the Earth's means.
>
> (1993: 2)

Enzo Scandurra and Alberto Budoni have stated the underlying premise for sustainability especially well and succinctly: "The planet cannot be considered as a gigantic source of unlimited raw materials, neither, equally, as a gigantic dump where we can dispose of all waste from our activities" (1995: 2). The environment is both a source and a sink, but its capacities to provide resources and to assimilate wastes are not limitless.

Timothy Beatley and Kristy Manning relate sustainable development to ecological planning. They note that "McHargian-style environmental analysis ... [has] become a commonplace methodological step in undertaking almost any form of local planning" (Beatley and Manning 1997: 86). The steps that follow attempt to provide a more comprehensive approach.

Step 1: identification of planning problems and opportunities

Human societies face many social, economic, political, and environmental problems and opportunities. Since a landscape is the interface between social and environmental processes, landscape planning addresses those issues that concern the interrelationship between people and nature. The planet presents many opportunities for people, and there is no shortage of environmental problems.

Problems and opportunities lead to specific planning issues. For instance, suburban development often occurs on prime agricultural land, a circumstance that local officials tend to view as a problem. A number of issues arise involving land-use conflicts between the new suburban residents and the farmers – such as who will pay the costs of public services for the newly developed areas. Another example is an area like an ocean beach or mountain town with the opportunity for new development because of its scenic beauty and recreational amenities. A key challenge would be that of accommodating the new growth while protecting the natural resources that are attracting people to the place.

Step 2: establishment of planning goals

In a democracy, the people of a region establish goals through the political process. Elected representatives will identify a particular issue affecting their region – a steel plant is closing, suburban sprawl threatens agricultural land, or a new power plant is creating a housing boom. After issues have been identified, goals are established to address the problem. Such goals should provide the basis for the planning process.

Goals articulate an idealized future situation. In the context of this method, it is assumed that once goals have been established, there will be a commitment by some group to address the problem or opportunity identified in Step 1. Problems and opportunities can be identified at various levels. Local people can recognize a problem or opportunity and then set a goal to address it. As well, issues can be national, international, or global in scope. Problem-solving, of which goal setting is a part, may occur at many levels or combinations of levels. Although goal setting is obviously dependent on the cultural–political system, the people affected by a goal should be involved in its establishment.

Goal-oriented planning has long been advocated by many community planners. Such an approach has been summarized by Herbert Gans:

The basic idea behind goal-oriented planning is simple: that planners must begin with the goals of the community – and of its people – and then develop those programs which constitute the best means for achieving the community's goals, taking care that the consequences of these programs do not result in undesirable behavioral or cost consequences.

(1968: 53)

There are some good examples of goal-oriented planning, such as Oregon's mandatory land-use law. However, although locally generated goals are the ideal, too often goals are established by a higher level of government. Many federal and state laws have mandated planning goals for local government, often resulting in the creation of new administrative regions to respond to a particular federal program. These regional agencies must respond to wide-ranging issues that generate specific goals for water and air quality, resource management, energy conservation, transportation, and housing. No matter at what level of government goals are established, information must be collected to help elected representatives resolve underlying issues. Many goals require an understanding of biophysical processes.

Step 3: landscape analysis, regional level

This step and the next one involve interrelated scale levels. The method addresses three scale levels: region, locality, and specific site (with an emphasis on the local). The use of different scales is consistent with the concept of levels-of-organization used by ecologists. According to this concept, each level of organization has special properties. Novikoff (1945) observed, "What were wholes on one level become parts on a higher one." Watersheds have been identified as one level of organization to provide boundaries for landscape and ecosystem analysis. Drainage basins and watersheds have often been advocated as useful levels of analysis for landscape planning and natural resource management.

Dunne and Leopold provide a useful explanation of watersheds and drainage basins for ecological planning. They state that the term *drainage basin*

is synonymous with *watershed* in American usage and with *catchment* in most other countries. The boundary of a drainage basin is known as the *drainage divide* in the United States and as the *watershed* in other countries. Thus the term *watershed* can mean an area or a line. The drainage basin can vary in size from that of the Amazon River to one of a few square meters drainage into the head of a gully. Any number of drainage basins can be defined in a landscape ... depending on the location of the drainage outlet on some watercourse.

(Dunne and Leopold 1978: 495)

Essentially, drainage basins and watersheds are the same thing – catchment areas – but in practical use, especially in the United States, the term *drainage basin* is generally used to refer to a larger region and the term *watershed* to a more specific area. Drainage basins cover a river and all of its tributaries, while watersheds generally encompass a single river or stream. Richard Lowrance and his colleagues, who have developed a hierarchical approach for agricultural planning, refer to watersheds as the landscape system, or ecologic level, and the larger unit as the regional system, or macroeco-nomic level. In the Lowrance *et al.* (1986) hierarchy, the two smallest units are the *farm system*, or *microeconomic level*, and *field system*, or *agronomic level*. The analysis at the regional drainage-basin level provides insight into how the landscape functions at the more specific local scale.

Drainage basins and watersheds, however, are seldom practical boundaries for Ameri-can planners. Political boundaries frequently do not neatly conform with river catchments, and planners commonly work for political entities. There are certainly many examples of plans that are based on drainage basins, such as water quality and erosion control plans. Several federal agen-cies, such as the US Forest Service (USFS) and the US Natural Resources Conservation Service (NRCS) regularly use watersheds as planning units. Planners who work for cities or counties are less likely to be hydrologically bound.

Step 4: landscape analysis, local level

During Step 4, processes taking place in the more specific planning area are studied. The major aim of local-level analysis is to obtain insight about the natural processes and human plans and activities. Such processes can be viewed as the elements of a system, with the landscape a visual expression of the system.

This step in the ecological planning process, like the previous one, involves the collec-tion of information concerning the appropriate physical, biological, and social elements that consti-tute the planning area. Since cost and time are important factors in many planning processes, existing published and mapped information is the easiest and fastest to gather. If budget and time allow, the inventory and analysis step may be best accomplished by an interdisciplinary team col-lecting new information. In either case, this step is an interdisciplinary collection effort that involves search, accumulation, field checking, and mapping of data.

Ian McHarg and his collaborators have developed a layer-cake model (Figure 11.2) that provides a central group of biophysical elements for the inventory or chorography of the place. Categories include geology, the surface terrain, groundwater, surface water, soils, climate, vegeta-tion, wildlife, and people (Table 11.1). UNESCO, in its Man and the Biosphere Programme, has developed a more exhaustive list of possible inventory elements (Table 11.2).

Land classification systems are valuable for analysis at this stage because they may allow the planner to aggregate specific information into general groupings. Such systems are based on inventoried data and on needs for analysis. Many government agencies in the United States and elsewhere have developed land classification systems that are helpful. The NRCS, USFS, the US Fish and Wildlife Service, and the US Geological Survey (USGS) are agencies that have been notably active in land classification systems. However, there is not a consistency of data sources even in the United States. In urban areas, a planner may be overwhelmed with data for inventory and analysis. In remote rural areas, on the other hand, even a Natural Resources Conservation Service survey may not exist, or the survey may be old and unusable. An even larger problem is that there is little or no consistency in scale or in the terminology used among various agencies. One helpful system that has been developed for land classification is the USGS Land Use and Land Cover Classification System (Table 11.3).

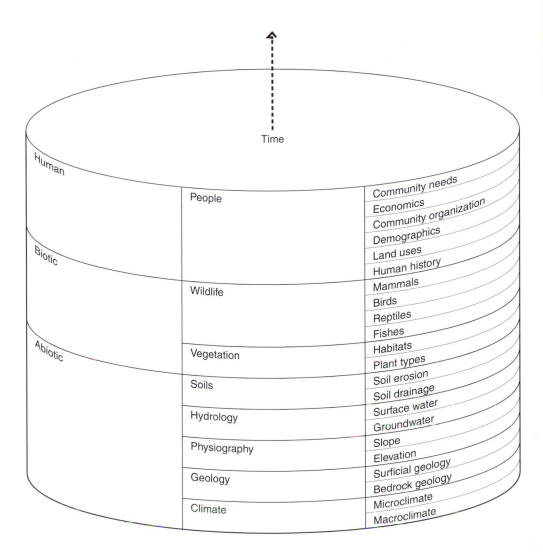

Figure 11.2
The layer-cake model. Source: Steiner, F. (2008) *The Living Landscape* **(2nd edition, paperback), Washington, DC: Island Press.**

The ability of the planner to inventory biophysical processes may be uneven, but it is far better than their capability to assess human ecosystems. An understanding of human ecology may provide a key to sociocultural inventory and analysis. Since humans are living things, *human ecology* may be thought of as an expansion of ecology – of how humans interact with each other and their environments. Interaction then is used as both a basic concept and an explanatory device. As Gerald Young, who has illustrated the pan-disciplinary scope of human ecology, noted:

> In human ecology, the way people interact with each other and with the environment is definitive of a number of basic relationships. Interaction provides a measure of belonging, it affects identity versus alienation, including alienation from the environment. The system of obligation, responsibility and liability is defined through interaction. The process has become definitive of the public interest as opposed to private interests which prosper in the spirit of independence.

(1976: 294)

Table 11.1 Baseline natural resource data necessary for ecological planning

CLIMATE. Temperature, humidity, precipitation, wind velocity, wind direction, wind duration, first and last frosts, snow, frost, fog, inversions, hurricanes, tornadoes, tsunamis, typhoons, Chinook winds

GEOLOGY. Rocks, ages, formations, plans, sections, properties, seismic activity, earthquakes, rock slides, mud slides, subsidence

SURFICIAL GEOLOGY. Kames, kettles, eskers, moraines, drift and till

GROUNDWATER HYDROLOGY. Geological formations interpreted as aquifers with well locations, well logs, water quantity and quality, water table

PHYSIOGRAPHY. Physiographic regions, subregions, features, contours, sections, slopes, aspect, insulation, digital terrain model(s)

SURFICIAL HYDROLOGY. Oceans, lakes, deltas, rivers, streams, creeks, marshes, swamps, wetlands, stream orders, density, discharges, gauges, water quality, floodplains

SOILS. Soil associations, soil series, properties, depth to seasonal high water table, depth to bedrock, shrink-swell, compressive strength, cation and anion exchange, acidity-alkalinity

VEGETATION. Associations, communities, species, composition, distribution, age and conditions, visual quality, species number, rare and endangered species, fire history, successional history

WILDLIFE. Habitats, animal populations, census data, rare and endangered species, scientific and educational value

HUMAN. Ethnographic history, settlement patterns, existing land use, existing infrastructure, economic activities, population characteristics

Source: Adapted from McHarg, I.L. (1997b) "Natural Factors in Planning," *Journal of Soil and Water Conservation* Vol. 51 (1): 13–17.

Note
The above natural resource factors are likely to be of significance in planning. Clearly the region under study will determine the relevant factors, but many are likely to occur in all studies.

Step 5: detailed studies

Detailed studies link the inventory and analysis information to the problem(s) and goal(s). One example of such studies is *suitability analysis*. As explained by Ian McHarg (1969), suitability analyses can be used to determine the fitness of a specific place for a variety of land uses based on thorough ecological inventories and on the values of land users. The basic purpose of the detailed studies is to gain an understanding of the complex relationships between human values, environmental opportunities and constraints, and the issues being addressed. To accomplish this, it is crucial to link the studies to the local situation. As a result, a variety of scales may be used to explore linkages.

Table 11.2 UNESCO total environmental checklist, components and processes

Natural environment – components

Soil	Energy resources
Water	Fauna
Atmosphere	Flora
Mineral resources	Microorganisms

Natural environment – processes

Biogeochemical cycles	Fluctuations in animal and plant growth
Irradiation	
Climatic processes	Changes in soil fertility, salinity, and alkalinity
Photosynthesis	
Animal and plant growth	Host–parasite interactions, and epidemic processes

Human population – demographic aspects

Population structure:
- Age
- Ethnicity
- Economic
- Education
- Occupation

Population size
Population density
Fertility and mortality rates
Health statistics

Human activities and the use of machines

Migratory movements	Industrial activities
Daily mobility	Commercial activities
Decision making	Military activities
Exercise and distribution of authority	Transportation
Administration	Recreational activities
Farming, fishing	Crime rates
Mining	

Societal groupings

Governmental groupings	Information media
Industrial groupings	Law-keeping media
Commercial groupings	Health services
Political groupings	Community groupings
Religious groupings	Family groupings
Educational groupings	

Products of labor

The built environment:
- Buildings
- Roads
- Railways
- Parks

Food
Pharmaceutical products
Machines
Other commodities

Culture

Values	Technology
Beliefs	Literature
Attitudes	Laws
Knowledge	Economic system
Information	

Source: Boyden, S. (1979) *An Integrated Ecological Approach to the Study of Human Settlement*, Paris: UNESCO.

Table 11.3 US geological survey land-use and land-cover classification system for use with remote sensor data

Level I	Level II
1 Urban or built-up land	11 Residential
	12 Commercial and services
	13 Industrial
	14 Transportation, communications, and services
	15 Industrial and commercial complexes
	16 Mixed urban or built-up land
	17 Other urban or built-up land
2 Agricultural land	21 Cropland and pasture
	22 Orchards, groves, vineyards, nurseries, and ornamental horticultural
	23 Confined feeding operations
	24 Other agricultural land
3 Rangeland	31 Herbaceous rangeland
	32 Shrub and brush rangeland
	33 Mixed forestland
4 Forestland	41 Deciduous forestland
	42 Evergreen forestland
	43 Mixed forestland
5 Water	51 Streams and canals
	52 Lakes
	53 Reservoirs
	54 Bays and estuaries
6 Wetland	61 Forested wetland
	62 Nonforested wetland
7 Barren land	71 Dry salt flats
	72 Beaches
	73 Sandy areas other than beaches
	74 Bare exposed rocks
	75 Strip mines, quarries, and gravel pits
	76 Transitional areas
	77 Mixed barren land
8 Tundra	81 Shrub and brush tundra
	82 Herbaceous tundra
	83 Bare ground
	84 Mixed tundra
9 Perennial snow ice	91 Perennial snowfields
	92 Glaciers

Source: Anderson, J.R., Hardy, E.E., Roach, J.T. and Witmer, R.E. (1976) *A Land Use and Land Cover Classification System for Use with Remote Sensor Data*, U.S. Geological Survey Professional Paper 964, Washington, D.C.: United States Government Printing Office.

A simplified suitability analysis process is provided in Figure 11.3. There are several techniques that may be used to accomplish suitability analysis. Again, it was McHarg (1969) who popularized the "overlay technique." This technique involves maps of inventory information super-imposed on one another to identify areas that provide, first, opportunities for particular land uses and, second, constraints (Johnson *et al.* 1979).

Numerous computer program systems, called *geographic information systems* (GIS), have been developed. Some of these programs are intended to model only positions of environmental processes or phenomena, while others are designed as comprehensive information

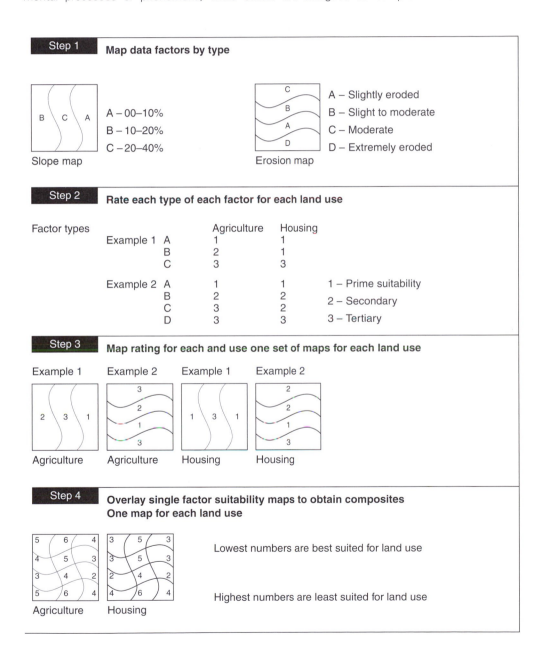

Figure 11.3
Suitability analysis procedure. Source: Steiner, F. (2008) *The Living Landscape* **(2nd edition, paperback), Washington, DC: Island Press.**

storage, retrieval, and evaluation systems. These systems are intended to improve efficiency and economy in information handling, especially for large or complex planning projects.

Step 6: planning area concepts, options, and choices

This step involves the development of concepts for the planning area. These concepts can be viewed as options for the future based on the suitabilities for the uses that give a general conceptual model or scenario of how problems may be solved. This model should be presented in such a way that the goals will be achieved. Often more than one scenario has to be made. These concepts are based on a logical and imaginative combination of the information gathered through the inventory and analysis steps. The conceptual model shows allocations of uses and actions. The scenarios set possible directions for future management of the area and therefore should be viewed as a basis for discussion where choices are made by the community about its future.

Choices should be based on the goals of the planning effort. For example, if it is the goal to protect agricultural land, yet allow some low-density housing to develop, different organizations of the environment for those two land uses should be developed. Different schemes for realizing the desired preferences also need to be explored.

The Dutch have devised an interesting approach to developing planning options for their agricultural land reallocation projects. Four land-use options are developed, each with the preferred scheme for a certain point of view. Optional land-use schemes of the area are made for nature and landscape, agriculture, recreation, and urbanization. These schemes are constructed by groups of citizens working with government scientists and planners. To illustrate, for the nature and landscape scheme, landscape architects and ecologists from the *Staatsbosbeheer* (Dutch Forest Service) work with citizen environmental action groups. For agriculture, local extension agents and soil scientists work with farm commodity organizations and farmer cooperatives. Similar coalitions are formed for recreation and urbanization. What John Friedmann (1973) calls a *dialogue process* begins at the point where each of the individual schemes is constructed. The groups come together for mutual learning so that a consensus of opinion can be reached through debate and discussion.

Various options for implementation also need to be explored, which must relate to the goal of the planning effort. If, for example, the planning is being conducted for a jurisdiction trying to protect its agricultural land resources, then it is necessary not only to identify lands that should be protected but also the implementation options that might be employed to achieve the farmland protection goal.

Step 7: landscape plan

The preferred concepts and options are brought together in a landscape plan. The plan gives a strategy for development at the local scale. The plan provides flexible guidelines for policymakers, land managers, and land users on how to conserve, rehabilitate, or develop an area. In such a plan, enough freedom should be left so that local officials and land users can adjust their practices to new economic demands or social changes.

This step represents a key decision-making point in the planning process. Responsible officials, such as county commissioners or city council members, are often required by law to adopt a plan. The rules for adoption and forms that the plans may take vary widely. Commonly in the United States, planning commissions recommend a plan for adoption to the legislative body after a series of public hearings. Such plans are called *comprehensive plans* in much of the United States but are referred to as *general plans* in Arizona, California, and Utah. In some states (like Oregon), there are specific, detailed elements that local governments are required to include in such plans. Other states permit much flexibility to local officials for the contents of these plans. On public lands, various federal agencies, including the USFS, the US National Park Service, and the US Bureau of Land Management, have specific statutory requirement for land management plans.

The term *landscape plan* is used here to emphasize that such plans should incorporate natural and social considerations. A landscape plan is more than a land-use plan because it addresses the overlap and integration of land uses. A landscape plan may involve the formal recognition of previous elements in the planning process, such as the adoption of policy goals. The plan should include written statements about policies and implementation strategies as well as a map showing the spatial organization of the landscape.

Step 8: continued citizen involvement and community education

In Step 8, the plan is explained to the affected public through education and information dissemination. Actually, such interaction occurs throughout the planning process, beginning with the identification of issues. Public involvement is especially crucial as the landscape plan is developed, because it is important to ensure that the goals established by the community will be achieved in the plan.

The success of a plan depends largely on how much people affected by the plan have been involved in its determination. There are numerous examples of both government agencies and private businesses suddenly announcing a plan for a project that will dramatically impact people, without having consulted those individuals first. The result is predictable – the people will rise in opposition against the project. The alternative is to involve people in the planning process, soliciting their ideas, and incorporating those ideas into the plan. Doing so may require a longer time to develop a plan, but local citizens will be more likely to support it than to oppose it and will often monitor its execution.

Step 9: design explorations

To design is to give form and to arrange elements spatially. By making specific designs based on the landscape plan, planners can help decision makers visualize the consequences of their policies. Carrying policies through to arranging the physical environment gives meaning to the process by actually conceiving change in the spatial organization of a place. Designs represent a synthesis of all the previous planning studies. During the design step, the short-term benefits for the land users or individual citizen have to be combined with the long-term economic and ecological goals for the whole area.

Since the mid-1980s, several architects have called for a return to traditional principles in community design. These "neotraditionals" or "new urbanists" include Peter Calthorpe, Elizabeth Plater-Zyberk, Andres Duany, Elizabeth Moule, and Stefanos Polyzoides. Meanwhile, other architects and landscape architects have advocated more ecological, more sustainable design; these include John Lyle, Robert Thayer, Sim Van der Ryn, Carol Franklin, Colin Franklin, Leslie Jones Sauer, Rolf Sauer, and Pliny Fisk. Michael and Judith Corbett, with others, helped merge these two strains in the Ahwahnee Principles (Local Government Commission 1991) (see Table 11.4).

Ecological design, according to David Orr, is "the capacity to understand the ecological context in which humans live, to recognize limits, and to get the scale of things right" (1994: 2). Or, as Sim Van der Ryn and Stuart Cowan note, ecological design seeks to "make nature visible" (1996: 16). These principles provide clear guidance for ecological design (Grant et al. 1996). While some designers and planners might object to the placement of design within the planning process, in an ecological perspective such placement helps to connect design with more comprehensive social actions and policies.

Step 10: plan and design implementation

Implementation is the employment of various strategies, tactics, and procedures to realize the goals and policies adopted in the landscape plan. The Ahwahnee Principles provide guidelines for implementation (Table 11.4). On the local level, several different mechanisms have been developed to control the use of land and other resources. These techniques include voluntary covenants, easements, land purchase, transfer of development rights, zoning, utility extension policies, and performance standards. The preference selected should be appropriate for the region. For instance, in urban areas like King County, Washington, and Suffolk County, New York, traditional zoning has not proved effective for protecting farmland. The citizens of these counties have therefore elected to tax themselves to purchase farmland preservation easements from farmers. In more rural counties like Whitman County, Washington, and Black Hawk County, Iowa, local leaders have found traditional zoning effective.

One implementation technique especially well suited for ecological planning is the use of performance standards. Like many other planning implementation measures, *performance standards* is a general term that has been defined and applied in several different ways. Basically, performance standards, or criteria, are established and must be met before a certain use will be permitted. These criteria usually involve a combination of economic, environmental, and social factors. This technique lends itself to ecological planning because criteria for specific land uses can be based on suitability analysis.

Table 11.4 **The Ahwahnee principles**

Preamble:

Existing patterns of urban and suburban development seriously impair our quality of life. The symptoms include more congestion and air pollution resulting from our increased dependence on automobiles, the loss of precious open space, the need for costly improvements to roads and public services, the inequitable distribution of economic resources, and the loss of a sense of community. By drawing upon the best from the past and the present, we can plan communities that will more successfully serve the needs of those who live and work within them. Such planning should adhere to certain fundamental principles.

Community Principles:

1. All planning should be in the form of complete and integrated communities containing housing, shops, work places, schools, parks, and civic facilities essential to the daily life of the residents.
2. Community size should be designed so that housing, jobs, daily needs, and other activities are within easy walking distance of each other.
3. As many activities as possible should be located within easy walking distance of transit stops.
4. A community should contain a diversity of housing types to enable citizens from a wide range of economic levels and age groups to live within its boundaries.
5. Businesses within the community should provide a range of job types for the community's residents.
6. The location and character of the community should be consistent with a larger transit network.
7. The community should have a center focus that combines commercial, civic, cultural, and recreational uses.
8. The community should contain an ample supply of specialized open space in the form of squares, greens, and parks whose frequent use is encouraged through placement and design.
9. Public spaces should be designed to encourage the attention and presence of people at all hours of the day and night.
10. Each community or cluster of communities should have a well-defined edge, such as agricultural greenbelts or wildlife corridors, permanently protected from development.
11. Streets, pedestrian paths, and bike paths should contribute to a system of fully-connected and interesting routes to all destinations. Their design should encourage pedestrian and bicycle use by being small and spatially defined by buildings, trees and lighting; and by discouraging high-speed traffic.

Regional Principles:

1. The regional structure should be integrated within a larger transportation network built around transit rather than freeways.
2. Regions should be bounded by and provide a continuous system of greenbelt/wildlife corridors to be determined by natural conditions.
3. Regional institutions and services (government, stadiums, museums, etc.) should be located within the urban core.

continued

Table 11.4 continued

Implementation Strategies:

1   The general plan should be updated to incorporate the above principles.
2   Rather than allowing for developer-initiated, piecemeal development, a local government should initiate the planning of new and changing communities within its jurisdiction through an open planning process.
3   Prior to any development, a specific plan should be used to define communities where new growth, infill, or redevelopment would be allowed to occur. With the adoption of specific plans, complying projects can proceed with minimal delay.
4   Plans should be developed through an open process and in the process should be provided with illustrated models of the proposed design.

Sources: Local Government Commission. (1991) *The Ahwahnee Principles*, Sacramento, California. Calthorpe, P., Corbett, M., Duany, A., Plater-Zyberk, E., Polyzoides, S., Moule, E. with Corbett, J., Katz, P. and Weissman, S. (1998) 'The Ahwahnee Principles' in *Creating Sustainable Places Symposium*, A.B. Morris (ed.), Tempe, Arizona: Herberger Center for Design Excellence, Arizona State University.

Step 11: administration

In this final step, the plan is administered. *Administration* involves monitoring and evaluating how the plan is implemented on an ongoing basis. Amendments or adjustments to the plan will no doubt be necessary because of changing conditions or new information. To achieve the goals established for the process, planners should pay special attention to the design of regulation-review procedures and the management of the decision-making process.

Administration may be accomplished by a commission comprising citizens with or without the support of a professional staff. Citizens should play an important role in administering local planning through commissions and review boards that oversee local ordinances. To a large degree, the success of citizens' boards and commissions depends on the extent of their involvement in the development of the plans they manage. Again, Oregon provides an excellent example of the use of citizens to administer a plan. The Land Conservation and Development Commission, comprising of seven members who are appointed by the governor and supported by its professional staff, is responsible for overseeing the implementation of the state land-use planning law. Another group of citizens, 1000 Friends of Oregon, monitors the administration of the law. The support the law has received from the public is evidenced by the defeat of several attempts to abolish mandatory state-wide land-use planning in Oregon. However, as Department of Land Conservation and Development staff member Ron Eber observes, "It is a myth that planning is easy in Oregon – it is a battle every day!" (personal communication 1999). For example, in the early 1990s, a counter-force to 1000 Friends of Oregon was organized; "Oregonians in Action" is a property-rights group that is opposed to the progressive state-wide planning program. Such opposition was successful in weakening Oregon's planning statutes in 2004 but the law was again strengthened in 2007. The debate continues in Oregon.

Working plans

A method is necessary as an organizational framework for landscape planners. Also, a relatively standard method presents the opportunity to compare and analyze case studies. To adequately fulfill responsibilities to protect the public health, safety, and welfare, the actions of planners should be based on a knowledge of what has and has not worked in other settings and situations. A large body of case study results can provide an empirical foundation for planners. A common method is helpful for both practicing planners and scholars who should probe and criticize the nuances of such a method in order to expand and improve its utility.

The approach suggested here should be viewed as a working method. The pioneering forester Gifford Pinchot advocated a conservation approach to the planning of national forests. His approach was both utilitarian and protectionist, and he believed "wise use and preservation of all forest resources were compatible" (Wilkerson and Anderson 1985: 22). To implement this philosophy, Pinchot in his position as chief of the US Forest Service required "working plans." Such plans recognized the dynamic, living nature of forests. In the same vein, the methods used to develop plans should be viewed as a living process. However, this is not meant to imply that there should be no structure to planning methods. Rather, working planning methods should be viewed as something analogous to a jazz composition: not a fixed score but a palette that invites improvization.

The method offered here has a landscape ecological – specifically human ecological – bias and as a result can be helpful in balancing equity, economic, and environmental concerns. As noted by the geographer Donald W. Meinig, "Environment sustains us as creatures; landscape displays us as cultures" (1979: 3). As an artifact of culture, landscapes are an appropriate focus of planners faced with land-use and environmental management issues. Ecology provides insight into landscape patterns, processes, and interactions. An understanding of ecology reveals how we interact with each other and our natural and built environments. What we know of such relationships is still relatively limited, but it is expanding all the time. As Ilya Prigogine and Isabelle Stengers have observed, "Nature speaks in a thousand voices, and we have only begun to listen" (1996: 77).

Questions for further consideration

1   In Steiner's eleven-step planning process the product of planning is purported to be the education of citizens, not the planning document itself. If substantive planning decisions are to be made by citizens, why do we need professional planners at all?

2   Steiner embraces the "weak" planning tradition of the United States, in comparison to the "strong" tradition of Europe, because it reflects our foundational cultural values related to property rights. Many advocates of sustainability have argued conversely, that the current environmental crisis requires new strong planning laws. Can Steiner's "applied human ecology" process be both "weak" and successful?

3   The systems approach to ecological planning advocated by Steiner, as introduced by Ian McHarg in the 1970s, has much in common with the "complexity theory" proposed by McDaniel and Lanham in Chapter 3. If the "planning" of complex adaptive systems requires constant and continual effort, what are the implications for the production of "city plans"?

4   The "feedback loops" inherent in Steiner's ecological planning method are analogous to those found in natural, self-correcting systems. Self-correction in human-dominated systems might best be called *politics*. Is social learning in the planning process a prerequisite for the kind of "solidarity" and social action proposed by Thompson in Chapter 1?

5   The framework of the "land plan" proposed by Steiner is both "goal-oriented" and experimental in that short-term feedback is intended to modify the goal as knowledge is gained in the system. It is imperative, he holds, that citizens remained engaged in the implementation process in order to continually assess intentions and outcomes. The process he proposes has, then, requirements for political structure and the distribution of political power. Are these consistent with the proposals of Jamison and Winner in Chapters 4 and 5?

Bibliography

Alinsky, S. D. (1946) *Reveille for Radicals*, Chicago, IL: University of Chicago Press.

Anderson, J. R., Hardy, E. E., Roach, J. T. and Witmer, R. E. (1976) *A Land Use and Land Cover Classification System for Use with Remote Sensor Data*, US Geological Survey Professional Paper 964, Washington, DC: United States Government Printing Office.

Beatley, T. and Manning, K. (1997) *The Ecology of Place: Planning for the Environment, Economy and Community*, Washington, DC: Island Press.

Bentham, J. (1864) *Theory of Legislation*, London: Trubner & Co.

Berry, W. (1972) *A Continuous Harmony, Essays Cultural and Agricultural*, New York: Harcourt Brace Jovanovich.

Boyden, S. (1979) *An Integrated Ecological Approach to the Study of Human Settlement*, Paris: UNESCO.

Calthorpe, P., Corbett, M., Duany, A., Plater-Zyberk, E., Polyzoides, S., Moule, E. with Corbett, J., Katz, P. and Weissman, S. (1998) "The Ahwahnee Principles," in A. B. Morris (ed.) *Creating Sustainable Places Symposium*, Tempe, AZ: Herberger Center for Design Excellence, Arizona State University.

Duchhart, I. (2007) *Designing Sustainable Landscapes from Experience to Theory*, Wageningen, The Netherlands: Wageningen University.

Dunne, T. and Leopold, L. B. (1978) *Water in Environmental Planning*, New York: W. H. Freeman.

Friedmann, J. (1973) *Retracking America*, Garden City, NY: Anchor Press/Doubleday.

Gans, H. (1968) *People and Plans*, New York: Basic Books.

Gore, A. (1992) *Earth in the Balance: Ecology and the Human Spirit*, New York: Houghton Mifflin.

Grant, J., Manuel, P. and Joudrey, D. (1996) "A Framework for Planning Sustainable Residential Landscapes," *Journal of the American Planning Association*, Vol. 62 (3): 311–344.

Hall, P. (1975) *Urban and Regional Planning*, New York: Halsted Press/John Wiley and Sons.

Humbach, J. A. (1989) "Law and a New Land Ethic," *Minnesota Law Review*, Vol. 74: 339–370.

Johnson, A. H., Berger, J. and McHarg, I. L. (1979) "A Case Study in Ecological Planning: The Woodlands, Texas," in T. Beatty, G. W. Petersen and L. D. Swindale (eds.) *Planning the Uses and Management of Land*, Madison, WI: American Society of Agronomy, Crop Science Society of America, and Soil Science Society of America.

Laslett, P. (ed.) (1988) *John Locke: Two Treatises of Government* (student edition), Cambridge, UK: Cambridge University Press.

Local Government Commission. (1991) *The Ahwahnee Principles*, Sacramento, CA.

Lowrance, R., Hendrix, P. F. and Odum, E. P. (1986) "A Hierarchical Approach to Sustainable Agriculture," *American Journal of Alternative Agriculture*, Vol. 1 (4): 169–173.

McHarg, I. L. (1969) *Design with Nature*, Garden City, New York: Doubleday/The Natural History Press.

—— (1997a) "Ecology and Design," in G. F. Thompson and F. Steiner (eds.) *Ecological Design and Planning*, New York: John Wiley and Sons.

—— (1997b) "Natural Factors in Planning," *Journal of Soil and Water Conservation*, Vol. 51 (1): 13–17.

—— (1981) "Human Ecological Planning at Pennsylvania," *Landscape Planning*, Vol. 8: 112–113.

Marsh, W. M. (1998) *Landscape Planning: Environmental Applications* (3rd edition), New York: John Wiley and Sons.

Meinig, D. W. (1979) "Introduction," in D. W. Meinig (ed.) *The Interpretation of Ordinary Landscapes*, New York: Oxford University Press.

National Commission on the Environment. (1993) *Choosing a Sustainable Future*, Washington, DC: Island Press.

Novikoff, A. B. (1945) "The Concept of Integrative Levels and Biology," *Science*, Vol. 101: 209–215 as quoted by Quinby, P. A. (1988) "The Contribution of Ecological Science to the Development of Landscape Ecology: A Brief History," *Landscape Research*, Vol. 13 (3): 9–11.

Opie, J. (1998) *Nature's Nation: An Environmental History of the United States*, Fort Worth, TX: Harcourt Brace & Company.

Orr, D. W. (1994) *Earth in Mind: On Education, Environment, and the Human Prospect*, Washington, DC: Island Press.

President's Council on Sustainable Development. (1996) *Sustainable America: A New Consensus for Prosperity, Opportunity, and a Healthy Environment for the Future*, Washington, DC: US Government Printing Office.

Prigogine, I. and Stengers, I. (1996) *Order Out of Chaos*, New York: Bantam Books.

Ricklefs, R. E. (1973) *Ecology*. Newton, MA: Chiron Press.

Scandurra, E. and Budoni, A. (1995) "For a Critical Revision of the Concept of Sustainable Development: Ten Years after the Brundtland Report," Paper presented to the 20th Annual Meeting, Boston, Massachusetts: Northeast Regional Science Association.

Steiner, F. (2008) *The Living Landscape* (2nd edition, paperback), Washington, DC: Island Press.

Stokes, S. W. A., Watson, E. and Mastran, S. (1997) *Saving America's Countryside: A Guide to Rural Conservation*, Baltimore: Johns Hopkins University Press.

Van der Ryn, S. and Cowan, S. (1996) *Ecological Design*, Washington, DC: Island Press.

Wilkerson, C. F. and Anderson, H. M. (1985) "Land and Resource Planning in National Forests," *Oregon Law Review*, Vol. 64 (1 & 2): 1–373.

World Commission on Environment and Development. (1987) *Our Common Future*, Oxford, UK: Oxford University Press.

Young, G. (1976) "Environmental Law: Perspectives from Human Ecology," *Environmental Law*, Vol. 6 (2): 289–307.

Editor's Introduction to Chapter 12

Supporters of sustainable development have encouraged the public to "Think globally and act locally." This slogan envisions urban sustainability as dependent upon the public maintenance of such basic goods as water supply. Beginning in the late nineteenth century, and continuing until the late twentieth century, water supply in the US evolved from a private responsibility to a public one. After 1990, in light of a deteriorated national infrastructure and portending scarcity, multinational water companies took up the call to act locally, but for much different ends. Critics of this transformation often claim that we have come full circle, from private to public and now back again to private ownership of basic infrastructures – a condition that, in their view, poses ethical dilemmas and threatens urban sustainability. The new century may have something different in store for municipal water supplies and delivery as fresh water becomes an increasingly scarce resource and a more profitable commodity. The line between water as a public good and water as a product always has been blurred, but never to the extent that it has been in recent years.

Beneath the immediate question of water scarcity, the meaning of *public* and *private* is the topic of historian Martin V. Melosi's chapter. When is a thing (water), or a service (water delivery), entirely public or private? Or, as Melosi suggests, is reality found in the tension between these idealized states? Dewey is again helpful here. He holds that when the consequences of any action are limited to the actors, the matter is a private one. But when actions have indirect consequences for others, the matter becomes public. Put directly, "the line between public and private is to be drawn on the basis of the extent and scope of the consequences of acts which are so important as to need control, whether by inhibition or by promotion" (Dewey 1927: 15). But Dewey also warns us that there is no automatic correlation between states organized in the name of the public good and the public itself. The problem that Americans have set about solving is how we locate the public in relation to private interests and the state. If we look for the public in some fixed principle we are, according to Dewey, looking in the wrong place because condition and the consequences of private action are dynamic. This observation may help us to understand why our estimation of the benefits derived from public vs private water infrastructure keep changing.

Chapter 12

Full Circle?

Public Responsibility versus Privatization of Water Supplies in the United States

Martin V. Melosi

Introduction

For much of the eighteenth and early nineteenth centuries, urban Americans acquired water through their own devices, from water merchants, or from public wells (some purchased by the local government). Beginning in the 1830s, many cities and towns developed centralized water systems managed and owned by the municipalities themselves. From that time until the late twentieth century, water was generally treated as a public good and providing it was regarded as a public responsibility, based on the assumption that market forces could not be depended upon to furnish services necessary to society (see Jacobson 2000: 3, 13, 22). At the same time, fresh water was a commodity to be bought and sold, whether controlled by private or public entities. Gail Radford suggested the implications of developing public water systems:

> Mundane as it might seem, providing water represented a sharp break for cities, which had previously confined themselves to supplying relatively indivisible public goods, such as police and fire protection, that did not lend themselves to the commodity form – that is, to being socially defined as objects bought and sold in markets. Water, by contrast, was generally charged for according to use. In a sense then, water opened Pandora's box. The widespread reliance on municipal provision of this vital substance enhanced the plausibility of following the same course for other goods.
>
> (Radford 2003: 872)

In the 1990s, however, privatization of the delivery of water to American cities appeared to be a viable option for the first time in many decades. How could such a long-standing commitment to a pioneering municipal service be challenged? And, more generally, what accounted for the change from private to public service and possibly back to private service again?

It may appear simplistic to create a scenario based on changes from private to public and then public to private water supply systems. As Charles Jacobson and Joel Tarr stated about infrastructure and city services, "Although it is widely believed that today's movement toward privatization represents the first major shift from public to private supply of infrastructure, history provides examples of many shifts in both directions." And they added that "a simple distinction" between what is "public" and what is "private" does not really "encompass the range of arrange-ments that has existed with respect to the ownership, financing, and operation of facilities." These might include plans where a government agency builds and operates a facility, contracts out the construction, or contracts out the operation. Funding provisions might rely on user fees, taxes, and assessments to abutters, bonds, or a combination of some or all of these (Jacobson and Tarr 1996: 2).

It should be noted that the focus of this chapter is on broad national trends in water supply only; not on all city services. A reasonable argument can be constructed using "public" and "private" construed quite generally to identify the biggest and most obvious changes over time. Furthermore, the privatization movement of the 1990s and beyond emerged out of circumstances much different from those in earlier times. Particularly significant has been the globalization of the water industry that has changed the organizational structure of water service in many parts of the world, and presents a major challenge to local or regional approaches to water delivery in the United States.

It is also useful to keep in mind that, especially with respect to water supply, a gap has existed in American cities between project design and long-range planning of systems. The munic-ipal embrace of public water systems in the nineteenth century was not carried out with long-term goals in mind – other than in developing a technical network that would function over many years. Such a view was built upon the assumption that the citizenry would invest in what was a very expensive infrastructure if there was a promise of its permanence and its longevity. Beyond that, little consideration was given to alternative technical approaches or to alternative management schemes other than centralized municipal control. Indeed, cities looked backward to what they believed to be the shortcomings of private franchises rather than to the future in asserting water as a public good. Many years later, consideration of privatization likewise looked back to the alleged weaknesses of publicly managed systems rather than to future alternatives.

In the previous chapter, Frederick Steiner made a clear distinction between temporal differences in planning agendas: "*Project planning* involves designing a specific object such as a dam, highway, harbor, or an individual building or group of buildings. *Comprehensive planning* involves a broad range of choices relating to all the functions of an area." This observation high-lights the limits of urban water-supply development and planning in the United States, and why, to a large extent, debates over public or private approaches have been so painful. Steiner's sugges-tions about the need for "ecological planning" also remind us that the debate over public or pri-vate water systems was conducted largely outside of a framework that took into account a major focus on sustainability.

Urban water supply before 1830

Prior to the 1830s many American cities faced the threat of fires, and suffered from poor sanitary conditions and the looming prospect of epidemic disease. A plentiful and pure water supply was a valued resource in such a setting. While some of the earliest city-wide water supply systems appeared at this time, few communities could boast of well-developed technologies of sanitation on the order of those constructed several decades later. Much of the responsibility for obtaining water rested in the hands of the individual, who acquired it from wells or nearby watercourses. In low-density areas in particular, these methods proved to be adequate, even efficient, and thus resisted change, obsolescence, or outright replacement. The practices most often were publicly regulated but rarely publicly managed or owned.

As the population grew larger, the number of structures increased, new technologies like the flush toilet (or water closet) came into use, water sources became polluted or infected, and/or local water supplies literally dried up, the traditional methods of acquiring water became less workable. The result – albeit somewhat slowly implemented – was the appearance of water-supply protosystems that placed emphasis on more sophisticated means of acquiring and delivering water than buckets and wells, were increasingly capital-intensive, and were publicly regulated and often publicly operated.[1]

European (especially English) experiences with water supply systems influenced US cities. Philadelphia became the first to complete a sophisticated waterworks and municipal distribution system in 1801, but it was an anomaly that did not spark an immediate nationwide trend.[2] Prior to the mid-nineteenth century, only about half of the major cities and towns had some type of waterworks and they were overwhelmingly private as Figure 12.1 shows (see Eddy 1932: 82; Croes 1885: 4–69).

Figure 12.1
American cities with waterworks, 1800–1830. Source: U.S. Bureau of Census, *Census of Population: 1960* **vol. 1,** *Characteristics of the Population* **(Washington, DC: Department of Commerce, 1961), Part A, pp. 1–14, 1–15, Table 8; Earle Lytton Waterman,** *Elements of Water Supply Engineering* **(New York: John Wiley and Sons, 1934), 6.**
Note: Cities = 2,500 or more population.

Year	# Works	# Cities	Cities with works	Public	Private
1800	17	33	51%	1	16
1810	27	46	59%	5	22
1820	31	61	51%	5	26
1830	45	90	50%	9	36

The rise of the public water utility, 1830–1920

Beginning in the 1830s, the scale of urban growth in the United States, the persistent fear of fire, increasing demand for water, and vague notions connecting waste with sickness led to the construction of several city-wide water supply systems. As Charles Jacobson stated, "[W]aterworks represented a critical element in a distinctively growth-oriented American style of city-building, elements of which have survived to the present day" (Jacobson 2000: 3). American cities were undergoing their first "sanitary awakening" between 1830 and 1880, a time when prevailing public health ideas attributed disease transmission to "miasmas," that is, decaying matter, foul smells, and bad air. Sanitarians, engineers, and city officials linked the new water systems to the goals of environmental sanitation, simply utilizing sensory tests of purity to seek out what they believed to be safe sources of water and to protect supplies from human and animal wastes. This strategy was crude and scientifically inaccurate – bacteria, not filth, transmitted disease – but waste removal and concern for water purity nonetheless had a salutary impact on making the delivery of water a high priority. It also placed responsibility for public improvement in human hands. The number of waterworks multiplied at an accelerated rate from forty-five in 1830 to 9,850 in 1924 (Melosi 2000: 73–89, 120; see also Jacobson *et al*. 1985: 9).

Leaders, especially in large cities, concluded that control of the sanitary quality of its water service would be difficult if the supply remained private. They also increasingly came to believe that a public water supply could be profitable for city government, and would keep a valuable resource from being controlled by businessmen. While many water companies had been profitable, capital investment in the modern systems escalated, and operating costs rose.[3] In addition, many private companies were accused of being inefficient or charging excessive rates. In essence, the push for municipal ownership had as much to do with the desire to influence the growth of cities as to settle disputes with private companies over specific deficiencies.[4] Thus, private owners increasingly were under pressure to sell their assets as several communities gradually phased out private service. Major cities tended to support public systems earlier and more uniformly than any other class of cities. They also tended to invest more heavily in water supply and distribution than had the privately owned companies. Whereas in 1830 only 50 percent of cities had public systems, in 1897 forty-one of the fifty largest cities (or 82 percent) had public systems; in 1924 70 percent of all cities went public. As Figure 12.2 shows, the most dramatic increase in public ownership occurred in the mid-1890s, during the Progressive Era, when promotion of government action in several spheres intensified (Committee on Municipal Administration 1898: 726–727; Griffith 1983: 180; Jacobson and Tarr 1996: 8).

Year	# Works	Public	Private	% Public	% Private
1830	45	9	36	20	80
1840	65	23	42	35.4	64.6
1850	84	33	51	39.3	60.7
1860	137	57	80	41.7	58.3
1870	244	116	128	47.5	52.5
1880	599	293	306	48.9	51.1
1890	1879	806	1,073	42.9	57.1
1896	3,197*	1,690	1,490	52.9	46.6
1924	9,850	6,900	2,950	70	30

Figure 12.2
Public versus private ownership of waterworks, 1830–1924. Source: Waterman, *Elements of Water-Supply Engineering*, 6. Note: *Includes 17 undocumented systems.

The desire of city leaders to convert private systems into public, or to build new public systems, rested on more than the will to do so. The central issue was the ability of cities to incur debt to fund major projects and to sustain the high costs of operation. As the nineteenth century unfolded, city finances underwent changes in scope and complexity that ultimately made the development of public water supply systems possible (see Anderson 1980: 106, 108, 112; Tarr 1984: 26, 30). The urban bureaucracy itself experienced substantial change, making it more responsive to developing city-wide sanitary services. Professional bureaucrats became firmly entrenched in municipal government, and helped shift power away from state capitals to city halls. Beginning slowly in the 1870s, several cities made efforts to move away from state interference in their affairs by demanding more "home rule." The movement took many forms, including efforts to increase the appointive power of mayors and to gain control of various service departments (see Teaford 1984: 7; Finegold 1995: 15).

"Home rule" – granted by legislatures or constitutions – proved viable in several states with large cities. In some cases, the cities demonstrated political clout which they could wield at the state level. In Colorado, Denver was granted some home rule powers in 1889, but this action was essentially a rubber stamp for powers the city had already accrued. When a new political party entered office, Denver temporarily faced the institution of state boards which cut into its local authority. In a quite different case, Louisiana granted statutory home rule to all cities in the state in 1896, except New Orleans. In some states with small cities, or where public service standards were high, legislatures often retained the right of special legislation, but wielded it carefully. By the end of the nineteenth century, the success of reform efforts in the cities and states made for a favorable political setting for greater home rule. More home rule did not insure political and financial stability for cities, but it did allow some latitude in setting local priorities, or at least in responding to perceived local needs (Griffith 1983: 215, 124–125, 128; Glaab and Brown 1976: 174–176; Teaford 1984: 105, 122).

By the late nineteenth century, faith in environmental sanitation as the primary weapon against disease lost followers as the "germ theory" of disease replaced the "filth theory."[5] Bacteriology placed more emphasis on finding cures for disease as opposed to prevention, which had been the mainstay of sanitary reform since the 1840s. The commitment to develop elaborate urban infrastructure for water services was not deterred by the changing notions of health and disease, since the need for pure and plentiful water was essential to city life. The technology of insuring the quality of the water supply changed with more emphasis on chemically testing, treating, and filtering water. By 1920 many American cities could boast about plentiful sources of pure water, and about water systems that took greater account of how to confront water-borne epidemics (Melosi 2000: 117–148).

In the era of bacteriology, water supplies increasingly relied upon centralized organizational structures and capital-intensive technical innovations which had been developing since the 1830s. The prevailing goal in the late-nineteenth and early-twentieth centuries was to transform the evolving systems into more comprehensive public, city-wide systems that afforded permanent solutions to the delivery of water. The price of public water infrastructure was high, but many officials and citizens came to believe it was worth the expense (see Jacobson 2000: 33–34, 61, 69).

Metering water usage became a powerful management tool in administering the water supply in public systems. Ostensibly employed as a way to set rates, the use of water meters was equally important as a means to check waste and to anticipate future expansions of the system. By 1920, metering had made notable strides. While only about 30 percent of the cities metered at the pump, more than 600 of 1,000 cities surveyed metered at the tap; 279 cities metered all taps ("Water-Supply Statistics of Metered Cities" 1920: 614–620; "Water-Supply Statistics of Metered Cities" 1921: 42–49).

Expansion of water supply systems, 1920–1945

From the end of World War I to the end of World War II, neither the quality nor character of water supply services underwent substantial change. The challenge for municipal officials, engineers, planners, and sanitarians was to adapt those services to urban growth increasingly characterized by metropolitization and suburbanization, on the one hand, and demand in numerous small towns and rural communities, on the other. Decision-making in this period was complicated by two major disruptions to American life: the Great Depression and World War II. Despite the fluctuations of the economy from the 1920s to the 1940s, national trends in the construction and expansion of waterworks continued to indicate steady growth. Many of the new systems were rudimentary ones in numerous small communities. In 1940, there were approximately 14,500 waterworks in the United States (Fuller 1927: 1588; Turneaure and Russell 1948: 9). Although the rate of growth was strongest from the 1890s through the early 1920s, increases in the 1930s were significant due to the infusion of federal funds during the New Deal ("Water-Supply Statistics for Municipalities of Less Than 5,000 Population" 1925: 185–191; March 1925: 309–323; April 1925: 435–445; May 1925: 555–565; June 1925: 665–677; July 1925: 47–59; Davis 1933: 92).

The relative stability of the waterworks business in the interwar years occurred with some significant changes in the management of the water supply systems. The need for greater cooperation between political entities in the acquisition and delivery of water was becoming obvious, especially in response to metropolitan and suburban growth patterns in major cities. In some parts of the country, special water districts sprouted up in the 1920s, especially for the development and delivery of water (see Siems 1925: 644–645).

Without question, the greatest change in the development, extension, and financing of water supply systems in the interwar years came with the new role of the federal government. Management, however, most often remained in the hands of local – or regional – public authorities.[6] During the New Deal, the Public Works Administration financed between 2,400 and 2,600 water projects with a price tag of approximately $312 million – half of the total expenditures for waterworks for all levels of government. The Federal Emergency Relief Administration, the Civil Works Administration, and the Works Progress Administration spent another $112 million for work relief on municipal water projects. Smaller communities realized the greatest impact of these funds; for the first time they were able to finance public systems, treatment facilities, and distribution networks. In fact, almost three-quarters of the projects financed went to communities with less than 1,000 people. While federal support stimulated development of new waterworks and provided resources for improving others, wartime priorities ultimately shifted federal funds away from local sanitary services (see Armstrong *et al.* 1976: 231–232; Daniels 1975: 9; Public Works Administration 1939: 170, 173–178; "Water Supplies Will be Widely Extended After the War" 1944: 18).

Metropolitan expansion and new demands on water supplies, 1945–1970

Relentless growth on the periphery and deterioration of the central city characterized post-World War II urban conditions, and placed increasingly stiff demands on the providers of water supply. Concern over decaying infrastructure, especially at the urban core, raised important questions about the permanence of the sanitary systems devised and implemented in the nineteenth and early-twentieth centuries. An array of mounting social ills – characterized as an "urban crisis" – increasingly shifted attention away from physical problems. The last of a series of *Fortune* articles on infrastructure (December, 1958) stated flatly that water supply and sewerage "remain a signal failure in public works" (Thompson 1958: 102). This assessment was harsh, but many older water supply and sewerage systems were in decline by the mid-1940s. The Committee on Public Information for the American Water Works Association reported in 1960 that of the approximately 18,000 functioning water facilities in the US, one in five had a deficient supply, two in five had inadequate transmission capacity, one in three had defective pumping, and two in five had weaknesses in its treating capacity (Hanna 1961: 22).

Decisions about improving water supply systems had to be made within a framework of rapid urban growth, increasing water usage, and growing financial pressures on cities. Further concentration of industry in metropolitan and unincorporated areas also increased the need for more water, as did demands for service in unincorporated residential communities (Bollens and Schmandt 1970: 176; Thompson 1958: 102).

New waterworks continued to come on line, especially in the expanding metropolitan periphery and in smaller cities and towns no longer able to depend on private wells and rudimentary water systems. In 1945 there were approximately 15,400 waterworks in the United States supplying about 12 billion gallons per day to ninety-four million people. By 1965, there were more than 20,000 waterworks supplying 20 billion gallons per day to approximately 160 million people. By the mid-1960s, 83.4 percent of water-supply facilities (in cities with 25,000 or more population) were publicly owned. Between 1956 and 1965, $10 billion was spent for new construction and additions in the United States. The annual value of the water placed waterworks within the nation's top ten largest industries (Babbitt and Doland 1949: 40; Fair *et al.* 1977: 14; US Department of Commerce 1975: 619, 621).

Distribution problems resulted from the location of water facilities at the cities' cores, which often serviced the larger metropolitan areas and outlying suburban communities. It was frequently in the interest of the central city to extend water lines to the suburbs to maintain a healthy economic climate in the metropolitan area. For suburbs, growth was impossible without adequate services. In some cases there was reluctance on the part of central cities to extend distribution lines outward, if there was no guarantee of future annexation. Often, real estate developers or alternative public entities constructed pipelines beyond the existing city limits to make outlying suburbs attractive to future annexation. In the 1960s the central plant in Chicago supplied water on a contract basis to approximately sixty suburban communities. The number of special districts and other administrative arrangements were increasing in number in response to the need for water. From the vantage point of the total water system, the cost of distribution represented as much as two-thirds of a utility's investment (Fleming 1967: 94–95; Bolton 1959: 67–68; Water Resources Council 1968: 5-1-3; Lavson 1968: 1316).

For water supply systems and other city services, the postwar economic boom and the dynamic expansion of metropolitan America obscured the chronic deterioration of the infrastructure and the inability of cities to keep pace with sanitary needs. Water supply systems were failing to live up to expectations and foretold an unsettling fear of a new era of adversity.

From infrastructure crisis to privatization, 1970–2000

In the wake of the so-called "infrastructure crisis" in the late twentieth century, water supply systems avoided the direst predictions about decay and deterioration. A 1987 report stated that a national water supply "infrastructure gap" of the magnitude that would require a substantial federal subsidy did not exist. Urban water supply systems as a whole, it concluded, "do not constitute a national problem" (National Council on Public Works Improvement 1987: 37–38). This assessment was based on comparisons with other components of the nation's infrastructure. Water needs appeared modest when compared with highway repair and replacement estimated in the mid-1980s to reach a 20-year "needs level" of approximately $2 trillion. Studies set price tags of $125 billion for water supply repairs, expansions, and improvements. The relatively small, but hardly insignificant, number masked problems that had been building for years. Some experts, looking beyond the statistics, charged that many drinking water systems were outdated, faced massive leaks, were poorly maintained, and relied on pipes 100 or more years old (Grigg 1986: 7–8; Everett 1996: 91; Ausubel and Herman 1988: 265).

Broadening federal regulatory authority over water pollution and the tightening of water quality standards were first steps in recognizing the severity and complex nature of water pollution in the 1970s, but added additional financial pressures to managing water systems at the local and regional level (Luken and Pechan 1977: 4; Environment and Natural Resources Policy Division 1980: 14; McClain 1994: 2-1, 2-2). Financing of water supply in the 1970s and 1980s largely remained at the local level. Statistics from the early 1980s indicate that state and local governments were primarily responsible for 83 percent of the expenditures for municipal water supplies. Federal funds for water projects were on the decline in the 1970s, and capital spending by all governments for water resources had fallen by 60 percent from the late 1960s to the late 1980s (American Public Works Association 1982: 11, 32; National Council on Public Works Improvement 1980: 31).

Regionalization of the water industry in the United States attracted considerable attention, especially the Metropolitan Water District in California and the Metropolitan Sanitary District of Greater Chicago (National Council on Public Works Improvement 1980: 16; Holtz and Sebastian 1978: 71; Grigg 1986: 1, 85). Moreover, efforts by several multinational companies to privatize water-supply delivery and treatment globally were gaining significant attention in the 1990s. American waterworks remained largely public ventures managed on the local level by the first decade of the twenty-first century, but privatization was a trend to reckon with (Ross and Levine 1996: 261).

In recent years, various observers have come to believe that fresh water will be the most contested commodity of the twenty-first century like oil had been in the twentieth (Swomley 2000: 6; Gaura 2002: A3; Gleick 2002: E8). Deep concern about this turn of events on a world scale grew out of several converging issues.

First, some have raised the specter of a "fresh water crisis," in much the same way as an "energy crisis" was proclaimed in the 1970s. In an article published in 2000, social ethics professor John M. Swomley predicted that a water crisis "looming on the horizon" could reach "dire proportions within the next ten to thirty years." It is unclear on what basis he made such a presumption (or if he has the expertise to do so) (Swomley 2000: 5). An article in a 2002 issue of *Nation* also sounded an alarm:

> The world is running out of fresh water. Humanity is polluting, diverting and depleting the wellspring of life at a starling rate. With every passing day, our demand for fresh water outpaces its availability and thousands more people are put at risk. Already, the

social, political and economic impacts of water scarcity are rapidly becoming a destabi-
lizing force, with water-related conflicts springing up around the globe. Quite simply,
unless we dramatically change our ways, between one-half and two-thirds of humanity
will be living with severe freshwater shortages within the next quarter-century.

(Barlow and Clarke 2002: 11)

Second, beyond the issue of scarcity there was growing unease that fresh water was being commodified, that is, being treated more as an economic as opposed to a social and environmental
good.[7] From this vantage point, water is not just another commodity or consumer product, but –
as one writer noted – it is "a shared resource and a public trust." A United Nations' committee
asserted that access to safe and affordable water must be a human right (Lenze 2003: C-12; Krisberg 2003: 15). Others echoed the notion that commodifying fresh water was ethically wrong. On
a practical level, treating water simply as a product leads to choosing the most profitable markets
for providing water service, leaving some areas – especially poor communities and those located
on the urban margins – without adequate service (Barlow and Clarke 2002: 13–14; Knickerbocker
2002: 1; Lee 2001: A1; Gleick 2004: 5). Such concerns, although raising legitimate questions about
equity, failed to take account that water historically has been treated as a product as well as a
public good, and that the actions of multinational water companies did not initiate the commodification of water.

Third, people especially in industrialized nations, have come to expect water delivered
efficiently and at low cost. However, local governments and regional authorities often face budg-
etary hardships – including reduced federal funding – and the increased cost of compliance with
environmental regulations to the extent that many historically profitable water supply systems are
difficult to maintain in the public arena.[8] Local leaders frequently must choose between maintaining services "in-house" that also may have political benefits versus substantial government spending that may have political costs. Given the predicament of many local authorities, private
companies are increasingly pursuing occasions to manage or to own local waterworks.[9]

In the United States "privatization" most often means governments contracting with
private companies to provide specific public services. For example, a public–private partnership
was established between Harrington Park, New Jersey, and United Water Resources through
which the city maintained ownership of the water utility, while the company managed the facilities. Selling off assets or complete liquidation of public holdings also is possible in some instances
(Lopez-de-Silanes and Vishney 1997: 447, 468; Nichols 1996: 8A; Schundler 1997: 45). From a
business perspective, water supply systems often represent a "hot investment." Johan Bastin,
with the European Bank for Reconstruction and Development in London, was reported as saying:
"Water is the last infrastructure frontier for private investors" (Fleming 1998: A1). Thus, the most
recent efforts of private water companies to penetrate the American market does not signal commodification of water per se, but rising expectations about new economic opportunities.

Fourth, critics are skeptical of claims that privatizing water supplies could revitalize the
systems, make them more efficient, and deliver the product at a reasonable cost once a city's
rate-setting ability is shifted to a private company. They also are concerned as to whether the private market can deal with issues related to the public good in addition to focusing on profits –
most likely to be taken out of the community. And they are particularly wary of multinational

companies with no local ties that are most often the driving force behind recent efforts at privatization of water supply systems (Fleming 1998: A1; Schundler 1997: 45; Gleick 2004: 5, 7. See also Shleifer 1998: 147; Runyan 2003: 38). As Maria Alicia Gaura stated in a 2002 edition of the *San Francisco Chronicle*, "The transformation of water delivery from prosaic necessity to hot investment trend has startled many US ratepayers, who never dreamed that stockholders in Europe would be wringing profits from their water bills" (Gaura 2002: A3).

Globalization of fresh-water service adds a significant layer of apprehension to the privatization trend in government. The rising influence of international water companies and their pursuit of local opportunities around the world do not take us "full circle" from individual and private water supplies before 1830, to public utilities established by the late-nineteenth century, and back again to private providers. They take us into a new era entirely.

Where public–private competition over water supply, waterworks, and treatment plants has been largely a local matter in the past, the potential impact of multinational – or transnational – water companies controlling vast numbers of systems represents a unique situation. Control over water supplies and water delivery is not a change from water as a public service to water as a commodity, but a fundamental erosion of local authority well beyond more traditional tensions between city and region, city and state, and the city and the federal government.

At the turn of the new century, privatization of water systems is much more widespread in Europe than in the United States. In 2003 only five percent of the water systems in the US were privately owned, and only about 15 percent of the population was served by corporate water. Of the 94 percent of water systems that are publicly controlled (about 5,000), most are municipal.[10] Between 1997 and 2003, however, the number of publicly-owned systems operated under long-term contracts by private companies has increased from 400 to 1,100.[11] The Center for Public Integrity – a non-profit advocacy group based in Washington, DC – estimated that before 2020, 65 to 75 percent of public waterworks in Europe and North America would be controlled by private companies, with Africa and Asia not far behind (Lenze 2003: 1; Cook 2002: 19–20; Elie 2003: 1; Jehl 2003: 14; Haarmeyer 1993: B5).

Leading the way to this potential sea change are ten major corporations,[12] several subsidiaries, and some smaller companies delivering water and wastewater services. The prospect of a long-term contract to monopolize a key resource has attracted substantial corporate attention. For their part, the World Bank and the International Monetary Fund provide backing to many of the larger ventures, especially in developing countries. Representatives of the World Bank have argued that governments in developing countries are too poor and too much in debt to subsidize water and sanitation services with public funds. International trade accords – such as the North American Free Trade Agreement – also incorporate provisions for governments to turn over control of fresh water supplies to global trade institutions, helping private companies gain access to those supplies. The bottled-water industry (Culligan, for example, is owned by Veolia) also must be included among water-for-profit enterprises, selling more than ninety billion liters of bottled water in 2002 alone. One report has noted that the annual profits of the water industry in recent years surpasses those in the pharmaceutical sector and is about 40 percent of the oil sector, although only about 5 percent of world's water is privately owned.

Two French companies dominate the international water industry, Veolia Environment and Suez.[13] Veolia, formerly Vivendi Environment, grew out of Generale des Eaux, which had been established by Napoleon III in 1852. Its first contract called for supplying water to the city of Lyons. Suez purchased Lyonnaise des Eaux, which was founded in 1880 with the sponsorship of the bank, Credit Lyonnais. Both Generale des Eaux and Lyonnaise des Eaux established the tradition of private water delivery in France and benefited from years of protectionism, and now have emerged as part of a powerful force on the world scene. Taken together, the two water giants – Veolia and Suez – provide service in more than 100 countries with approximately 200 million customers. Only RWE/Thames comes close to them, benefiting from Margaret Thatcher's privatization of water in Great Britain in 1989. In many cases, low margins in the European water market have encouraged the multinationals to spread their financial risk into other parts of the world.[14]

Some American-based corporations attempted to challenge Veolia and Suez – most notably Azurix, which was a subsidiary of the now much maligned energy-trading company Enron. Enron had hoped to be a major player in the fresh water market on a scale equal to its core businesses in natural gas and electricity. It met with little success, however, because it could not raise sufficient capital to operate effectively in both the water and energy markets.[15] In 1999, American Water Works Company was the leading water company in the United States, serving sixteen million customers in twenty-nine states, but its revenue was less than 10 percent of Veolia's. German conglomerate RWE AG purchased American Water Works for $8.6 billion, which has further taken American water companies outside the leadership of the industry. Through its ownership of US Filter, Veolia is the largest private wastewater firm operating in the United States ("Savoir Faire" 2003: 7; Lenze 2003: C12).

The water giants have not been without their failures as well as successes. Allegations of corruption and unfair business practices regularly dog them. Ventures in developing companies generally have been less successful than elsewhere. In 1998 Bolivian authorities – under pressure from the World Bank – gave a contract for water service in the city of Cochabamba to a consortium of private investors (English, Italian, Spanish, American, and Bolivian), who promptly raised water rates by 35 percent. Water then cost more than food! In 2000 a general strike and transportation stoppage ensued. Despite mass arrests and several deaths, the protesters continued to demand "deprivatization" of water, and ultimately the consortium abandoned the project and the government revoked the privatization legislation. In neighboring Rio de Janeiro, an effort to auction off the state's water system was canceled by the Federal Supreme Court because of a clash between city and state authorities over ownership of the assets. In Argentina, government officials terminated a contract granted to the city of Tucuman after water rates doubled and water quality worsened (Swomley 2000: 7; Barlow and Clarke 2002: 13–14; Fleming 1998: A1; Runyan 2003: 36; Gleick 2002: E8).

In the wake of difficulties in developing countries, Suez retrenched, especially in Asia and Latin America, while Veolia proved more successful, focusing on Eastern Europe and North America. The China market appears promising, but has yet to be effectively penetrated. And little attention is given to places such as sub-Saharan Africa where the need for water is great, but where the business of water seems less profitable ("Savoir Faire" 2003: 7).

A wholesale trend toward privatization of water supplies and water supplies management has yet to occur in the United States. However, in 1999 alone there were $15 billion in acquisitions in the US water industry. For example, Suez purchased Nalco Chemical Company of

Illinois – a water treatment group – for $4.1 billion, and also acquired Calgon Corporation – the third largest water-conditioning company, which is based in Pittsburgh – for $425 million. The 1996 Safe Drinking Water Act and other federal and state laws requiring renovation or improvement of deteriorating water systems place a financial burden on several cities, which are now ready to explore a relationship with a private water company. Also, a 1997 executive order, tax-rule changes by the Internal Revenue Service, and privatization advocates in Congress have opened up the possibility of more shifts from public to private service. Cities such as Indianapolis, Milwaukee, and Gary, Indiana contracted with private companies to manage their waterworks (Barlow and Clarke 2002: 12–13; Jehl 2003: 14; *St. Petersburg (Florida) Times* (June 29 1999) 2E; Iskandar 1999: 37; Hairston 1999: 3B; Taylor 1998: 19; Helton 1997: 5C).

In the United States, as elsewhere, the global water company juggernaut has not always prevailed. Atlanta officials struck a 20-year operations and maintenance contract with United Water, Inc. (a subsidiary of Suez) in 1998, which paid the company $21.4 million per year. What had been one of the first large privatization awards in the US, however, was terminated in 2003, ostensibly because of faulty contract provisions, but also because of poor service and the protest (and lawsuits) of environmentalists over the construction of suburban reservoirs. As one journalist noted, "The decision, in many ways, takes Atlanta back to square one" (Jehl 2003: 14). While the action was a setback for privatization of water, and cities such as New Orleans (before Katrina), Louisiana, and Stockton, California were rethinking plans to privatize (or to further privatize in the case of New Orleans), Atlanta's decision was not likely to have long-range implications for water privatization in the United States.[16]

Conclusion

Many environmental activists have encouraged the public to "Think globally, act locally." Multinational water companies have taken up that call, but for much different ends. The historical record about urban water service in the United States has long been viewed from the vantage point of the triumph of public control over private action – a model in many cases unique in the world. A deeper look at that record suggests that a wholesale shift from private means of water delivery to public means is a little too simplistic, since historians are most comfortable demonstrating the shades of gray that make up much of our lives. Nonetheless, for a very long time municipal control or oversight of water service has been part of the local fabric of cities – a venture that set precedents for many other services to follow. The new century may have something different in store for municipal water supplies and delivery as fresh water becomes an increasingly scarce resource and a more profitable commodity. The line between water as a public good and water as a product always has been blurred, but never to the extent it has been in recent years.

Questions for further consideration

1   We tend to see the structure of basic infrastructural systems as somehow neutral and natural and thus dismiss the likelihood that they might have shown up in different form. Melosi's account of water systems in North America should disabuse us of such misconception. The question remains, however: to what degree can we apply Melosi's finding to other forms of infrastructure – transportation, power generation, or housing?

2   Like Allen *et al.* in Chapter 6, Melosi recognizes the tension between conceiving durable systems designed to last indefinitely and flexible systems designed to be regularly adapted to changing conditions. He also documents the political crisis which ensued when expensive, durable systems proved too expensive to modify. On the basis of Melosi's findings, should we conclude that technical decisions about infrastructure are really disguised political decisions?

3   Many argue that the commodification of water is ethically wrong, that it violates the "public trust" inherent in a democratic society. In this light the debate over water privatization illustrates Oden's reasoning in Chapter 2. Others, however, argue that without valuing water more highly we will only encourage overconsumption. How might this problem be resolved using Steiner's ecological planning process discussed in Chapter 11?

4   In Melosi's view, the benefits of public vs private water supply are contextual – meaning that benefits depend on constantly changing local and global conditions. Should we construe the absence of an *a priori* "right" to be an endorsement of flexible, adaptive systems?

5   If there are no fixed principles by which planners and citizens can make choices about things so fundamental as water supply, how can we hope to design sustainable cities?

Notes

I would like to thank Tom McKinney for research on privatization that he completed for the last section of the chapter.

1   "Protosystem" connotes an original system or "first in rank or time" as opposed to a primitive system. For a more thorough discussion of water supplies and waterworks in the United States, see Melosi 2000. See also Jacobson and Tarr 1996: 7.

2   After examining various options, the city leaders chose the proposal of English-born engineer Benjamin Henry Latrobe, who recommended building a steam-powered pumping plant that would distribute water to the city from the protected Schuylkill River located more than one mile away. Latrobe began the task in 1799 and completed it in 1801. In 1811 the city's Watering Committee replaced the original plant, pumping water to a reservoir atop Fairmount rise and then releasing the water by gravity to the city. The Fairmount Waterworks served Philadelphia until 1911. See Jackson 1989: 635; McMahon 1988: 25–26; Gibson 1988.

3   In the early years, several waterworks were operated by state chartered corporations financed by private investors. In some small communities, private firms and municipal government were not antagonistic and developed long-term relationships. See Jacobson 2000: 25; Jacobson and Tarr 1996: 7.

4   For a general discussion of municipal ownership as a public issue, see Griffith 1983: 86–87.

5   The germ theory purported that microscopic organisms – or bacteria – were the cause of epidemic disease. A contagionist disease paradigm was replacing a noncontagionist paradigm.

6   The states, more than the municipalities or the federal government, were the centers of action for new legislation to control stream pollution. See Vesilind 1981: 26; Micklin 1970: 131; Tarr 1985: 1059, 1064; Warrick 1933: 496; Monger 1926: 790; Hinderlider 1926: 606–608; Besselievre 1931: 325–344; Skinner 1939: 1332. For regional systems, see Elkind 1998.

7   This, of course, is ahistorical since water had been commodified long before the onset of the twenty-first century. On the recent claim of the commodification of water, see Gleick 2004.

8   See Grunsky 2001: 17–18; C. Runyan (2003) "Privatizing Water," *World Watch* 16, January–February: 36–37; J. Lanza (1992) "Cities Mull Privatizing Waterworks," *Boston Business Journal* 12, May 11: 1; Gleick 2002: E8; Hyman 1992: 52).

9   In a few cases the reverse has occurred. For example, city officials in Marysville, Ohio were preparing to initiate eminent domain proceedings against Ohio Water Service Company in 1990 in an effort to purchase the private company. See Ball 1990: 10.

10   Estimates do vary. Some observers argue that only about 85 percent of waterworks are publicly owned. See Gaura 2002: A3.

11   In many cases the private water companies are agreeing upon long-term contracts (20–25 years) to manage and operate a particular city's waterworks. This has been more typical in recent years than outright purchases.

12   Included here are Veolia Environment, Suez, Bouygues Saur, RWE-Thames Water, and Bechtel-United Utilities, and several other smaller companies.

13   They also have holdings in other businesses as well.

14   See Grunsky 2001: 14; Barlow and Clarke 2002: 12–13; Veolia Environment; Veolia Environment website; Defending the Internal Water Empire; Glassman 1999: E1; Tolhurst 1999: 39.

15   Enron was interested in water company acquisitions within the US borders and throughout other parts of the world. For example, they attempted to invade the markets in Rio de Janeiro, Berlin, and Panama, and thus posed a threat to the French companies. Fleming 1998: A1; Warsh 2001: E2; Taylor 1998: 19.

16   Powers and Rubin 2003: 14–15; Brooks 2003: C4; Rosta 2003: 12; Carr 2003: 8. On other debates, see Davis 1999: 4; Hightower 2002: 8; Cook 2002: 20–21; Russell 2003: 1.

Bibliography

American Public Works Association (1982) *Proceedings of the National Water Symposium: Changing Directions in Water Management*, Washington, DC: APWA.

Anderson, L. (1980) "The Diffusion of Technology in the Nineteenth Century American City," PhD dissertation, Northwestern University.

Armstrong, E., Robinson, M. and Hoy, S. (eds.) (1976) *History of Public Works in the United States*, Washington, DC: American Public Works Association: 231–232.

Ausubel, J. H. and Herman, R. (eds.) (1988) *Cities and Their Vital Systems: Infrastructure Past, Present, and Future*, Washington, DC: National Academy Press.

Babbitt, H. E. and Doland, J. J. (1949) *Water Supply Engineering.* New York: McGraw-Hill.

Ball, B. R. (1990) "Marysville Seeks Control of Private Water System," *Business First-Columbus* 6, February 12: 10.

Barlow, M. and Clarke, T. (2002) "Who Owns Water?" *Nation* 275, September 2: 11.

Besselievre, E. B. (1931) "The Disposal of Industrial Chemical Waste," *Chemical Age* 25, December 12: 325–344.

Bollens, J. C. and Schmandt, H. J. (1970) *The Metropolis: Its People, Politics, and Economic Life*, New York: Harper and Row.

Bolton, C. M. (1959) "A Metropolitan Water Works Is Best," *American City* 74, January: 67–68.

Brooks, R. (2003) "Deals and Deal Makers: A Deal All Wet," *Wall Street Journal*, January 31: C4.

Carr, M. (2003) "Water Board Hopes to Learn from Atlanta: City's Privatization Venture Went South," *New Orleans Times-Picayune*, April 17: 8.

Committee on Municipal Administration (1898) "Evolution of the City," *Municipal Affairs* 2, September: 726–727.

Cook, C. D. (2002) "Drilling for Water in the Mojave," *Progressive* 66, October: 19–20.

Croes, J. J. R. (1885) *Statistical Tables from the History and Statistics of American Water Works*, New York: Engineering News: 4–69.

Daniels, R. (1975) "Public Works in the 1930s: A Preliminary Reconnaissance," in *The Relevancy of Public Works History: 1930s – A Case Study*, Washington, DC: Public Works Historical Society.

Davis, C. V. (1933) "Water Conservation – The Key to National Development," *Scientific American* 148, February: 92.

Davis, J. (1999) "Furor over Privatization Stirs Debate Over its Merits," *Kansas City Business Journal* 17, June 11: 4.

Dewey, J. (1927) *The Public and Its Problems*, Athens, OH: Ohio University Press.

Eddy, H. P. (1932) "Water Purification – A Century of Progress," *Civil Engineering* 2, February: 82.

Elie, L. E. (2003) "Privatization Argument has Its Leaks," *New Orleans Times-Picayune*, March 31: 1.

Elkind, S. S. (1998) *Bay Cities and Water Politics: The Battle for Resources in Boston and Oakland*, Lawrence, KS: University Press of Kansas.

Environment and Natural Resources Policy Division (1980) Congressional Research Service, *Nonpoint Pollution and the Area-Wide Waste Treatment Management Program Under the Federal Water Pollution Control Act*, Washington, DC: GPO.

Everett, C. T. (1996) "So Is There an Infrastructure Crisis or What?" *Public Works Management and Policy* 1, July.

Fair, G. M., Geyer, J. L. and Okun, D. A. (1977) *Elements of Water Supply and Wastewater Disposal*, New York: Wiley.

Finegold, K. (1995) *Experts and Politicians: Reform Challenges to Machine Politics in New York, Cleveland, and Chicago*, Princeton, NJ: Princeton University Press.

Fleming, C. (1998) "Sofia's Choice: Water Business is Hot as More Cities Decide to Tap Private Sector," *Wall Street Journal*, November 9: A1.

Fleming, R. R. (1967) "The Big Questions . . .," *American City* 82, June: 94–95.

Fuller, G. W. (1927) "Water-works," *Proceedings of the American Society of Civil Engineers* 53, September: 1588.

Gaura, M. A. (2002) "Water a Hot Commodity," *San Francisco Chronicle*, December 1.

Gibson, J. M. (1988) "The Fairmount Waterworks," *Bulletin of the Philadelphia Museum of Art* 84, Summer: 2–40.

Glaab, C. N. and Brown, A. T. (1976) *A History of Urban America*, New York: Macmillan Publishing.

Glassman, J. K. (1999) "In Europe, Going for the Water," *Washington Post*, April 7: E1.

Gleick, P. H. (2002) "The Big Idea Water, Water-Where?" *Boston Globe*, January 6: E8.

—— (2004) *Executive Overview, The New Economy of Water: The Risks and Benefits of Globalization and Privatization of Fresh Water*. Online, available at: www.pacinst.org/reports/new_economy_overview.htm.

Griffith, E. S. (1983 [1974]) *A History of American City Government: The Progressive Years and Their Aftermath 1900–1920*, Washington, DC: University Press of America.

Grigg, N. S. (1986) *Urban Water Infrastructure*, New York: Wiley.

Grunsky, S. (2001) "Privatization Tidal Wave," *Multinational Monitor* 22, September: 17–18.

Haarmeyer, D. (1993) "Privatize Seattle Water? Study has Wrong Answer," *Seattle Times*, December 27: B5.

Hairston, J. B. (1999) "Treatment Plant Bidding Could Be Fierce," *Atlanta Constitution*, April 9: 3B.

Hanna, G. P. Jr. (1961) "Domestic Use and Reuse of Water Supply," *Journal of Geography* 60, January: 22.

Helton, C. (1997) "Atlanta's Sewer Problems," *Atlanta Constitution*, March 4: 5C.

Hinderlider, M. C. and Meeker, R. I. (1926) "Interstate Water Problems and Their Solution," *Proceedings of the American Society of Civil Engineers* 52, April: 606–608.

Hightower, J. (2002) "The Water Profiteers," *Nation* 275, September 2: 8.

Holtz, D. and Sebastian, S. (eds.) (1978) *Municipal Water Systems: The Challenge for Urban Resource Management*, Bloomington, IN: Indiana University Press.

Hyman, U. (1992) "Wastewater Partnerships," *American City & County* 107, April: 52.

International Consortium of Investigative Journalists (2003) *Defending the Internal Water Empire*. Online, available at: www.icij.org/water.

Iskandar, S. (1999) "Suez Buys Calgon," *Financial Times (London)*, June 16: 37.

Jackson, D. C. (1989) "The Fairmount Waterworks, 1812–1911," *Technology and Culture* 30, July.

Jacobson, C., Klepper, S. and Tarr, J. A. (1985) "Water, Electricity, and Cable Television: A Study of Contrasting Historical Patterns of Ownership and Regulation," *Technology and the Future of Our Cities* 3, Fall.

Jacobson, C. D. (2000) *Ties That Bind: Economic and Political Dilemmas of Urban Utility Networks, 1800–1990*, Pittsburgh, PA: University of Pittsburgh Press.

Jacobson, C. D. and Tarr, J. A. (1996) *Public or Private? Some Notes from the History of Infrastructure: A Report to the World Bank*, unpublished manuscript.

Jehl, D. (2003) "As Cities Move to Privatize Water, Atlanta Steps Back," *New York Times*, February 10: 14.

Knickerbocker, B. (2002) "Privatizing Water: A Glass Half Empty?" *Christian Science Monitor*, October 24.

Krisberg, K. (2003) "Privatizing Water Systems Draws Mixed reviews," *Nation's Health* 33, March: 15.

Lanza, J. (1992) "Cities Mull Privatizing Waterworks," *Boston Business Journal* 12, May 11: 1.

Larson, T. E. (1968) "Deterioration of Water Quality in Distribution Systems," *Journal of the American Water Works Association* 58, October: 1316.

Lee, P. (2001) "The Wellspring of Life, or Just a Commodity," *Ottawa Citizen*, August 16: A1.

Lenze, A. (2003) "Liquid Assets," *Pittsburgh Post-Gazette*, September 16: C-12.

Lopez-de-Silanes, F. A. S. and Vishny, R. W. (1997) "Privatization in the United States," *RAND Journal of Economics* 28, Autumn: 447–468.

Luken, R. A. and Pechan, E. H. (1977) *Water Pollution Control: Assessing the Impacts and Costs of Environmental Standards*, New York: Praeger.

McClain, W. E. Jr. (ed.) (1994) *US Environmental Laws*. Washington, DC.

McMahon, M. (1988) "Makeshift Technology: Water and Politics in 19th-Century Philadelphia," *Environmental Review* 12, Winter: 25–26.

Melosi, M. V. (2000) *The Sanitary City: Urban Infrastructure in America from Colonial Times to the Present*, Baltimore, MD: Johns Hopkins University Press.

Micklin, P. P. (1970) "Water Quality: A Question of Standards," in R. A. Cooley and G. Wandesforde-Smith (eds.) *Congress and the Environment*, Seattle.

Monger, J. E. (1926) "Administrative Phases of Steam Pollution Control," in *Journal of the American Public Health Association* 16, August.

National Council on Public Works Improvement. (1987) *The Nation's Public Works: Executive Summaries of Nine Studies*. Washington, DC: National Council on Public Works Improvement: 37–38.

Nichols, J. (1996) "Chance to Save Lures Cities to Private Sector," *Cleveland Plain Dealer*, June 22: 8A.

Powers, M. B. and Rubin, D. (2003) "Severed Atlanta Water Contract was Tied to Unclear Language," *Engineering News-Record* 25, February 10: 14–15.

Public Works Administration (1939) *America Builds*, Washington, DC: US Government Printing Office.

Radford, G. (2003) "From Municipal Socialism to Public Authorities: Institutional Factors in the Shaping of American Public Enterprise," *Journal of American History* 90, December.

Ross, B. H. and Levine, M. A. (1996) *Urban Politics: Power in Metropolitan America*, Itasca, IL: F.E. Peacock.

Rosta, P. (2003) "Stockton Mulls Outsourcing After Atlanta Changes Course," *Engineering News-Record* 250, February 24: 12.

Runyan, C. (2003) "Privatizing Water," *World Watch* 16, January–February: 36–37.

Russell, G. (2003) "S&WB Adds New Duties for Privatization Bidders," *New Orleans Times-Picayune*, April 4: 1.

"Savoir Faire" (2003) *Economist* 368, July 19.

Schundler, B. (1997) "City Chooses Private Manager for its Water Utility," *American City & County* 112, March: 45.

Shleifer, A. (1998) "State versus Ownership," *Journal of Economic Perspectives* 12, Autumn: 147.

Siems, V. B. (1925) "The Advantages of Metropolitan Water-Supply Districts," *American City* 32, June: 644–645.

Skinner, H. J. (1939). "Waste Problems in the Pulp and Paper Industry," *Industrial and Engineering Chemistry* 31 (November): 1332.

—— (1999) *St. Petersburg (Florida) Times*, June 29: 2E.

Swomley, J. M. (2000) "When Blue Becomes Gold," *Humanist* 60, September/October: 6.

Tarr, J. A. (1984) "The Evolution of the Urban Infrastructure in the Nineteenth and Twentieth Centuries," in R. Hanson (ed.) *Perspectives on Urban Infrastructure*, Washington, DC: National Academy Press.

—— (1985) "Industrial Wastes and Public Health," *American Journal of Public Health* 75, September.

Taylor, A. (1998) "Enron Steps into Global Water Market," *Financial Times (London)*, July 25: 19.

Teaford, J. C. (1984) *The Unheralded Triumph: City Government in America, 1870–1900*, Baltimore, MD: Johns Hopkins University Press.

Thompson, E. T. (1958) "The Worst Public-Works Problem," *Fortune* 58, December: 102.

Tolhurst, C. (1999) "Drinking at the Front of Opportunity," *Australian Financial Review*, May 18: 39.

Turneaure, F. E. and Russell, H. L. (1948) *Public Water-Supplies: Requirements, Resources, and the Construction of Works*, New York: John Wiley and Sons.

US Department of Commerce, Bureau of the Census (1975) *Historical Statistics of the United States: Part 2*, Washington, DC: Department of Commerce.

Vesilind, P. A. (1981) "Hazardous Waste: Historical and Ethical Perspectives," in J. J. Peirce and P. A. Vesilind (eds.) *Hazardous Waste Management*, Ann Arbor, MI. Public Citizen, "Veolia Environment." Online, available at: www.citizen.org/cmep/Water/general/major water/veolia/index.cfm.

Veolia Environment. Online, available at: www.vivendienvironment.com/en/activities/water.

Warrick, L. F. (1933) "Relative Importance of Industrial Wastes in Stream Pollution," in *Civil Engineering* 3, September.

Warsh, D. (2001) "What Enron Got Right," *Boston Globe*, December 9: E2.

Water Resources Council (1968) *The Nation's Water Resources*, Washington, DC: GPO: 5-1-3.

"Water-Supply Statistics of Metered Cities" (1920) *American City*, December: 614–620.

"Water-Supply Statistics of Metered Cities" (1921) *American City* 24, January: 42–49.

"Water-Supply Statistics for Municipalities of Less Than 5,000 Population" (1925) *American City* 32, February.

"Water Supplies Will be Widely Extended After the War" (1944) *Scientific American* 171, July: 18.

Civil Society, Industry, and Regulation

Editor's Introduction to Chapter 13

In opening this final section on *civil society, industry, and regulation*, STS scholar David J. Hess documents the existence of four pathways through which citizen activists can make positive environmental change. These are not ideal types of political thought deduced from a theoretical perspective, but types of action that seem to be successful from an empirical political economic perspective on sustainability. These four "alternative pathways" for social change serve as laboratories of innovation that test alternative designs of organizations, technologies, and infrastructures that would enable a transition to a more just and sustainable society.

Hess finds industry will struggle to undermine environmental regulations and will continue to focus on growth at the expense of the environment. Social movements and other forms of social change action provide a source of ongoing pressure for change and experimentation with alternatives. Through a process of incorporation and transformation, reformers often achieve mixes of partial victory and cooptation.

There are two significant assumptions in Hess' analysis that are consistent with Dewey's assessment of *The Public & Its Problems*: first, the interests of industry are not necessarily congruent with those of the public. In cases where private judgment has adverse consequences for other citizens, the state exists to regulate such actions on behalf of public well-being. But second, the distinction between private matters and those public ones regulated by the state doesn't cover all possible associations.[1] There is a political or experimental space in between where some associations among citizens come into being in order to advocate for norms that are not commonly held. In such cases the public, or "civil society" as Hess prefers, anticipates improved alternative futures and works toward the rational acceptance of new norms by a majority of citizens. The most valued characteristic of a democratic society, for Dewey and Hess both, is the manner in which experimental thought within civil society becomes, through public talk and over time, the norm to be regulated by the state. By imagining a "civil society society," Hess too argues for the creative power of the public to construct new habits.

Note

1   Dewey, John. *The Public & Its Problems*. (New York [reprinted in Athens, Ohio]: H. Holt [reprinted by Swallow Press, Ohio University Press], 1927), 23–29.

Chapter 13

A Political Economy of Sustainability

Alternative Pathways and Industrial Innovation

David J. Hess

Introduction

A political economic approach to sustainability begins with the fundamental question: is a sustainable society possible within a political and economic system dominated by large, publicly traded corporations? Certainly the greening of industry is occurring, and many of the technologies that would reverse the ecological crises of global warming, resource depletion, and polluted ecosystems are available. However, as accumulation theorists have argued, to date the greening of industry takes place within an economic system that emphasizes ongoing growth as measured both by macroeconomic indices and ecological deposits and withdrawals. The growth of production and consumption overwhelms the forward steps of industrial greening with the backward steps of the aggregate impact of humans on the global ecosystem.[1]

Social scientists cannot predict the state of future society any more than climatologists can predict the climate, but we can extrapolate on trends. Under the more pessimistic scenarios that examine global conditions in a future seventh generation, economic growth will continue, technological innovation will enable new forms of environmental withdrawal and deposit, regulation will fail to keep pace with environmental damage, conversion to renewable energy will be little and too late, resource wars and terrorism will proliferate, civil liberties will continue to erode, cancer incidence will continue to climb, and the wealthy will pay an increasingly steep price for the "inverted quarantine" of access to clean air, water, and food, not to mention the security of life in gated communities and cloistered workplaces. The prospect of general civilizational collapse may not necessarily come to pass, but under the pessimistic scenarios there are likely to be increasingly large areas of the world characterized by slums, political chaos, starvation, epidemics, warfare, and genocide.[2]

If ongoing growth in consumption and environmental degradation are likely to continue to outpace ecologically oriented technological innovation, then the central political and economic issue in any discussion of sustainability is the transformation of an economic system based on ongoing growth in resource use. At the heart of that system is an amoral financial system that structures the goals of the publicly traded corporation around revenue and earnings growth. Advocates of eco-innovation argue that the self-correcting mechanisms of the market will generate increasing investments in green technologies, and there is some evidence that firms have shifted to practices that lessen their ecological footprints while also finding new sources of profit. However, studies of the greening of industry suggest that the primary causal factor behind eco-innovation is regulatory push rather than profitability pull. Even while some large, publicly traded corporations are making environmentally significant changes in their products and production processes, other corporations are finding new ways to exploit the environment.[3]

If the market alone cannot solve the problem, regulation is needed. However, the government, like the market, is likely to fail at providing adequate technological and economic change in a timely manner. Since the 1970s, the trend has been for governments to adopt neoliberal policies in support of increased privatization, as Melosi described in the previous chapter, and decreased government regulation. As a result, the potential for many governments to steer the economy in a more sustainable direction is weak. Even where there is little overt hostility to the fundamental proposition that some environmental regulation is needed, the regulatory interventions of most nation-states and international treaties have been inadequate to reverse ecological crises such as climate change, ongoing habitat destruction, and pervasive chemical pollution. Furthermore, some international agreements, such as the North American Free Trade Agreement, have significantly reduced the capacity for national and subnational governments to develop environmental regulations.

If one accepts the two basic arguments – that the publicly traded corporation has a growth logic that is at odds with significant restoration of ecological balance, and that neither the self-correcting mechanisms of the market nor the regulatory push of the nation-state have to date generated an adequate response – then one is left with little hope for significant change led by industrial and political elites. Although they are responding to environmental change by sanctioning a greening process, their responses have been inadequate to address the crisis. Given the absence of adequate leadership from elites, grassroots efforts have played and continue to play a role in generating the political will to make more significant reforms. Although social movements often lack the power to have a transformative effect on society, they can, at some historical junctures, raise effective challenges to the legitimacy of the dominant institutions, and as a result the action of social movements can lead to some changes. Whether those changes can be of great enough significance to reverse the flow of greenhouse gases into the atmosphere and toxic chemicals into the biosphere is impossible to determine. However, an analysis of the diversity, trajectories, and impacts of those movements may provide some insight into how they can be made more effective.

A typology of sustainability movements

The social movement literature, especially as it has developed in the English-speaking countries, is rich and complex, but in some ways it is also too narrowly focused for the study of sustainability politics. For example, it is too easy to circumscribe prematurely the object of study, the social movement, and to exclude from the horizon of analysis other forms of action aimed at societal change, especially the role of innovation that appears in the nonprofit sector, informal community networks, entrepreneurial businesses, and hobbies. A broader category of action is needed. Some

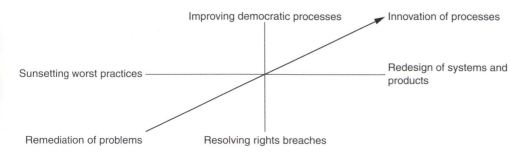

Figure 13.1
Sustainability as a
field of contestation.

of the leading social movement theorists have recognized the problem and suggested the term "contentious politics," but not all of the interesting action that will be discussed here is recognizably politics, and not all of it is contentious. As a result, I use "alternative pathways" as a general umbrella term for the wide range of sustainability-related movements to be discussed here.[4]

Sustainability is understood here as a political value that is situated in a contested field of action that can be conceptualized as having an environmental and social axis (see Figure 13.1). Along the environmental axis there is a range of possible positions, from remedial approaches such as sunsetting worst practices to radical technological innovation such as the redesign of product lifecycles, as occurs in the zero waste and industrial ecology fields. Likewise, along the social axis there is a parallel range of possible positions, from remedial approaches that correct lapses in human rights such as exposure of low-income communities to toxic chemicals to more process-oriented approaches that focus on making political and economic institutions more democratic, participatory, and deliberative. Together, the two axes form a field of potential and existing change action that would move society toward a state of "just sustainability," that is, a society that has not only solved its worst abuses of environmental and human degradation but has designed new technologies and institutions that would solve the environmental crises in a democratic way. Notice that in this conceptualization the "economic" is not a third axis, but instead a means toward achieving the value of a justly sustainable society.[5]

Business and government elites tend to define the politics of sustainability in a reductionist way. First, they often ignore the connection between environmental sustainability and social justice so that sustainability becomes a one-dimensional environmental issue, and second, they tend to define the environmental problem in terms of remediation rather than a fundamental rethinking of technological design and economic organizations. From the minimalist perspective of significant sectors of the elites, sustainability tends to be defined in terms of sunsetting various worst practices, such as immediately threatening pesticides, particulate emissions from diesel engines, or high levels of carbon dioxide. The project of moving to new designs – a chemical industry freed from organochlorines or a transportation sector powered by renewable energy – are often relegated to long-term research, such as the hydrogen-powered vehicle. By making sunsetting the short-term goal and redesign the long-term goal, the prospect of building a sustainable society is deferred to some future time, and short-term profits are left unthreatened. In contrast, the wide range of social movements and other types of social change action help keep alive a more dynamic and broader understanding of the vision of building a more justly sustainable society.

To get some handle on the wide range of movements related to the broad vision of sustainability, I have developed a somewhat specific nomenclature that allows some comparison across the historical instances of social change action oriented toward justice and/or environmental sustainability. First, a social movement is understood here to have broad scope in terms of organizational diversity and temporal duration; an intention to change society from below, that is, by groups that are not part of the ruling elites; and repertoires of action that include extrainstitutional strategies such as protest. When the effort to change society occurs within an industry or a profession and utilized institutionalized repertoires of action, I use the term industrial or professional "reform movement." When the scope is smaller than a movement, I use the term "activist" for groups that use extrainstitutional protest and "advocates" for those who work more within the system. The term "interest group" is reserved for groups that do not seek to change society but instead hope to gain resources for a specific segment of society. The terms are only ideal types that serve as guideposts for understanding some differences of emphasis in an empirical field that is constituted by mixed types along a continuum. The terms are based on relatively common usage and are unlikely to be highly controversial, but at the same time they may have some value in making comparisons somewhat more precise. The term "alternative pathway" provides a broader umbrella for discussing movements, activists, and advocacy groups, but it can also include networks of reform movements that bridge civil society and industry, including entrepreneurs. Thus, whereas social movement theory often explores the oppositional relationship between movements and industries, I prefer to open up the field of inquiry to include the partnerships among activists, advocates, hobbyists, and entrepreneurs.[6]

Utilizing the definition of a justly sustainable society given above, social change action can be divided into four major types associated with the poles of the two axes in Figure 13.1. Industrial opposition movements (IOMs) focus on bringing about the sunsetting of worst environmental practices. They function most recognizably as social movements because of their broad temporal and organizational scope and their use of repertoires of protest aimed at the state and industry. Alternative industrial movements, of which only technology- and product-oriented movements (TPMs) will be discussed here, focus more on designing and diffusing alternative technologies and products that embed an alternative view of society, the environment, and their relationship in systems of organizational and technological innovation. The TPMs are generally professional and/or industrial reform movements, with a component in nonprofit advocacy or trade association organizations and a component in for-profit firms that develop, produce, and market the alternative technology. Access movements and action focus on the rights dimension of the social axis; they demand greater access to goods, or reduced exposure to toxic substances, usually for the less well-off sectors of society. The organizations tend to be nonprofits that are rooted in extrainstitutional protest histories such as the civil rights movement but have often shifted into charitable and service-delivery roles due to devolution and privatization. Finally, democratic movements focus on changing fundamental patterns of deliberation, participation, and ownership. In this chapter I will focus on one type: localist action, which involves action oriented toward increased local ownership and control of the economy, again a "movement" that involves organizational mixes and includes the business sector.

Utilizing the typology of the four forms of social change action, one can develop an overview of various "alternative pathways" across different industrial fields. Table 13.1 lists some examples for four types of alternative pathways in the United States during the period from the 1960s to the present. The restrictions of period and country are based largely on the accessibility

Table 13.1 Alternative pathways for social change

Field of action:	Industry-oriented alternative pathways		Justice-oriented alternative pathways	
	Industrial opposition	Technology- and product-oriented	Access	Localism
Food and agriculture:	Pesticides, GMOs	Organic	Anti-hunger, community gardens	Local agricultural networks
Energy:	Nuclear energy	Renewable energy	Fuel banks	Home power, community power
Waste:	Pollution and toxics reduction	Recycling, zero waste	Thrift	Reuse and resale
Infrastructure:	Highways, development projects	New urbanism	Transit access, fair housing	Local sources, cohousing, ecovillages

of the information, and the analysis would be deepened by an historical and comparative perspective. Not all of the actors and organizations would endorse the full spectrum of a justly sustainable society as has been outlined here. In fact, many focus on specific corners of that field, and in some cases they work at cross purposes with each other or fail to recognize the contributions of other groups.

The analysis that follows summarizes part of the argument of a larger work that analyzes in detail various alternative pathways in science and industry. The space constraints of this chapter prohibit providing detailed histories of the trajectory of each of the sixteen boxes in Table 13.1. Instead, the discussion will develop a synthetic view of sustainability action and movements in the United States and their overall historical trajectory and impacts since the 1960s. One benefit of a synthetic analysis is to foster a greater appreciation for the contributions, limitations, and complementarities of the different approaches to building a more just and sustainable society.[7]

The Industrial Opposition Movements

The IOMs are most easily identified as social movements because of their broad scope and tendency to utilize protest as a repertoire of action directed against governments and large corporations. In some cases specific corporations are targeted, such as Monsanto in the case of genetically modified food or Mitsubishi and Citigroup in the case of rainforest degradation. In other cases, such as the movement against nuclear energy, government policies that supported the nuclear industry were a primary target. Community-based opposition to highways, cell phone towers, airports, and nuclear reactors was directed against specific construction projects.

The central goal of most IOMs is to develop a moratorium on an industrial process, project, or product. The organizations demand an end to an undesirable object, such as pesticides, genetically modified food, nuclear energy, air and water pollutants, organochlorines, and specific sites for highways, cell phone towers, or other development projects. When elites conclude that they cannot ignore the demands and will have to respond to them, the grassroot goals undergo a process of incorporation and transformation. However, frequently the outcome is only a partial moratorium. By negotiating a partial moratorium, elites avoid the worst confrontations and often split movements into accommodationist and radical wings. In many cases, movements can claim a degree of victory because some of the most egregious environmental problems are remediated. However, the concessions occur within a context of continued resource utilization and technological innovation that generates a new generation of hazards, risks, and oppositional mobilization.

Industrial opposition movements in the food and agriculture field have centered on agricultural waste, pesticides, and genetically modified food. Concern with agricultural waste has grown from the health effects of pesticides on farm workers to the effects that drifting pesticides and animal waste products have on the air and water supply of nearby residents. Both the growth of cities into former agricultural land and the increasing industrialization of meat production have added to the concerns. Pesticides in food and the ecosystem have been of general concern since the publication of *Silent Spring*, which directed attention to problems of industrial pollution. By the 1980s there was an international Pesticide Action Network that drew public attention to food issues, and by the 1990s the network could claim the victory of having convinced governments to ban several of the worst pesticides in food. During the 1990s the organization's mission diversified to include support of a broad coalition to limit or ban genetically modified food; however, achievement of a moratorium on genetically modified food proved to be more difficult than for some pesticides. One reason is that some of the genetically modified food allows reductions in pesticides, so industry may argue that there are some environmental benefits, and another reason is that the health risks are less clear, except for a few allergens, which have been banned from human food supplies.[8]

In the energy field the most salient IOM in the late twentieth century was the anti-nuclear energy movement, which had its origins in the 1950s and achieved widespread public mobilizations during the 1970s. By the mid-1970s the movement had shifted from a strategy of improving nuclear reactor safety to a call for a complete moratorium, and repertoires of action had diversified to include direct action from local groups such as the Clamshell and Abalone Alliances. Although protest action had some effect on the nuclear industry, the elimination of construction work in progress laws (which allowed utilities to charge customers for new construction on their utility bills) and the increase in interest rates shifted the underlying economics of nuclear reactor construction. With the achievement of a partial moratorium – the cancellation of new orders but not the closure of existing plants – many of the leaders and organizations shifted to anti-nuclear weapons activism.[9]

Waste and pollution were a central focus of the second wave of environmental organizations, such as the Environmental Defense Fund, Friends of the Earth, Greenpeace, the Natural Resources Defense Council, and the post-1960s Sierra Club. From the 1970s to the present those organizations dedicated resources to programs and campaigns in support of clean air, clean water, and toxics, as did science-based organizations such as the Union of Concerned Scientists, consumer organizations such as Public Citizen, and some of the older, "first wave" preservationist and conservationist organizations. During the 1970s support for environmental issues was widespread and to some degree bipartisan, and the environmental movement grew on a crest of legislative successes. Its repertoire of action tended to be more institutionalized, although street protest also occurred. However, by the 1980s the IOM in this field increasingly fought a rearguard battle that was focused less on new regulations and more on making sure that existing regulations were enforced or not watered down by neoliberal political leaders. Some of the most dangerous industrial pollutants have been limited, and emissions standards for vehicles have continued to improve (such as for diesel buses), but overall air and water quality remains at risk due to loopholes in laws, emissions trading, and continued growth. Furthermore, increasing attention and energy has focused on the unequal burden of pollution, especially across geographical, race, and class lines. The third wave of the environmental movement, the environmental justice movement, saw substantial growth during and after the 1980s, and with the development of community-based environmental justice and antitoxics organizations, localist and access goals became prominent. Notwithstanding ongoing support, both the wave of mainstream environmental organizations and the subsequent wave of environmental justice organizations have faced a situation of partial victory and partial moratoria. Often achievement of victory in one policy arena or community leads to a shift of burden and struggle to another arena or locale.[10]

During the 1960s and 1970s, the IOMs in the infrastructure field targeted new highway construction inside cities, which provoked significant opposition in some cities. Frequently, low-income and ethnic minority neighborhoods were targeted for demolition, and campaigns to stop highways were sometimes successful, particularly when multi-ethnic, multi-neighborhood coalitions coalesced, as in the cases of Boston and San Francisco. By the 1990s, highway projects through dense urban areas were drawing to a close, and mobilization against infrastructure projects shifted to targets such as big-box superstores, expansions of airports, and cell phone towers. In the process, the class address shifted more to middle-class homeowners who were concerned with the impacts of development on quality of life and housing values, and, in the case of big-box superstores, to independent retailers, who sometimes joined with neighborhood associations to halt construction of "category killing" retail outlets. Again, the outcomes have been mixed, with victories in one locality sometimes resulting in a shift of the project to another community.[11]

Over time there has been a tendency for some of the IOMs to take on a localist flavor. The anti-nuclear energy mobilizations against the siting of new plants, the environmental justice and antitoxics mobilizations, and most of the anti-infrastructure campaigns had a strong NIMBY (not-in-my-backyard) component, and some of the mobilization in opposition to pesticides has involved conflicts between farms and local residents over the drifting of pesticides, odors, and other agricultural waste into nearby communities. The localization of IOMs may occur partly because there are greater opportunities to develop public support when the threat is made more proximate and concrete, and partly because the political opportunity structure at the national and international level was more open during the 1970s than in the 1980s through the early 2000s.

The technology- and product-oriented movements

Like the IOMs, the TPMs target industry for change, but they tend to operate more as reform movements within the system, with relatively little evidence of repertoires of direct action and protest. There is often a symbiotic relationship between the IOMs and TPMs. Because IOMs are particularly vulnerable to the delegitimating claim that they are "negative" – that they do not propose a solution to the problem – members of the IOMs can point to the TPMs as the alternative to business as usual. Likewise, the IOMs tend to create opportunities for the TPMs, such as by educating consumers and the corporate sector about the availability of alternatives and by freeing up funding for research and development that support the TPMs.

Organizationally, TPMs are mixtures that include a reform movement side, often in the form of advocacy organizations, and a private sector side. From the movement perspective, the private sector side is a vehicle for social change, whereas from the private sector side, the movement can be a spur for market development. Some TPMs begin more as movements and develop toward the private sector over time, and likewise in some cases the private sector side sometimes begins as entrepreneurial firms and ends up being acquired by or displaced by large corporations. As a result, the relationship with large corporations is oppositional in the sense that the TPMs are creating alternative products and markets, but as the incorporation and transformation process unfolds, the relationship can evolve into partnership and cooptation.[12]

The incorporation and transformation process for TPMs works through two main mechanisms. In the first, entrepreneurial firms become publicly traded corporations, are purchased by them, or are marginalized by competing products developed by the corporate sector. An example is Cascadian Farms, which began as a back-to-the-land, organic, hippie farm and ended as a division of General Mills. In the second mechanism, countervailing industries sometimes step in to develop and transform the alternative technologies and products. An example is support from the energy industry for solar and wind energy when the electric power industry opposed it.[13]

To begin with the food and agriculture field, the organic food and agriculture movement in the US began largely as a gardening movement and then shifted into farming due to the influence of the post-1960s counterculture. During the 1980s, organic farming increasingly attracted larger growers who entered the industry because of new market opportunities that opened as a result of pesticide scares in food. During the 1990s, federal standards came to replace the patchwork of state-level organic standards and to facilitate the design change of organic food toward processed organic foods such as frozen foods and cereal bars. As the category of organic became a market niche for the food industry, profits shifted along the commodity chain from farmers to food producers. Smaller, more "alternative" farmers reframed their mission increasingly as one of environmental stewardship and local ownership (e.g., "sustainable local agriculture"), and some opted to develop networks of trust with local consumers rather than certify as organic.[14]

During the 1970s, a network of small-scale inventors and entrepreneurs began developing renewable energy, especially solar energy. Unlike in the agricultural field, where federal government recognition and support of organic farming did not develop until the 1980s, federal government support for renewable energy development in the US began in the 1970s. However, small-scale entrepreneurs – many of whom combined social movement goals of off-grid, independent power generation with their start-up businesses – found themselves pushed aside in favor of projects developed by industry. Afraid of widespread, decentralized power generation, the industry developed an alternative, on-grid vision of solar energy technology design. In contrast to solar, wind energy in the US has a longer industrial history, dating back to the nineteenth century. Wind energy has also provoked its own environmental backlash movement in the form of preservationist organizations that are concerned with bird kill and NIMBY groups concerned with viewshed pollution from wind farms. However, like solar energy, federal funding during the 1970s and after primarily supported designs oriented toward on-grid production, such as large turbine design that could be utilized in wind farms. The result in the cases of both solar and wind energy was an incorporation and transformation process that made the alternative energies compatible with centralized, corporate ownership and transmission via the grid. However, as in the case of the organic food industry, alternative designs compatible with the original movement goals of decentralized, locally controlled production also continued to be developed.[15]

As with organic food and wind energy, one can trace a history of recycling in the US that dates back to the nineteenth century, but during the 1970s a new recycling movement emerged as an off-shoot of second-wave environmentalism. It had a typical TPM mix of voluntary organizations and small firms, both of which collected and channeled materials to the reuse and remanufacturing industries. During the 1970s the recycling movement went through various ups and downs, and by the 1990s the small, nonprofit and independent operations were increasingly displaced by curbside programs run by city sanitation services or privatized waste management companies. Some recycling activists shifted into the zero waste movement, which focused on the upstream issue of product design and called for the replacement of nonrecyclables (such as toxic materials in computers) with greener materials. Some firms have responded to campaigns for product redesign and take-back programs, but at the same time industry in the US has generally opposed European-style mandates for extended producer responsibility. As the recycling movement became incorporated into the waste industry, some of the original recycling activists also formed reuse centers, which were generally locally owned businesses or nonprofit organizations that accepted household products such as furniture, appliances, cabinets, wood, and plumbing fixtures.[16]

In the infrastructure field, TPMs have emerged generally as professional reform movements that have advocated alternative forms of infrastructure development. In the 1960s, the reformers Jane Jacobs and Herbert Gans developed critiques of the subservient position of planning with respect to urban growth coalitions, and a variety of alternative planning organizations, often linked to tenants' rights struggles, emerged. In the 1980s, a more moderate reform movement emerged under the banners of new urbanism and smart growth, which called for transit-oriented development, urban growth boundaries, infill, mixed income building, and mixed used zoning. New urbanists encountered substantial criticism, especially from the more activist and radical planners, who argued that their projects tended to lead to gentrification and displacement of renters. In addition, some of the new urbanist projects have been incorporated and transformed by suburban housing developers, who have selected some of the neotraditional principles, often setting aside the goals of mixed income buildings and transit-oriented development, to make upscale and expensive developments for the wealthy.[17]

In general, TPMs can leverage considerable change in industry by carving out alternative categories of products and infrastructure, developing new markets, creating innovative designs, and drawing attention to the inadequacies of the status quo. They have been a significant force in the greening of industry because they have provided a profitability pull motivation that complements the regulatory push motivation that the IOMs tend to support. However, TPMs play an intense game of cooptation, not only because the alternative start-up firms tend to be displaced and acquired by large corporations but also because the dominant industrial corporations tend to redesign the original alternative technologies and products to make them more compatible with existing systems. One can view such outcomes from a glass-half-full or glass-half-empty perspective, but the achievements tend to be, as in the case of IOMs, only partial transformations that rarely match the ambitions of the activists and innovators.

Access movements and advocacy

Access organizations work along the vertical axis of the just sustainability field to develop awareness of the need for social change that addresses human rights. The work in this area spans a spectrum from activism to charitable work, that is, from social movement organizations to interest groups and charities that redistribute resources to the poor but do not articulate a social change agenda. However, the latter can develop a social change agenda over time, and conversely activist organizations can become captured by charitable and service-provisioning goals. In all cases, the organizations are generally nonprofit entities, and their relationship with large corporations can vary from opposition – when the corporations are seen as responsible for rights violations – to partnership, when the corporations are donors to organizational efforts to provide needs.

The incorporation and transformation process of access movements tends to occur as a long-term shift from a period of advocacy and even activism, when rights and recognition are demanded from the state and industry, toward a phase of service delivery, when the organizations become conduits for the flow of materials from the state and private sector to those in need. The process is most visible in the antihunger and fair housing fields, and it is not uniformly evident across the access pathways. The historical change is associated with the downward and outward shift of welfare-related policies that occurred with the rise of neoliberal ideologies after 1980. In other words, welfare obligations have been devolved downward from the federal government to state and local governments through the block-granting process, and likewise they have been privatized through incentives that link access to government or foundation funding to matching support from the private sector. The devolution and privatization process can coincide with the incorporation of some organizations into welfare networks and the transformation of their missions from justice goals to service provisioning. However, the process may in turn lead to a new generation of organizations that resurrect the older, rights values when service provisioning arrangements come under threat due to cuts in government budgets.

In the food and agriculture field, the anti-hunger movement seeks to provide food to those who are hungry or have inadequate access to food on a regular basis. During the 1980s cutbacks in federal entitlement programs and a recession triggered rapid growth of anti-hunger organizations, and from that period to the present, most anti-hunger organizations reported that demand outstripped supply. Hunger and food security organizations channeled food from government, individual, and corporate donors through food banks to distribution centers such as pantries, soup kitchens, and homeless shelters. The large anti-hunger organizations that operated at a national level have, like the nationally oriented environmental organizations, diversified to occupy different niches. Some are best characterized as charitable organizations, whereas Bread for the World, RESULTS, and the Food Research and Action Center have a more political, social change mission.

Since the mid-1990s, a coalition of organizations represented by the Community Food Security Council has attempted to shift the hunger agenda toward local self-reliance based on institutions such as the farmers' markets and food cooperatives in low-income neighborhoods. The agenda is also consistent with the movement to develop community gardens, which complement hunger organizations as a second access pathway in the food sector. Whereas the historical transformation of anti-hunger organizations has tended to involve a shift from activism to service provisioning, in the case of community gardening the parallel transformation since the 1960s has been institutionalization through partnerships between grassroots community gardening organizations and city departments (such as a department of parks or neighborhoods) and local foundations. In cities where land values have risen dramatically, community gardens have been forced to secure land tenure either through purchases supported by local foundations or by moving to city-owned land such as parks and school grounds.[18]

In the energy field, federal support for energy access was inaugurated in 1981 under the Low Income Home Energy Assistance Program. Under the block grant system, federal funds were channeled to the state and local governments, and public–private partnerships developed through a system of energy banks or fuel funds that were analogous to food banks. At the national level, advocacy work was much less developed than in the food field, and at the time of writing it appeared to be limited largely to two organizations: the National Low-Income Energy Consortium and the National Fuel Funds Network. There is limited evidence in this field for an historical process of incorporation and transformation, perhaps because government support for energy assistance has been relatively consistent over time.[19]

Access pathways in the waste field overlap considerably with localist pathways in the rapidly growing resale sector of the retail industry. The nonprofit thrift industry, such as the Salvation Army and Goodwill, operates stores that provide clothing and other household materials and serve as the equivalent of food and energy banks; indeed, a specialized segment has emerged under the rubric of "furniture banks." Increases in income equality and changes in welfare benefits have fueled the growth of the broader resale sector, which includes both the thrift sector and for-profit, second-hand stores. Although the broad resale sector is more oriented toward the access goal of providing usable goods at very low prices, environmental concerns have been a prominent motivation in one segment of the resale sector: reuse centers. Reuse centers may be set up as for-profit businesses, but many that we surveyed were nonprofit organizations that have an environmental and/or community development mission, and some provide job training to low-income residents.[20]

In the infrastructure field a parallel access pathway was the growth of community development corporations (CDCs). The first generation of organizations had a business development orientation, but over time they came to focus more on providing affordable housing. President Nixon's Community Development Block Grant Program was intended to open up funding to the non-poor, but advocacy organizations proved to be good at recapturing the funding. Cutbacks under the Reagan administration and after resulted in increased privatization of funding as well as the professionalization of community development and housing advocacy organizations. In contrast, access-oriented action in support of improved public transportation remained closer to its roots in the civil rights movement. The concept of "transit justice" has been developed as an infrastructural counterpart to environmental justice, and grassroots mobilization has emerged over the emissions levels of public transit. However, transit justice organizations also focus on fundamental access issues such as resisting fare increases, improving the frequency and extent of service, and reducing funding disparities between bus service to low-income neighborhoods and commuter rail.[21]

Access pathways serve to remind theorists of sustainability and design that for a large proportion of the population, even in wealthy countries such as the United States, access to the basic requirements of life – food, energy, clothing, furniture, housing, and transportation – remains a much more pressing issue than saving the environment. To date, the access pathways have tended to operate apart from sustainability considerations, but there are various points where a convergence can be found: the links between local agricultural networks and local hunger networks, the continuing development of sustainable practices in community gardens, the availability of weatherization and energy conservation programs for low-income energy consumers, the articulation of environmental and social justice goals that occurs in the reuse centers and some other corners of the resale industry, and the small but growing attention to the greening of affordable housing and public transportation. In the "beggars can't be choosy" world of access economics and politics, green access may be considered an unaffordable luxury, but thinking through what it can involve could help ignite powerful synergies between the social justice and environmental sustainability agendas.

Localism

Localism is only one among many pathways that aim to strengthen and redesign democratic institutions and processes. Other approaches include demarchy (random selection of citizens as in juries) and various deliberative and participatory institutions, as well as structural reforms such as campaign finance reform and media reform. Localism enhances democracy by developing alternative institutions that would strengthen the local economy and revitalize local ownership; in other words, it represents one response to the loss of democratic control over the economy that has occurred during an era of economic and political globalization. Localist firms are privately held, locally owned, independent businesses, such as family stores and service businesses. Unlike the large, publicly traded corporation, for localist businesses growth and profitability are often less important overarching goals than merely maintaining an adequate revenue stream to cover wages and other expenses. Other localist organizations include regional nonprofit organizations and the service agencies of the local government, such as publicly-owned utilities and transit agencies, where a mission broader than growth of revenue and profits is generally explicit. The most typical localist organizations tend to be in the retail, service, and agricultural sectors, whereas in the manufacturing sector economies of scale may require firms to compete in nonlocal markets, grow rapidly to take advantage of product innovation, and seek nonlocal capital to fuel the growth.[22]

In some cases, networks of localist organizations seek consumer boycotts in favor of their products and, implicitly or explicitly, boycotts of corporate products. For example, one finds "buy local" campaigns in some of the affiliate organizations of the two main national networks of alternative, local business associations (the American Independent Business Alliance and the

Business Alliance for Local Living Economies). Main street retailers who are under competition from big-box stores and small farmers who are trying to develop local direct marketing networks tend to be the main sources of support for buy local campaigns, but there are also interesting examples of the use of import substitution in city government purchases that are designed to help develop a local industry.[23]

The incorporation and transformation process in the localist segment of social change action depends greatly on organizational form. Small businesses are especially vulnerable to displacement by the chains, and they often must differentiate their products from those of the chains in order to stay in business. When they are pushed out of conventional markets, they can form niches oriented to green, fair trade, and other products that appeal to progressive, middle-class consumers, or they can diversify into the reuse and service sectors. Nonprofit organizations and public agencies are more able to resist direct acquisition or displacement by large firms, but nonprofits may undergo shifts toward professionalization that include higher levels of participation by nonlocal elites on the governing boards.

In the food and agriculture field, the case for localism has been especially easy to make because of the concern of some middle-class shoppers with supporting local farms to slow the demise of the countryside, and because high-quality, fresh, local produce is generally superior to the varieties offered in the supermarket. Frequently, localism in agriculture is combined with sustainable production, and the "sustainable, local agriculture movement" is in some ways the heir to what was formerly called the organic movement. However, localism in agriculture, as with other localist alternative pathways, is not necessarily environmentally sustainable; the primary feature is local ownership and control. Local agricultural networks are built around a mixture of institutions, some old and some new, including farmers' markets, retail food cooperatives, community-supported agriculture (subscription-based farming), local food labels, and restaurants and cafeterias that emphasize local food purchases. In all cases there is quantitative evidence of growth from the 1980s to the present, but in absolute terms each example of agricultural localism has achieved only a relatively small percentage of total market share. Most of the institutions have been relatively resistant to incorporation and transformation; the strongest case for incorporation and transformation is with food cooperatives, which are being displaced by the natural foods grocery chains and natural foods sections in mainstream supermarket chain stores.[24]

In the United States most of the electric utilities are locally-owned public power agencies, but investor-owned utilities serve most of the large cities and the preponderance of consumers. Because many public power agencies possess little or no generation capacity, they must buy their electricity from electricity generators and in effect are electricity retailers. However, some of the larger public power utilities have significant generation capacity and have provided models of renewable energy innovation. For example, Seattle City Light claims to have become the first carbon neutral utility in the country, largely because of its significant hydropower sources but also because of investments in wind and other renewable energy sources. In San Francisco there was a heated grassroots campaign to replace the investor-owned utility with local government ownership, but proponents of public power lost the referendum. San Francisco, like other cities, then pursued the alternative pathway of aggregating their customers and seeking competitive bids from investor-owned utilities that are willing to provide a specified portion of the portfolio through renewables or cleaner energy. The San Francisco aggregation may result in significant new construction of local, distributed renewable energy generation. In the case of public power, there is again evidence of an incorporation and transformation process, which occurred as the strategy of conversion to public power has given way to community aggregation. In the latter, communities aggregate all customers after an opt-out period, then they negotiate a group contract with an electricity service provider. In San Francisco, community choice aggregation has been coupled with the city's bond authority to create investment in hundreds of megawatts of locally-owned renewable energy and energy conservation developments.[25]

The ideal typical form of localism in the waste field would involve the capture of local waste by locally-owned or controlled organizations to produce products for sale on local markets. One can find some examples of such operations in city-owned composting, small-scale recycling and remanufacturing operations that sell to local markets, and arts and crafts enterprises that make products from recycled or reused products. However, the remanufacturing industry as a whole tends to operate at a larger scale, where inputs tend to come from local and nonlocal sources, and markets are continental if not international. Instead, localism in the waste field can be found in yard sales and other aspects of the resale sector already mentioned. About 20 percent of all Americans have held a yard sale in the past year, and the resale sector claims to be the fastest growing sector of retail. In this case the access and localist pathways are very closely interwoven.[26]

One example of localism in the infrastructure field is sourcing to local businesses for infrastructure projects. For example, in Chattanooga the public transit agency helped to develop a local electric bus manufacturing company by shifting its purchases to the company, and in Seattle the transit agency has purchased biodiesel blends, much of which is produced locally. Likewise, in some cases building construction can substitute local materials, and points are given in the LEED certification process for buildings that use local materials. In addition to import substitution, localism in infrastructure also involves organizational innovations that have resituated the small domestic unit in larger living arrangements that allow cooperative, local arrangements to recapture labor that has been previously outsourced to the market, such as collective childcare and cooking arrangements. Cohousing provides greater opportunities for communal activities such as meal sharing, whereas ecovillages take the additional step of attempting to combine work and living arrangements. Both cohousing and ecovillage units tend to be innovative in terms of energy efficiency and other sustainable building practices.[27]

Localism has the advantage of building on widespread grassroots dissatisfaction with the loss of economic sovereignty that has accompanied the globalization of the economy. Localist projects tend to construct alternative markets in a manner similar to the TPMs, but the localist alternative flags ownership rather than green product design as the main portal to social change. Furthermore, localism can also substitute nonmarket activity, such as home improvements and collective domestic labor arrangements, for services that were previously purchased on the market. Because of the emphasis on the invigoration of the local community, localist pathways have the advantage of being able to attract support across traditional left–right political boundaries. Although localism can devolve into enclavism, it can also be opened up to alternative trade networks, which also emphasize purchasing locally-owned, privately held businesses throughout the world. The complex politics of localism are explored elsewhere, but it is worth noting that, as in the case of access pathways, localist pathways are not necessarily linked to sustainability values.

For example, not all local farms use sustainable agricultural practices, and not all off-grid home power projects use renewable energy. However, there are numerous points of convergence in the worlds of sustainable local agricultural networks, public power companies, distributed and off-grid energy, the local second-hand economy, and alternative living arrangements. The localist pathways have the advantage of reminding theorists of sustainability that issues of democratic, bottom-up political organization may be important for thinking through the fundamental social changes that are needed to solve environmental and social justice problems.[28]

Conclusion

As an economic system capitalism has often been defined as based on production for profit, but under conditions of monopolistic competition in the global knowledge economy, it is more accurate to say that capitalism is also production to standard. The most ubiquitous standards are those generated by groups of large corporations to capture a price premium and customer loyalty for their differentiated brands, but governments and intergovernmental organizations also develop standards. The wide range of alternative pathways discussed in this chapter provide public input into the process of defining standards and products, and they open up a public debate on "object conflicts," or definitional struggles among firms, states, and civil society organizations over the design and shaping of the material culture of society.

The IOMs are probably the most transparent example of the role that social change actors play in conflicts over technologies, products, and their design and standards. Conflicts over pesticides in food, nuclear energy safety, cell phone tower locations, and acceptable air quality or emissions standards involve social movement and advocacy organizations as representatives of societal and environmental interests in negotiations with firms and states over standards. Where negotiations are not successful and standards are inadequate, demonstrations and consumer boycotts can emerge, and the result can be a moratorium or partial moratorium on a technology, infrastructure design, or other aspect of the material culture. The achievement of a partial moratorium is only a partial victory, because it shifts the contours of a technological field and the development of material culture and design in a new direction but sets the stage for a new generation of conflicts.

In the TPMs, the outcome of the incorporation and transformation process is a double-edged process whereby established industrial firms may change to accept the alternative technologies and products, but the alternative technologies rarely replace those of the mainstream. Instead, a complementarization process often emerges, whereby the alternative is redesigned into a technology and/or product that is compatible with those produced by the dominant corporations of the industrial field. An example is solar and wind energy, which the power industry originally saw as very frightening because it raised the specter of transmission lines coming down due to off-grid power production. Over a multidecade process of change, the industry has instead incorporated and transformed the technology in two ways. First, the concept of distributed generation allowed formerly off-grid technologies to become grid interconnected, with the grid serving as a bank for deposits and withdrawals of energy from local sources. Second, the technology itself was redesigned – especially in the case of wind farms but increasingly also in the case of solar farms – so that it could be utilized for grid-based production. This is not to say that the original, localist variant of alternative, small-scale wind turbine designs has disappeared; rather, it has become marginalized as capital investments have flowed into designs that are more compatible with existing technological systems and investments. Another example is organic food, which has gone from a fresh, directly marketed, local whole food anchored in local agricultural networks to a product category for food that can be produced on large farms, transformed into processed food, transferred through global commodity chains, and sold through mass channels such as supermarkets. Again, as the object of "organic food" is incorporated into the existing industrial system, it undergoes a change in design whereby it is made increasingly complementary to existing forms of industrial food production and products. In particular, the localism drops out, and the whole foods dimension is relegated to one option among many.

Access and localist organizations focus less on the design of products and industrial processes and more on organizational design, that is, how economic systems can be designed to ensure goals such as meeting basic human rights and providing for enhanced democratic control of the economy. Object conflicts in access pathways tend to occur around organizational mission. For example, is the mission of an antihunger organization to relieve hunger or reduce inequality in society that is at the basis of hunger? The definition of the object of access has implications for how food production and distribution systems are organized. Likewise, in the localist pathways there are many conflicts emerging over definitions of localism, such as the extent to which local business networks will also be committed to sustainability and justice goals. As in the case of the IOMs and TPMs, there are conflicts over design, but in this case the conflicts are more focused on organizational design than material culture and production processes.

Behind the range of object conflicts is a general question of how the economy should evolve if societies are to move more rapidly toward solving the ecological crises and problems of social justice that they currently face. As accumulation and treadmill-of-production theorists have noted, among the publicly traded corporations there is little evidence for the emancipation of environmental and social values from the paramount value of profitability and growth. Indeed, the financialization of the economy tends to place an ever-greater emphasis on those goals. In the large corporate and financial organizations, the technological and discursive shifts associated with ecological modernization take place within a context of investor interest in continued profitability. Change in their paramount value of profitability growth would require significant shifts in state regulations so that large, publicly traded corporations would be required to set general societal benefit concerns above the interest in maximizing profits for shareholders.[29]

From the broader historical perspective of world history and ecological anthropology, a global economy based on an amoral, growth-oriented, economic organization might be viewed as a long-term problem of ecological adaptation of the economy. Shifts in sectoral dominance in human societies have occurred over time: in the earliest human societies, kinship relations encompassed the economic and political "systems," whereas in the urban civilizations and empires, centralized states (in some cases theocracies) dominated the economic sector.[30] The current configuration of society, in which the large corporations of the private sector dominate the state, civil society, and domestic sphere, is not necessarily the endpoint of historical development of human societies. The various alternative pathways discussed here provide experimental models of a way to organize the economy and society that would enable issues of sustainability and justice to encompass that of amoral profit-seeking. Organizationally, one can see examples where public mission encompasses profit-seeking in revenue-generating state agencies, such as transit agencies and publicly-owned utilities; nonprofit organizations that derive a portion of their revenue stream from market activity, such as nonprofit farms and reuse centers; domestic units or networks of domestic units, as found in cohousing facilities and community gardening groups; and privately held, locally owned, for-profit firms that have endorsed social and environmental values over growth. In those organizations, goals traditionally associated with civil society organizations – social justice and environmental sustainability – meet the market through the production and sale of goods and services. They raise the possibility of a "civil society society" as a next step beyond the capitalist society.

If such a transformation were to occur, it would require a significant rethinking of how financial markets operate and how corporate charters are defined. Any attempts to redefine highly profitable organizational forms that benefit elites will likely be dismissed, marginalized, and suppressed. The alternative pathways serve as demonstration projects and educational fora that teach the feasibility of significant societal change; they are, in a sense, research and development centers for the innovation of new organizational, technological, and market relationships that might be capable of producing a more just and sustainable future. However, to bring the demonstration projects to full scale, significant reforms would be required in the standards by which publicly traded corporations are organized and the objects that they are allowed to produce. Such changes would be unlikely to occur unless severe social and environmental disruptions were to endanger the survival of elites. At that point, the alternative pathways would come to serve as resources for redefining what is left of society and the environment.

Acknowledgments

This chapter summarizes research that is discussed in more detail in David J. Hess, *Alternative Pathways in Science and Industry* (MIT Press, 2007), with prior contractual permission from MIT Press (www.mitpress.edu).

Questions for further consideration

1   As did historian Martin V. Melosi in the previous chapter, STS scholar David J. Hess documents in this chapter the messy distinctions between matters of private and public concern. Hess' view toward change is, however, more like Jamison's proposal for "change-oriented research" discussed in Chapter 4, in which private citizens advocate for the adoption of new public norms. Hess proposes, however, methods of successful action rather than norms per se. Is there a difference?

2   There is a fundamental disagreement between those, like McDaniel and Lanham in Chapter 3, who see liberal capitalism as a "self-correcting system," and those like Hess, Jamison, Winner, and Feenberg who make strong arguments for strong regulation. What, if anything, do these authors share?

3   Hess' analysis is inductive, meaning that he sought to reconstruct and categorize those sustainability practices in the private sector that had been relatively successful. This is a very different investigation than that conducted by historian Andrew Jamison, who worked more or less deductively to discover the nature of "green knowledge." Although these contributors share a common attitude toward action-oriented research, their research methods could not be more different. Does it matter?

4   Like his colleague Langdon Winner, Hess sees the development of new "green technologies" as a field of struggle where "the process of defining standards and products" is contested by at least three parties: the citizens who use them, the corporations who make them, and the governments who struggle to regulate them. And like Oden in Chapter 2, Hess argues that corporations have disproportionate power in non-economic spheres of life because they dominate decisions about what things we are going to make and how we make them. Is Hess's proposal for redistributing choice inherently democratic? If so, how might the market be democratized beyond the superficial practice of market research?

5   The contested territory of "standards and products" documented by Hess has few clear winners and losers. Rather, standards are constantly revised, co-opted, or compromised in response to the rapidly changing conditions theorized by McDaniel and Lanham in Chapter 3. STS scholar Guy in Chapter 7, and Architect Canizaro in Chapter 9, suggest that the conflict is not only a pre-design power struggle about defining the product or standard *a priori*, but the conflict is embedded in the manner we design the world in which we hope to live. Guy's point "is not to abandon judgment" when design begins, "but ... avoid closing down the evaluative process prematurely, to always be open to other design possibilities." What are the implications of these insights for the design disciplines?

Notes

1   Schnaiberg and Gould 1994 and York and Rosa 2003.
2   Davis 2006 and Meadows *et al.* 2004. On the inverted quarantine, see Szasz 2007.
3   Bayliss *et al.* 1998a, 1998b; DeSimone *et al.* 1997; Florida 1996; Hawken *et al.* 1999.
4   On contentious politics, see McAdam *et al.* 2001. On alternative pathways, see Hess 2007a as well as Gottlieb 2001 and similar concepts in Brown 2001; Daley-Hughes 2002; Henderson 1996; Korten 1999; Pinderhughes 2004.
5   On just sustainability, see Agyeman *et al.* 2003. See also Campbell 1996; McGranahan and Sattherhwaite 2000; O'Connor 1998.
6   Flacks 2004; McAdam and Snow 1997; Tarrow 1998.
7   Hess 2007a. For a similar historical perspective, see Hård and Jamison 2005.
8   Brieger 2002; Carson 1962; Reisner 2001.
9   Gusterson 1996; Joppke 1993; Moyer *et al.* 2001; Wellock 1998.
10   Bullard 1994; Cole and Foster 2000; Dowie 1995; Gottlieb 1993; Heiman 1990; Kline 2000; Mazmanian and Kraft 1999; Summit II National Office 2002; Szasz 1994.
11   Issel 1999; Mitchell 2006; Mohl 2004; Norman 2009; Regional Commission on Airport Affairs 2009.
12   For a more detailed discussion of TPMs, see Hess 2005, 2007a.
13   Pollan 2001.
14   Gottlieb 2001; Guthman 2004; other sources in Hess 2004, 2007a.

15   Asumus 2001; Reece 1979; Righter 1996.
16   Lounsbury *et al.* 2003; Palmer and Walls 2002; Seldman 1995; Weinburg *et al.* 2000.
17   Congress for the New Urbanism 2002; Gans 1959; Hoffman 1989; Jacobs 1961; Pyatok 2000.
18   Allen 2004; Eisenger 1998; Gottlieb 2001; Poppendieck 1998.
19   National Fuel Funds Network 2009 and National Low Income Energy Consortium 2009. Some utility companies also provide assistance to low-income customers and assistance for weatherization.
20   Hess 2009; Horne and Maddrell 2002; National Association of Resale and Thrift Shops 2009; Warren 1999.
21   Bullard *et al.* 2000, 2004; Dreir 1997; Ferguson and Dickens 1999; Hess 2007b.
22   Carson and Martin 2002; Fischer 2000; Sclove 1995; Shuman 2000; Williamson *et al.* 2002.
23   Mitchell 2006 and Shuman 2006.
24   A. Brown 2001, 2002 and Stevenson *et al.* 2004. For more detailed literature reviews and sources, see Hess 2007, 2008, 2009.
25   Fenn 2009 and Hess 2009.
26   Hess 2007a, 2009; Lach 2000.
27   Cassidy 2003; Jackson and Jackson 2004; McCamant *et al.* 1994.
28   Hess 2009.
29   Mol 1996; Mol and Spaargaern 2000; Pellow *et al.* 2000; Scheinberg 2003; Schnaiberg and Gould 1994. There is an exchange about the extent to which one can empirically support a claim that there has been an emanicipation of environmental values from the paramount value of profitability. Clearly, such an emancipation, when it will occur, will depend on significant regulatory changes.
30   Chase-Dunn and Hall 1997.

References

Agyeman, J., Bullard, R., and Evans, B. (2003) *Just Sustainabilities: Development in an Unequal World*, Cambridge, MA: MIT Press.

Allen, P. (2004) *Together at the Table: Sustainability and Sustenance in the American Agrifood System*, University Park, PA: Pennsylvania State University Press.

Asmus, P. (2001) *Reaping the Wind: How Mechanical Wizards, Visionaries, & Profiteers Helped Shape Our Energy Future,* Washington, DC: Island Press.

Bayliss, R., Connell, L., and Flynn, A. (1998a) "Sector variation and ecological modernization: towards an analysis at the level of the firm," *Business Strategy and the Environment*, 7, 3: 150–161.

—— (1998b) "Company size, environmental regulation, and ecological modernization: further analysis at the level of the firm," *Business Strategy and the Environment* 7, 5: 285–296.

Brieger, T. (2002) "Pesticide Action Network's first twenty years: an interview with Monica Moore," *Global Pesticide Campaigner* May: 18–21.

Brown, A. (2001) "Counting farmers' markets," *Geographical Review* 91, 4: 655–674.

—— (2002) "Farmers' market research 1940–2000: an inventory and review," *American Journal of Alternative Agriculture* 17, 4: 167–176.

Brown, L. (2001) *Eco-economy: Building an Economy for the Earth*, New York: W.W. Norton.

Bullard, R. (1994) *Dumping in Dixie: Race, Class, and Environmental Quality*, Boulder, CO: Westview Press.

Bullard, R., Johnson, G., and Torres, A. eds. (2000) *Sprawl City: Race, Politics, and Planning in Atlanta*, Washington, DC: Island Press.

Bullard, R., Johnson, G., and Torres, A. eds. (2004) *Highway Robbery: Transportation Racism and New Routes to Equity*, Boston, MA: South End Press.

Campbell, S. (1996) "Green cities, growing cities, just cities? Urban planning and the contradictions of sustainable development," *American Planning Association Journal* 62, 3: 296–312.

Carson, L., and Martin, B. (2002) "Random selection of citizens for technological decision making," *Science and Public Policy* 29, 2 (April): 105–113.

Carson, R. (1962) *Silent Spring*, Boston, MA: Houghton-Mifflin.

Cassidy, R. (ed.) (2003) "The basics of LEED," *Building Design and Construction* November (supplement): 8–12.

Chase-Dunn, C., and Hall, T. (1997) *Rise and Demise: Comparing World Systems*, Boulder, CO: Westview Press.

Cole, L., and Foster, S. (2000) *From the Ground Up: Environmental Racism and the Rise of the Environmental Justice Movement,* New York: NYU Press.

Congress for the New Urbanism (2002) "Charter of the New Urbanism." Online, available at: www.cnu.org/charter (accessed May 15 2009).

Daley-Hughes, S. (2002) *Pathways Out of Poverty*, Bloomfield, CT: Kumarian Press.

Davis, M. (2006) *Planet of Slums*, London: Verso.

DeSimone, L., and Popoff, F., with the World Business Council for Sustainable Development. (1997) *Eco-Efficiency: The Business Link to Sustainable Development*, Cambridge, MA: MIT Press.

Dowie, M. (1995) *Losing Ground: American Environmentalism at the End of the Century*, Cambridge, MA: MIT Press.

Dreier, P. (1997) "The new politics of housing: how to build a constituency for a progressive federal housing policy," *Journal of the American Planning Association* 63, Winter: 5–27.

Eisinger, P. (1998) *Toward an End to Hunger in America*, Washington, DC: Brookings Institution.

Fenn, P. (2009) "Local Power." Online, available at: www.local.org/local.html (accessed May 10 2009).

Ferguson, R., and Dickens, W. (eds.) (1999) *Urban Problems and Community Development*, Washington, DC: Brookings Institution.

Fischer, F. (2000) *Citizens, Experts, and the Environment: The Politics of Local Knowledge*, Durham, NC: Duke University Press.

Flacks, R. (2004) "Knowledge for what? Thoughts on the state of social movement studies," in J. Goodwin and J. Jasper (eds.) *Rethinking Social Movements: Structure, Meaning, and Emotion*, Lanham, MD: Rowman and Littlefield, pp. 135–153.

Florida, R. (1996) "Lean and green: the move to environmentally conscious manufacturing," *California Management Review* 39, 1: 80–105.

Gans, H. (1959) "The human implications of current redevelopment and relocation planning," *Journal of the American Institute of Planners* 25, 1: 15–25.

Gottlieb, R. (1993) *Forcing the Spring: The Transformation of the American Environmental Movement*, Washington, DC: Island Press.

——. (2001) *Environmentalism Unbound: Exploring New Pathways for Change*, Cambridge, MA: MIT Press.

Gusterson, H. (1996) *Nuclear Rites: A Weapons Laboratory at the End of the Cold War*, Berkeley, CA: University of California Press.

Guthman, J. (2004) *Agrarian Dreams: The Paradox of Organic Farming in California*, Berkeley, CA: University of California Press.

Hård, M., and Jamison, A. (2005) *Hubris and Hybrids: A Cultural History of Technology and Science*, New York: Routledge.

Hawken, P., Lovins, A., and Lovins, J. H. (1999) *Natural Capitalism: Creating the Next Industrial Revolution,* Boston, MA: Little, Brown, and Co.

Heiman, M. (1990) "From 'not in my backyard!' to 'not in anybody's backyard!': grassroots challenge to hazardous waste facility siting," *Journal of the American Planning Association* 56, 3: 359–362.

Henderson, H. (1996) *Creating Alternative Futures*, Bloomfield, CT: Kumarian.

Hess, D. J. (2004) "Organic food and agriculture in the U.S.: object conflicts in a health-environmental movement," *Science as Culture* 13, 4: 493–513.

——. (2005) "Technology and product-oriented movements: approximating social movement studies and science and technology studies," *Science, Technology, and Human Values* 30, 4: 515–535.

——. (2007a) *Alternative Pathways in Science and Industry: Activism, the Innovation, and the Environment in an Era of Globalization*, Cambridge, MA: MIT Press.

——. (2007b) "What is a clean bus? Object conflicts in the greening of urban transit," *Sustainability: Science, Practice, and Policy* 3, 1: 1–14.

——. (2008) "Localism and the Environment," *Sociology Compass* 2, 2: 625–638.

——. (2009) *Localist Movements in a Global Economy: Sustainability, Justice, and Urban Development in the United States*, Cambridge, MA: MIT Press.

Hoffman, L. (1989) *The Politics of Knowledge: Activist Movements in Medicine and Planning*, Albany, NY: The State University of New York Press.

Horne, S., and Maddrell. A. (2002) *Charity Shops: Retailing, Consumption, and Society*, New York: Routledge.

Issel, W. (1999) "Land values, human values, and the preservation of the city's treasured appearance," *Pacific Historical Review* 68, 4: 611–646.

Jackson, H., and Jackson, R. (2004) "Global eco-village network history, 1990–2004," Gaia Trust. Online, available at: www.gaia.org/mediafiles/gaia/resources/HJackson_GEN-History.pdf (accessed May 15 2009).

Jacobs, J. (1961) *The Death and Life of Great American Cities*, New York: Vintage Books.

Joppke, C. (1993) *Mobilizing against Nuclear Energy: A Comparison of Germany and the United States*, Berkeley, CA: University of California Press.

Kline, B. (2000) *First Along the River*, San Francisco, CA: Acada Books.

Korten, D. (1999) *The Post-Corporate World: Life after Capitalism*, West Hartford, CT: Kumarian.

Lach, J. (2000) "Welcome to the hoard fest," *American Demographics* 22, 4: 8–9.

Lounsbury, M., Ventresca, M., and Hirsch, P. (2003) "Social movements, field frames, and industry emergence: a cultural-political perspective on U.S. recycling," *Socio-Economic Review* 1, 1: 71–105.

McAdam, D., and Snow, D. (eds.) (1997) *Social Movements: Readings on their Emergence, Mobilization, and Dynamics*, Los Angeles, CA: Roxbury Publishing Co.

McAdam, D., Tarrow, S., and Tilly, C. (2001) *Dynamics of Contention*, Cambridge, MA: Cambridge University Press.

McCamant, K., and Durrett, C., with Hertzman, E. (1994) *Cohousing: A Contemporary Approach to Housing Ourselves*, Berkeley, CA: Ten-Speed Press.

McGranahan, G., and Satterthwaite, D. (2000) "Environmental health or ecological sustainability? Reconciling the brown and green agendas in urban development," in C. Pugh (ed.) *Sustainable Cities in Developing Countries*, London and Sterling, VA: Earthscan, pp. 73–90.

Mazmanian, D., and Kraft, M. (eds.) (1999) *Toward Sustainable Communities: Transition and Transformations in Environmental Policy*, Cambridge, MA: MIT Press.

Meadows, D., Randers, J., and Meadows, D. (2004) *Limits to Growth: The Thirty-Year Update*, White River Junction, VT: Chelsea Green.

Mitchell, S. (2006) *Big-Box Swindle: The True Cost of Mega-Retailers and the Fight for America's Independent Businesses*, Boston, MA: Beacon.

Mohl, R. (2004) "Stop the road: freeway revolts in American cities," *Journal of Urban History* 30, 5: 674–706.

Mol, A. (1996) "Ecological modernization and institutional reflexivity: environmental reform in the late modern age," *Environmental Politics* 5, 2: 302–323.

Mol, A., and Spaargaren, G. (2000) "Ecological modernisation theory in debate: a review," *Environmental Politics* 9, 1: 17–49.

Moyer, B., with McAllister, J., Finley, M., and Soifer, S. (2001) *Doing Democracy: The MAP Model for Organizing Social Movements*, Gabriola Island, BC: New Society.

National Association of Resale and Thrift Shops (2009) "About NARTS," retrieved 15 May 15 2009: www.narts.org/press/.

National Fuel Funds Network (2009) "Mobilization for charitable energy assistance." Online, available at: www.nationalfuelfunds.org/mobilizationforcharitableenergyassistance/index.html accessed May 15 2009:

National Low Income Energy Consortium (2004) "What is NLIEC?" Online, available at: www.nliec.org/what.htm (accessed May 15 2009).

Norman, A. (2009) "About Sprawl-Busters." Online, available at: www.sprawl-busters.com/aboutsb.html (accessed May 15 2009).

O'Connor, J. (1998) *Natural Causes? Essays in Ecological Marxism*, New York: Guilford.

Palmer, K., and Walls, M. (2002) "The product stewardship movement: understanding costs, effectiveness, and the role of policy." Online, available at: www.rff.org/RFF/Documents/RFF-RPT-prodsteward.pdf (accessed May 15 2009).

Pellow, D., Schnaiberg, A., and Weinberg, A. (2000) "Putting the ecological modernization theory to the test: the promises and performances of urban recycling," *Environmental Politics* 9: 109–137.

Pinderhughes, R. (2004) *Alternative Urban Futures*, Lanham, MD: Rowman and Littlefield.

Pollan, M. (2001) "Naturally," *New York Times Magazine*, May 13, pp. 30ff.

Poppendieck, J. (1998) *Sweet Charity? Emergency Food and the End of Entitlement*, New York: Viking.

Pyatok, M. (2000) "The Politics of design: the new urbanists vs. the grassroots," *Housing Policy Debate* 11, 4: 803–814.

Reece, R. (1979) *The Sun Betrayed*, Boston, MA: South End Press.

Regional Commission on Airport Affairs (2009) "Airport community groups and cities." Online, available at: www.rcaanews.org/exchange.htm (accessed May 15 2009).

Reisner, A. (2001) "Social movement organizations' reactions to genetic engineering in agriculture," *The American Behavioral Scientist* 44, 8: 1389–1404.

Righter, R. (1996) *Wind Energy in America*, Norman, OK: University of Oklahoma Press.

Scheinberg, A. (2003) "The proof of the pudding: urban recycling in North America as a process of ecological modernization," *Environmental Politics* 12, 4: 49–75.

Sclove, R. (1995) *Democracy and Technology*, New York: Guilford.

Schnaiberg, A., and Gould, K. (1994) *Environment and Society: The Enduring Conflict*, New York: St. Martin's.

Seldman, N. (1995) "Recycling: a history in the United States," in A. Bisio and S. Boots (eds.) *Encyclopedia of Energy, Technology, and the Environment*, New York: Wiley, pp. 2352–2368.

Shuman, M. (2000) *Going Local: Creating Self-Reliant Communities in a Global Age*, New York: Routledge.

——. (2006) *The Small Mart Revolution: How Local Businesses are Beating the Global Competition*, San Francisco, CA: Berrett-Koehler.

Stevenson, S., Lass, D., Hendrickson, J., and Ruhf, K. (2004) "CSA across the nation: findings from 1999 and 2001 national surveys." Online, available at: www.cias.wisc.edu/economics/csa-across-the-nation-findings-from-the-1999-and-2001-csa-surveys (accessed May 15 2009).

Summit II National Office (2002) "Summit II briefing: celebrating our victories, strengthening our roots: our challenge for the twenty-first century." Online, available at: www.ejrc.cau.edu/summit2/EJSummitIIBriefing.pdf (accessed May 15 2009).

Szasz, A. (1994) *Ecopopulism: Toxic Waste and the Movement for Environmental Justice*, Minneapolis, MN: University of Minnesota Press.

——. (2007) *Shopping Our Way to Safety: How We Changed from Protecting the Environment to Protecting Ourselves*, Minneapolis, MN: University of Minnesota Press.

Tarrow, S. (1998) *Power in Movement: Social Movements and Contentious Politics,* second edition, Cambridge, UK: Cambridge University Press.

Warren, T. (1999) "Onward Christian soldiers," *Washingtonian* 35, 3: 86–89.

Weinberg, A., Pellow, D., and Schnaiberg, A. (2000) *Urban Recycling and the Search for Sustainable Community Development*, Princeton, NJ: Princeton University Press.

Wellock, T. (1998) *Critical Masses: Opposition to Nuclear Power in California, 1958–1978*, Madison, WI: University of Wisconsin Press.

Williamson, T., Imbroscio, D., and Alperovitz, G. (2002) *Making a Place for Community*, New York: Routledge.

York, R., and Rosa, E. (2003) "Key challenges to ecological modernization theory," *Organization and Environment* 16, 3: 273–288.

Editor's Introduction to Chapter 14

In the previous chapter David J. Hess argued that the markets and governments of North America have failed to turn the tide of environmental degradation. From this perspective only civil society would appear to have the capacity to think experimentally and act successfully. But in this chapter, Sean B. Cash and Samuel D. Brody argue from a perspective that is seemingly opposite – that successful ecosystem management requires the presence of corporate landowners at the table. Can these differing perspectives be reconciled under the philosophical canopy of pragmatism?

The danger of *a priori* dispositions regarding the status of markets and governments is that we tend to forget that, in the end, such institutions are comprised of individuals whom are also citizens. This is to say that we wear many hats in any given day and should resist essentializing social contexts and how people will act in them. Through the study of particular cases, Cash and Brody have empirically documented situations in which corporate actors will willingly participate in transboundary management if their interests are recognized and respected – if actions taken are, in their eyes, successful. And since corporations own sixty-eight million acres of forestland in North America that includes the most critical ecological habitat, it is only prudent to rationally experiment with citizen participation at all levels of society.

The authors proceed in this task by first outlining the importance of multiparty collaboration in ecosystem approaches to management and the increasing significance of industry as a key stakeholder in the management process. Next, they specify a framework of ten factors that may stimulate industry to engage in transboundary ecosystem management efforts. These motivating factors are drawn from findings in previous literature, recent survey results, and the authors' own insights. Finally, this framework is applied empirically through a survey of the thirty-eight largest landholding forestry corporations in North America.

In the end it is the empirical foundation of the chapter that allows us to productively consider its findings alongside those of the previous chapter without lapsing into postmodern relativism. Pragmatism, as Larry Hickman has argued, allows us to consider the problem of "global citizenship" by recognizing a "strain of human commonality" that trumps ideological difference (Hickman 2001: 65–81). And likewise, Andrew Light has previously argued that "environmental pragmatism [is] the best framework within which to make competing political theories compatible in practice" (Light 1996: 161). These pragmatists are, then, less concerned with the ideological orientation of particular players than with the possibility that long-term success may derive from their differing interpretations of reality.

Chapter 14

Bringing Corporate Stakeholders to the Table in Collaborative Ecosystem Management

Sean B. Cash and Samuel D. Brody

Introduction

Shelter Bay Forests (SBF) was a private company managing approximately 500,000 fragmented acres of forest lands along the shores of Lake Superior in the Upper Peninsula of Michigan. While not critical to its core business, SBF invested time and money to play a leading role in the Eastern Upper Peninsula Partners in Ecosystem Management (EUPPEM) project. This group was comprised of government agencies, forest product companies, and the Nature Conservancy, a leading environmental NGO. The partners (composed of eight public and private landholders) collectively managed 2.6 million acres of land in the EUP. Despite varying resource management goals and activities, group members formed a collaborative venture to facilitate the sustainable management of the EUP ecosystem over the long term. The mission of the EUPPEM was to "facilitate complementary management of public and private lands for all appropriate land uses through a large-scale, landscape–ecological approach to maintaining and enhancing sustainable representative ecosystems in the EUP of Michigan" (Draft EUPPEM 1997).

EUPPEM meetings were held periodically (from two to four times a year) to discuss management issues of mutual interest and to work toward cooperative approaches to management of the members' respective landholdings. While group members agreed to cooperate on a wide range of issues, no formal MOU was ever signed nor were there regulations mandating specific collaborative arrangements. Instead, partners worked informally, stressing communication, understanding and cooperation, rather than formal procedures and protocol. Through this approach, the group created a working environment built on trust in which presumably open, honest communication could occur on a regular basis (Beyer *et al.* 1997).

During its participation in EUPPEM, SBF developed an amicable relationship with the Nature Conservancy, which owned an adjacent parcel of land. When SBF wanted to access harvestable timber by utilizing an existing road that traversed the Nature Conservancy preserve, it was able to call upon what was now considered to be an old friend. SBF and the Nature Conservancy capitalized upon their previously established relationship to quickly negotiate an arrangement allowing the forest management company to access its timber stand through the existing road, rather than spend the time and money to build several miles of new road through a naturally occurring wetland. In the absence of a prior relationship, a request to use a road on protected land for logging purposes may have quickly been rejected, but in this instance both parties recognized the opportunity to collaborate to reduce the overall environmental impact on the area. Without the presence of trust and spirit of collaboration created through the EUPPEM, a solution that met the interests of both parties may have never been reached. Although such a transaction could not be anticipated, it demonstrates the value of forming solid relationships with neighboring stakeholders to both attain natural resource management goals and realize financial gain.

The example of SBF's participation in EUPPEM illustrates that there are opportunities where the private interests of industry may be in line with the public good. In contrast to Hess' exposition of pathways for social change outlined in Table 13.1 of the previous chapter, we argue that there are also process-oriented pathways that can harness multiple stakeholders' interests, including those of industry. While we agree that there is a crucial need for government to regulate industry to protect the public good, we contend there is also a role for government to foster collaborative processes that can result in sustainable forms of resource management. This chapter examines how industry incentives can be harnessed to promote sustainability within the context of ecosystem management.

The ecosystem approach to management

An ecosystem approach to management is holistic in addressing natural resource issues by focusing on the interaction between human communities and entire ecological systems (Grumbine 1994). Because natural systems, such as watersheds or eco-regions often transcend lines of ownership, collaboration among multiple parties is required. Ecosystem approaches to management thus broaden a manager's geographic focus beyond a single property and necessitate collaborative problem-solving. In general, the practice of ecosystem management is transboundary, interagency, and multi-party (Yaffee et al. 1996).

In recent years, resource-based industries (e.g., forestry, agriculture, fishery operations) have been identified as key stakeholders in effective ecosystem planning initiatives, as they not only have a large impact on critical natural resources, but also because much of the critical habitat in the US is located on privately held land (O'Connell 1996; Hoffman et al. 1997; Brody 2003). Approximately one-third of US land is classified as forestland (Holt and Warren 1998). Sixty-five percent of this land (483 million acres) can be further classified as commercial forestland. Of this commercially viable forestland, approximately sixty-eight million acres are owned and managed by industrial landowners (Holt and Warren 1998). Hence, the timber industry, along with other natural resource-based industries, controls and impacts a significant amount of critical natural resources that must be incorporated into landscape-level management initiatives.

While the impacts of industry participation on the quality of local ecosystem-oriented plans have been examined, an understanding of what motivates large resource-intensive corporations to engage in ecosystem approaches to management and the perceived benefits to these organizations has never been clearly articulated (Brody 2003). In response, this chapter seeks to establish a better understanding of the motivations for resource-based industry to participate in ecosystem management projects. First, we briefly outline the importance of multiparty collaboration in ecosystem approaches to management and the increasing significance of industry as a key stakeholder in the management process. Next, we identify ten factors that may stimulate industry to engage in transboundary ecosystem management efforts. These motivating factors are drawn from findings in previous literature, recent survey results, and our own insights. Finally, we empirically test these motivating factors through a survey of the thirty-eight largest landholding forestry corporations in North America.

The importance of collaboration in ecosystem management

As mentioned on p. 261, ecosystem approaches to management increasingly depend on collaboration across administrative and ownership boundaries (Blumenthal and Jannink 2000). Because the planning unit in this case is the ecological system, inter-organizational collaboration across jurisdictions, agencies, and land ownership is often necessary to achieve effective management of critical natural resources. Management decisions must be made collectively, because in most cases no single entity has jurisdiction over all aspects of an ecosystem. The need to integrate the values and knowledge of a broad array of organizations and individuals translates into a need to focus on collaborative planning efforts among land owners, managers, and resource users (Cortner and Moote 1999; Wondolleck and Yaffee 2000).

The organizational design literature long identified the need for inter-organizational and inter-sectoral collaboration to solve major environmental problems (Cooperrider and Passmore 1991). Such collaborations, which include a variety of inter-jurisdictional partnerships and public–private alliances, have been viewed as critical to effective management outcomes that meet the needs of all interested parties (Westley and Vredenburg 1997). In this sense, collaborations induced by shared visions are intended to advance the collective good of the stakeholders involved in solving the problem (Bryson and Crosby 1992). Emery and Trist initially argued that problem domains (ill-defined problems that depend on multiple perspectives for their solution) could be stabilized by inter-organizational collaboration (Emery and Trist 1965). These so-called "meta-problems" transcending the boundaries of single organizations or jurisdictions must be addressed cooperatively. Others have also noted that multiple stakeholders in different sectors, having different viewpoints, interests, and values, must cooperate to solve problems whose parameters are transboundary or not clearly defined (Brown 1991; Clark 1989).

Because ecosystem management often requires a transboundary, multi-party approach to solving "meta-problems," participation and collaboration of key stakeholders is widely viewed as the single most important element of a successful outcome (Grumbine 1994; Westley 1995; Duane 1997). Participation of stakeholders from the beginning of a planning initiative increases trust, understanding of, and support for ecosystem-based policies (Yaffee and Wondolleck 1997). Furthermore, including key parties in the decision-making process helps to build a sense of ownership over the planning outcome and ensures that all interests are reflected in the final management plan (Innes 1996; Daniels and Walker 2001). Furthermore, organizations and individuals often bring to the process valuable knowledge and innovative ideas about their community that can increase the quality of adopted plans (Moore 1995; Beierle and Konisky 2001; Brody 2003). For example, Innes examined the role of consensus building through case studies of environmental problems involving multiple issues that cut across jurisdictional boundaries (Innes 1996). She found that collaboration not only increased trust, communication and the development of public–private networks, but also resulted in stronger outcomes or plans that were beneficial to the resource or to the natural system as a whole. In a survey of ecosystem management initiatives in the US, Yaffee *et al.* found that collaboration of key stakeholders was the single most important factor which enabled projects to reach a quality outcome (Yaffee *et al.* 1996). Also, Kennedy *et al.* found in their analysis of 100 cases involving watershed management in the US that collaboration by stakeholders was a key feature in improving resource management (Kennedy *et al.* 2000).

While the literature supports collaboration as beneficial to managing ecological systems, there are also arguments against forming collaborative arrangements (Coglianese 1999; Conley and Moote 2003). For example, bringing together multiple stakeholders to solve common-pool resource problems may increase conflict and reduce the chances that a plan will be adopted. Even if solutions are agreed upon, the outcome of collaboration may be a "watered-down," inappropriate, or an ineffective management plan. In addition, collaboration around natural resource management can be expensive and time-consuming, result in a loss of control by government officials, reinforce negative stereotypes, and meet the needs of only a few parties (Kennedy *et al.* 2000).

Role of industry

The majority of the literature on stakeholder participation in ecosystem approaches to management is written from a public sector perspective, where the influence of government or non-government organizations is the focus of inquiry. The participation of industry does not receive a great deal of attention in arguments for collaborative ecosystem management, despite the fact that industry has a significant impact on our natural resource base and that much of the critical habitat in the US is located on privately-owned lands. Industry land holdings (a subset of privately-held lands in the US) include many important elements of ecosystem diversity, particularly in the eastern part of the country, and comprise approximately two-thirds of the land base of the continental US. For example, approximately 57 percent of forests in the US are privately owned. In regions such as the southeast and Texas, private ownership comprises up to 90 percent of the land base. Furthermore, 90 percent of the more than 1,200 listed endangered and threatened species occur on nonfederal lands and more than 5 percent, including nearly 200 animal species, have at least 81 percent of their habitat on nonfederal lands (Wondolleck and Yaffee 2000). As a result, government should encourage industry participation in order to adequately protect ecological systems over the long term (O'Connell 1996; Vogt *et al.* 1997).

Consistent with this line of thinking, Cortner and Moote (1994) assert that a fundamental requirement for effective ecosystem management is the coordination of public and private interests. Similarly, Hoffman, Bazerman, and Yaffee argue that because much of the critical habitat in the US lies on privately-owned land, including this stakeholder in the decision-making process is critical to achieving successful management outcomes (Hoffman *et al.* 1997). These arguments are supported by case study analysis conducted by Beyer *et al.* (1997), who observed that the informal participation of industrial forest stakeholders was one of the keys to the perceived success of the Eastern Upper Peninsula of Michigan Ecosystem Management Project described above. More recently, Brody empirically examined the impact of resource-based industry participation on the quality of local plans associated with managing ecological systems in Florida (Brody 2003). Quantitative results from this study show that the presence of industry during the planning process significantly improves the quality of adopted plans to manage ecological systems.

Ten motivating factors for participation in ecosystem management

The previous sections outline much of the empirical and theoretical evidence for why regulators should seek to encourage industry participation in ecosystem management. What has not been clearly articulated in the literature, however, is why industry should be interested in committing the resources necessary in formulating ecosystem management plans, or accepting the possible restrictions on their operations that may result from these plans. It is obvious that if participation ultimately results in significantly reduced profitability, few companies will find it in their best interest to voluntarily participate in ecosystem management regimes. Yet, there are several ways in which participation can possibly augment profitability and other corporate goals that should be taken into account by organizations considering such involvement.

While arguments have been put forth for the importance of corporations looking beyond their boundaries,[1] little has been published on a clear rationale for resource-intensive industries to pursue ecosystem management when it is not part of their core business. Ecosystem management involves a unique set of issues and problems related to sustainability that needs to be addressed more thoroughly. We build on the research related to environmental strategy and management to identify a series of motivators (both external and internal) that will help explain the reasons for industry participation in collaborative ecosystem management initiatives.

We suggest the following ten motivating dimensions for participation: (1) effective resource management; (2) direct financial gain; (3) good public relations; (4) good partnerships with stakeholders; (5) acquisition of data; (6) technical assistance; (7) employee satisfaction; (8) reduction of media criticism; (9) an attractive alternative to litigation; and (10) an attractive alternative to command-and-control regulations. These motivating characteristics serve as a conceptual framework to quantitatively assess the factors driving large resource industry landholders to engage in collaborative ecosystem management initiatives.

Effective resource management

Because ecological systems often extend beyond a single parcel, collaboration with adjacent landowners may be an essential part of effectively managing corporate landholdings and maintaining the economic value of a resource base. A company involved in resource management may want to look beyond its boundaries and consider activities or impacts occurring on adjacent lands. Key wildlife species, hydrological features, pollutants, and diseases are constantly moving across areas of ownership. Working with adjacent property owners to maintain the ecological integrity of their resources is thus part of effectively managing the ecological unit as a whole. Participation in ecosystem management initiatives demonstrates recognition that the critical natural resources upon which these companies' core business rests are regional in nature and may require collective efforts to maintain economic value well into the future. The decision to participate in this sense is based on a desire to build a solid base of natural capital.

Direct financial gain

Researchers in the field of strategy and management have also begun to indicate reasons for corporate involvement in environmental activities (Arora and Carson 1996; King and Lenox 2000; Welch *et al.* 2000). The positive relationship between ecological sustainability and economic performance are becoming more clearly understood. Sharma and Vrendenburg, for example, argue that proactive corporate environmental strategy can lead to firm competitiveness (Sharma and Vrendenburg 1998). Financial profitability has also been linked to ecologically sustainable practices (Porter and van der Linde 1995; Klassen and McLaughlin 1996; Judge and Zandbergen 1998). Hartman and Stafford take this concept one step farther by arguing for "market-based environmentalism" where industry and business integrate environmental activities with market-driven goals (Hartman and Stafford 1997). For example, eco-labeling is one technique that may lead to improved financial performance (Amacher *et al.* 2004).

Good public relations

Positive public relations are another important motivation for companies to participate in ecosystem management. Companies are increasingly more receptive to the expectations of their stakeholders, adjacent landholders, and the general public (Fineman and Clarke 1996; Rajan 2001). The motivation to be "good corporate citizens," particularly regarding environmental activities, may lead companies to engage in ecosystem management activities that involve collaboration with neighboring property owners and associated organizations. Fostering positive environmental perceptions may also help buffer adverse reactions to management decisions made in the future (e.g., deciding to harvest a particularly visible forest stand). In general, forestry operations are increasingly less insulated from the scrutiny of other stakeholders and the public. Strong public relations may be viewed as a means for cultivating a positive image that may in turn make it easier for a company to conduct business in the long run. For example, Vogt *et al.* argue that the timber industry will be motivated to participate in ecosystem management in part due to the perceptions of how the timber industry is managing their timberlands (Voght *et al.* 1997). They state that public perceptions and media attention will drive management policies and practices.

Solid partnerships with stakeholders

Perhaps the most important and least-realized benefit to participating in collaborative ecosystem management projects is the development of personal relationships (Khanna and Anton 2002). As mentioned on p. 264, firms are increasingly recognizing that they lie within a broader network of interests and interaction with these outside interests is essential to effective management

(Hoffman 2000). Developing relationships based on trust and reciprocity with neighboring land-holders can help a company attain its resource management and financial goals. There are strong links between the levels of trust organizations have in others, the effort others make in building trustworthy reputations, and the likelihood parties will reciprocate good will (Ostrom 1998). In sum, when relationships are formed among multiple interests, there is a good chance that those interests will collaborate with each other to reach common natural resource goals sometime in the future. Reciprocity is particularly important for corporate landholders whose neighbors are controlling and impacting what can often be considered the same natural system. In their survey of large landholding forestry companies in the US, Brody *et al.* found that collaborative partnerships is a statistically significant motivating factor for industry parties to participate in ecosystem management projects (Brody *et al.* 2006).

Acquisition of data

Collaborating with outside parties often entails an exchange of information and data relevant to effectively managing natural resources. Corporate entities can gain valuable knowledge regarding habitat locations, species movement, silvaculture techniques, the presence of pollutants, etc. This knowledge can increase a company's capacity to effectively manage natural resources within their landholdings and contribute to financial performance over the long term.

Technical assistance

Collaborative arrangements can also lead to technical assistance that cannot be acquired elsewhere. Nongovernmental and government organizations can provide technical assistance and databases that can be useful to managing timber or other types of natural resources. For example, in the EUPPEM case, SBF gained access to GIS data and received technical assistance that may prove useful in maximizing harvesting operations. In this respect, a collaborative effort provides a forum for learning that can translate into more effective management within ownership boundaries.

Employee satisfaction

Collaborative ecosystem approaches to management that makes the long-term ecological sustainability of the natural resource a priority can boost employee satisfaction. Managers often feel better about their work when it promulgates environmental concerns rather than seeks to solely maximize financial gain. For example, Dyke *et al.* found that several forestry companies believed that ecosystem management "is the right thing to do" and instills employees with a great deal of personal satisfaction (Dyke *et al.* 2005).

Reduction of media criticism

Participation in collaborative ecosystem management and other sustainability projects may come as a reaction to media criticism. Companies are increasingly more receptive to media coverage. For example, Darnall states that pressure exerted through these outside channels may be a viable policy option for influencing corporate decisions (Darnall 2002). Engaging in high-profile, environmentally sustainable practices may serve as a defensive maneuver for a company interested in negating unfavorable environmental perceptions from shareholders and the general public. Positive press can reduce public opposition to commercial harvesting operations, increase the firm's customer base, and make it easier to conduct core business practices (Rajan 2001). For example, Brody *et al.* found that positive public relations are a statistically significant motivation for participating in ecosystem management projects (Brody *et al.* 2006). They studied the largest landholding forestry management corporations and found that over 90 percent of the sample had received publicity regarding their role in resource stewardship over the last five years, most notably on sustainable forest management practices and the management of wildlife. Sixty-three percent reported they have been involved in controversial resource management issues in the recent past.

An attractive alternative to litigation

Collaboration among multiple parties is often an attractive alternative to courtroom litigation (Bacow and Wheeler 1984; Crowfoot and Wondolleck 1990). Lawsuits over environmental issues can be costly, time intensive, and reinforce adversarial relationships. In contrast, if environmental and natural resource-based disputes can be successfully resolved through a consensus-building process, the time and resources expended on maintaining the value of corporate holdings can be considerably less. Conflict management techniques can also yield outcomes that maximize all parties' interests (Wondolleck and Yaffee 2000).

An attractive alternative to command-and-control regulations

From an industry perspective, participation in collaborative ecosystem management initiatives can offer an attractive alternative to command-and-control style government regulation and reduce the need for strict regulatory controls in the long run. Many companies are opposed to stringent regulations and lack of control in the regulatory process. The practice of collaborative ecosystem management could help decrease the burden of governmental controls and improve the current regulatory structure by educating regulators about sustainable corporate practices. If the forest and timber industry can demonstrate to regulators that it is working to improve environmental standards, companies can show they are capable of setting and abiding by their own high management standards. A collaborative approach may reduce operational costs and provide the flexibility corporations need to sustainably manage their natural resource base. Dyke *et al.* quote a company representative who claims, "[t]he original intent of our regulatory system is laudable, but the resultant system is too heavy on process and paperwork with less and less time for professional decision-making in the forest. We could achieve better results simply by being smart business folks and being aware of our neighbors and communities" (Dyke *et al.* 2005).

Survey results

To examine the importance of the ten motivating factors described above, we conducted a telephone survey of the thirty-eight largest landholding forest management corporations in North

America.[2] Together, these companies own or control an average of approximately 1.4 million acres, much of it in large blocks, and have an average of 251 employees engaged in resource management activities.

As shown in Table 14.1, while all of the companies surveyed were familiar with the term collaborative ecosystem management, there was variation in the degree of participation in these initiatives, the role companies played, and the motivations for involvement. Approximately three-quarters of the respondents had participated in one or more ecosystem management projects, but more than half of the sample declined at least one opportunity to participate in a project during the last ten years. When asked why companies did not or would not participate, respondents listed concerns over the initiator's agenda, unclear goals and objectives of the project, time constraints, anti-trust issues, and a general lack of funding.[3] When a company did participate in an ecosystem management project, it was usually as an active member or leader of the planning process. Of the twenty-eight companies that participated in ecosystem management projects, 57 percent considered their role to be project initiators and over 35 percent assumed the role of collaborator.

Table 14.1 Participation in ecosystem management and collaborative decision-making

Familiarity with collaborative ecosystem management planning	100%
Company involvement in collaborative ecosystem management projects/ initiatives in the past 10 years?	71%
Company involvement in collaborative ecosystem management projects/ initiatives in the past 5 years?	74%
For companies which listed projects (28 out of 38 surveyed), what was the average number of projects listed?	3.11 (range from 1–7)
Number of companies participating in each role	Initiator – 57% Collaborator – 35% Respondent – 3% Observer – 3%
In the past 10 years, has the company decided not to participate in a collaborative ecosystem management program it had the opportunity to participate in?	52%

Table 14.2 shows that of the ten motivating factors to participate in collaborative ecosystem management projects described above, good public relations and an alternative approach to command-and-control regulations ranked the highest (both averaging 5.97 out of 7 on a Likert-type scale, where 7 indicates "strongly agree"). The development of stakeholder partnerships, collaboration as a more attractive alternative to litigation, and obtaining data from other parties were also seen as prominent motivating factors. Participating in collaborative ecosystem management for direct financial gain was the least cited motivation. Finally, when asked whether there are other motivators not listed in the survey, respondents listed, among other factors, market access and ethical obligations.

Table 14.2 **Possible motivators for collaborative ecosystem management participation**

Alternative to command-and-control regulations	5.97
Public relations	5.97
Stakeholder partnership	5.61
Alternative to litigation	5.32
Data collection	5.01
Effective resource management	4.92
Personal satisfaction	4.55
Technical assistance	4.53
Decrease media pressure	4.30
Financial gain	3.79

Note

Average responses on a scale of 1–7; 1 being strongly disagree, 7 being strongly agree.

We provide further insight into the importance of these motivating factors by examining how the stated importance of each factor correlated with the actual decision to participate in ecosystem management activities. These results are shown in Table 14.3. Three of the ten motivating factors are statistically significant at the five percent level of significance. More effective resource management was the motivating factor most strongly correlated with the decision to participate in collaborative ecosystem management initiatives. Positive public relations is also a statistically significant motivation for participating in ecosystem management projects. This result is not surprising when one considers that over 90 percent of the sample had received publicity regarding their role in resource stewardship over the five years prior to the survey. Finally, establishing good partnerships with stakeholders is another significant motivator at the five percent level. Other notable correlations for participating in collaborative ecosystem initiatives ($p \leq 0.10$) were found for personal satisfaction and an attractive alternative to litigation.

Table 14.3 **Correlations between motivating factors and forest industry participation in collaborative ecosystem management**

Variable name	Spearman rank correlation coefficient	P-value
Good partnerships	.434	.00
Public relations	.411	.01
Effective resource management	.401	.01
Personal satisfaction	.272	.09
Alternative to litigation	.256	.10
Alternative to command-control regulation	.202	.22
Technical assistance	.182	.27
Reduce media pressure	.130	.44
Financial gain	.117	.45
Data	.111	.50

Respondents' views of the results of their organizations' participation in EM projects are summarized in Table 14.4. For the vast majority of the sample, participation in collaborative ecosystem management resulted in important benefits for the company, including such factors as relationship building with other stakeholders, better management practices, regulatory predictability and stability, and economic incentives. Benefits also accrued to other stakeholders and to the health of the natural resource itself. These planning processes were generally more formal than informal and the outcomes were adopted plans, memoranda of understanding, or some other forms of agreement. While 96 percent of participants indicated they incurred costs, only 19 percent believed these costs outweighed the long-term benefits of involvement in collaborative initiatives. Additionally, all participating companies responded they would participate in another ecosystem management project in the future. Perhaps most importantly, of all the respondents in the sample, whether they participated in ecosystem management or not, 89 percent believed it is a useful process for industry–government relations because of reciprocal relationships and trust developed through collaboration and decreased regulations resulting from stakeholders working together on common resource management problems.

Table 14.4 **Results of ecosystem management participation**

Participants felt the ecosystem management projects their company had participated in were more formal than informal in nature	72%
Participation resulted in an adopted plan, memorandum, or some other agreement	78%
The company benefited by participating	87%
The project was successful	87%
The company incurred costs by participating	96%
Company believed costs outweigh the benefits of participating	19%
Company believed other participants benefited by company's participation	95%
Company believed initial goals and objectives were met by collaborating parties	88%
Company believed any agreement reached by collaborating parties has been or will be implemented	98%
Company believed the health of natural resource/ecosystem has improved as a result of the initiative	81%
Company would participate in a collaborative ecosystem management project again or in the future	100%

Conclusion

The results of this study indicate that collaborative ecosystem management is an important aspect of the forest and timber industry in North America. From a corporate perspective, participation in ecosystem management initiatives fosters communication and collaboration among multiple interests, leading to more sustainable management practices, effective business strategies, and mutually beneficial relationships with outside stakeholders. The results of our survey can provide guidance for effective corporate environmental strategy associated with resource-based industries.

Resource-based industry participation is a necessary condition for effective collaborative ecosystem management. Industry brings critical knowledge and capacity to the table, and is frequently the owner of key ecosystem components. Business managers may, however, be skeptical of voluntarily participating in processes that generally seek to limit their activities or with stakeholders who view them as opponents. Despite these obstacles, natural resource industries were motivated by specific factors to take part in ecosystem management initiatives. In this chapter, we developed a conceptual framework for understanding these motivations, and investigated their relevance to participation in ecosystem management. It is telling that all of the forest industry managers we surveyed indicated that they would be willing to participate in future ecosystem management collaborations. Understanding what brings companies to the table, and what will bring them back, is critical to protecting the integrity of the ecological systems in which these industries operate.

Acknowledgments

The authors gratefully acknowledge the financial support of the College of Architecture Research and Interdisciplinary Council Grant program at Texas A&M University. We also want to thank Jennifer Dyke and Sara Thornton who, as research assistants on this study, contributed greatly to data collection and analysis. Without their help, the project could never have been completed.

Questions for further consideration

1   Pragmatists in general tend to see "pragmatism" as more a method of problem-solving than an ideological position. But, is it coherent to place the method proposed in this chapter under the same tent as critiques of liberal capitalism offered by Oden in Chapter 2, Jamison in Chapter 4, Winner in Chapter 5, and Hess in Chapter 13?

2   As did Melosi in Chapter 12, this chapter investigates the fuzzy boundary between public and private interests. Rather than argue the merits and demerits of private vs public management of natural resources in a deductive manner, Cash and Brody simply set that volatile question aside and ask what "transboundary actions" are likely to be successful. Is avoiding the deeper question helpful, or will that question come back to haunt participants?

3   American environmentalists like Aldo Leopold have argued for decades that we must instill a new "land ethic" in citizens before much can be done to turn back environmental degradation. But, the ten "motivating factors" identified by Cash and Brody are designed to change the habits of corporate managers rather than change their minds about the relationship between humans and the ecosystem. Can such a seemingly superficial approach succeed?

4   The authors endorse collaborative decision-making, not only because participants "buy into" decisions which they have coauthored, but because they also believe that the presence of diverse experience around the decision-making table contributes to the crafting of better solutions to common problems. Given such assertions, would the process described be improved by the presence of wood-cutters and heavy equipment operators at the table, or would such inclusion only add to conflict and "watered-down" compromise?

5   In Chapter 4 Jamison describes "green knowledge" as combining the philosophical critique of technology (which derives from Habermas and others) with the ontology and critique of science (which derives from the environmental movement). In this chapter, however, there is no critique of either technology or science. Is such a critique necessary to produce relevant new knowledge?

Notes

1   For example, Freeman 1984.
2   For a more complete discussion of this survey, see Dyke *et al.* 2005.
3   For more information on industry participation, see Brody *et al.* 2006.

Bibliography

Amacher, G., Koskela, E., and Ollikainnen, M. (2004) "Environmental Quality Competition and Eco-labeling," *Journal of Environmental Economics and Management*, 42: 284–306.

Arora, S. and Carson, T. (1996) "Why do Firms Volunteer to Exceed Environmental Regulations? Understanding Participation in EPA's 33/50 Program," *Land Economics*, 72(4): 413–432.

Bacow, L. and Wheeler, M. (1984) *Environmental Dispute Resolution*, New York: Plenum Press.

Beierle, T. C. and Konisky, D. (2001) "What Are We Gaining From Stakeholder Involvement? Observation from Environmental Planning in the Great Lakes," *Journal of Environmental Planning C: Government and Policy*, 19: 515–527.

Beyer, D. E., Homan, L., and Ewert, D. N. (1997) "Ecosystem Management in the Eastern Upper Peninsula of Michigan: A Case History," *Landscape and Urban Planning*, 38(3–4): 199–211.

Blumenthal, D. and Jannink, J. L. (2000) "A Classification of Collaborative Management Methods," *Conservation Ecology*, 4(2): 13.

Brody, S. D., Cash, S. B., Dyke, J., and Thornton, S. (2006) "Motivations for the Forest Industry to Participate in Collaborative Ecosystem Management Initiatives," *Forest Policy and Economics*, 8: 123–134.

Brody, S. D. (2003) "Evaluating the Role of Resource-Based Industries in Ecosystem Approaches to Management: An Evaluation of Comprehensive Plans in Florida," *Society and Natural Resources*, 16 (7): 625–641.

Brown, L. D. (1991) "Bridging Organizations and Sustainable Development," *Human Relations*, 44(8): 807–831.

Bryson, J. M. and Crosby, B. (1992) *Leadership for the Common Good: Tackling Public Problems in a Shared-Power World*, San Francisco, CA: Jossey-Bass.

Clark, W. C. (1989) "Managing Planet Earth," *Scientific American*, 261(3): 46–57.

Coglianese, C. (1999) "The Limits of Consensus," *Environment*, 41(3): 28–33.

Conley, A. and Moote, M. A. (2003) "Evaluating Collaborative Natural Resource Management," *Society and Natural Resources*, 16: 371–386.

Cooperrider, D. and Passmore, W. (1991) "The Organization Dimension of Global Change," *Human Relations*, 44: 763–787.

Cortner, H. and Moote, M. (1999) *The Politics of Ecosystem Management*, Washington, DC: Island Press.

—— (1994) "Trends and Issues in Land and Water Resources Management: Setting the Agenda for Change," *Environmental Management*, 18(2): 167–173.

Crowfoot, J. and Wondolleck, J. (1990) *Environmental Disputes: Community Involvement in Conflict Resolution*, Washington, DC: Island Press.

Daniels, S. E. and Walker, G. (2001) *Working Through Environmental Conflict: The Collaborative Learning Approach*, Westport, CT: Praeger.

Darnall, N. (2002) "Motivations for Participating in a US Voluntary Environmental Initiative: the Multi-State Working Group and EPA's EMS Pilot Program," in Sharma, S. and Starik, M. (eds.) *Research In Corporate Sustainability: The Evolving Theory and Practice of Organizations in the Natural Environment*, Northampton, MA: Edward Elgar, Ltd.

Draft EUPPEM Two-Hearted River Sub-Group Report. October 1, 1997.

Duane, T. (1997) "Community Participation in Ecosystem Management," *Ecology Law Quarterly*, 24(4): 771–797.

Dyke, J., Cash, S. B., Brody, S. D., and Thornton, S. (2005) "Examining the Role of the Forest Industry in Collaborative Ecosystem Management: Implications for Corporate Strategy," *Corporate Social Responsibility and Environmental Management* 12: 10–18.

Emery, F. and Trist, E. (1965) "The Causal Texture of Organizational Environments," *Human Relations*, 18: 21–35.

Fineman, S. and Clarke, K. (1996) "Green Stakeholders: Industry Interpretations and Response," *Journal of Management Studies*, 33(6): 71–82.

Freeman, E. (1984) *Strategic Management: A Stakeholder Approach*, Boston, MA: Pitman.

Grumbine, E. (1994) "What Is Ecosystem Management?" *Conservation Biology*, 8(1): 27–38.

Hartman, C. and Stafford, E. (1997) "Green Alliances: Building New Business with Environmental Groups," *Long Range Planning*, 30(2): 184–196.

Hickman, Larry A. (2001) *Philosophical Tools for a Technological Culture: Putting Pragmatism to Work*, Bloomington, IN: Indiana University Press.

Hoffman, A. (2000) *Competitive Environmental Strategy: A Guide to the Changing Business Landscape*, Washington, DC: Island Press.

Hoffman, A., Bazerman, M., and Yaffee, S. (1997) "Balancing Business Interests and Endangered Species Protection," *Sloan Management Review*, Fall: 59–73.

Holt, B. and Warren, S. (1998) "Integrated Planning Across Ownerships," *Forest Management into the Next Century: What will make it work?* Madison, WI: Forest Products Society.

Innes, J. (1996) "Planning Through Consensus Building: A New View of the Comprehensive Planning Ideal," *Journal of American Planning Association*, 62: 460.

Jennings, P. D. and Zandbergen, P. (1995) "Ecologically Sustainable Organizations: An Institutional Approach," *Academy of Management Review*, 20(4): 1015–1052.

Judge, W. Q. and Zandbergen, P. A. (1998) "Performance Implications of Incorporating Natural Environmental Issues into the Strategic Planning Process: An empirical assessment," *Journal of Management Studies*, 35(2): 241–262.

Kennedy, D. S., McAllister, S. T., Caile, W. H., and Peckham, J. S., (2000) *The New Watershed Source Book*, Natural Resources Law Center, University of Colorado School of Law, Boulder, CO.

Khanna, M. and Anton, W. R. (2002) "What is Driving Corporate Environmentalism: Opportunity or Threat?" *Corporate Environmental Strategy*, 9(4): 409–417.

King, A. and Lenox, M. (2000) "Industry Self-regulation Without Sanctions: The chemical industry's responsible care program," *Academy of Management Journal*, 43(4): 698–716.

Klassen, R. D. and McLaughlin, C. P. (1996) "The Impact of Environmental Management on Firm Performance," *Management Science*, 42(8): 1199–1214.

Light, Andrew and Eric Katz, eds. (1996) *Environmental Pragmatism,* London and New York: Routledge.

Moore, N. C. (1995) *Participation Tools for Better Land-Use Planning: Techniques and Case Studies*, Sacramento, CA: Local Government Commission.

O'Connell, M. (1996) "Managing Biodiversity on Private Lands," in Szaro, R. and Johnston D. (eds.) *Biodiversity In Managed Landscapes: Theory and Practice*, Oxford, UK: Oxford University Press.

Ostrom, E. (1998) "A Behavioral Approach to the Rational Choice Theory of Collective Action: Presidential Address, American Political Science Association, 1997," *American Political Science Review*, 92(1): 1–22.

Porter, M. E. and van der Linde, C. (1995) "Green and Competitive," *Harvard Business Review*, September–October: 120–134, 196.

Rajan, R. (2001) "What Disasters Tell Us About Environmental Violence: The case of Bhopal," in Peluso, N. and Watts, M. (eds.) *Violent Environment*, Ithaca, NY: Cornell University Press.

Selin, S. and Carr, D., (2000) "Modeling Stakeholder Perception of Collaborative Initiative Effectiveness," *Society and Natural Resources* 13: 735–745.

Sharma, S. and Vrendenburg, H. (1998) "Proactive Corporate Environmental Strategy and the Development of Competitively Valuable Organizational Capabilities," *Strategic Management Journal*, 19: 729–753.

Vogt, K. A., Gordon, J. C., Wargo, J. P., and Vogt, D. J. (1997) *Ecosystems*, New York, Springer-Verlag.

Welch, E., Mazur, A., and Bretschneider, S. (2000) "Voluntary Behavior by Electric Utilities: Levels of adoption and contribution of the climate change program to the reduction of carbon dioxide," *Journal of Public Policy Analysis and Management*, 19(3): 407–425.

Westley, F. (1995) "Governing Design: The Management of Social Systems and Ecosystems Management," in Gunderson, L., Holling, C. S., and Light, S. S. (eds.) *Barriers and Bridges to the Renewal of Ecosystems and Institutions*, New York: Columbia University Press, 391–427.

Westley, F., and Vrendenburg, H. (1997) "Interorganizational Collaboration and the Preservation of Global Biodiversity," *Organizational Science*, 8(4): 381–403.

Wondolleck, J. and Yaffee, S. (2000) *Making Collaboration Work: Lessons from Innovation in Natural Resource Management*, Washington, DC: Island Press.

Yaffee, S. and Wondolleck, J. (1997) "Building Bridges Across Agency Boundaries," in Kohm, K. A. and Franklin, J. F. (eds.) *Creating A Forestry for the 21st Century*, Washington, DC: Island Press.

Yaffee, S., Phillips, A., Frentz, I., Hardy, P., Maleki, S., and Thorpe, B. (1996) *Ecosystem Management in the United States: An Assessment of Current Experience*, Washington, DC: Island Press.

Editor's Introduction to Chapter 15

In this final chapter, philosopher Andrew Feenberg challenges the reasoning of both environmental pessimists and optimists. Pessimists claim we must revert to premodern crafts to save the planet and optimists reply that the problems can all be solved within the existing system at modest cost. Both, however, argue that environmental quality comes at the expense of other goods. Their only disagreement concerns how much of these other goods must be sacrificed to achieve environmental goals. Feenberg rejects a vision of environmentalism based on the notion of unavoidable trade-offs and offers a different approach to environmental politics.

His "critical constructivist" approach is based on two fundamental points. First, the technological past was not a succession of rational decisions about the most efficient way to do things, but the result of social choices between alternative paths with different environmental consequences. This realization suggests that, second, incorporating changed social values in future technical codes is not necessarily inefficient. Regulation can, he holds, lead to technological changes and codes that enhance economic activity rather than obstruct it, as we have seen in recent years in several domains. What is required today is conscious participation in a technological revolution we are already living unawares.

As Feenberg has argued elsewhere, technological change is not a predetermined pathway, but "a scene of struggle" in which old expectations and desirable new habits are tested and reconciled. Sustainability is but the most recent criteria for testing bad habits.

Chapter 15

Incommensurable Paradigms

Values and the Environment

Andrew Feenberg

The trade-off theory

The dominant environmental discourse is based on the notion that environmental quality comes at the expense of other goods. Just how seriously we take the environmental crisis will then determine how much prosperity we are prepared to sacrifice. A lot say the ones, a little say the others.

The goal of this chapter is to criticize this trade-off theory and to suggest a different way of thinking about environmental politics. A great deal is at stake in this debate. Trade-off theory supports conservative attitudes and has led a significant fraction of the environmental movement to call for such unpopular and self-defeating notions as a return to preindustrial ways. I will begin by discussing the origins of the environmentalist version of this position before turning at length to more familiar conservative arguments.

In the early 1970s, Paul Ehrlich argued that environmental crisis was caused by both economic and population growth. He advocated "de-development" of the advanced societies to reduce over-consumption (Ehrlich and Harriman 1971). This suggestion found support in *The Limits to Growth*, a famous study of the prospects for industrial collapse due to resource exhaustion and pollution (Meadows *et al.* 1972). No-growth ideology influenced many early discussions of alternative technology. These critics argued that since industrial society is inherently destructive of the environment, we must return to preindustrial crafts to survive.

To claim that society must choose between industry and crafts is to concede that the existing industrial system is the only possible one, an essentially determinist position. This excludes a reform of modern industrialism leading to the invention of alternative technologies compatible with the health of the environment. Such a reform would reconstruct the industrial system through the incorporation of new values into industrial design.

The risk of confusion between these two very different conceptions of technical change is evident in Robin Clarke's list of utopian characteristics of what he calls soft technology (Dickson 1979: 103–104). The list includes dozens of pairs of hard and soft attributes. Some, like the following, could guide either the reconstruction of industry or a return to crafts.

Ecologically unsound	Ecologically sound
Alienation from nature	Integration with nature
Centralist	Decentralist
Technological accidents frequent and serious	Technological accidents few and unimportant

But alongside these ecumenical objectives, Clarke lists such things as:

Mass production	Craft industry
City emphasis	Village emphasis
World-wide trade	Local bartering
Capital intensive	Labor intensive

Figure 15.1
Robin Clarke's list of utopian characteristics.

These latter attributes determine a strategy of radical deindustrialization.

Why is it important to draw a sharp line between anti-industrialism and a program of alternative industrialism? There is a significant issue here which has to do with the value we place on modern life. The individualism and freedom we value so highly depend not only on political democracy but also on the technological achievements that support communication and transportation, and leave time for education in childhood and beyond. In sum, modernity and technology are mutually interdependent. It is inconceivable that people living in small impoverished villages could sustain the values and the form of life we associate with modernity. When Clarke valorizes the village and local bartering over the city and worldwide trade, he is thus implicitly questioning our identity as modern human beings.

I am firmly convinced that we need to develop a critical, democratic politics of technology within and not against the general project of modernity. This is a much contested position, both by those who despair of modernity and those who see no need for serious criticism of its accomplishments. I defend a critical modernism here in opposition to both these positions.

Costs and benefits

If regression to traditional village life is the solution, can the problem be worse? This is most people's reaction to arguments for de-development. Its main effect is to bring grist to the conservative mill of those opposed to "excessive" environmental regulation. Cost/benefit ratios are obviously unfavorable if industry as such must be sacrificed for environmental quality. The common view, therefore, holds that it would be better to adjust to the risks rather than surrendering all the advances of modern life out of exaggerated fears of remote disasters. Accordingly, the trade-off theory has emerged as the standard conservative response to environmentalism.

Despite its modern neo-liberal dress, these conservative arguments go way back. They pose the dilemma Mandeville mocked in a famous bit of doggerel at the end of the eighteenth century. In the preface to his poem, he denounced those silly enough to complain about the major environmental problem of his day, the filth of London's streets. In demanding cleanliness, they wish away the very prosperity of the city, which is the cause of the filth. The poem concludes:

> ...Fools only strive To make a Great an honest Hive.
> Bare Vertue can't make Nations live In Splendour;
> They that would revive A Golden Age,
> Must be as free For Acorns, as for Honesty.

(Mandeville 1970: 76)

Cost/benefit analysis of regulations is supposed to be able to precisely quantify and compare alternatives along the continuum of choice between Mandeville's "splendour" and a diet of acorns. For example, each incremental increase in the cleanliness of the air produces an incremental decrease in the number of respiratory illnesses. The policy choice is clarified by estimating the cost of improving the air, for example by tightening the standards for automobile exhaust, then estimating the benefits of reduced medical costs, and comparing the two figures.

But how credible are the results? There are enough problems with cost/benefit analysis to cast doubt on its claims. The current value we place on the various elements of trade-offs may not make much sense in scientific or human terms. Organizations tend to hide or exaggerate costs that might interfere with their plans, and it is difficult to know how to place a monetary value on such things as natural beauty and good health. But these values must be translated into economic terms to enter the calculation. When environmental reforms are proposed, biased cost/benefit analyses can be devised to show that they interfere with economic performance. Trade-off arguments are thus often based on flimsy estimates of costs and benefits.

The alternative is simply to impose environmental standards. Naturally, costs will come up in the debate over standards, but they will be evaluated much more flexibly and alternative arrangements designed to deal with them discussed much more freely if the issues are not boiled down to a set of numbers pretending to have scientific status.

The question I will address in the rest of this chapter is whether cost/benefit analysis can supply us with an environmental philosophy. When so generalized it has been used, along lines anticipated by Mandeville, to argue that too much environmentalism will end up impoverishing society. But do we really understand the issues when we start out from the notion that there are trade-offs between environmental and economic values? While there are obvious practical applications of cost/benefit analysis, I will argue that it fails as a basis for environmental philosophy. In this I agree with an extensive critical literature on problems of quantification.[1] To this literature I will add a discussion of the technological aspects of the trade-off approach.

Behind the trade-off approach lies an implicit philosophy of technology which I argue is incorrect. Once it falls, the limits of the approach it supports become apparent. That philosophy of technology assumes two connected principles, technological determinism and the neutrality of technology. I discuss these assumptions here in relation to several historical examples. In my conclusion I argue that environmentalism is not essentially about trade-offs. The question it poses concerns the kind of world we want to live in, not how much we want of this or that.

Background assumptions

Economics is based on the proposition that multiple variables cannot be optimized at the same time. To optimize A, some of B must be sacrificed. While this seems obvious in daily life, it involves some questionable background assumptions in policy applications.

In the first place, it is necessary that the options in a trade-off be clearly defined. But defined by whom? There is an unfortunate ambiguity on this point. The trade-off concept has an obvious source in common experience where the agent who chooses between the options also defines them. But when it is incorporated into economics, it borrows plausibility from that common experience while overstepping its limits. Economists can deploy technical tools that enable them to extend the notion of trade-offs to include purely theoretical alternatives that figure in no actual calculus of well-being. This confuses the issues in public debate over live options.

Now, there may sometimes be good reasons for the economists' extension of the concept, but it is very important not to mix the ordinary and this technical sense of the concept of trade-offs. Most people would not consider the failure to earn income through prostitution as a trade-off of moral principles for money for the simple reason that prostitution is not a live option for them. Similarly, well-established environmental and safety standards are not up for grabs and their theoretical cost, which may sound impressive, is irrelevant to present concerns.

There is a second assumption in the background of the trade-off approach. To make sense of talk about trade-offs, all other things must remain equal. This assumption is called "*ceteris paribus.*" If laws change, if prices change, if the relation between goods changes, then it makes no sense to talk about trade-offs. *Ceteris paribus* may be plausible in some short-run economic decisions. When one composes a personal budget it is reasonable to assume that all other things will be equal, that one will not win the lottery, or be struck by lightning, or discover unexpected mutual dependencies between goods. But, extend the time horizon to historical spans and it is not at all plausible that things will remain equal. It is thus not surprising to find that the trade-off approach fails to explain cases such as the abolition of child labor that resemble contemporary environmental regulation. The changes involved cannot be understood on the model of a personal budget.

There is a good reason for this: *ceteris paribus* is confounded by cases in which pursuing one good unexpectedly makes it possible to obtain another competing good. In such felicitous cases what looks like a trade-off is something very different. This is a historical commonplace since obstacles to linear progress such as resource scarcities and regulation often lead to the emergence of new paths of development and new relations between goods. For example, the initial response of automobile makers to pollution controls reduced fuel efficiency, an undesirable trade-off. Later innovations culminating in electronic fuel injection successfully combined emission controls and fuel efficiency. Here, clearly, all things are not equal and the trade-off dissolves in the face of technical advances.[2]

Applied uncritically, *ceteris paribus* overlooks the possibility of such advances. Thus it implies that development proceeds along a fixed track from one stage to the next without the possibility of branching out in new directions inspired by political interventions. This view is called technological determinism.

Deterministic applications of trade-off theory serve not only to challenge environmentalism but many other technological reforms. For example, until recently most management theorists were convinced that there was a trade-off between worker participation and productivity. Technological imperatives supposedly condemned us to obedience at work (Shaiken 1984). Similar arguments in medicine keep patients in a passive role. In the early 1970s women demanding changes in childbirth procedures were often told they were endangering their own health and that of their babies. Today many of the most controversial changes have become routine, for example, partners admitted to labor and delivery rooms. When AIDS patients in the 1980s sought access to experimental treatment they were told they would impede progress toward a cure. Their interventions did not prevent the rapid discovery of the famous "drug cocktail" that keeps so many patients alive today (Feenberg 1995: chapter 5). Over and over technological reform is condemned as morally desirable perhaps, but impractical. Over and over the outcome belies the plausible arguments against reform.

Determinism is often accompanied by the belief in the neutrality of technology. As pure means the only value to which technology conforms is the formal value of efficiency. The neutrality thesis is familiar to us from the gun-control debate where it is expressed in the slogan: "Guns don't kill people, people kill people." Guns are neutral and values are in the heads of the people who choose the targets.

Together, technological determinism and the neutrality thesis support the idea that progress along the one possible line of advance depends exclusively on rational judgments about efficiency. Since only experts are qualified to make those judgments, environmentalists obstruct progress when they impose their ideological goals on the process of development. Where goals conflict, one or the other must be sacrificed, environmental protection or technological advance – in Mandeville's terms, virtue or prosperity.

I will discuss an alternative view later in this chapter. Anticipating my conclusion, I will argue that technological development can switch tracks in response to constraints. On its new track, it may achieve several goals that were originally in conflict along its old one. Before introducing a philosophy of technology which supports this proposition, I want to discuss two historical examples in some detail.

Two historical examples

The first case concerns child labor. It is fascinating to go back to the British Parliamentary Papers and read the debates on the law regulating the labor of women and children. The issue arose because manufacturing took more and more children off the land and put them in factories. No one worried about the children so long as they worked on their parents' farm or shop. But the morality of child labor was questioned when they were employed in big anonymous institutions without parental supervision.

Lord Ashley was the leading speaker for regulation in the parliamentary debates of 1844. Today we would call his arguments ideological. He referred to no economic benefit of abolishing child labor or limiting the labor of women but instead emphasized the moral importance of motherhood. He worried that the factory system would result in a generation growing up without the tender care of a mother. He even complained that the mothers, once they were sent to work in factories, could be heard using foul language.

The response to Lord Ashley came from Sir J. Graham who complained about international competition, inflation, and technological imperatives, just like those who resist environmental regulation today. Why international competition? Regulation makes no sense in a globalized economy in which other nations continue to employ child labor. Why inflation? Because children cost less to feed and therefore can be paid less. If you replace their labor with adult labor, costs and prices go up. And who will that hurt? The poor, the very people who need help! So Sir J. Graham argued that the abolition of child labor is based on "a false principle of humanity that is certain to defeat itself" (*Hansard's Debates* 1844: 1123).

Finally, this early opponent of regulation comes to the question of technology. His argument is vague but there is a famous old photograph by Lewis Hine which helps to understand his concerns.[3] This photograph shows a little girl in front of the equipment she uses in a cotton mill. She looks about ten years old, standing there in a white dress in front of ranks of machines going back into the distance. At first glance the picture seems quite ordinary. But soon one notices something strange about it: the machines are built to her height. The whole mill was designed for operation by children four feet tall. Industrial technology, like the chairs in an elementary school classroom, was designed for little people. The machines would be obsolete without the children to operate them. Thus technological imperatives required child labor.

This sort of argument is all too familiar. We have all heard about environmental Luddites out to destroy industry. Well, it is an old refrain. But what actually happened when new laws regulated the labor of women and children? In fact child labor was phased out in all the industrial countries. Regulation and economics did not conflict as factory owners feared. The intensity of labor increased and productivity went up, more than compensating for the higher wages paid to adults. Since children went to school for longer periods, they entered the labor force with more skills and discipline, which also improved productivity. A vast historical process unfolded, partly stimulated by the ideological debate over how children should be raised, and partly economic. It led eventually to the current situation in which nobody dreams of returning to cheap child labor in order to cut costs, at least not in the developed countries.

Determinism misses the cultural dimension of this historical change. In developed countries, child labor violates fundamental assumptions about the nature of childhood. Today we see children as consumers, not as producers. Their function is to learn, insofar as they have any function at all, and not to make money. This change in the definition of childhood is the essential advance that has occurred as a result of the regulation of labor.

In sum, although the abolition of child labor was promoted for ideological reasons, it was part of a larger process that redefined the direction of progress. In the child labor case all other things were not equal because a new path of development emerged. On this path regulation actually contributed to increasing social wealth. Technology was not neutral in this case. It established the meaning of childhood and embodied that meaning in machines. The low machines suited to operation by the ten-year-old girl made a statement about what it is to be a child. The value society places on childhood is embodied in the design of the equipment.

Here is a second example. Steamboat boilers were the first technology regulated in the United States (Burke 1972). In the early nineteenth century the steamboat was a major form of transportation like the automobile or airlines today. The US was a big country with few paved roads and lots of rivers and canals. Steamboats were essential means of transportation.

But steamboats blew up when the boilers weakened with age or were pushed too hard. After several particularly murderous accidents the city of Philadelphia consulted in 1816 with experts on the design of safer boilers. This was the first time an American governmental institution interested itself in the regulation of technology, but in the end nothing was done and the accidents continued. In 1837, at the request of Congress, the Franklin Institute issued a detailed report and recommendations based on rigorous study of boiler construction. Some representatives wanted to impose a safe boiler code on the industry but boilermakers and steamboat owners resisted and Congress hesitated to interfere with private property.

It took from that first inquiry in 1816 to 1852 for Congress to pass effective laws regulating the construction of boilers. In that time 5,000 people were killed in steamboat accidents. Once Congress imposed a code requiring thicker walls and safety valves, the epidemic of explosions abruptly ceased. To us it seems obvious that regulation was needed. But apparently it was not obvious in the early part of the nineteenth century. The situation was puzzling. Consumers kept on buying tickets despite the rising toll. At the same time people voted for politicians who demanded regulation. It was reasonable to ask what people really wanted, cheap travel or safety.

The controversy was finally settled at another level. To understand how, we need to consider the case from another angle. In everyday life, our goals are nested in hierarchies. But sometimes, particular actions or objects we pursue belong to several different hierarchies, some individual, some communal. In such cases, an individual decision may well differ from a communal one because the community relates the options to different goals than do the individuals. Trade-offs are further complicated where these goals are associated with different decision procedures, each procedure introducing a different bias into the choice. This complication is relevant to the steamboat case. Individual market-based decisions led to different conclusions than collective political decisions because individuals and governments situate safety in different goal hierarchies.

Individual travelers simply wanted to reach their destinations cheaply. Like drivers who fail to fasten their seatbelts today, they ignored the personal risk in their own individual case. But politics brought in other considerations besides personal risk. The basis for regulation is the commerce clause of the Constitution under which the government controls interstate transportation. This is not just a matter of economics but concerns national unity. Like the highway system today, the canals and rivers of the early nineteenth century unified the territory of the United States. The movement of people, ideas, and goods, troops, all the things that define a nation depend on transport and, in that period, most especially on steamboats. National unity is not an individual economic concern but a collective political one. Safe transport had obvious individual benefits, and indeed most of the congressional debate concerned those benefits, but it was also a legitimate national issue. For example, senators from the West argued that they should not have to fear for their lives in traveling back and forth between the nation's capital and their constituents.

From an individual standpoint the imposition of regulation traded off ticket prices for safety, but at the collective level something quite different was at stake. The infrastructure of national unity lies beyond the boundaries of the economy. It cannot be traded off for anything. Once security of transport is treated as essentially political, it ceases to figure in routine economic calculations. It no longer makes sense to worry about the slight increase in ticket prices once the principle of national interest in safe transportation is established. Just as we don't worry about all the money we are losing by not marketing our bodies for sex, so the cost of insuring a certain minimum security of transportation figures in no one's account books.

The steamboat case shows how economic considerations are sometimes undercut by the instability of the problem definition associated with particular technologies. For there to be a trade-off account, the options must be stabilized. But in the steamboat case the options were not stable. There were two slightly different and competing problem definitions, one at the individual and the other at the collective level, and it was not clear what the problem was until it was finally settled. In this case the decision about what kind of technology to employ could not be made on the basis of efficiency because efficiency is relative to some known purpose. If the purpose is in question, efficiencies cannot be compared.

A constructivist approach

There is a philosophy of technology that acknowledges these difficulties. Various versions of constructivism argue against technological determinism that there are many paths of development and that the choice between them is social and political and not a simple matter of efficiency (Pinch *et al.* 1989). A way of life is expressed in design. Values are thus embedded in technology. I will come back to the environmental question from a constructivist perspective in the conclusion to this chapter, but let me first explain this alternative view of technology.

Constructivist technology studies grow out of an earlier revolution in science studies, and it is in fact reminiscent of Thomas Kuhn's famous theory of scientific revolution. Kuhn showed that important scientific advances may appear purely rational, that is to say, uniquely determined by evidence and arguments, but they are actually underdetermined by rationality since they also respond to changes in the very idea of evidence and arguments (Kuhn 1962).

Technology is similar. The regulation of child labor appeared to have unacceptable costs but once put into effect it released new sources of wealth. The boiler code appears purely rational – surely a safer boiler is better from an engineering standpoint. But history shows that the decision to make safer boilers took forty years, and then the moving force behind the change was politics not engineering. We thus have the same kind of problem in understanding the development of technology that Kuhn had with scientific development: progress is not reducible to a succession of rational choices because criteria of rationality are themselves in flux.

Kuhn's solution to this conundrum was the notion of paradigms, by which he meant a model for research. Such models have tremendous influence on those who come afterward. For example, physicists found in Newton not just a correct theory of gravitation, but a way to do physics that prevailed for several hundred years.

Normal science, Kuhn argued, is research within the established paradigm. The technological equivalent is the pursuit of efficiency in conformity with what I call technical codes, the codes that govern technical practice (Feenberg 1999: 87–89). These codes materialize values in technical disciplines and design.

Revolutions in both science and technology involve fundamental changes in values reflected in the paradigms or codes that control the normal pursuit of truth or efficiency. Progress proceeds within a paradigm through the continuous advance of research and development, but there is discontinuity between paradigms. They open up incommensurable worlds.

This approach has consequences for our understanding of the rationality and autonomy of the technical professions. At every stage in the history of their discipline experts inherit the results of earlier revolutions growing out of technical controversies and struggles. Engineering students do not have to learn how this or that regulation was translated into a design specification. The results are technically rational in themselves and presented as such. This gives rise to a characteristic illusion of autonomy. In fact the autonomy of these disciplines is limited. Their past is not a succession of decisions identifying the scientifically validated "one best way," but rather it is the result of social choice between several good ways with different social consequences. There is thus what might be called a technological unconscious in the background of these disciplines. This is what makes determinism so plausible, but it also leaves it vulnerable to historical refutation.

Environmental values

Now let me return to the question of the relation between environmental values and the economy with this constructivist argument in mind. I have identified several problems with the trade-off approach.

First, it ignores the significance of the shifting boundaries of the economy. We do not mourn the cost of using adult labor instead of child labor for the simple reason that children are culturally excluded from the category of workers.

Second, the trade-off approach assumes the fixity of the background, *ceteris paribus*, but technological change over the long time spans of history invalidates that assumption. All things are not equal in history since cultural change and technological advance alter the terms of the problem.

Third, the trade-off approach obscures differences in problem definition and goals reflecting different contexts of decision. There is no absolute context from the standpoint of which an unbiased evaluation is possible. It is thus deceptive to compare such things as the risk of death in an automobile accident with the risk of death from a nuclear accident since the one case involves individual responsibility and the other collective responsibility.

Fourth, the trade-off approach confuses short-run economic considerations with civilizational issues. These latter concern identity, who we are and how we want to live. This is a different proposition from getting more of A at the expense of B.

For all these reasons we need another way to think about environmental values. Here is a constructivist approach to an example that concerns a current environmental issue, the case of air pollution and asthma. Asthma attacks are treated as a cost in cost/benefit calculations. One study of the revised clean air act valued asthma attacks at an average $32 (Rowe and Chestnut 1986). Obviously, the lower the cost of attacks, the less benefit is recovered by decreasing their frequency. Although calculations of this sort are offensive to anyone with asthma, it makes some kind of sense to the extent that our society is not fully committed to the struggle against this disease, which has modest medical costs.[4]

But it is entirely possible that we will respond to the rapidly rising incidence of asthma and the rising death rate associated with it by attempting to eliminate pollution as a causative factor. This would mean treating asthma the way we currently treat waterborne diseases such as cholera and dysentery. In that case health-based standards would place asthma beyond the boundaries of economic controversy, and we would eventually arrive at a state of affairs that would seem obvious and necessary both technically and morally.

The relevant polluting methods would be replaced gradually by clean ones. Spare parts for the old polluting devices would be unavailable and they would gradually go out of service if they were not simply outlawed. After a while, the substitutes would be better in many respects, not just environmentally, since all later progress would be designed for them. It would not occur to our descendants to save money by going back to the old polluting machinery in order to cheapen industrial production or transportation. They would say, "We are not the kind of people who would trade off the health of our children for money," much as we would immediately reject the suggestion we supplement the family budget by sending our children out to work in a factory. This would be a civilizational advance in the environmental domain.

This leads to the question of why environmental values appear as values in the first place. Indeed, why is it at all plausible to claim that environmentalism is an ideology intruding on the economy? This is explained by the fact that our civilization was built by people indifferent to the environment. Environmental considerations were not included in earlier technical disciplines and codes and so today they appear to come from outside the economy. It is this heritage of indifference that makes it necessary to formulate concern for the environment as a value and to impose regulation on industry.

This charge of indifference need not imply an overly harsh judgment of our predecessors. Not only are we richer and better able to afford environmental protection, but the immense side effects of powerful technologies that have come into prominence since World War II have made environmental regulation imperative for us (Commoner 1971).[5] However, it does imply a harsh judgment of contemporaries who rely on specious arguments to justify blocking and dismantling regulations we can well afford today and desperately need. However powerful these conservative ideologues may look at the moment, we can expect their current offensive to fail as the severity of environmental problems make an obvious mockery of their claims.

From this standpoint it seems likely that the ideological form of environmental values is temporary. These values will be incorporated into technical disciplines and codes in a technological revolution we are living unawares today. Environmentalism will not impoverish our society. We will go on enriching ourselves but our definition of prosperity and the technologies instrumental to it will change and become more rational in the future judgment of our descendants. They will accept environmentalism as a self-evident advance. Just as images of Dickens in the boot-black factory testify to the backwardness of his society, so will images of asthmatic children in smog-ridden cities appear to those who come after us.

What we have seen with child labor and boiler safety standards is just as true of environmental standards. Once they are established, the old options drop out of sight. No one thinks about saving money by getting rid of seat belts in cars and few car owners disable pollution control devices to improve performance. The only "trade-off" in which yesterday's bad designs play a role is in the head of conservative commentators. As zealous accountants they may insist that we monetize all these considerations and mark them down as expenses. But when the boundaries of the economy shift, so many cultural and technical consequences follow that it makes no sense to look back with an eye to costs and benefits. In the only sense in which it is significant for policy, effects on social wealth must be measured with respect to the fulfillment of actual desires, not theoretical constructions.

To be sure, we should be interested in economists' calculation of risks of which people are temporarily ignorant such as the consequences of smoking. But that concerns a future in which live options can be expected to appear. Once the case is settled, the dead options are no longer relevant. And since it is impossible to put a price on revolutionary changes in the direction of progress, cost/benefit analysis can play only a minor role in such debates.

One might object that in failing to appreciate theoretical trade-offs, we ignore economic realities, but that is a short-term view. This type of cultural change is eventually locked in by technical developments.[6] For example, in the abstract one could redo all the calculations of labor costs taking into account the savings that might be made with cheap child labor, but that is an economic absurdity since developed economies presuppose the educated and disciplined products of schooling and could not be operated by children. Priorities change too so it is impossible to compare the value of something like cleaner air or water to other goods on a constant basis over historical time.

It is thus a misrepresentation to claim that we are spending a specific sum such as $100 billion a year on environmental protection as though this money could be made available for other purposes. No doubt most of it went into improved design standards we now take for granted, for example, proper toxic waste disposal, safer water supplies, and so on. Economics regards these as "goods" and they do indeed have costs that may be controversial at first, but once they have been integrated to the culture and the prevailing technical environment we do not think about those costs any more than New Yorkers conceive of Central Park as a piece of real estate they could sell if they wanted to buy something else for a change. In sum, economics can help us navigate the flow of wealth but it cannot tell us where to place the dams that change the course of that flow.

Conclusion

Technological revolutions look irrational at first but in fact they establish another framework of rationality, another paradigm. Thus it is neither rational nor irrational in some absolute sense to build a safer boiler. Constructivists would say that the decision to do so is "underdetermined" by pure considerations of technical efficiency because it also depends on a decision about the meaning of transportation and the significance of safety. As we have seen, that is a value question settled through political debate. Similarly, withdrawing children from the labor process and putting them in school was an enormous change, a change of civilization. Such a change is bound to generate a different path of technological development. With environmentalism we are again witnessing the opening of a new path.

Although its progress is slow and there are setbacks, environmentalism has the temporality of a revolution. Revolutions represent themselves as fully real in the future and criticize the present from that imagined outcome. The French revolutionary Saint-Just asked what "cold posterity" would someday have to say about monarchy even as he called for its abolition (Saint-Just 1968: 77). With history as our guide, we too can overleap the ideological obstacles to creating a better future by realizing environmental values in the technical and economic arrangements of our society.

Acknowledgements

I want to take this opportunity to thank Simon Glynn for first setting me the task of explaining my views on the environment, and Michael Benedikt and Andrew Light for challenging me to explain myself more clearly, and Arne Elias for advice on an early draft.

Questions for further consideration

1   Feenberg discounts the "trade-off theory" in the long run, arguing that we have historically chosen to make certain ethical decisions outside of the economy. In the short run, however, don't individuals make "trade-off" decisions every day? If so, what are the implications for Feenberg's position?

2   Feenberg holds that, far from being a neutral or merely aesthetic practice, "a way of life is expressed in design," whether or not designers intend certain consequences. In other words, the design of artifacts anticipates their use in particular ways that have both intended and unintended outcomes. Does this reasoning suggest that the design disciplines should be more regulated than they now are?

3   By rejecting the *ceteris paribus* clause of traditional experimental science – which holds that, all things being equal, outcomes must follow a path determined by the manipulation of selected variables – is Feenberg arguing for the indeterminacy of history, or is he arguing that history is more malleable than we have dared to claim?

4   An extension of Feenberg's reasoning suggests that environmental and other types of regulation are both an index of changing social values and a strategy to enforce those values. At bottom they are social rather than "technological codes." If we accept this reasoning, what are the implications for the education of engineers, architects and other technical experts?

5   Traditional economists tend to argue that human societies make choices within the constraints of fixed economic rules. Feenberg is making the opposite argument – that economic choices are made within ever-changing social rules. Is Feenberg's attempt to secularize economics parallel to the proposals by Light in Chapter 8 and Canizaro in Chapter 9 to secularize nature?

Notes

1   See, for example, Venkatachalam (2004) and Kopp *et al.* (1997).

2   Gilbert Simondon describes such cases as "concretizations" (Simondon 1958). For more on concretization, see Feenberg (1999: 216ff).

3   See www.eastman.org/ar/letchild/m197701810015_ful.html#topofimage.
4   Stranger still is the notion that, since individual wealth correlates positively with life expectancy, regulations "induce" deaths by reducing disposable income. This "cost" of regulation was brought before the court in a challenge to the Clean Air Act, but the judge was not impressed. For further discussion of the costs of asthma, see "The Benefits and Costs of the Clean Air Act, 1990 to 2010."
5   For more on Commoner's argument for this point, see Commoner (1971) and Feenberg (1999: chapter 3).
6   This is an argument for a culturally informed version of the notion of path dependence (Arthur, B. 1989).

Bibliography

"The Benefits and Costs of the Clean Air Act, 1990 to 2010," Appendix: "Valuation of Human Health and Welfare Effects of Criteria Pollutants." Online, available at: http://yosemite.epa. gov/ee/epa/eermfile.nsf/vwAN/EE-0295A-13.pdf/$File/EE-0295A-13.pdf.

Arthur, Brian (1989) "Competing Technologies, Increasing Returns, and Lock-In by Historical Events," *The Economic Journal*, 99.

Burke, J. (1972) "Bursting Boilers and the Federal Power," in M. Kranzberg and W. Davenport (eds.) *Technology and Culture*, New York: New American Library.

Commoner, B. (1971) *The Closing Circle*, New York: Bantam.

Dickson, D. (1979) *The Politics of Alternative Technology*, New York: Universe Books.

Ehrlich, P. and Harriman, R. (1971) *How To Be a Survivor*, New York: Ballantine.

Feenberg, Andrew (1995) *Alternative Modernity: The Technical Turn in Philosophy and Social Theory*, Los Angeles, CA: University of California Press.

—— (1999) *Questioning Technology*, New York: Routledge.

Hansard's Debates, Third Series: Parliamentary Debates 1830–1891, vol. LXXIII.

Kopp, R. J., Pommereline, W. W., and Schwarz, N., eds. (1997) *Determining the Value of Non-marketed Goods: Economic, Psychological, and Policy Relevant Aspects of Contingent Valuation Methods*, Boston, MA: Kluwer Academic Publishers.

Kuhn, Thomas (1962) *The Structure of Scientific Revolutions*, Chicago, IL: University of Chicago Press.

de Mandeville, Bernard (1970) *The Fable of the Bees*, Baltimore, MD: Penguin.

Meadows, D. and D. J. Randers and W. W. Behrens III (1972) *The Limits to Growth*, New York: Universe Books.

Pinch, Trevor, Hughes, Thomas, and Bijker, Wiebe (1989) *The Social Construction of Technological Systems*, Cambridge, MA: MIT Press.

Rowe, R. D. and Chestnut, L. G. (1986) "Oxidants and Asthmatics in Los Angeles: A Benefits Analysis – Executive Summary," Prepared by Energy and Resource Consultants, Inc. Report to the US EPA, Office of Policy Analysis. EPA-230-09-86-018. Washington, DC.

de Saint-Just, Louis-Antoine (1968) *Oeuvres Choisies*, Paris: Gallimard.

Shaiken, Harley (1984) *Work Transformed*, Lexington, MA: DC Heath.

Simondon, Gilbert (1958) *Du Mode d'Existence des Objets Techniques*, Paris: Aubier.

Venkatachalam, L. (2004) "The contingent valuation method: a review," *Environmental Impact Assessment Review*, Vol. 24, No. 1: 89–124.

Index

Note: page numbers in *italics* denote figures or illustrations, those in **bold** denote tables.